Medieval Marvels and Fictions in the Latin West and Islamic World

Medieval Marvels and Fictions in the Latin West and Islamic World

Michelle Karnes

THE UNIVERSITY OF CHICAGO PRESS
CHICAGO AND LONDON

The University of Chicago Press, Chicago 60637
The University of Chicago Press, Ltd., London

For more information, contact the University of Chicago Press, 1427 East 60th Street, Chicago, IL 60637.
Published 2022
Printed in the United States of America

31 30 29 28 27 26 25 24 23 22   1 2 3 4 5

ISBN-13: 978-0-226-81974-7 (cloth)
ISBN-13: 978-0-226-81975-4 (paper)
ISBN-13: 978-0-226-81976-1 (e-book)
DOI: https://doi.org/10.7208/chicago/9780226819761.001.0001

The University of Chicago Press gratefully acknowledges the generous support of the Institute for Scholarship in the Liberal Arts in the College of Arts and Letters at the University of Notre Dame toward the publication of this book.

Library of Congress Cataloging-in-Publication Data

Names: Karnes, Michelle, author.
Title: Medieval marvels and fictions in the Latin West and Islamic world / Michelle Karnes.
Description: Chicago ; London : The University of Chicago Press, 2022. | Includes bibliographical references and index.
Identifiers: LCCN 2022000986 | ISBN 9780226819747 (cloth) | ISBN 9780226819754 (paperback) | ISBN 9780226819761 (ebook)
Subjects: LCSH: Literature, Medieval—History and criticism. | Comparative literature—Western and Arabic—History and criticism. | Curiosities and wonders in literature.
Classification: LCC PN682.C85 K37 2022 | DDC 809/.02—dc23/eng/20220324
LC record available at https://lccn.loc.gov/2022000986

♾ This paper meets the requirements of ANSI/NISO Z39.48-1992 (Permanence of Paper).

For David and Jessica

Contents

Note to the Reader

In the text that follows, I provide my own translations unless otherwise noted. I often alter the translations that I cite, though I do so without comment. I provide the original language for all medieval sources, but not for modern studies. I have regularized the letters *s*, *f*, *u*, and *v*, as well as capitalization, but I otherwise preserve the form of the editions, which differ in their orthography. I have expanded manuscript and print abbreviations silently. I cite editions along with their editors except where none is given. For poetry, I provide line numbers, but otherwise I cite page numbers except in a few cases that are explained in the notes.

I transliterate the Arabic quotations literally, without marking *al-ḥurūf al-shamsīya* or other elisions. For instance, I leave elidible *alif*s in, except in the presence of proclitics like *wa-* and *fa-*. I don't include initial hamzas. Following convention, I use the English form of common Arabic words such as "Quran" and "sharia," including names like Avicenna and Averroes. For the transliteration of individual letters, I follow the American Library Association and Library of Congress (ALA-LC) Romanization table (https://www.loc.gov/catdir/cpso/roman.html).

Introduction

The prominence of marvels in medieval culture, whether in its literature, philosophy, religion, or visual art, is well known. Indeed, one can easily find marvelous creatures like phoenixes or dragons in the period's texts or in its visual art. Such prominence is more likely to be overstated than understated, hence "the medieval West was submerged in [*l'Occident médiéval baigne dans*] what is usually called the marvelous," and it has earned marvels a great deal of scholarly attention, particularly in recent decades.[1] What distinguishes this book, at least with respect to scope, is its analysis of marvels in their cross-disciplinary and cross-cultural abundance, although it confines itself to written sources rather than painted or sculpted ones.[2] With that qualification, it studies marvels where they congregate, namely, in natural philosophy, travel literature, romance, and similar genres, beginning in the twelfth century in the Latin West and centuries earlier in Arabic texts.[3] Writers in one discipline refer explicitly to marvels in the others, as we will see, and they take an interest in the same marvels as well. To view marvels as the shared property of the different disciplines is to raise an obvious question. Natural philosophy focuses on things that are or might be part of the natural world, whereas literature comfortably invents objects and events that do not exist. Put simply, one deals with real things, the other with invented ones. How can marvels at once motivate scientific inquiry and support literary fantasy?

1. Lecouteux, "Introduction à l'étude du merveilleux médiéval," 273. In the 1990s, scholars noticed a heightened interest in marvels. See Bynum, "Miracles and Marvels," 799–801; and Freedman and Spiegel, "Medievalisms Old and New." Such interest has not waned.

2. "Discipline" is a medieval as well as a modern term, and I use it for that reason. Alexander Neckham, for instance, refers to each of the seven liberal arts as a different discipline (*disciplina*) in *De naturis rerum* 2.173, ed. Wright, 301.

3. As Bynum notes, "there is general agreement among scholars that the late twelfth–early thirteenth century saw an increased interest in marvels" in the Latin West ("Miracles and Marvels," 801n11).

The chapters that follow will qualify the association of natural philosophy with the "real," since nature as a concept encompasses the possible as well as the actual. They will also argue against the temptation to understand marvels as either true or false, which has been an impediment to the study of them, as several scholars studying marvels outside of the Latin West have recognized. Persis Berlekamp, for instance, writes, "Today, we define wonder and wonders through post-Enlightenment polarities such as religious-scientific, fantastic-real, and legendary-historical," and though likely inadequate in any period, they are clearly ill suited to the study of marvels in the Middle Ages.[4] David Shulman, in his analysis of South Indian literature, likewise writes that wonder "defies standard analysis in terms of truth-claims," and the same is true of the marvels that produce it.[5] They are, instead, creative or imaginative possibilities, according to a technical definition of imagination that I lay out in the first two chapters.

As a faculty, imagination is not restricted to either the true or the false, the real or the invented. Rather, it heightens qualities like vividness that might belong to both. It thrives where ontological boundaries are least clear and specializes in creating phenomena that are similarly indeterminate, whether in literature or philosophy. On the one hand, philosophers' marvels are more powerful for resembling literary inventions. Prophecy, for instance, relies on the same faculty (imagination) and the same cognitive process as dreams. For one who accepts its validity, it is a true thing that acts like a made-up one and exercises the power of a fictive thing to inspire wonder.[6] Literature, on the other hand, situates purely fanciful creatures alongside nature's most improbable creations. Together, they make the point that spectacular things, whether real or invented, can resemble one another so strongly that it is difficult, and perhaps unnecessary, to distinguish them. Whether in literature or in philosophy, marvels are unlikely phenomena that demand scrutiny and investigation. They mark out the outer boundaries of nature's capabilities and challenge philosophers to think through the limitations of logical possibility. In literature, they are enigmas that, steadfastly inexplicable, demand a lover's faith and play with

4. Berlekamp, *Wonder, Image, and Cosmos in Medieval Islam*, 8. Travis Zadeh also faults Enlightenment binarism for distorting our understanding of medieval marvels; see his *Mapping Frontiers across Medieval Islam*, 6.

5. Shulman, *More Than Real*, 63.

6. I discuss medieval definitions of wonder in the Latin West in "Wonder, Marvels, and Metaphor in the *Squire's Tale*," 463–66. Lara Harb offers a similar definition with respect to Arabic texts (*Arabic Poetics*, 6–12). Both rely on the same key Aristotelian sources.

the reader's expectations. Precisely because they are hard to classify, they enliven the intellect and stimulate imagination.

It is the job of marvels to create not conviction but cognitive uncertainty. Dante describes Sordello responding to the news that Virgil himself stands before him "as one does who suddenly sees before him a thing that makes him marvel, who both believes and does not, saying, 'it is; it is not.'"[7] Marvels tend to inspire doubt. Dreams might be confused with experiences as illusions might be mistaken for perceptions, in part because all rely on imagination. As imagination produces phenomena that resist easy categorization, so it is enlivened by them. For instance, in his commentary on Aristotle's *Poetics*, Averroes comments on images that are easily confused with objects. His examples are constellations called "crab" and "spear-bearer," which so closely approximate the objects for which they are named that they create uncertainty in the one imagining them: "whenever these things that are imagined are most likely to create doubt, they resemble each other most strongly."[8] In other words, the more that the astral and terrestrial images resemble one another within the soul, the more likely they are to create confusion, and in Averroes's view, that is a productive state. Marvels can operate similarly, leading one to ask whether they reside only within the soul, as in the case of hallucinations, or correspond to something in the external world, as happens in the case of perception.

Imagination not only accounts for the likeness between illusory and perceived things but, in medieval theories of the faculty, it can actually alter the world through its images. According to a famous medieval example, imagining the fall of a camel might make the camel fall. In a case like that, imagination breaches the divide between the soul and the world outside, shaping the external world through the force of its images. That capacity, not typically granted to imagination in contemporary philosophy, contributes to the faculty's power to confuse the boundary between the soul and the world beyond. It also gives imagination almost supernatural potency, to the extent that philosophers ask, as we will see, whether God or human imagination might take the credit for some spectacles. Imagination's

7. Dante, *Purgatorio* 7.10–12, ed. and trans. Durling: "Qual è colui che cosa innanzi sé/ sùbita vede ond' e' si maraviglia,/ che crede e non, dicendo: 'Ella è, non è.'"

8. Averroes, *Talkhīṣ kitāb al-shiʿr*, ed. Butterworth and Harīdī, 91: "kullamā kānat hādhihi al-mutawahhamātu aqraba ilā wuqūʿi al-shakki kānat atamma tashbīhan." Averroes addresses the estimative power rather than the imaginative power here, closely linked powers that I discuss in chapter 2. As is often the case, the Latin translation prefers imagination: such images "create uncertainty in the one imagining them" ("inducant ambiguitatem imaginanti," ed. Valgimigli et al., *De arte poetica*, 59).

potential power expresses itself in and defines itself through the marvels it creates.

This book explores writings from the Latin West as well as from Islamic communities, in part because the treatment of marvels in Latin natural philosophy expressly emerges from Arabic sources, as indeed Latin natural philosophy itself is strongly indebted to them. Their shared philosophical, Aristotelian foundations facilitated the transmission of ideas: "The European Christian and Islamic traditions concerning wonder and wonders both flourished at approximately the same time," from the twelfth to eighteenth centuries, and "drew on some of the same sources."[9] They were similarly committed to marvels as opportunities for investigation, and equally intrigued by the marvels of creation.[10] Moreover, "many of the same creatures and tales that inhabit classical Arabic and Persian letters found their way into the collections of curiosities, bestiaries, isolarios, and secrets of nature that filled the libraries of monasteries, universities, and courts in Latin Christendom."[11] This is not to deny the significance of other traditions that were similarly invested in marvels, but simply to privilege the one whose influence was the most overt and, arguably, extensive.[12]

With respect to travel literature and romance, the lines of influence are far hazier. In these contexts, I draw on texts that, so far as we know, were not available in the Latin West. Limiting study of Arabic philosophy and literature to the texts we know to have been translated into Latin necessarily distorts our understanding of them, even when the translations are faithful.[13] Partitioning the two traditions also hampers the study of marvels in the Latin West, whose aims are more clearly viewed through a wider lens. This book identifies an elastic but ultimately coherent theory of marvels that consists, above all, in understanding them as creative and unlikely possibilities that display the full powers of imagination. They are inherently interdisciplinary, boundary resistant, and perplexing, realizing the highest capacities of both nature and the human intellect. They are near-

9. Berlekamp, *Wonder, Image, and Cosmos in Medieval Islam*, 9.

10. Throughout his *Géographie humaine du monde musulman*, André Miquel emphasizes these two aspects of Arabic writings on marvels. See, for instance, 1:42 and 1:180.

11. Zadeh, *Wonders and Rarities*, chap. 5. I look at Persian sources only insofar as they circulated in Arabic, but Zadeh focuses on both, along with Sanskrit and Turkish sources.

12. Especially in the early chapters, footnotes point to some of the many contributions by Jewish philosophers to the views I describe.

13. It is also highly likely that more texts were translated than survive. Charles Burnett gives the examples of Albertus Magnus and Arnold of Saxony, who rely on Arabic philosophical texts whose full Latin translations have not been discovered ("Arabic into Latin," 383).

impossibilities that cannot be conclusively discounted, and that is essential to their power.

Some comments about terminology are in order. The "Latin West" is a widely used phrase that is also, at least for now, relatively uncontroversial. As a concept, it was formed in contrast with the Greek East and referred to the parts of Western Christendom where Latin was a prominent form of communication.[14] It has its failings, as all such descriptors inevitably do. Is al-Andalus, the Arabic name for Islamic Iberia, part of the Latin West? Some scholars include it and some do not. When defining people not according to kingdom or empire—which is not an option in these cases—but according to religious, linguistic, or vaguely cultural affiliation, there will always be some imprecision. Within the units so defined, especially in the Middle Ages, a range of ethnicities, religious beliefs, and languages is certain to exist. Labels, of course, are formed on the basis of likeness, which necessarily means de-emphasizing heterogeneity and, in this case, potentially disenfranchising minority (and sometimes majority) populations.

When it comes to Islamic cultures, the issue of labels is especially complicated, and was in the Middle Ages as well. The term "Saracen" preceded Islam and continued to be imprecise, if consistently offensive, well beyond the Middle Ages.[15] Alexander Bevilacqua, for instance, begins his study of the seventeenth and eighteenth centuries by observing that "Europeans lacked a standardized terminology for identifying Muslims in their religious, cultural, and linguistic communities."[16] They lacked such terminology in the Latin West as well. Among other flaws, alternatives like "Oriental" and "Arab" are similarly imprecise, as Bevilacqua explains. The shifting geographical boundaries of Muslim-identified areas in the Middle Ages—what is typically referred to as the classical or postclassical period by scholars who specialize in it—rules out geographical descriptors, including those based on cardinal points such as the "East."[17] Further, since Persia was thought to be at the center of the world according to Arabic and Persian sources, and Islamic communities extended in every direction around

14. The terms specifically divide the Christian world, as noted by Louth, *Greek East and Latin West*, 2–3.

15. See Beckett, *Anglo-Saxon Perceptions of the Islamic World*, 116–39; and Rajabzadeh, "The Depoliticized Saracen." "Muslim" and "Islam" were not yet circulating in the Latin West.

16. Bevilacqua, *The Republic of Arabic Letters*, ix.

17. I acknowledge that applying the labels "medieval" and "Middle Ages" to Arabic texts expresses a cultural bias since the terms are coined to describe a period in the Latin West. "Classical" and "postclassical," however, are potentially confusing, given the different definition of "classical" in the Western tradition.

it, "East" is woefully inaccurate.[18] The shifting and fragmenting centers of power mean that we cannot rely terminologically on dynasties or caliphates when we speak about broad historical periods either. Were I to focus only on texts written within the periods of Umayyad or Abbasid rule, such designations would be useful, but the period I discuss extends beyond them. As a relatively neutral adjective, language is an appealing and popular option.[19] I too use such phrases as "Arabic philosophers" and "Arabic texts" often, but when applied to cultures rather than genres and texts, such usage excludes Persian and Turkish, among others, as well as the many multilingual communities. The ethnic marker "Arab" is not suitable for a host of reasons, not least because many people in these areas were not Arab, and religion is not ideal either. Even in areas ruled by Islamic law, the *dhimmī* (non-Muslim citizen) and *musta'min* (non-Muslim foreigner) accounted for large portions of some Islamic communities. Further, Muslims were not always in power, nor were they necessarily the majority community, in the areas designated as "Islamic."[20]

This long-standing terminological conundrum has led to the introduction of various alternatives in recent decades, including "Islamdom," "Islamicate," and "dār al-Islām." "Islamdom," proposed by Marshall Hodgson in 1974 and obviously formed on the pattern of "Christendom," was meant to characterize Islamic society, as opposed to its religion or culture, but it did not catch on.[21] "Islamicate," also coined by Hodgson, was meant to designate Islamic culture as opposed to its religion or society, and it still circulates, though Shahab Ahmed's criticism of the term is quite devastating. As he writes, it depends on the notion of "an Islam-concentrate whose presence in greater or lesser dilution may then be measured," as though religion and culture are always distinguishable, and as though culture is less Islamic than religion.[22] In its continued use, "Islamicate" does not necessarily name culture as opposed to religion, but it has to mean something other than "Islamic," and that difference is often left unarticulated. *Dār al-Islām*, a medieval phrase that means "land of Islam" or "where Islam lives," has been adopted by some

18. On Persia's centrality, see Ṣā'id al-Andalusī, *Kitāb tabaqāt al-umam*, ed. Cheikho, 15. Trans. Salem and Kumar, *Science in the Medieval World*, 15.

19. Richard Taylor and Peter Adamson, for instance, prefer the adjective "Arabic" to "Islamic" or "Arab" ("Introduction," in Adamson and Taylor, eds., *Cambridge Companion to Arabic Philosophy*, 3–4). Cynthia Robinson, too, following María Rosa Menocal, advocates for distinguishing cultures by language rather than religion (*In Praise of Song*, 17).

20. As Giovanna Calasso notes; see her introduction to Calasso and Lancioni, eds., *Dār al-Islām/ dār al-ḥarb*, 5.

21. See Ahmed, *What Is Islam?* 159.

22. Ahmed, *What Is Islam?* 175. See his discussion of the term, 157–75.

scholars in Western Europe and North America. In medieval sources, it is used especially by jurists who oppose it to the *dār al-kufr* or *dār al-ḥarb*, that is, the land of the infidels or the land of war (of those who are at war with Islam).[23] The opposition it implies is a compelling reason not to use it, as is the overreliance on Islamic law and its categories in the study of Islamic communities.[24] I am left, then, using "Islamic communities" or "cultures," with the plural reflecting recent scholarly trends.[25] It is easy to object to an adjective that prioritizes religion above every other feature of a community and homogenizes a heterogeneous culture, and it is admittedly an imperfect option, but I choose it in the absence of a better one.[26]

The different sources in this book intersect most visibly and extensively at the point of philosophy, and specifically Aristotelian natural philosophy. Although there is little evidence of direct influence within the realm of travel writing, the genre is active in both cultures, even more so in Islamic communities, and comparisons are productive. With respect to romance, there are some explicit similarities, particularly with respect to Alexander romances, along with many shared features. For sustained attention to marvels, the *Thousand and One Nights* stands out, although it is a text that is hard to place generically. Grouped with "*ʿajāʾib*" or "wonder" literature, it is often placed alongside cosmologies and geographies. The *sīra*, a prosimetric genre that consists of heroic narratives, also turns to marvels often, and for that reason it figures into my final chapters along with the *Thousand and One Nights*. Although both have been disparaged, based on a common belief that "poetry is the only respectable genre [of literature] for the Arabs," they have begun to attract the more serious attention that they deserve.[27]

In comparative work such as this, there is always the risk of assimilation, of making the Arabic materials suit an argument that does not proceed organically from them. Such scholarship can perpetuate a colonialist project that subordinates cultures outside the Latin West and casts them in its shadow.[28] That risk is especially acute when the attention paid to the

23. See Calasso, "Constructing and Deconstructing the *dār al-islām/ dār al-ḥarb* Opposition," in Calasso and Lancioni, eds., *Dār al-Islām/ dār al-ḥarb*, as well as the other articles in the collection.

24. As discussed by Ahmed, *What Is Islam?* 113–29.

25. I use "Islamic world" in the singular in my title, although the plural has also become common, because I think that the notion of "world" includes variety and multiplicity. For more on this issue, see Denoix, "Des culs-de-sacs heuristique."

26. On terminology, see also Zadeh, "Postscript," 607–14.

27. Rodinson, "La place du merveilleux," 179.

28. Edward Said famously fleshed out these implications in *Orientalism*. Among the many important responses to his argument from medievalists, see Akbari, *Idols in the East*, 5–11; and Phillips, *Before Orientalism*, 15–27.

different literatures is unequal, as it is in this book. Further, whereas Arabic writings about marvels took precedence in the Middle Ages and were transmitted to the Latin West, without reciprocation so far as we know, here the writings from the Latin West take precedence. Were I equally competent in both traditions, I would remedy that imbalance and address them equally, or privilege the Arabic texts, but the value of broadening the book's parameters beyond the Latin West, even imperfectly, is greater than the harm done by restricting it.[29] Occluding the Arabic conversation perpetuates a false image of intellectual insularity in the Latin West, and integrating the two better reflects the active migration of ideas in the Middle Ages. I should add that I do not study Western Christian representations of Muslims or of Islamic communities in this book. While undoubtedly valuable and often theoretically savvy as well, the scholarship devoted to such representations tends to illuminate Western Christians and their prejudices more than the communities that they perceived. It is more productive, I think, to broaden our focus and study texts across languages and cultures.

The relevance of Arabic materials to the conception of marvels in the Latin West is no secret, either in its own period or in later ones, but it introduces a sticky problem.[30] Foundational to Western Orientalism was the appeal of Western Europeans to the "Orient" for shocking, lurid, or simply irrational content, and marvels were a part of that project. In fact, that movement produced many of the translations of literature, travel and otherwise, that I draw on.[31] As Travis Zadeh explains in his magisterial study of marvels in Islamic thought, "the endless marvels of the Orient became a foil for defining the rationality of Christian Europe."[32] In other words, there is a well-known body of Western scholarship that turns to Arabic sources specifically on the topic of marvels, but it provides no roadmap to follow. Marvels were, from its perspective, exoticized imports that belonged properly to a superstitious past or to a benighted, foreign, and backward

29. As Kathleen Kennedy writes, "to be interdisciplinary demands risk-taking, and that means that we will sometimes fail," even if we fail only to meet our own highest standards ("Moors and Moorishness," 251).

30. Reto Bezzola points to early nineteenth-century scholars who recognized such influence (*Les origines et la formation de la littérature courtoise en Occident*, 1:184). Examples of medieval and early modern philosophers who do the same appear in this book's first two chapters.

31. Recent years have seen the translation of many Arabic works—philosophical and fictional—into Western European vernaculars, but the early focus fell more narrowly on geographies and fiction, in part because they contained in abundance the marvels that were made to define the "Orient."

32. Zadeh, *Wonders and Rarities*, introduction.

present, and this attitude toward marvels persists.[33] It is easy to spot, for instance, in the claim that the *Thousand and One Nights* appealed to Western European Christians because it offered them the thrill of illicit magic, magic that "Christian orthodoxy, as defined by Thomas Aquinas's thought, must reject."[34] I agree that Aquinas was emblematic of Christian orthodoxy with respect to magic, but only insofar as he embraced and directed considerable intellectual energy toward it rather than rejecting it. Marvels were as thoroughly integrated into the Christian cultures that this book studies as the Islamic ones. It is certainly the case that Arabic sources were crucial to the treatment of marvels in the Latin West, but not because they were irrational or exotic. Instead, it was Arabic philosophers' rationalistic, natural philosophical approach to marvels that influenced philosophers in the Latin West, partly because it was based in Greek philosophical sources that were integral to both traditions.[35] Marvels themselves belonged no more to the one religion than to the other.

In recent years, there has been little effort to study the two traditions in tandem, even though the same marvels often appear in both.[36] Perhaps because they grapple openly with phenomena that are strange and unfamiliar, marvels traveled unusually well across both geographical and conceptual space. For that reason, they offer an ideal vantage point from which to understand intercultural—albeit largely unidirectional—contact. In this context, the differences between the traditions are as useful as the similarities. In support of applying categories from modern literary criticism to the study of medieval literature, Julie Orlemanski writes of the "critical energy to be drawn from the friction of concepts."[37] Comparing concepts across cultures in the same time period provides a similar energy, enriching our understanding through unlikeness as well as likeness.

DEFINING MARVELS

Marvels are difficult to define, and not for lack of attempts in the recent or distant past. The difficulty, rather, is that the category can be so broad as to exclude hardly anything within nature. Thomas of Cantimpré, quot-

33. Muslim reformists repudiate such materials because of a similar belief that they are retrograde; see Zadeh, *Wonders and Rarities*, conclusion.

34. Warner, *Stranger Magic*, 43.

35. See Kieckhefer, "The Specific Rationality of Medieval Magic."

36. The most progress has been made in the study of travel literature. See, for instance, Chism, "Facing the Land of Darkness"; and Pinto, *"Mandeville's Travels": A "Rihla" in Disguise.*

37. Orlemanski, "Who Has Fiction?" 148.

ing Aristotle, proclaims that "there is something marvelous in all things of nature."[38] The thirteenth-century *De mirabilibus mundi* likewise declares that "everything is full of marvels," and "nobody can say that everything is not full of marvelousness."[39] Jacques de Vitry writes that "all the works of God are marvels."[40] The thirteenth-century philosopher al-Qazwīnī begins his *'Ajā'ib al-makhlūqāt*, or *Wonders of Creation*, with the marvel of the beehive's honeycomb—"how small animals create equilateral hexagons the likes of which a skillful engineer could not make with a compass and a ruler"—and concludes that "everything in the universe in this manner" is a marvel (*'ajab*).[41] As he shows, the regular operations of nature, such as the mating habits or diets of different animals, can be construed as marvels in this general sense. The Bible too was thought to be full of *mirabilia*, as suggested even by the title of the seventh-century *De mirabilibus sacrae scripturae*. Peter Comestor describes any number of biblical events as marvels or marvelous, including Samson's feats, the Israelites' escape from Egypt, the crossing of the Jordan, and Isaac's birth and death.[42] The Quran not only contained wonders but was itself thought to produce wonder.[43]

We might read such comments as evidence that "marvel" carried different meanings, one general and one technical. However, even where philosophers investigate individual marvels, presumably understanding "marvel" in its most narrow sense, the category still threatens to include too much. Thus Nicole Oresme describes as *mirabilia* people who do not feel the pain of a burn, the tendency of pepper to act as a laxative in small

38. Aristotle, *De partibus animalium* 1.5, 645a16–17, ed. Henderson, 99; and Thomas of Cantimpré, *Liber de natura rerum*, Prologue, ed. Boese, 4: "in omnibus rebus naturalibus est mirabile."

39. *De mirabilibus mundi*, Prologue, ed. Sannino, 97: "res unaquaeque est plena mirabilibus"; and 96: "Non potest aliquis dicere, quod omnis res non sit plena mirabilitate."

40. Jacques de Vitry, *Historia orientalis* 92, ed. Donnadieu, 406: "omnia Dei opera mirabilia sunt."

41. Al-Qazwīnī, *'Ajā'ib al-makhlūqāt*, Introduction, ed. Sa'd, 31: "al-ḥayawānu al-ḍa'īfu kayfa aḥdatha hādhihi al-musadasāta al-mutasāwīyata al-aḍlā'a allatī 'ajaza 'an mithlihā al-muhandasu al-ḥādhiqu ma'a al-firjāri wa-l-misṭarati" . . . "wa-kullu mā fī al-'ālami bi-hādha al-mathābati." Qazwīnī here addresses *'ajā'ib*, but his title also includes *gharā'ib*, or oddities, and it should be noted that the two terms, often paired, differ in meaning. See Zadeh, "Postscript," 615–24, and Harb, *Arabic Poetics*, 5n11 and 8n20. There has been a good deal of resistance to the notion that the terms *'ajā'ib* and *gharā'ib* might be considered synonymous with or subsumed under the notion of the "fantastic" in Western scholarship (see, for instance, Abu-Deeb, *The Imagination Unbound*, 8–13). My definition of "imagination" (I do not use "the fantastic" substantively) is deliberately constructed to apply to both traditions.

42. Petrus Comestor, *Historia scholastica*, *PL* 198: 1105B, 1129D, 1155D, 1262A, and 1288A.

43. See Harb, *Arabic Poetics*, 203–51.

quantities but as a diuretic in large ones, the existence of monsters, the fact that one person can like a certain flavor and someone else the opposite one, the ability of some people to speak languages they never learned, the preference of some men for black women (*aliquos qui habent placentiam circa nigras*), and the fact that a man might be impotent with a beautiful woman (*pulchra muliere*) but not with an ugly one (*turpi*).[44] Marvels could be minor quirks or monstrous aberrations. He includes phenomena both spectacular and mundane, perhaps all unusual in his view, but united above all by their inconsistency with respect either to how they manifest themselves or to how others respond to them. It is the irregularity that seems to demand explanation.

Oresme expressly defends the everyday marvel, which in his view has as strong a claim to marvelousness as the evil eye. His inclusiveness is mirrored in works of natural philosophy that happen upon the most striking marvels casually, interspersing them in discussions of other natural phenomena instead of bracketing them out or distinguishing them in any clear way from usual matters. Such organization suggests little interest in managing marvels' boundaries. That is due, in large part, to the fact that "marvel" is a subjective concept—as Daniel Poirion writes, the marvelous does not refer "to an objective quality of the world"—and as such it is necessarily untidy.[45] Not all people consider the same things to be marvelous. As Jacques de Vitry evenhandedly writes, a Cyclops might be no less surprised by someone with three eyes than with two, and Pygmies might consider humans to be giants. Perspectives differ. Also addressing race, he writes, "we think that black Ethiopians are ugly, but among themselves, they judge the one who is more black to be more beautiful."[46] His prejudice is obvious even to himself, and with his vague "we" he shares it with others. Marvels are defined by the wonder of the one who perceives them, which makes the concept mutable and unstable.

There are, nonetheless, some criteria that help to define the narrower sense of marvels. They are typically natural phenomena that are not sufficiently understood, usually ones that seem especially hard to explain, that appear to transgress the known operations of nature. A middle-of-the-road definition is offered by the *De mirabilibus mundi*, a very popular text that was misattributed to Albertus Magnus in the Middle Ages and early modern period.

44. Oresme, *De causis mirabilium*, ed. Hansen, *Nicole Oresme and the Marvels of Nature*, 136, 192, 222, and 244.

45. Poirion, *Le merveilleux dans la littérature française du Moyen Age*, 4.

46. Jacques de Vitry, *Historia orientalis* 92, ed. Donnadieu, 406: "Nos autem nigros Ethiopes turpes reputamus, inter ipsos autem qui nigrior est pulchior ab ipsis iudicatur."

> What is marvelous is that whose cause has generally been hidden from view . . . However, when someone sufficiently inspects the thing or the cause of the thing, they marvel not at all. Therefore, something is marvelous if it is unusual or rare or has never been seen. It is not just marvelous because its cause is unknown, but because it has been discovered to be exceedingly rare . . . And something is also marvelous that is not unusual, but often seen, and its cause is not totally unknown, but it does not seem that the effect can follow from the cause . . . In the first category are the most marvelous things, in the second the middle sort, and in the third are most marvels.[47]

From this perspective, marvels are things that are unexplained, unexplained because rare, or insufficiently explained because the effect seems mismatched to the cause. In any case, there is a deficiency of explanation. The idea that wonder results from things not fully understood is very easy to find in medieval sources.[48] Roy Mottahedeh, citing al-Iṣfahānī's definition of *ʿajab* and *taʿajjub* (wonder and astonishment) as "ʿstates which come to a person at the time of that person's ignorance of the *sabab* (cause) of something,'" notes that "a definition along these lines becomes standard in the scholastic tradition."[49] It opens al-Qazwīnī's *Wonders of Creation*: "the marvel appears confusing to someone because they lack knowledge about something's cause or about the nature of its effect."[50] Marvels produce wonder because they resist explanation in some respect. According to the Anglo-Norman jurist Gervase of Tilbury, "we call those things marvels which do not submit to our understanding, even though they are natural."[51]

47. *De mirabilibus mundi*, ed. Sannino, 151–52: "Mirabile est illud, cuius causa removetur a conspectu communiter . . . Cum vero res aut rei causa sufficiens aspicitur, nihil miratur. Est igitur aliquid mirabile quod inconsuetum aut rarum aut numquam visum est. Unde non solum est mirabile, quia causa ignoratur, sed et ipsum rarissime est inventum . . . Et est aliquid mirabile, quod nec ipsum inconsuetum est, sed saepe visum, nec eius causa totaliter ignoratur, sed non apparet quod ex ea causatus effectus possit exire . . . In primo genere sunt maxima mirabilia, in secundo medio modo, in tertio sunt maiora."

48. Bert Hansen provides an extensive but not exhaustive list of references in *Nicole Oresme and the Marvels of Nature*, 64–69.

49. Mottahedeh, "ʿAjāʾib in *The Thousand and One Nights*," 30.

50. Al-Qazwīnī, *ʿAjāʾib al-makhlūqāt* Introduction, ed. Saʿd, 31: "al-ʿajabu ḥayratun taʿruḍu li-l-insāni li-quṣūrihi ʿan maʿarifati sababi al-shayʾi aw ʿan maʿarifati kayfīyati taʾthīrihi fīhi." On the complicated textual history of this work, see Zadeh, *Wonders and Rarities*.

51. Gervase of Tilbury, *Otia imperialia*, Preface to Book 3, ed. and trans. Banks and Binns, 558–59: "Mirabilia vero dicimus que nostre cognicioni non subiacent, etiam cum sunt naturalia." Miracles, in contrast, are beyond nature (*preter naturam*), 558.

They *seem* unnatural but are not. In that sense they constitute a provocation, showing philosophers who could not account for them that their understanding of nature was insufficient and challenging them to know more. Such philosophers return again and again to the same marvels, like the basilisk that kills with its sight alone or the women in Bythia with the same power. They engage in a conversation about the mechanisms of marvels that crosses space and time.[52]

Among marvels are products of magic like illusions and transmutations as well as the special properties of natural things like curative herbs and unusual stones.[53] They are defined in part by the wonder they create. As Caroline Walker Bynum notes, "the wonderful . . . was never the *merely* strange or the *simply* inexplicable. It was a strange that mattered, that pointed beyond itself to meaning . . . Wonder was a response to something novel and bizarre that seemed both to exceed explanation and to indicate that there might be reason . . . behind it."[54] Marvels necessarily provoke wonder, if not to everyone equally, and they are often unusual. Augustine notes that a thoughtful person might find cause for wonder in any created thing, but wonder is most often reserved for phenomena that are rare.[55] In addition, they are often foreign. Elly Truitt writes that automata typically relied on knowledge "from long ago or far away," and the same is true of marvels more generally.[56] Their origins are frequently placed at a temporal or spatial distance from the one who writes about them. Finally, marvels are often entertaining, a feature that is easily appreciated in visual art, but has not been associated as often with the period's written marvels.[57] Thomas of Cantimpré, for instance, acknowledges that some of the marvels he describes defy belief, but defends their inclusion in part because "new things in one's mouth might soften the ears of the sluggish."[58] They divert and move their readers where "the well-worn and often-heard matters of scripture" do not.[59] Vincent of Beauvais makes a similar point, defending

52. As Travis Zadeh notes with respect to Persian and Arabic philosophy, "writings on the wonders of creation, like descriptive geography, often recycle a set corpus of material," *Mapping Frontiers across Medieval Islam*, 139.

53. It is more often natural than demonic magic that furnishes such marvels. On the distinction between them, see Kieckhefer, *Magic in the Middle Ages*, 1–15; Kaye, "Law, Magic, and Science"; and Bartlett, *The Natural and The Supernatural*, 21–23.

54. Bynum, "Wonder," 23–24.

55. Augustine, *De civitate Dei* 21.8, ed. Dombart and Kalb, *CCSL* 48:772.

56. Truitt, *Medieval Robots*, 5.

57. I thank Jessica Wolfe for this observation.

58. Thomas of Cantimpré, *Liber de natura rerum*, Prologue, ed. Boese, 5: "nova in ore suo pigritantium aures demulceant."

59. Thomas of Cantimpré, *Liber de natura rerum*, Prologue, ed. Boese, 5: "sepius audita de scripturis et inculcata non movent."

his inclusion of non-Christian sources in order to satisfy those who "would take delight in knowledge of such things."[60] Marvels are hard to believe, and they are meant to be enjoyed. It is safe to conclude that the two features are related: marvels create pleasure at least in part through their unlikeliness.

Although the opposition between natural marvels and supernatural miracles is common in scholarship on the Latin West, both need to be qualified.[61] Augustine specifically denied that any action performed by God within the natural world was unnatural, even though it might exceed our understanding. "A portent happens not contrary to nature, but contrary to what we know of nature," he wrote.[62] Various medieval philosophers embraced the idea, hence Thomas Aquinas: "God does nothing contrary to nature."[63] Nature instead accommodates God. In this strict sense, miracles too are natural, but they do not need to follow the normal laws of nature. For their part, marvels might be supernatural in the sense that spiritual beings produce them. Jacques Le Goff, for instance, writes that "one characteristic of the marvelous is of course that of being produced by supernatural forces or beings."[64] All the same, even in cases of demonic possession and prophetic inspiration, as we will see, the natural mechanisms of marvels—the ways in which they involve the intellect or nature more generally—can be grasped by the rational intellect. They are in a basic sense knowable, which sets the foundation for a sturdier contrast. Because marvels operate through nature and follows its laws, they can potentially be understood, whereas miracles typically cannot, at least not in this life.[65] This distinction, though by no means firm, is reflected in how much medieval philosophy is dedicated to explaining how marvels work and how little is similarly directed at miracles.

UNDERSTANDING MARVELS

The scholarship on medieval marvels is vast. Nonetheless, it is possible to identify three basic approaches that have governed the study of them in the Latin West. The first rests on the conviction that marvels were widely

60. Vincent of Beauvais, *Speculum naturale* Pro.18, in *Speculum quadruplex* 1:15C: "talium notitia delectantur."

61. On the opposition, see Bartlett, *The Natural and the Supernatural*, 1–33; and Bynum, "Miracles and Marvels," 802–5.

62. Augustine, *De civitate Dei* 21.8, ed. Dombart and Kalb, *CCSL* 48:771: "Portentum ergo fit non contra naturam, sed contra quam est nota natura."

63. Aquinas, *Summa contra Gentiles* 3.100.1, in *Opera omnia* 14:310: "nihil tamen facit contra naturam."

64. Le Goff, *L'imaginaire médiéval*, 22.

65. See Daston and Park, *Wonders and the Order of Nature*, 93–124; and Bynum, "Miracles and Marvels."

believed, and believed as a matter of faith. Claude Lecouteux, for instance, writes that the marvel, like the miracle, "pertains to the act of faith."[66] A people who were deferential to authority accepted what they were told by the church or otherwise without much resistance.[67] In that spirit, they were quick to accept marvels as facts. As Jacques Le Goff writes, the people of the period were "fed from the outset with legends that they took for truths."[68] For this reason, marvels flourished particularly among the less educated, forming part of "popular religion," that amorphous entity often made responsible for ideas that might now seem embarrassing.[69] The simple-minded gullibility that fueled marvels in the Middle Ages dissipated with the passage of time and was decisively rejected during the Enlightenment, a period that "is still defined in part as the anti-marvelous."[70] A more critical attitude toward marvels appeared, then, with a more critical attitude toward Christianity, further suggesting that religious belief conditioned people to be credulous with respect to them. They were appropriate to an age of faith, and stayed roughly within its boundaries. Although the roots of this approach are now several decades old, it is still prominent, maybe even dominant, certainly in popular culture. When David Brooks, for instance, writes that "the medievals had a tremendous capacity for imagination and enchantment," and that, for them, "material things were consecrated with spiritual powers," he echoes this approach.[71]

The second approach holds that people in the Middle Ages interpreted marvels allegorically. It was "an era that understood every phenomenon as figurative," in which "significance is more important—even more striking—than existence."[72] From this perspective, the truth of marvels is relatively unimportant. What matters is the deeper spiritual truth that a given marvel might symbolize. The pelican's piercing of itself in order to feed its young represents Christ's sacrifice, whether or not the pelican actually wounds itself so dramatically. The same attitude might be applied to travel literature, where spiritual truths outweigh geographical realities.[73]

66. Lecouteux, "Introduction à l'étude du merveilleux médiéval," 276–77.

67. Patty Ingham describes and disputes this depiction in *The Medieval New*, 1–7.

68. Le Goff, "L'Occident médiéval," 283.

69. On the appeal of marvels to the less educated, see Le Goff, "L'Occident médiéval"; and Poirion, *Le merveilleux dans la littérature française*, 5–6. In *Imagination, Meditation, and Cognition*, I discuss the critical tendency to assign meditational literature to the same ill-defined group, 12–14.

70. Daston and Park, *Wonders and the Order of Nature*, 368. See also Bynum, "Wonder," 4.

71. Brooks, "The Great Escape."

72. Campbell, *The Witness and the Other World*, 83.

73. Le Goff, "L'Occident médiéval," 283.

Finally, scholars have embraced the Middle Ages and its marvels as foundational to modern science.[74] Insofar as natural philosophers sought to understand the natural mechanisms of marvels, they might be seen to drive a wedge between religion and science so that science might prosper. Although not particularly disposed toward experimentation, they might appear to anticipate other elements of the scientific method. This approach can be traced back to Pierre Duhem's *Le système du monde*, where he disputes the once-common notion that science began with the end of the Middle Ages. It privileges the work of the Oxford calculators along with the medieval study of motion and mechanics more generally. With respect to marvels, it is sometimes selective. For instance, Duhem, translating portions of Abū Ma'shar's most popular work on astronomy, stops when he devolves into explanations that are "purely fantastic."[75] He sanitizes medieval writing about marvels here, stripping it of what might be considered unscientific content in order to establish its seriousness.

I confine my study to the Middle Ages and seek to understand the role that marvels occupied within it rather than reading them forward. A great deal of evidence shows that writers did not habitually assume that marvels were true, as we will see. Rather, the stakes concerning marvels were usually low: whether they might or might not be believed was a matter of individual choice. In both traditions, they were sometimes elided with miracles, in which case belief ceased to be optional, but when distinct from them, they were more playful and hypothetical than dogmatic or doctrinal. I argue that marvels represent creative, often far-fetched possibilities that invite inspection in large part because of their ontological uncertainty. Possibly real and possibly not, they pique imagination because they resist easy classification. This reading has more in common with scholarship on medieval Arabic, Persian, and Sanskrit marvels than with that on marvels in the Latin West. For instance, Travis Zadeh focuses expressly on how marvels in Arabic and Persian texts "harmoniously fuse together seemingly disparate levels of discourse," such as philosophy, geography, Quranic exegesis, poetry, and literary criticism.[76] The disciplinary heterogeneity that surrounds marvels, not just in a single text but across them, is central to this study. The fact that medieval writers regularly cross disciplinary boundaries when they write about them opens the door for critics who seek to

74. Hence Grant, *The Foundations of Modern Science in the Middle Ages*; Lindberg, *The Beginnings of Western Science*; Weisheipl, *Nature and Motion in the Middle Ages*; Maier, *On the Threshold of Exact Science*; Clagett, *The Science of Mechanics in the Middle Ages*; and Truitt, *Medieval Robots*.

75. Duhem, *Le système du monde*, 2:385.

76. Zadeh, "Wiles of Creation," 25.

understand their methods. It shows from the outset that the truth or falsehood of marvels is not essential to them. Otherwise, their philosophical and poetic forms would resist comparison.

Insofar as this book focuses on the role of imagination in the operation of marvels, it rejects a reductive understanding of the faculty that associates it only with mental picture-making.[77] In this sense, too, scholarship on imagination in other cultures is helpful. David Shulman, for instance, notes that "any simplistic divide between the 'real' and the 'imagined' has to be set aside from the outset" in order to understand the concept of imagination in early South Indian literature, and the same is true in the Latin West and in medieval Islamic cultures.[78] He argues that "imagination requires a high-grade, tensile suspension in which reality and unreality come together in the mind of the listener or spectator without resolving the contradiction between them," which is a perspective I largely share.[79] Marvels depend on this irresolution for their existence as unlikely possibilities that, in most cases, cannot be definitively proven either to exist or not to exist.

PHILOSOPHY, LITERATURE, AND MARVELS

Following Aristotle, medieval writers expressly linked philosophy to literature on the basis of wonder.[80] It is hard to think of another topic where the two disciplines' interests overlap so overtly. In the second chapter of his *Metaphysics*, Aristotle writes that "it is owing to their wonder that men both now begin and at first began to philosophize . . . [E]ven the lover of myth is in a sense a lover of wisdom, for myth is composed of wonders."[81] Commenting on the much-cited lines, in both Latin and Arabic sources, Aquinas explains, "the reason why the philosopher is compared to the poet

77. I acknowledge the anachronism of the term "mental" and, elsewhere, "extramental," since only according to a later, Cartesian sense does the concept of the mind include representations in the senses, such as imagination.

78. Shulman, *More Than Real*, 17.

79. Shulman, *More Than Real*, 60. Maxime Rodinson makes a similar point about the mental representation of real and invented things with respect to Arabic writings about marvels ("La place du merveilleux," 168).

80. Instead of "literature," medieval sources typically speak of "poets" and "poetry," which is not precisely the same as "myth" or "mythographers," but as the subsequent quotation from Aquinas shows, the two were considered roughly equatable. On the meaning of poetics in the Arabic tradition, see Harb, *Arabic Poetics*, 124–25, as well as the collected articles in Kennedy, ed., *On Fiction and* Adab *in Medieval Arabic Literature*.

81. Aristotle, *Metaphysica* 1.2, 982b12–19, ed. Vuillemin-Diem, 16: "Nam propter admirari homines et nunc et primum inceperunt philosophari . . . philomitos philosophus aliqualiter est; fabula namque ex miris constituitur." Trans. Barnes, *The Complete Works of Aristotle*, 2:1554.

is that both are concerned with wonders. For the myths with which the poets deal are composed of wonders, and the philosophers themselves were moved to philosophize as a result of wonder."[82] In Aquinas's view, poets seek to preserve or inculcate wonder, while philosophers are motivated by it and seek to replace it with knowledge. As engines of wonder, marvels fall to the purview of both. However, in literature wonder also inspires investigation, as we will see. Is that a fairy? Is she benevolent or not? Is that an actual beast or just an apparition? Marvels provoke inquiry from both characters and readers.[83]

Such like-mindedness should not obscure the differences between the disciplinary contexts.[84] Nonetheless, the recognition that poets and philosophers share marvels as a source of inspiration appears in a variety of texts. In *Le chemin de longue étude*, for instance, Christine de Pizan has her main character visit the Fountain of Wisdom that sits beneath Mount Parnassus. The nine Muses cavort in it, and both poets and philosophers begin their path of long study, for which the poem is named, there.[85] Christine explains that Aristotle, Hermes, and Avicenna had their start at the fountain, along with Homer, Virgil, and Orpheus.[86] The path begins with Constantinople, and it reveals "more than a thousand marvels" that are familiar from travel literature, including distant lands, strange animals, giants, and the trees of the sun and moon.[87] Such marvels appeal to philosophers and poets who would cultivate wonder in response to the created world and praise their creator in the hope of ascending to heaven.

Not only similarly motivated by marvels, poets and philosophers also write about some of the same marvels. For instance, the French romance *Floire et Blancheflor* features a well that tests virginity. If a virgin washes

82. Aquinas, *In Metaphysicam Aristotelis Commentaria* 3.55, ed. Cathala, 20: "Causa autem, quare philosophus comparatur poetae, est ista, quia uterque circa miranda versatur. Nam fabulae, circa quas versantur poetae, ex quibusdam mirabilibus constituuntur. Ipsi etiam philosophi ex admiratione moti sunt ad philosophandum."

83. Lara Harb writes about the similarities between the wonder produced by knowledge and by poetry in *Arabic Poetics*, 75–134.

84. Consider Elly Truitt: "Because accounts of automata in historical chronicles, travel narratives, and encyclopedias emerge from the same wellspring as accounts of automata in romances, epic poems, and drama, all can be read as historical texts that offer insight into medieval beliefs and practices" (*Medieval Robots*, 5). See also Baldwin, *Aristocratic Life in Medieval France*, 77.

85. As Christine notes (*Le chemin de longue étude*, 1128, ed. and trans. Tarnowski), the phrase "path of long study" comes from Dante (*Inferno* 1.83).

86. Sarah Kay writes that Christine departs from literary tradition in associating the fountain with both poets and philosophers (*Place of Thought*, 163).

87. Christine de Pizan, *Le chemin de longue étude*, 1285, ed. and trans. Tarnowski: "merveilles plus de mile."

her hands in it, the water will not protest, but it will respond to an impure woman by screaming and turning red. According to the Middle English version:

> Nou is the welle of so mochel eye,
> Yif ther cometh ani maiden that is forleie,
> And hi [she] bowe to the grounde
> For to waschen here honde,
> The water wille yelle als hit ware wod [crazy],
> And bicome on hire so red so [as] blod.[88]

The particular marvel of the well, its "eye," is its ability to identify the woman who is "forleie," who has transgressed literally by lying with a man.[89] The marvel is symbolically rich, with a woman so polluted that she corrupts the water she touches. Her sin is insoluble, and so she turns water blood-red in imitation of her ruptured hymen. Christian exegesis unravels the symbolism further. When Longinus pierced Christ's side, the water and blood that spilled out were cleansing. Thus the *Glossa ordinaria* on Jn 19:34: "this blood was poured out for the remission of sins. Water offers both bath and drink."[90] The potent purity of Christ's water and blood, foundational to the sacraments of baptism and the Eucharist, creates a strict contrast with the impurity of the bloodstained water on the woman's hands. Through Christ's death, Eve's wound was healed—citing Theophilus, the Gloss writes, "through the side wound, the wound of the side, here Eve is healed"—and so Christ's side wound sanitizes specifically female transgression.[91] In line with that tradition, virgins might purify water. Bevis of Hampton, for instance, is restored by falling into a well that a virgin had bathed in, a well that reappears in the first book of Spenser's *Faerie Queene*.[92] The impure maiden instead undoes Christ's work and re-immerses herself in original sin.

Philosophers too wrote a good deal about marvels that test virginity. Albertus Magnus in his *Mineralium*, for instance, describes nearly a dozen

88. *Floris and Blancheflour*, 664–69, ed. Sands, *Middle English Verse Romances*.

89. "Eye" here is etymologically related to "awe" (OED awe, n., 1). The coincidence of forms between this and the ocular "eye" is a happy linguistic accident that invests the marvel with the sense of spectacle.

90. *Bibliorum Sacrorum cum Glossa Ordinaria*, ed. Feuardent et al., 5:1316E: "Ille sanguis fusus est in remissionem peccatorum. Aqua et lavacrum praestat et potum."

91. *Bibliorum Sacrorum cum Glossa Ordinaria*, ed. Feuardent et al., 5:1316F: "per saucium latus, vulnus lateris, hoc est Eva sanatur." The representation of the side wound (*vulnus*) as a vagina (*vulna*) has received a great deal of scholarly attention. For a recent example, see Bynum, *Dissimilar Similitudes*, 202–11.

92. *Bevis of Hampton*, 2804–6, in *Four Romances of England*, ed. Herzman et al.

ways to determine whether a woman is a virgin. When discussing the stone *gagates*, or jet, he writes:

> They say, too, that experience shows that if the stone is placed in water and the water is strained and then given with some scrapings of the stone to a virgin, having drunk, she will retain the liquid, so that she does not urinate. But if she is not a virgin, she urinates immediately. And this is how one should prove whether a woman is a virgin.[93]

The marvel is less flashy, but it follows similar principles: the water somehow rejects the nonvirgin and shows her to be corrupt, here by causing her to produce urine. In other words, her uncleanliness expresses itself in the waste she expels. If the two sources are read in tandem, one can surmise that the *Floire*'s Emir lined his well with this or another stone in order to give it its special power, but that is hardly revelatory. More interesting is the belief here expressed that nature like poetry loves a symbol. Even in cases where poetry and philosophy intersect less explicitly, marvels remain expressions of creativity that invite cross-disciplinary comparison.

MARVELS AND FICTION

Travis Zadeh writes that "fiction" mischaracterizes literature that contains marvels, since it "tends to predetermine for us the place and significance of the marvelous or uncanny."[94] It is potentially simplifying, and it also focuses attention on whether they exist, which is equally unhelpful. That was not the question that drove interest in them, and it does not help us to understand them. I persist, nonetheless, with using the term "fiction," although I want to suggest some modifications to its standard definition.[95] Medieval literature does not qualify as fiction according to some literary theorists, and I have argued elsewhere against this exclusion.[96] I use it in this book to characterize literature, with the goal not of assimilating medieval literature to that of later periods but of identifying some key distinctions.[97] The first

93. Albertus Magnus, *Mineralium* 2.2.7, in *Opera omnia*, ed. Borgnet, 5:37: "Aiunt autem de expertis esse, quod si colatura et ejus lotura cum rasura detur virgini, bibita retinebit eam, quod non minget. Si autem non est virgo, statim minget: et sic debet probari an aliqua sit virgo." Trans. Wyckoff, *Book of Minerals*, 93.

94. Zadeh, *Mapping Frontiers across Medieval Islam*, 7.

95. For definitions of "fable" and "fiction" in the Latin West, see Vance, *From Topic to Tale*, 20–22. On poetry in the Arabic tradition, see Harb, *Arabic Poetics*, 25–134.

96. Karnes, "The Possibilities of Medieval Fiction."

97. For inclusive definitions, see Orlemanksi, "Who Has Fiction?"; and Ashe, "1155 and the Beginnings of Fiction."

is that medieval fiction does not always depend on a firm contrast between facts and fables, whereas "the primary categorical division in our textual universe is between 'fiction' and 'nonfiction,'" according to Catherine Gallagher.[98] It is a distinction we police assiduously, as when we punish those (like James Frey) who market fiction as nonfiction. Umberto Eco helps to conceptualize the medieval alternative when he describes what he characterizes as an encyclopedic approach to knowledge in the Latin West. His contrast is with ancient philosophers, for whom knowledge was about classification, about identifying genera and species and then filing "man" under "animal" and "daisy" under "flower." For them, knowledge was a dictionary, but in the encyclopedic Middle Ages, understanding a rock did not mean properly locating it in a classificatory system, but rather understanding its qualities more broadly. The result was something more like an encyclopedia entry, but distinct from a modern encyclopedia in one key respect: the medieval encyclopedist, following Pliny, "does not make the slightest effort to separate reliable empirical information from legend."[99] That is, he does not categorically distinguish fact from fiction.

Even limited exposure to medieval natural philosophy shows what he means. Thomas of Cantimpré, describing animals in sequence, includes *caco*, or Cacus, the fire-breathing giant killed by Hercules, alongside *capra* (she-goat) and *cefusa* (monkey).[100] Jacques de Vitry transitions from camels to mythical creatures like manticores and eales and then back to hyenas without observing any difference in kind between them.[101] The transition from scientific information to creatures from legend can be jarring because a fundamental organizing principle in the contemporary Western classification of knowledge, as Eco notes, is that the two should be partitioned, the real from the imaginary.[102] He does not claim that people in the period or its encyclopedists *failed to recognize the difference* between, say, manticores and hyenas, and that point is worth stressing. Neither does he pretend that his observation holds across disciplines. His would not be a fair characterization of medieval Christian theology, surely. Nonetheless, his analysis shows that the medieval deprivileging of the opposition between truth and falsehood might be viewed as a choice, even an aesthetic choice. It does not need to imply a gullible people who believed what they were told, a nondiscriminating people who thought mythical creatures were real, or a simple people who were slow to make rational judgments.

98. Gallagher, "Rise of Fictionality," 336.
99. Eco, *From the Tree to the Labyrinth*, 26.
100. Thomas of Cantimpré, *Liber de natura rerum* 4.19–21, ed. Boese, 120–21.
101. Jacques de Vitry, *Historia orientalis* 88, ed. Donnadieu, 360.
102. Eco, *From the Tree to the Labyrinth*, 28.

When fiction is not categorically cordoned off from the real, there is more room to appreciate objects and phenomena that resist classification, such as marvels. They blur the boundary between what exists in the mind and what exists in the world, with the consequence that invented things might resemble real ones and real things might act like inventions. Of course, realism relies on the former possibility, but it is the reciprocity that bears stressing. As I mentioned above, prophecy is more vivid for resembling nonprophetic dreams. Both might be enlivened by the similarity between them. As Matilda Bruckner writes of romance, "reality is enhanced and extended by the play of fiction," and the same might be said of philosophy and travel literature, especially in the context of marvels.[103] Where the two are not firmly partitioned, the similarities between them are more easily appreciated. Such is the work of the faculty of imagination, which excels in highlighting qualities shared by real and fanciful things.

Building on this is the other distinctive feature of medieval fiction, in my view: spectacular things, whether real or not, have a great deal in common. Several philosophers, as we will see, explain that nature is as creative as any poet, and that the creations of one can be as startling as the creations of the other. For instance, al-Dimashqī, describing a beaver as a sort of weasel of the sea, a "water dog" (*kalb al-mā'*), retells a famous story about its defense mechanism.[104] Outfitted with two sets of testicles, one internal and one external, the beaver removes his spare set to keep would-be attackers at bay. "If the attackers do not witness this mutilation and instead persist with their chase, then the beaver will stretch out on his back in order to show his pursuers that his testicles have been removed and they, seeing the blood, will leave."[105] The beaver will then replace his missing testicles with the two latent ones. The story of the self-mutilating beaver is familiar from Pliny, and versions of it are easy to find in the Latin West.[106] The similarity between the Latin term for beaver, *castor*, and *castratio*, although the two are etymologically unrelated, encouraged them. The avid traveler Gerald of Wales, for instance, citing Cicero, Juvenal, and Bernardus Silvestris in his support, suggests that the beaver removes his testicles because he recognizes that his castor sacs, thought to be located in the testicles, are considered valuable for medicinal and other purposes. The beaver might therefore sacrifice the part of himself most likely to be desired, appeasing

103. Bruckner, *Shaping Romance*, 117.

104. Al-Dimashqī, *Nukhbat al-dahr* 5.6, ed. Mehren, 147.

105. Al-Dimashqī, *Nukhbat al-dahr* 5.6, ed. Mehren, 147: "fa-in lam yarahā wa-jaddū fī ṭalabihi, istalqā 'alā ẓahrihi li-yurīhim annahā quṭi'at fa-yarū al-dama fa-yatarakūhu." French trans. Mehren, *Manuel de la cosmographie*, 195.

106. Pliny, *Natural History* 32.13, ed. Jones, 9:480.

his pursuers and preserving his life.[107] It is easy to see how he became an emblem of asceticism for Christian allegorists.

The story is incorrect with respect to behavior and biology (beavers' testicles are internal), but that hardly matters. The platypus is equally implausible, and that makes the point. Nature's feats can be just as unlikely as a story invented from scratch, as its marvels testify. As al-Ghazālī famously put it, in lines that rhyme, "in all that is possible there is nothing more wondrous than what is."[108] Even marvels that are openly fabricated can help to illustrate the power of those that might actually exist. The fact that philosophers compare natural marvels to those in literature, and that authors like Chaucer appeal to the marvels of natural philosophy within their poems, suggests that for writers in either camp their truth or falsehood was not essential to them. When later readers ask whether their predecessors thought they were real, they focus on a question that medieval writers did not foreground. As they challenge binaristic thinking, medieval marvels are also constructive insofar as they reveal a more fluid understanding of disciplines than is offered by the modern division of sciences.

THE CHAPTERS

The first two chapters of this book argue that the faculty of imagination was essential to the operation of marvels according to Arabic and Latin natural philosophy, and that it helped to define their character. Understanding the relationship requires understanding imagination properly, which is the first project. Focusing on the philosophers al-Kindī, Avicenna, Albertus Magnus, Thomas Aquinas, and William of Auvergne, chapters 1 and 2 highlight imagination's role in the creation of marvels. They are divided into two categories only implicitly distinguished in medieval sources. The first is interior marvels—phenomena such as veridical dreams, visions, illusions, and prophecy. The second, taken up by chapter 2, is externally directed marvels whose root is at least partly in imagination but whose ultimate effect is in the extramental world. The most popular scenarios have imagination exercising influence, through intermediaries, on foreign bodies, including people and animals, but its power could also extend to nature and affect both weather and the elements. Where both categories of marvels involve imagination, they harness its maximal and exceptional powers. All are rare and set the outer boundaries of imagination's capacity, which can only be

107. Gerald of Wales, *Itinerarium Cambriae* 2.3, in *Opera*, ed. Brewer et al., 6:114–18.

108. Cited in Griffel, *Al-Ghazālī's Philosophical Theology*, 226: "laysa fī al-imkān abdaʿ mimmā kān." Griffel also comments there on the controversy that this line created, with references.

reached when a series of conditions is met. Nonetheless, whether an author wanted to augment or limit its power, imagination became a staple in the scholastic treatment of various marvels, so much so that its centrality to them eventually became an express topic of debate.

At their most basic level, the first two chapters reveal the dependence of Latin discussions of marvels on Arabic ones, and specifically on their notion of the marvel-performing imagination. They argue that imagination helps to define the character of medieval marvels, which rely on the faculty for their status as unlikely possibilities that defy cognitive certainty. They explain how imagination has the capacity to confuse images within the soul with those in the external world, and also how imagination might in certain circumstances act on bodies within the world. As the imagination of a pregnant woman might alter the shape of her fetus, so the imagination of an envious old woman might deform a child viewed at a distance. In both cases, imagination endows marvels with the indeterminacy and import that come to characterize them.

Chapter 3 focuses on references to poets' marvels within medieval natural philosophy. It begins by defining marvels as creative possibilities rather than truths. More precisely, it argues that, for natural philosophers, they are nonimpossibilities, or phenomena that simply have yet to be proven impossible, that have at least a toehold on the ledge of logical possibility, terms that the chapter defines. Some are certain, like magnets or particular medicinal herbs, but logical possibility is the feature that all share. The fact that philosophers appeal self-consciously to poets' marvels shows that questions of truth or falsehood did not determine their thinking about them. For instance, when Avicenna describes fossils, he claims that they are the result of animals who turn into stone, referring to what al-Masʿūdī describes as a "well-known story" about a species of crab that becomes stone once it reaches land.[109] After citing Avicenna's description approvingly, Albertus Magnus offers the example of Medusa, who turns animals into stone as a matter of course. In both the Latin and Arabic traditions, then, marvels travel from literature to philosophy and back again. By purposefully placing invented marvels, extracted from poetry, alongside those that are found within the natural world, philosophers define marvels as creative possibilities, and nature, who produces them, as a poet.

Anyone who writes a book on marvels is bound to discover that the topic can expand seemingly endlessly, and so I have set some boundaries with

109. Al-Masʿūdī, *Kitāb murūdj adh-dhahab* 16, ed. de Meynard and de Courteille, *Les prairies d'or*, 1:345; and Avicenna, *Kitāb al-shifāʾ*, ed. Holmyard and Mandeville, *De congelatione et conglutinatione lapidum*, 74.

respect to these early chapters that delve into the philosophy of marvels. I do not include automata, which have been brilliantly studied by others, most recently by Elly Truitt. In general, I privilege marvels that appear in nature over those that are crafted or handmade, although that boundary is often fuzzy, and it is undeniably true that automata often accompany such marvels, especially in literature. I do not delve into alchemy or astronomy, although I readily admit that both would enhance this study. In both Latin and Arabic sources, there is a great deal of interest in cosmological and alchemical marvels, and they present contexts in which Arabic materials influenced Latin ones extensively. Some works on alchemy were even versified, as though asking to be considered from a philosophy-and-literature perspective. However, the alchemical and cosmological material is simply too abundant to include here; it would need its own book.[110]

The remaining three chapters focus directly on literature. The fourth chapter analyzes medieval travel literature, with particular attention to Marco Polo, *Mandeville's Travels*, al-Dimashqī, and al-Masʿūdī. Travel literature puts invented places next to real ones in a way that has long inspired accusations of readerly gullibility or authorial duplicity. Were people so credulous as to believe that Amazons exist? Were people lying when they claimed to have seen them? I argue that the heterogeneity of such accounts, with their combination of factual and imaginary geographies, instead shows with special clarity how marvels create a state of suspension that depends on their possibly being real and possibly not. Together, the more and less likely claims of the traveler help to mark out the range of what is possible for nature, allowing its most spectacular features to resonate in its most mundane ones. Instead of proving that the medieval world view was limited or enchanted, as Max Weber claimed, they show authors making conscious efforts to enliven the imagination and access the full range of its powers.

The fifth and sixth chapters turn to romance and genres that similarly place marvels in fully fictional contexts. Chapter 5 begins with the question of marvels' place in literary history and then proceeds to the ambiguous status of marvels within *Mélusine*, *Partonopeu de Blois*, *Cligés*, *Sayf ibn Dhī Yazan*, and others. I point to episodes in which authors call into question the believability of marvels, beginning with Jean d'Arras's prologue, where he depends on his readers to be skeptical precisely as he seems to encourage credulity. He plays with marvels' confused truth status. Similary, char-

110. Among the many studies on these topics, and for references to more, see Haq, *Names, Natures and Things*; Zadeh, *Wonders and Rarities*, chap. 6; Rampling, *The Experimental Fire*; North, *Chaucer's Universe*; and DeVun, *Prophecy, Alchemy, and the End of Time*.

acters such as Mélusine and Melior inspire wariness through the marvels they produce, making others doubt their benevolence. The indeterminacy of marvels is reflected in the suspicion that greets their makers, and it becomes a test that determines the faithfulness of their lovers. Raymondin and Partonopeu need to believe in the fairies' goodness precisely because it is uncertain, as marvels are uncertain, and both fail. The chapter also considers the prophets Merlin and ʿĀqila, who manipulate their audiences directly by using their doubts against them. In these cases, marvels ask to be inspected, by both characters and readers.

Chapter 6 begins with the common claim that marvels are enchanting and redefines it by showing that they inspire scrutiny. Focusing particularly on the Syrian manuscript of the *Thousand and One Nights*, *Sir Orfeo*, and *Flores y Blancaflor*, it shows that marvels are emblems of change that play openly with readers' expectations. Although the popularity of marvels in the Middle Ages has long been recognized, scholars have not made a corollary observation, namely, that the people who inhabited such cultures were informed consumers of marvels. The repurposing of them in the texts discussed in this chapter shows that their authors expected readers to be both familiar with marvels and able to identify more or less subtle alterations to them. They play with the absence of expected marvels and the addition of unexpected ones. For instance, analyzing *Sir Orfeo* in conjunction with medieval lapidaries shows how Orfeo is defined in the poem by the absence of expected marvels regarding stones, those that furnish the fairy king with his powers of enchantment. It shows how received scripts about marvels invite refashioning. Change is conceptualized both in and through them.

As a whole, the chapters show how marvels function for both philosophers and writers of literature as creative possibilities in a way that challenges a sharp disciplinary division between them. It could even be argued that marvels constitute their own genre, one that crosses disciplinary boundaries and encourages comparisons between fictive and nonfictive texts. At the same time, as unlikely and spectacular possibilities, marvels conceptualize a space between truth and falsehood that invites play, experimentation, uncertainty, and, of course, wonder.

[CHAPTER 1]

Marvels and the Philosophy of Imagination

True Dreams, Prophecy, and Possession

According to an Aristotelian dictum much quoted in the Middle Ages, understanding anything requires understanding its causes.[1] To understand marvels, then, one ought to understand their sources, among them the faculty of imagination. Predictably, the human imagination only participates in marvels that concern people, whether they produce or are altered by them, but so customary does the association become that, as we will see, nature's own imagination is credited with marvels involving plants and other animals. This chapter studies imagination's role in marvels of the human interior, such as veridical dreams, prophecy, and demonic possession.[2] I argue that all bear the imprint of the faculty that helped to create them. Imagination is not restricted by the distinction between real and nonreal things, which happily cohabitate in the form of images within it. That, along with its unique talent for muddying the boundary between things existing within the soul and those in the world outside, helps to produce marvels' indeterminacy and import. Both are essential features of marvels: they resist classification and they seem to be significant. Marvels in turn cast light on the operations of imagination when it

1. See, for instance, Aristotle, *Posterior Analytics* 1.2, 71b9–11, in *Analytica Posteriora*, ed. Minio-Panuello and Dod, 7: "We think that we know something in its essence, and not in the sophistical mode that is according to accidents, when we believe that we know the cause because of which something is" ("Scire autem opinamur unumquodque simpliciter, sed non sophistico modo qui est secundum accidens, cum causam que arbitramur cognoscere propter quam res est").

2. Following Greek tradition, medieval Arabic and Latin philosophers thought that prophecy relied on the natural mechanisms of the soul, which is presumably why they often analyzed prophecy alongside marvels, and why it can be analyzed as a marvel in turn.

is at its most powerful. It became so enmeshed in medieval discussions of marvels that, by the mid-fourteenth century, Nicole Oresme could warn that "imagination does not have as much power as some people think" with respect to them.[3] Nonetheless, imagination's central role in the production of medieval marvels, especially in the Latin West, has received relatively little attention.[4] Imagination figures prominently in classical Arabic literary criticism because it is directly theorized, which is not the case in the Latin West. As Wolfhart Heinrichs writes, al-Jurjānī in the eleventh century was the first to identify *takhyīl*, roughly translatable as "make-believe" or "the imaginary," as a literary phenomenon.[5] Such scholarship helps to illuminate its behavior in natural philosophy, but it is still the case that the marvel-performing imagination in both traditions has been understudied. This and the following chapter, therefore, focus on how marvels reflect the influence of imagination, and in their course argue for a richer understanding of the faculty itself.

A fundamental claim of this book is that marvels are imaginative phenomena, with "imaginative" understood in a specific sense. I mean not just that they often depend on the faculty of imagination, but that they have the status of imaginary beings, much like fictive beings, and in that respect they represent possibilities neither true nor false. This book is called *Medieval Marvels and Fictions* because, I argue, the two have similar status within the mind and depend on imagination in similar ways. As Avicenna writes when defining the compositive imagination—that is, the one that composes images, often fanciful ones, rather than simply storing perceptions—"we know with certainty that it is in our nature to combine sensory images with one another and to separate them from one other, not according to the form that we found externally, and not with belief [*taṣdīq*] with respect to the existence or nonexistence of any of them."[6] The compositive imagination makes no judgment with respect to such a thing's real-

3. Oresme, *De configurationibus* 2.38, ed. Clagett, *Nicole Oresme and the Medieval Geometry of Qualities and Motions*, 384: "nec quod tantam habeat potentiam [ymaginatio] ut aliqui putant." Trans. Clagett, 385.

4. See Thorndike, "Imagination and Magic"; Compagni, "*Artificiose operari*"; Zambelli, "L'immaginazione"; the articles of Béatrice Delaurenti cited in the bibliography; and *Phantasia—imaginatio*, ed. Fattori and Bianchi.

5. Heinrichs, "Takhyīl," *Encyclopaedia of Islam*, 2nd ed. See also Harb, *Arabic Poetics*, 25–134; Abu-Deeb, *Imagination Unbound*, 5–35; Key, *Language between God and the Poets*, 196–240; and Takhyīl, *The Imaginary in Classical Arabic Poetics*, ed. Van Gelder and Hammond.

6. Avicenna, *De anima* 4.1, ed. Rahman, 165–66: "qad naʿlamu yaqīnan an fī ṭabīʿatinā an nurakkiba al-maḥsūsāti baʿḍahā ilā baʿḍin wa-an nufaṣṣila baʿḍahā ʿan baʿḍin lā ʿalā al-ṣūrati allatī wajadnāhā ʿalayhā min khārijin wa-lā maʿa taṣdīqin bi-wujūdi shayʾin minhā aw lā wujūdihi." Latin trans., ed. Van Riet, 6. Taneli Kukkonen notes that *al-quwwa*

ness or unrealness. Its instinct is to make different categories of phenomena resemble one another, as dreams might resemble perceptions, more than it is to separate them. As imaginary creatures, then, marvels are often uncertain, possibly real and possibly not. Chaucer writes about Fortune's penchant for change as, paradoxically, her most constant feature, and in a similar way, indeterminacy—whether with respect to their realness or their mechanisms—defines marvels.

Nonetheless, it was conventional then, as it is now, to oppose imagination to reality or truth, and this requires some clarification. For instance, Oresme contrasts magic that takes place "in imagination" (*in ymaginatione*) with that which occurs "in reality" (*in re*), and Albertus Magnus opposes a "fantastic deed" (*opus . . . phantasticum*; fantastic because from *phantasia*, the ancient Greek term for "imagination") to "true" (*vera*) ones or "truth" (*veritatem*) proper.[7] The beginning of Richard Rolle's *Incendium amoris* offers another well-known example: "for the first time, I indeed felt my heart grow warm, and burn as though with sensible fire in a true and not imaginary way."[8] However, imaginary phenomena are not necessarily spectral. In the sources I have just cited, they lack reality in the sense that they remain within the soul, but they still exist in the way that thoughts and desires, for instance, exist. Further, as we will see, they did not have to confine their activity to the soul. Various marvels require images to act on the world beyond, and so the opposition between the real and the imagined is itself unstable.

As David Shulman notes, "the question of reality—as distinguished from truth—comes up naturally whenever the mind, and the imaginative faculty in particular, is discussed."[9] Granted that imaginative events actually occur, albeit within the soul, the distinction between them and objects in the outside world still stands. The legitimacy of the distinction is,

---

al-mutakhayyila signifies the compositive imagination for Avicenna ("Ibn Sīnā and the Early History of Thought Experiments," 445).

7. Oresme, *De configurationibus* 2.28, ed. Clagett, *Nicole Oresme and the Medieval Geometry of Qualities and Motions*, 342; and Albertus Magnus, *Summa theologiae* 2.30.1.1, ed. Borgnet, *Opera omnia*, 32:320–21.

8. Richard Rolle, *Incendium amoris*, Prologue, ed. Deanesly, 145: "siquidem sentivi cor meum primitus incalescere, et vere non imaginarie, quasi sensibile igne estuare."

9. Shulman, *More Than Real*, 9. Harb too notes the challenge posed by the fact that "the notions of the 'imaginary' and 'falsehood' are sometimes conflated in modern scholarship" (*Arabic Poetics*, 50). Some scholars seek to avoid this problem by introducing a different term. Jean Michot, for instance, uses *imaginale* rather than *imagination* to sidestep the problem (*La destinée de l'homme*, 19n71). In the same note, he quotes Henry Corbin: "We cannot avoid the fact that, in current and instinctive usage, the term 'imaginary' is equivalent in sense to 'unreal'" ("Mundus imaginalis," 3). As we have seen, the reflex to oppose imagination to reality is also a medieval one, although the opposition is far from tidy.

in a basic sense, incontestable. Although imagination possesses a bodily organ, its images are fundamentally unlike the bodies we perceive through our external senses. However, to oppose the two outright is to simplify a complicated relationship, aside from the fact that imagination's images can accurately represent the extramental world. As the quotation from Rolle suggests, imagined objects can also generate the same affective, intellectual, and physical effects as perceived objects, which is why he calls internal burning real. Imagination also intervenes in the world by exercising influence over foreign bodies, as the next chapter will discuss, so to say that marvels are imaginative is to say that they might exist solely within the soul or also outside of it. The two sorts of phenomena resemble one another, as illusions resemble perceptions, so much so that they are sometimes hard to distinguish. Marvels frequently depend on such blurring to make one ask whether something is as it appears to be, and they do not usually admit of easy answers.

Imagination is a sensory faculty that performs a wide range of functions according to medieval philosophy. Its location, range of functions, mechanisms, and even unity were all matters for debate. Beginning with Neoplatonic commentaries on Aristotle, it was often subdivided into a lower and higher power, sometimes called the *virtus imaginativa* or *imaginatio* and *phantasia* in Latin, but the terms and their referents varied.[10] They could be used in more or less narrow senses, with one late thirteenth-century philosopher defining the broadest option: "'imagination' is taken in a general sense to refer to all the higher powers of the sensitive soul."[11] Insofar as it helps to produce marvels, imagination is typically at the height of its power. At this pinnacle, it displays some of its distinctive features with unusual clarity, particularly its capacity to confuse the boundary between what lies within the soul and what lies outside it. Many marvels, like magnets or cosmological anomalies, involved imagination not at all, while others, like automata and other technological wonders, relied more on its normal operations than its extraordinary ones. These early chapters are concerned with the extraordinary imagination. The marvels under its control can only be accomplished when a series of conditions are met, as detailed below. It is also worth noting

10. *Imaginatio* became the standard Latin translation for the Greek term, but the transliterated *phantasia* also remained in use. On the role of imagination in such commentaries, see Blumenthal, "Neoplatonic Interpretations of Aristotle on 'Phantasia'"; and Watson, *Phantasia in Classical Thought*, 96–133. On the use of the terms in the Middle Ages, see Black, "Imagination and Estimation"; and Hamesse, "*Imaginatio* et *phantasia* chez les philosophes du XIIe et du XIIIe siècle."

11. Pseudo-Rigauld, *Quodlibeta* 2.11, ed. Delaurenti, "Les franciscains et le pouvoir du regard," 181: "ymaginationem large accipiendo pro omnibus viribus superioribus sensitivis."

that, in the production of marvels, imagination never acts independently, but rather interacts variously with the external senses and other faculties of the soul, as well as the passions, vapors, humors, and spirit. The precise patterns of influence differ depending on a given philosopher's theory of the soul. Nonetheless, it is common for philosophers to speak of it as though it were an independent agent, and I isolate it for analysis here.

It is well known that late medieval philosophers sought diligently to identify natural causes for natural events, including marvels, but imagination's contributions to this project have been relatively neglected in the scholarship.[12] I emphasize those philosophers most explicit in their attention to the marvel-making imagination, from both the Arabic and Latin traditions. In the context of natural philosophy, the influence of the former tradition on the latter is unmistakable, acknowledged through frequent citations. If anything, the influence tends to be overstated, especially in retrospect, and especially with respect to imagination. In the seventeenth century, the Cambridge philosopher Henry More thus comments on the powers that had been attributed to imagination by philosophers contemporary and past:

> There are some, and they of no small note, that attribute so wonderful effects to . . . imagination, that they affirm that it will not onely alter a mans own Body, but act upon anothers, and that at a distance; that it will inflict diseases on the sound, and heal the sick; that it will cause Hail, Snows and Winds; that it will strike down an Horse or Camel, and cast their Riders into a ditch; that it will doe all the feats of Witchcraft, even to the making of Ghosts and Spirits appear, by transforming the adjacent Aire into the shape of a person that cannot onely be felt and seen, but heard to discourse, and that not onely by them whose Imagination created this aiery *Spectrum*, but by other by-standers, whose Fancy contributed nothing to its existence. To such an extent as this have *Avicenna*, *Algazel*, *Paracelsus*, *Pomponatius*, *Vaninus* and others, exalted the power of humane Imagination.[13]

He joins two Arabic philosophers, Avicenna and al-Ghazālī, to the Renaissance philosophers Paracelsus, Pomponazzi, and Vanini, the latter

12. On the methods of late medieval natural philosophy, see Grant, *The Nature of Natural Philosophy*; and Rashed, "Natural Philosophy." On the effort to explain marvels through natural means, see Daston and Park, *Wonders and the Order of Nature*, 109–34; and Zadeh, *Wonders and Rarities*.

13. More, *The Immortality of the Soul*, 386–87. For more on imagination in More's philosophy, see Vermeir, "Imagination between Physick and Philosophy."

two of whom were especially well known for their theories of a powerful imagination.[14] More's collection of imaginative wonders had been assembled long before he wrote, and all of its elements minus the witches will be discussed below.[15] Together, they came to constitute a canon of imaginative marvels thought to have been inherited from Arabic philosophy. Thus More's contemporary, Meric Casaubon, writes of the "Enthusiast Arabs, as Avicenna and some others, . . . who did ascribe so much to the strength of imagination."[16] Arabic philosophers in fact appealed to imagination frequently, and sometimes to the estimative faculty instead, but in the Latin philosophy of marvels, the estimative power takes second place to imagination.

Magical practices and marvels are often ascribed to foreigners,[17] and so while scholars in the Latin West look to Arabic sources, Persian and Arabic writers look to Indian ones. Thus the ninth-century Persian geographer Ibn Khurdādbih writes, "Indians claim that they can, through their enchantments, accomplish all that they want, even poison those who are distant, or cure those they have poisoned. Through the estimative power and thought, they can unbind and bind, cause harm and give aid. They create images in the imagination (*al-takhāyīl*) that confuse the most clever person; they claim that they are able to prevent rain and hail."[18] Notice that imagination is crucial to the operation of marvels as Ibn Khurdādbih describes them. In both cases, the Christian and the Islamic, ideas about magic were in fact imported, even if altered in transmission. In the case of the Latin West, insofar as scholastics sought natural explanations for marvels and placed them on the same continuum as everyday phenomena, they followed the

14. Vermeir, "Castelli in aria," 104.

15. This is not to deny interest in witches or their association with imagination in the Latin West. For instance, the much cited *Canon episcopi*, a short text on witchcraft that was incorporated into Gratian's *Decretum*, repeatedly attributes supposed witchcraft to phantasms. See *Decretum Gratiani* 2.26.5.12, *PL* 187:1349B–51B. Albertus Magnus, as we will see below, links witchcraft to imagination explicitly. It simply had not become conventional to include witchcraft in lists of imaginative marvels. On medieval theories concerning witches, see Bailey, "The Feminization of Magic"; Kieckhefer, *European Witch Trials*; and Peters, *The Magician, The Witch, and the Law*.

16. Casaubon, *A Treatise Proving Spirits, Witches, and Supernatural Operations*, 103.

17. See, for instance, Fraser, "Roman Antiquity," 125.

18. Ibn Khurdādbih, *Kitāb al-masālik wa'l-mamālik*, ed. de Goeje and Sezgin, 71–72: "wa-l-hindu taz'umu anhā tadruka bi-l-ruqīya mā arādu wa-yasqūna bihi al-samma wa-yakhrujūnuhu mimman suqiya wa-lahum al-wahmu wa-l-fikru wa-yaḥillūna bihi wa-yaqidūna wa-yaḍurrūna wa-yanfa'ūna wa-lahum iẓhāru al-takhāyīli allatī yataḥayyaru fīhā al-arība wa-yadda'ūna ḥabsa al-maṭari wa-l-baradi." French trans., 52–53.

lead of Arabic works on marvels.[19] With respect to content as well, they built on various theories they imported, some of which rely on imagination. However, as the next chapter discusses, Latin scholastics expanded the marvelous powers associated with imagination, and that is not the only alteration they made. Aside from the inevitable changes wrought by selective translation and by unstable manuscript transmission, some philosophers in the Latin West deliberately altered the texts' original context and meaning.

The programmatic translation of Arabic philosophical works into Latin made the borrowings discussed in these first two chapters possible. Its essential prerequisite was the translation of Greek philosophical works into Arabic. Starting in the eighth century, "almost *all* non-literary and non-historical secular Greek books that were available throughout the Eastern Byzantine Empire and the Near East were translated into Arabic," along with significant translations into and out of Syriac, Persian, and Sanskrit.[20] This enormous and lengthy project depended on the vast expansion of the Islamic empire; the availability of multilingual scholars, including Syriac-speaking Christians; the acquisition of paper-making technology from Chinese prisoners of war in 751; the relocation of the capital from Damascus to Baghdad under the Abbasids; and the Abbasids' active patronage.[21]

Ancient Greek philosophical texts, including Aristotle's, might have been found in Constantinople, Antioch, Pisa, and elsewhere, but the Arabic texts were often preferred as the basis of translation because they were, in many cases, more reliable, and they also came with highly valued commentaries.[22] The earliest Latin text containing information from Arabic sources is from the tenth century,[23] but the translation of Arabic texts into Latin, alongside translations into and out of Hebrew, hit its stride in the twelfth and thirteenth centuries. Toledo—where the predominant language was Arabic, libraries contained a bevy of Arabic manuscripts, Latin-speaking Christian clergy were in abundance, and many Jewish scholars took refuge—became the capital of the movement.[24] Frederick II, king

19. See Kieckhefer, *Magic in the Middle Ages*, 16–18; Metlitzki, *The Matter of Araby*, 51–55; and Saif, *The Arabic Influences*, 70–94.

20. Gutas, *Greek Thought, Arabic Culture*, 1, his emphasis.

21. See Gutas, *Greek Thought, Arabic Culture*, 1–27. On the making of paper, see Bloom, *Paper before Print*.

22. See Burnett, "Arabic into Latin," 375.

23. Burnett, "The Translating Activity in Medieval Spain," 1039.

24. Burnett, "Arabic into Latin," 373. For more on the Jewish translators, see Sirat, "Les traducteurs juifs." The Christian conquest led to the destruction of many Arabic texts.

of Sicily and later Holy Roman Emperor, supported a systematic translation program in the thirteenth century. Himself a polyglot, he encouraged Arabic-speaking scholars to collaborate with Christians and Jews.[25] As Charles Burnett has shown, the translators themselves often grew up or studied in multilingual areas and bounced from one intellectual center to another, part of "an intellectual community which was not confined by religious or political boundaries."[26] For instance, Master Theodore, philosopher to Frederick II, appears to have been a Jacobite Christian from Antioch who moved to Mosul and then Armenia before joining Frederick's court.[27] In both translation movements, translators often relied on scholars fluent in the relevant languages. Al-Kindī, for instance, paid Syriac Christians to translate materials for him, as Michael Scot relied on the help of a Jew named Abuteus or Andreas Levita.[28] Within schools too, scholars from different religions crossed paths. Muslim intellectuals like Ibn Yūnus admitted Jewish and Christian students into their classes, and Christian and Jewish communities in different Islamic societies ran schools that would sometimes educate students of other faiths.[29] Within this vast constellation of activity, works on medicine, astronomy, natural philosophy, and other topics were translated into Latin. Among other things, the newly available texts sparked unprecedented interest in the mechanisms of marvels in the Latin West.

Scholars have recognized that the power of marvels depends on their crossing of typically maintained boundaries. According to Lorraine Daston and Katharine Park, "to register wonder was to register a breached boundary, a classification subverted."[30] Caroline Walker Bynum writes that wonder is most reliably created when "ontological and moral boundaries are

25. Burnett, "Arabic into Latin," 381.

26. Burnett, "Master Theodore," 225. Scholars have become wary, rightly, of overstating the degree of tolerance and multicultural harmony in this period, which also saw the development of a "persecuting society" in Western Europe, as Robert Moore famously argued (*The Formation of a Persecuting Society*). For a helpful collection of articles on the state of some longstanding scholarly debates about *convivencia* and the study of al-Andalus, see *Journal of Medieval Iberian Studies* 11, no. 3 (2019), ed. Fancy and García Sanjuán.

27. Burnett, "Master Theodore." Translators like Theodore, who were elevated to the rank of court philosopher, were so valuable that some were included in trade negotiations (250). See also Ṣā'id al-Andalusī's fulsome praise for good translators, who were clearly held in high esteem (*Kitāb tabaqāt al-umam*, ed. Cheikho, 36–37).

28. Brentjes, *Teaching and Learning the Sciences*, 42–43; and Minio-Paluello, "Michael Scot," 361.

29. Brentjes, *Teaching and Learning the Sciences*, 11, 104.

30. Daston and Park, *Wonders and the Order of Nature*, 14.

crossed, confused, or erased."[31] Imagination operates at some of the same boundaries. Like marvels, it can blur the distinction between mental representations and bodies. A spectacular appearance might result from bodily transmutation—for instance, various scholastics insisted that Pharaoh's magicians in fact transformed rods into serpents—or it might occur only within the soul, as in hallucination. Imagination is a natural faculty, but its susceptibility to demonic or angelic influence places it in league with higher powers. Marvels might themselves be strictly natural, as when a magnet moves another object without being in physical contact with it, or rely on the aid of demons, as medieval theories of witchcraft typically held. Acting on both sides of boundaries crucial to various marvels, and even on occasion helping to traverse them, imagination contributes significantly to marvels' marvelousness.

Part of imagination's role is to create a pocket of excess significance that is never wholly depleted. In mundane matters, imagination often makes events and images seem more consequential than they are. We experience such imaginary inflations often. A slight whiff of a campfire can lead to images of your house burning down, and a shadow in the distance is easily imagined into some nefarious creature. It is imagination's tendency to augment events and images so that a trivial one seems impressive. However, the same quality also allows it to express the ungraspable, transcendent significance of truly impressive feats. In the case of prophecy, for instance, it obscures as it illuminates, relying on metaphor and other potentially confounding devices as it depicts with vivid intensity whatever content has been transmitted to it. Such devices create the impression that one's understanding is always partial. As Thomas Aquinas explains in passages analyzed below, prophecy is by definition beyond one's reach. Whether in mundane or extraordinary matters, then, imagination suggests residual import that cannot be fully grasped. This is either a distortive feature (illusions might seem real) or a legitimately awe-inspiring one (prophecy is a phenomenon that necessarily transcends the individual), and it can be difficult to determine which is the case. However, to say that imagination is *either* deceptive *or* revealing is to miss the point: as it generates and responds to marvels, it has the potential to be either, and its elusiveness is much of its power.

Considering the remarkable capabilities allotted to it in medieval philosophy, the exceptionally robust imagination not surprisingly became a topic of contention in the Latin West, especially insofar as it furnished a natural explanation for phenomena that might otherwise be judged divine.

31. Bynum, "Wonder," 21.

Thus Thomas Bradwardine, discussed in the next chapter, was eager to discount any supposedly natural explanation for works properly deemed divine. He considered imagination to be a dangerous lure, a temptation that led people to believe their natural powers more extensive and God's powers more limited than they were. The idea that imagination defines natural *as opposed to* supernatural phenomena is still with us, perhaps most visibly in the tendency to accuse those people who favor supernatural explanations for phenomena of having overactive imaginations. The individual who thinks that a cosmological anomaly is a miracle rather than an act of nature, for instance, is easily labeled credulous. One who interprets a dream as prophecy might likewise be accused of misjudgment. Either could be accused of succumbing to imagination, which is simply to say that the person attributes too much to supernatural influence. Similarly, when the Middle Ages as a historical period is deemed imaginative, the implication is that it too readily favors supernatural over natural explanations.[32] Supernatural causation is reinterpreted as imaginative.

While the tendency to position imagination-based explanations against supernatural ones persists, however, it is worth noting a fundamental difference: the modern tendency often subsumes God under imagination, so that accounts that rely on him are, properly viewed, purely imaginative. A reliance on imagination from this skeptical perspective is also a repudiation of reason and a symptom of error. It therefore bears stressing that, in the context of medieval theories of marvels in the Latin West, supernatural explanations are often viable alternatives to imaginative ones. When it takes the lead in the construction of marvels, imagination represents human power at its pinnacle, and it ought to be stressed that accounts that rely on it are not self-evidently mistaken. The medieval philosophers who turned to it intended to articulate a scientifically sound philosophy.

NATURAL PHILOSOPHY AND MARVELS

Before I proceed, some words are in order about marvels and their place in medieval Latin natural philosophy (*philosophia naturalis*), which medieval philosophers also refer to as natural science (*scientia naturalis*) or physics (*physica*). Since late medieval natural philosophy was fundamentally Aristotelian, its emergence depended on access to Aristotle's texts, specifically his *libri naturales*. Reintroduced to the Latin West beginning in the twelfth

32. On the Latin Middle Ages as imaginative rather than rational, see Bundy, *The Theory of Imagination*, 87–92. On suspicion toward imagination in the early modern period, see Lobsien, "Faculties and Imagination."

century and later installed in university curricula, such works made nature a topic of serious philosophical investigation. As Hans Thijssen writes, "one of the new domains of philosophy created by the introduction of Aristotle's works into the curriculum was natural philosophy."[33] Whereas Plato "denied the status of true 'scientific' knowledge to any theory of the natural world," Aristotle disagreed.[34] His famous definition of nature—one that "every schoolboy knew . . . by heart"—is that "nature is the principle and cause of motion and rest in those things, and those things only, in which it inheres primarily and *per se*, not accidentally."[35] Natural philosophy studies beings that come to be by nature rather than, for instance, by art or chance, and it seeks to isolate their natural rather than miraculous causes.[36]

Essential to natural philosophy, and the subject of many works written by medieval natural philosophers, is motion. This is not simply motion through space, but motion understood as a species of change, specifically change in a thing's accidents. Aging is a sort of motion from this perspective, as is the cooling of water or the yellowing of grass. Aquinas explains: because natural things possess matter, and "because everything that has matter is mobile, it follows that mobile being (ens mobile) is the subject of natural philosophy."[37] In other words, natural philosophy studies the principle of motion and, where relevant, the principle of rest within material things.[38] The goal of the natural philosopher is to understand their natural causes. Why does a particular herb cure infertility? How does the basilisk reproduce? As Albertus Magnus has it, "the task of natural science is not simply to accept what has been said, but to inquire into the causes of natural things."[39] The quest for causes is basic to the discipline.

33. Thijssen, "Late-Medieval Natural Philosophy," 160.

34. Weisheipl, "Aristotle's Concept of Nature," 143.

35. Weisheipl, "Aristotle's Concept of Nature," 146; Aristotle, *Physics* 2.1, 192b21–23; Latin translation from Aquinas, *Commentaria Physicorum Aristotelis,* in *Opera omnia,* 2:54: "Est igitur natura principium alicuius et causa moviendi et quiescendi in quo est primum per se et non secundum accidens."

36. Aquinas contrasts nature as cause to the causes of art and chance in his *Commentaria Physicorum Aristotelis* 2.1.3, in *Opera omnia,* 2:56. Trans. Blackwell et al., *Commentary on Aristotle's Physics,* 75.

37. Aquinas, *Commentaria Physicorum Aristotelis* 1.1.3, in *Opera omnia,* 2:4: "quia omne quod habet materiam mobile est, consequens est quod *ens mobile* sit subiectum naturalis philosophiae." Trans. Blackwell et al., *Commentary on Aristotle's Physics,* 2.

38. Not all material things rest, a point that Aquinas supports with the example of celestial bodies; *Commentaria Physicorum Aristotelis* 2.1.5. Trans. Blackwell et al., *Commentary on Aristotle's Physics,* 77.

39. Albertus Magnus, *Mineralium* 2.2.1, in *Opera omnia,* ed. Borgnet, 5:30: "Scientiae enim naturalis non est simpliciter narrata accipere, sed in rebus naturalibus inquirere causas." Trans. Wyckoff, *Book of Minerals,* 69. He offers another helpful definition earlier in the work: "according to the property of natural science, we seek causes that are suited

Natural philosophy was a divinely sanctioned science that, according to the *Secretum secretorum*, God established through Greek philosophers: "among other philosophers, exalted God most inspired the Greeks to seek after knowledge and to know the classes of natural things."[40] The notion that creation is meant to be wondered at was widely held by Christian and Muslim philosophers in the Middle Ages. As Lara Harb writes, "marveling at God's creations was a spiritual duty."[41] In his cosmology, al-Qazwīnī writes that, after someone leaves childhood and begins to explore the world, "only when he suddenly sees a strange animal or plant or a miraculous phenomenon does his mouth burst forth, saying 'God be praised.'"[42] The marvels of creation lead one to its creator, and investigating them encourages devotion. Further, he explains that it is precisely by marveling at the marvels of creation that one is led to "the greatest book," the Quran, and is there introduced to further marvels.[43] The Bible too encourages people to ponder creation and learn from it.[44] As Peter Comestor puts it, "man is taught by marveling at the works of God."[45] What especially shines forth in creation is God's power, wisdom, and goodness, a claim that writers in the Latin West repeated with precision.[46] Another lesson that the observer of nature learns is how to read the very Bible that encouraged their inquiries, since its secrets are hidden (*velate*) "under symbols and figures of the properties of natural and artificial things."[47] Nature is both object and symbol, worthy of study as a fascinating thing in itself and also as a means to know God.

---

to their effects, and especially matter changing univocally" ("Nos autem secundum proprietatem naturalis scientiae causas quaerimus suis effectibus proprias & maxime materiam et univoce transmutantem"), *Mineralium* 1.1.4, in *Opera omnia*, ed. Borgnet, 5:6.

40. *Secretum secretorum* 2.1, ed. Steele, *Opera hactenus inedita Rogeri Baconi*, 5:64: "Deus excelsus inter ceteros philosophos Grecos magis inflammavit ad sciencias inquirendas et rerum naturalium genera cognoscenda."

41. Harb, *Arabic Poetics*, 7.

42. Al-Qazwīnī, *'Ajā'ib al-makhlūqāt*, Introduction, ed. Sa'd, 32: "ra'ā baghtatan ḥayawānan gharīban aw fi'lan khāriqan li-l-'ādāti inṭalaqa lisānuhu bi-l-tasbīḥi fa-qāla subḥāna allāhu."

43. Al-Qazwīnī, *'Ajā'ib al-makhlūqāt*, Introduction, ed. Sa'd, 32: "al-kitāba ajallahu."

44. See, for instance, Isidore of Seville, *De natura rerum*, Preface, ed. Fontaine, *Traité de la nature*, 167–69.

45. Petrus Comestor, *Historia scholastica*, Liber Genesis 9, *PL* 198:1063A: "instruitur admirando opera Dei."

46. See, for instance, Neckham, *De naturis rerum*, Book 2 Prologue, ed. Wright, 125; Vincent of Beauvais, *Speculum naturale*, Prologue 6, in *Speculum quadruplex* 1:5C–D; and Bonaventure, *De itinerarium mentis ad Deum* 1.11, in *Opera omnia*, 5:298.

47. Bartholomaeus Anglicus, *De proprietatibus rerum*, Preface, ed. van den Abeele, 1:51: "engimata Scripturarum, que sub symbolis et figuris proprietatum rerum naturalium et artificialium." Vincent of Beauvais makes a similar point, quoting Augustine in support of it; see *Speculum naturale*, Prologue 6, in *Speculum quadruplex* 1:5D–E.

According to Alexander Neckham, creation resembles a letter written to people so that they might know and praise God. In his metaphor, Christ is a scribe who with his "reed-pen" (*calamus*) quickly wrote the created world as the wisdom of the Father ordained: "as the whole world has been written down, so the whole is a letter, but to one who possesses understanding and investigates the natures of things in order to know and praise the Creator."[48] The writtenness of creation implies an obligation for people to study and interpret it. To do so is to accept the gift they have been given and use it for its intended purpose, which is to see God within it. According to Aquinas, creatures relate to God as artwork (*artificiata*) to its artist (*artificem*), and indeed "the whole of nature is like a work of art created by the divine mind."[49] Nature is a concept deliberately fashioned as an object. Like a work of art, it entices its observer and asks to be pondered. Marvels, then, like other natural phenomena, are meant to be studied.

Natural philosophy is far larger than marvels, and marvels are hardly confined to natural philosophy, but these early chapters focus on their intersection. They privilege the natural philosophy of the universities over encyclopedias and other collections that gathered the most sensational marvels. An interest in identifying natural causes unites both, but the philosophers' texts tend to be more detailed, and the detail is useful to me. This is not a value judgment, or a repudiation of the "popular," which is worth mentioning because there is an unmistakable snobbery in some of the scholastic texts. Nicole Oresme, for one, writes of the "simple folk, who are ignorant of the nature of things."[50] The fact that natural philosophers focused on the operations of nature that were not self-evident necessarily meant that they sought knowledge hidden from the average person. In some respects, Nature makes her operation so accessible that "even the vulgar know it," according to Alexander Neckham, but in other respects she hides her treasures, "as if Nature were saying, 'It's my secret! It's my secret!'"[51] Marvels often belong to the latter category. Alexander continues by promising to keep knowledge unsuited to the vulgar out of their hands. Expressing the same conviction that the unlearned cannot grasp marvels,

48. Neckham, *De naturis rerum*, Book 2 Prologue, ed. Wright, 125: "Sicut autem totus mundus inscriptus est, ita totus littera est, sed intelligenti et naturas rerum investiganti, ad cognitionem et laudem Creatoris."

49. Aquinas, *Summa contra Gentiles* 3.100, in *Opera omnia*, 14:311: "Unde tota natura est sicut quoddam artificiatum divinae artis." Trans. Bourke, 3.2:81.

50. Oresme, *Livre de divinacions* 12, ed. and trans. Coopland, 100: "simple gens, qui sont ignorans la nature des choses."

51. Neckham, *De naturis rerum* 2.99, ed. Wright, 184: "eo quod notae vulgo sunt," "ac si dicat natura, 'Secretum meum mihi, secretum meum mihi!'" "Secretum meum mihi" is a quotation of Isaiah 24:6. I thank Steve Justice for calling my attention to it.

the ninth-century philosopher al-Jāḥiẓ explains that only those with the requisite knowledge (*fī al-ʿilmi aṣlun*) and clarity of thought (*tabayyun*) can attempt to understand nature's marvels.[52] Were marvels simply fodder for stupefaction, no such care would be required.

TRUE DREAMS AND PROPHECY

True or veridical dreams were thought to depend on imagination uncontroversially, as were all dreams, and so they provide a useful starting point for a discussion of the marvel-making imagination.[53] As al-Kindī notes, imagination "is stronger in dreams than it is when one is awake."[54] In this passage, he refers to imagination as the "formative power" (*quwwatu . . . al-muṣawwirati*), and he is explicit about their equivalence in an earlier reference: "this power, which is called formative . . . is that which the wise ancients called *phantasia*."[55] Al-Kindī is usually named the first Arabic or Arabo-Islamic philosopher because he incorporated Greek philosophy into Islamic thought in a manner that characterized much Arabic philosophy in the following centuries. His brief *Liber de somno et visione*, translated into Latin in the twelfth century by Gerard of Cremona, helpfully links imagination's vivacity in everyday dreams to its power in marvelous, prophetic ones. What makes dreamed images difficult to distinguish from perceived ones is their vivacity, and the same quality invests veridical dreams with due import. Constructed of images even more powerful than perceptions, prophetic dreams appear more significant than present-tense, external reality.

Al-Kindī arrives at prophetic dreams and visions, which he conflates,

52. Al-Jāḥiẓ, *Kitāb al-ḥayawān*, ed. Hārūn, 3:238.

53. See Kruger, *Dreaming in the Middle Ages*, 40–41.

54. Al-Kindī, "Risālat fī māhīyat al-nawm wa-l-ruʾyā," ed. Abū Rīdah, 1:295: "fī al-nawmi aẓhara fiʿlan wa-aqwā minhā fī al-yaqaẓa." Latin trans., ed. Nagy, *Liber de somno et visione*, 15. English trans. Adamson and Pormann, *The Philosophical Works of Al-Kindi*, 125. For an introduction to the text's content, see Jolivet, *L'intellect selon Kindī*, 128–32; and Adamson, *Al-Kindī*, 135–43.

55. Al-Kindī, "Risālat fī māhīyat al-nawm wa-l-ruʾyā," ed. Abū Rīdah, 1:295: "quwwatun yusammā al-muṣawwirata . . . huwa allatī yusammīhā al-qudamāʾa min ḥukamāʾi al-yūnānīyina al-fanṭāsīā." Latin trans., ed. Nagy, *Liber de somno et visione*, 13–14. English trans. Adamson and Pormann, *The Philosophical Works of Al-Kindi*, 125. Avicenna also writes that imagination, though for him the retentive imagination, is often called the formative or formal power; see *De anima* 4.1, ed. Rahman, 165; and Adamson notes that "imagination" goes by many names in al-Kindī's work (*Al-Kindī*, 135). Medieval philosophers often distinguished the retentive imagination, which stores sensory impressions, from the compositive imagination, which rearranges sensory impressions or creates original images, although not in those terms.

through analysis of unexceptional dreams. His procedure of moving from the ordinary to the extraordinary is characteristic of the naturalistic approach to marvels in Arabic philosophy, which places marvels on the same continuum as everyday phenomena and explains them in some of the same terms. Regarding regular dreams, al-Kindī explains that the vividness of their images indicates imagination's strength. The faculty transforms thoughts it receives from the soul into images with greater vibrancy and clarity than those transmitted by the external senses, which are more encumbered by matter.[56] What one sees in imagination is thus "purer, clearer, and better than the form of sense perception."[57] During waking hours, imagination typically occupies itself with images furnished by the external senses, but in al-Kindī's view, they hamper imagination, which thrives when independent of their input, as during sleep. Then, imagination "does not receive that which it receives except through the bare soul, and therefore neither confusion nor corruption befalls it."[58] Not beholden to the external senses, imagination can outperform them by creating more arresting images. As a result, a dreamed image can better suggest an extramental object than a sensory image created from the perception of that object.

For al-Kindī, the vivacity of imagination's images is an expression of the faculty's strength, which is in turn a function of its source. The superior source—the "bare soul" instead of the external senses—yields the more vivid, though not necessarily the more reliable image. Dreamed images, after all, need not correspond to anything outside the soul. However, prophetic dreams, drawn from a superior source still, combine reliability with power. They originate in the soul's innate treasury of knowledge. As al-Kindī explains, "knowledge of things is within the soul by nature, and it contains all sorts of sensible and rational things."[59] Like Plato, he uses the doctrine of innate knowledge to explain prophetic dreams. In his view, the soul imprints forms that convey insight onto imagination, and imagination

56. Al-Kindī, "Risālat fī māhīyat al-nawm wa-l-ru'yā," ed. Abū Rīdah, 1:295–97. Latin trans., ed. Nagy, *Liber de somno et visione*, 15–17.

57. Al-Kindī, "Risālat fī māhīyat al-nawm wa-l-ru'yā," ed. Abū Rīdah, 1:297: "anqā wa-abyana wa-azkā min al-maḥsūsati." Latin trans., ed. Nagy, *Liber de somno et visione*, 15. English trans. Adamson and Pormann, *The Philosophical Works of Al-Kindi*, 126.

58. Al-Kindī, "Risālat fī māhīyat al-nawm wa-l-ru'yā," ed. Abū Rīdah, 1:297: "yanāluhā bi-l-nafsi al-mujarradati. fa-laysa ya'aruḍu fīhā 'akarun wa-lā fasādun." Latin trans., ed. Nagy, *Liber de somno et visione*, 15. English trans. Adamson and Pormann, *The Philosophical Works of Al-Kindi*, 126.

59. Al-Kindī, "Risālat fī māhīyat al-nawm wa-l-ru'yā," ed. Abū Rīdah, 1:301: "mā al-nafsu min al-'ilmi bihā bi-l-ṭab'i wa-annahā mawḍi'un li-jamī'i anwā'i al-ashīā'i al-ḥissīyati wa-l-'aqlīyati." Latin ed., trans. Nagy, *Liber de somno et visione*, 18. English trans. Adamson and Pormann, *The Philosophical Works of Al-Kindi*, 128.

joins with thought in deciphering them.[60] When the soul's impression is strong and unimpeded, then it "sets things out as they will be before they occur."[61] In this case, imagination does not invent. It reconfigures true content, using the same techniques that it uses in normal dreams to bring images to life. In other words, it gives truth the force of invention. The same attribute that makes regular dreamed images compelling, namely, their vivacity, is also what creates the hyperreality of prophetic ones. In this case, that quality expresses the extraordinariness of prophetic insight.

Part of what gives imagination such power is the ambiguity it creates, not least by making unexceptional and prophetic dreams difficult to distinguish. Al-Kindī hints at the problem by using the same term, *ru'yā*, to characterize both.[62] Avicenna, known by the honorific *al-shaykh al-ra'īs*, or top master, more explicity associated imagination's prophetic power with its obfuscations. Among the writings on prophecy from Islamic communities, his had the greatest influence in the Latin West.[63] His *De anima*, a section of his massive *Kitāb al-Shifā'*, was widely read in Arabic but it was also "the most frequently copied and quoted" of his texts in Latin.[64] It most fully communicated his views about prophecy and imagination to Christian philosophers, and no philosopher became more closely associated with the exceptionally potent imagination than he, to the extent that he was credited with views on the topic that he did not espouse. Thanks to a mistranslation, his Latin readers even made him a king, giving him a position that suited his intellectual stature.[65]

Further illuminating Avicenna's views and included in my discussion here is Abū Ḥāmid al-Ghazālī's *Maqāṣid al-falāsifa*, literally *Doctrines of the Philosophers* but more commonly known as his *Metaphysics*, which is a précis of Avicenna's philosophy that "quickly penetrated the Christian schools."[66] Although scholars have long recognized that the text expresses

60. See al-Kindī, "Risālat fī māhīyat al-nawm wa-l-ru'yā," ed. Abū Rīdah, 1:303–4. Latin trans., ed. Nagy, *Liber de somno et visione*, 18.

61. Al-Kindī, "Risālat fī māhīyat al-nawm wa-l-ru'yā," ed. Abū Rīdah, 1:303: "tanbī bihā bi-a'yānihā." Latin trans., ed. Nagy, *Liber de somno et visione*, 18. English trans. Adamson and Pormann, *The Philosophical Works of Al-Kindi*, 129.

62. The Latin translation preserves the likeness by using *visio* in both instances.

63. Hasse, *Avicenna's* De anima *in the Latin West*, 230.

64. Hasse, *Avicenna's* De anima *in the Latin West*, v. The text was translated into Latin once in the twelfth century and once in the thirteenth, together leaving more than one hundred surviving manuscripts (4–9). For a short introduction to his influence in the Latin West, see d'Alverny, "L'Introduction d'Avicenne en Occident."

65. Hasse, "King Avicenna."

66. Alonso, "Influencia de Algazel," 372.

Avicenna's philosophy more than al-Ghazālī's, it is still a common error, originating in the Middle Ages, to attribute its views to al-Ghazālī, and for that reason some explanation is in order. The Persian al-Ghazālī is now best known in the West for his *Incoherence of the Philosophers (Tahāfut al-falāsifa)*, a criticism of twenty philosophical theories drawn from the work of al-Fārābī and Avicenna.[67] However, for much of the Middle Ages, the work was unknown in the Latin West, which was left instead with his *Metaphysics*, written between 1091 and 1095, and translated by Gundissalinus and Abraham ibn Daud in the twelfth century. Formerly considered "an intelligent reworking" of Avicenna's Persian *Dānish-nāma-i'alā'ī*, it is now typically regarded as a "slightly interpretative translation" in which al-Ghazālī sometimes removes material, adds examples, and varies terminology but is largely faithful to Avicenna's text.[68] He wrote it out of the laudable desire to understand Avicenna's philosophy before he set to evaluating it, and his prologue communicated his plans, but it was neglected by copyists and quickly disappeared from view.[69] Avicenna's source text was not available in Latin translation, so the Latin West was left with the misimpression that al-Ghazālī was only a follower and not also a critic of Avicenna.[70] Al-Ghazālī's *Metaphysics* and Avicenna's *De anima* were translated in the same place (Toledo), by the same people, and at roughly the same time, between 1150 and 1166.[71] They were often cited together, and I discuss the works in tandem here.

Like al-Kindī's, Avicenna's theory of veridical dreams develops from his theory of regular ones. In both cases, what links imagination's normal and exceptional operations is its ability to obscure the difference between what is imagined and what is perceived. Dreams give imagination the opportunity to act freely, to do what comes naturally to it ("tataṣarrafa 'alayhi").[72] Its penchant is to create images so vivid that "they seem to have being extrinsically."[73] When dominant during waking activities, as during times

67. He is also famous for his efforts to summon jinn to his aid; see Zadeh, "Commanding Demons and Jinn."

68. Alonso, "Influencia de Algazel," 374; and Janssens, "Al-Ghazālī and His Use of Avicennian Texts," 43. Frank Griffel agrees with Janssens; see "Al-Ghazālī."

69. D'Alverny, "Algazel dans l'Occident Latin," 8.

70. Al-Ghazālī was criticized in kind; see d'Alverny, "Algazel dans l'Occident Latin," 8.

71. Delaurenti, "Pratiques médiévales de réécriture," 357.

72. Avicenna, *De anima* 4.2, ed. Rahman, 172. Latin trans., ed. Van Riet, 17. Avicenna's imagination is usually subject to the oversight of either the estimative power or reason; see Black, "Estimation (*Wahm*) in Avicenna," 228.

73. Avicenna, *De anima* 4.2, ed. Rahman, 173: "fa-tarā ka-annahā mawjūdatan khārijan." Latin trans., ed. Van Riet, 18. Avicenna explains this effect as the result of imag-

of illness or intense emotion, it behaves similarly. For instance, hallucinations can cause the infirm to reach out to grab things that they mistakenly think are real.[74] According to al-Ghazālī's *Metaphysics*, intense fear can lead one to imagine a frightening creature and believe it exists, a process that he uses to account for the jinn, fairy-like creatures from Islamic theology.[75] It is thus the nature of the unchecked imagination to invest its creations with the cognitive status of perceived objects.

All such phenomena belong to the nonprophetic, compositive imagination, but they form the foundation for the first of three sorts of prophecy distinguished by Avicenna, "the prophecy particular to the compositive imagination."[76] It includes visions while awake or asleep as well as true dreams, and it is reserved for those with unusually potent imaginations undistracted by the senses.[77] Necessary as well is a soul uncorrupted by lying. The prophet's soul must instead be habituated to the truth.[78] As for al-Kindī, so for Avicenna prophecy originates in an authoritative source. While al-Kindī roots it in the soul's innate knowledge, Avicenna roots it in the celestial souls, that is, the souls of the celestial spheres that move the cosmos and therefore know things past, present, and future.[79] Imagination acts with relative freedom during regular dreams and during illness, but the prophetic imagination submits to the soul's higher powers. Prophecy occurs when the celestial spheres communicate with the practical intellect,

---

ination sending its images to common sense, which is what truly perceives; see Hasse, *Avicenna's* De anima, 158; as well as al-Ghazālī, *Maqāṣid al-falāsifa* 2.5.8, ed. al-Kurdī, 3.70. (The Arabic edition includes three volumes in one text, and each is paginated separately. 3.70 refers to page 70 in vol. 3. All references to the text follow the same pattern.) Latin trans., ed. Muckle, *Algazel's Metaphysics*, 192.

74. Al-Ghazālī, *Maqāṣid al-falāsifa* 2.5.8, ed. al-Kurdī, 3.70. Latin trans., ed. Muckle, *Algazel's Metaphysics*, 193.

75. Al-Ghazālī, *Maqāṣid al-falāsifa* 2.5.8, ed. al-Kurdī, 3.70. Latin trans., ed. Muckle, *Algazel's Metaphysics*, 193.

76. Avicenna, *De anima* 4.2, ed. Rahman, 173: "al-nubūwatu al-khāṣṣatu bi-l-quwwati al-mutakhayyilati." Latin trans., ed. Van Riet, 19: "prophetia virtutis imaginativae." For an introduction to Avicenna's theory of prophecy, see Rahman, *Prophecy in Islam*; Hasse, *Avicenna's* De anima, 154–74; and Michot, *La destinée de l'homme*, 118–39. On this particular branch of prophecy, see also Gutas, "Imagination and Transcendental Knowledge in Avicenna," and "Intellect without Limits."

77. Much as Avicenna discusses prophetic visions and veridical dreams in tandem, he does not, as Hasse notes, characterize such dreams as themselves prophetic (Hasse, *Avicenna's* De anima, 158). Avicenna, *De anima* 4.2, ed. Rahman, 177–78.

78. Avicenna, *De anima* 4.2, ed. Rahman, 181.

79. Avicenna, *De anima* 4.2, ed. Rahman, 177. See also his *Ishārāt*, ed. Forget, *Le livre des théorèmes et des avertissements* 2.10, 210–11. On the common belief that the celestial spheres determine events on earth and make foreknowledge of them possible, see North, "Medieval Concepts of Celestial Influence."

which transmits the data it receives to imagination.[80] There is no intermediary; the prophet "directly receives all intelligible emanations."[81] However, the intellect has no bodily organ and therefore requires the assistance of imagination to convert the content of the vision into images that might be recorded.[82] Those images can appear as living things, even angels, and so al-Ghazālī writes that imagination translates the message received from celestial souls into beautiful images that speak in the manner typical of dreamed images.[83]

It is important to note that, for Avicenna, the prophet is distinguished by intellectual insight. For him, "Prophet, Mystic or Philosopher . . . at the highest point are all one at the intellectual level."[84] Nonetheless, some uncertainty accompanies prophecy. Al-Ghazālī's comment about speaking images points to two ways in which imagination contributes to it. First, prophecy resembles other sorts of imaginative phenomena, rendering it difficult to distinguish between them. While there are basic differences in the mechanisms behind imagination's regular (albeit heightened) and prophetic operations—behind hallucinations and angelic visions, for instance—the experience of them is potentially the same. In both cases, someone mistakenly thinks something to be out in the world, whether an angel or an object, because it shines vividly in imagination. The inability to discriminate conclusively between the imaginative experiences is a measure of their power.

Second, imagination regularly distorts prophetic communication. Sometimes that distortion is innocuous or even appealing, as in the case of the pretty speaking images, but more often it is destructive. Influenced by al-Fārābī, Avicenna explains that it is imagination's nature to veer from the topic at hand, to move from one image to another, according to a logic that he does not pretend to understand fully. The soul struggles because of imagination's peregrinations:

80. On some occasions, Avicenna writes that the celestial souls communicate directly with imagination, and Herbert Davidson takes this to be Avicenna's doctrine (*Alfarabi, Avicenna, and Averroes on Intellect*, 123), but others argue convincingly that it communicates instead with the practical intellect. See Gutas, "Imagination and Transcendental Knowledge," 338–44; Hasse, *Avicenna's* De anima, 448; and Michot, *La destinée de l'homme*, 121–25.

81. Rahman, *Prophecy in Islam*, 34.

82. Gutas, "Imagination and Transcendental Knowledge," 350. See also Rahman, *Prophecy in Islam*, 36–39.

83. Al-Ghazālī, *Maqāṣid al-falāsifa* 2.5.9, ed. al-Kurdī, 3.75. Latin trans., ed. Muckle, *Algazel's Metaphysics*, 196. On imagination's role in making prophecy audible, visible, and symbolic, according to Avicenna, see Michot, *La destinée de l'homme*, 129–32.

84. Rahman, *Prophecy in Islam*, 35. There is also some discussion of philosophers as prophets in the Latin West; see Even-Ezra, *Ecstacy in the Classroom*, 44–52.

> Rational cogitation is in torment because of this power [imagination], and it is preoccupied with its misdirections. Whenever it takes to itself some form which tends toward a certain object, imagination moves quickly to something dissimilar, and from it to a third thing, so that the soul forgets the first [form] from which this began, and then the soul needs to recollect and is led to reverse its analysis until it returns to the beginning.[85]

Such is the soul's cross to bear. It solicits an image or form from imagination, imagination traipses from one form to another according to its largely inscrutable logic, and the intellect has to expend great effort simply to return to the original form it desired.

Imagination exhibits the same tendency to swap one image for another in the context of imaginative prophecy. It translates celestial foreknowledge into images, altering the original message and perhaps occluding it as well. Focusing especially on visions received during sleep, Avicenna returns to imagination's penchant for creative association:

> Often it happens that what appears from the heavens stands as the head and beginning, but afterward imagination prevails over the soul so that it distracts it from following what it has seen and the soul is afterward moved by movement after movement, which movements do not accord with what appeared from the heavens, which has been lost. And this is the sort of dream in which a little interpretation is necessary.[86]

As Deborah Black writes, "the central feature that emerges in Avicenna's theory of the compositive imagination is its restlessness and randomness."[87] If imagination meanders, then the dream will require interpretation.[88] Al-

85. Avicenna, *De anima* 4.2, ed. Rahman, 175: "al-fikra al-nuṭqī mamnūwun bi-hādhihi al-quwwati, wa-huwa min gharīrati hādhihi al-quwwati fī shughli shāghilin, fa-innahu idhā istiʿamiluhā fī ṣūratin mā istiʿamālan muwajjihan naḥwa gharaḍin mā intiqalat bi-ṣurʿatin ilā shay'in ākharin lā yunāsibuhu wa-minhu ilā thālathin wa-ansat al-nafsa awwala mā ibtida'at ʿanhu ḥattā taḥūja al-nafsu ilā al-tadhakkuri fāziʿatun ilā al-taḥlīli bi-l-ʿaksi ḥattā taʿūda ilā al-mabda'i." Latin trans., ed. Van Riet, 22.

86. Avicenna, *De anima* 4.2, ed. Rahman, 176: "wa-yataffaqa kathīran an yakūna mā yarā min al-malakūti shay'an ka-l-ra'isi wa-ka-l-ibtida'i fa-yustawlā al-takhayyulu ʿalā al-nafsi istīlā'an yaṣrifuhā ʿan istitmāmin mā tarāhu wa-tantaqilu baʿdahu intaqalan baʿda intiqālin lā tuḥākā bi-tilka al-intiqālāti shay'an mimmā yarā min al-malakūti idh dhālika qad inqaṭaʿa, fa-yakūnu hādhā ḍarban min al-ru'yā innamā mawḍiʿu al-ʿibārati minhu shay'un ṭafīfun." Latin trans., ed. Van Riet, 24–25.

87. Black, "Rational Imagination," 65.

88. For al-Kindī, the need for interpretation is instead an indication that the "instrument," or brain, was not sufficiently receptive to the prophetic message and did not take its impression strongly enough. As a result, a dream might be symbolic, indicating an

Ghazālī thus writes that imagination might convert a man into a tree or an enemy into a serpent, leaving the soul to reconstruct through interpretation the truth contained within the dream.[89] Some dreams also contain their own correct interpretation. However, if imagination's movements are too erratic, then no amount of interpretation will undo the damage it has wrought. Memory will store imagination's misrepresentations, and the original vision will be lost.[90] More often, however, imagination distracts the intellect so that it cannot receive input from the celestial souls in the first place, in which case dreams are just run-of-the-mill dreams. The unfettered imagination at such moments occupies the mind with insignificant images. It serves prophecy better when it "moderates its impulses" and curbs its enthusiasm.[91]

Avicenna carefully distinguishes the manner in which each sort of dream is produced, but offers no system by which one might be distinguished from another at the level of experience. The blurriness that he creates at the boundaries of various imaginative phenomena seems not only inevitable but constructive. We have seen that imagination gains a good deal of power from its ability to mimic, and even outdo, perceptions, and thus to confuse the difference between mental representations and bodies. Such confusion can extend to imagination's offspring, which resemble each other because of their shared vivacity. Whatever the consequence of that vivacity—whether something imagined seems to exist in the extramental world or in fact derives from an authoritative, external source—it allows events to mean more than the images in which they are based. Where that "more" ends is decidedly unclear. I have mentioned that the heightened imagination tends to elevate an event's significance, and we now see how it lends the same quality to prophecy. Because it cannot be precisely delimited, prophecy claims more-than-human import. Even when broken down into its component parts and subjected to in-depth philosophical analysis, it retains its defining mystery.

---

upcoming journey, for instance, by showing the dreamer an image of himself flying. See "Risālat fī māhīyat al-nawm wa-l-ru'yā," ed. Abū Rīdah, 1:304. Latin trans., ed. Nagy, *Liber de somno et visione*, 21.

89. Al-Ghazālī, *Maqāṣid al-falāsifa* 2.5.5, ed. al-Kurdī, 3.67. Latin trans., ed. Muckle, *Algazel's Metaphysics*, 189.

90. Avicenna, *De anima* 4.2, ed. Rahman, 175–76. Latin trans., ed. Van Riet, 23. Rahman sees a fundamental contradiction in Avicenna's thought between the agency and passivity he variously demands of imagination (*Prophecy in Islam*, 76), but Hasse disagrees. In his reading, Avicenna calls for an active imagination during the transmission of the vision and a passive one after the fact, when the vision is being stored in memory (*Avicenna's* De anima, 160–61).

91. Michot, *La destinée de l'homme*, 126.

As these comments make clear, imagination is essential to Islamic theories of prophecy. The "second master" al-Fārābī, in a work not translated into Latin, likewise makes "imagination . . . the seat of prophecy and divination."[92] The works that did reach the Latin West influenced Christian theories of prophecy profoundly. Various Latin scholastics responded to them not by disavowing them but by reclassifying them. They distinguished a natural brand of prophecy, investigated by Arabic philosophers, from a supernatural one, to use Aquinas's terms.[93] Jean-Pierre Torrell credits Albertus Magnus with introducing the distinction, which he articulates with the opposing terms *philosophi* and *sancti*.[94] Philosophical prophecy involves the apprehension of hidden things, "knowledge of which is not above man," while for the *sancti* prophecy comes from God and communicates knowledge that people could not otherwise attain.[95] Identifying the latter with true prophecy, Albertus, Aquinas, and others criticized Avicenna for failing to acknowledge it or its divine source.[96] In the following analysis, I privilege Aquinas's views because his treatment of prophecy was especially influential and because he analyzed at length its dependence on imagination. In one respect, he embraced imagination's obfuscations in terms that underscore a point already made: the power of prophecy depends on its elusiveness, which imagination specializes in generating. In other ways, he attempted to curb imagination's meanderings and clarify its operations. In both respects, however, he showed that it was imagination's nature to defy containment, and that prophecy relied on it accordingly.

Avicenna conceived of prophecy in terms of intellectual and specifically cognitive proficiency, and Aquinas too defined it as a fundamentally cognitive act: "prophecy perfects understanding."[97] He responds not just to Islamic but also to Greek and Jewish traditions by keeping prophecy wedded to both cognition and imagination.[98] He hews closely to the Aristote-

92. Walzer, "Al-Fārābī's Theory of Prophecy and Divination," 143. On this point, he influenced both Avicenna and Maimonides (Hasse, "The Soul's Faculties," 317).

93. Aquinas, *De veritate* 12.3, ad 8, in *Opera omnia*, 22.2:378.

94. Torrell, *Recherches sur la théorie de la prophétie*, 179.

95. Albertus Magnus, *De prophetia* 2.2.109, cited in *Recherches sur la théorie de la prophétie*, ed. Torrell, 147.

96. Their complaint about the neglect of God in writings about prophecy was not unique to Christians. Had al-Ghazālī's *Incoherence of the Philosophers* been available to them, they would have seen that he anticipated it.

97. Aquinas, *De veritate* 12.1, ad 4, in *Opera omnia*, 22.2:370: "prophetia enim perficit intellectum." Trans. McGlynn, *Truth*, 2:109. On the cognitive orientation of late medieval theories of prophecy, see Ottaviani, "Le prophétie comme achèvement intellectuel à la fin du moyen âge."

98. Aquinas's views on prophecy, including imagination's role in it, were powerfully influenced by Moses Maimonides. See Wohlman, *Thomas d'Aquin et Maïmonide*, 267–

lian doctrine that every act of understanding requires imagination, and he faithfully inserts imagination into the act of prophecy as a result.[99] A strong imagination is a prerequisite for Avicenna's prophet, but for Aquinas's it is merely requisite. God makes the prophet, not the exceptional qualities of the individual, which means that prophecy is given rather than earned. As God can make bleared eyes see clearly, so he can strengthen the imaginative power in one whom he selects to prophesy.[100]

Aquinas divides supernatural prophecy into three species, bodily, imaginative, and intellectual. Bodily prophecy occurs when the senses perceive divinely or angelically crafted objects or images, as when King Baltasar sees a scribbling hand in the book of Daniel. It involves imagination insofar as the senses perceive bodies whose images then become imprinted on imagination, awaiting interpretation by the intellect. In imaginative prophecy, images are imprinted on imagination in the first instance. Aquinas privileges this category as "the sort of prophecy that all who are listed in the ranks of prophets had."[101] So defined, it not surprisingly receives the bulk of his analysis. Intellectual prophecy instead involves the direct illumination of the intellect without the prior impression of images on imagination.[102] It is the highest form of prophecy, enjoyed by both David and Moses.[103] Through it, the intellect operates "above its natural capacity" and sees intelligible substances like God and angels in their essence.[104]

Aquinas nonetheless disqualifies intellectual prophecy as prophecy, strictly defined. Strikingly, the reason why it "exceeds the mode of proph-

---

317; and Elders, "Les rapports entre la doctrine de la prophétie de saint Thomas et le *Guide des égarés* de Maïmonide."

99. On Aquinas's attention to cognitive images in his theory of prophecy and its root in Aristotle's cognitive psychology, see Torrell, *Recherches sur la théorie de la prophétie*, 207. On Avicenna's theory of prophecy and its possible indebtedness to ancient Greek philosophy, see Pines, "Arabic Recension," 124–26.

100. The analogy is Aquinas's; see *De veritate* 12.4, ad 2, in *Opera omnia*, 22.2:382. Albertus Magnus also believed that a prophet needed a strong imagination. See *De somno et vigilia* 3.1.5, ed. Borgnet, in *Opera omnia*, 9:183.

101. Aquinas, *Summa theologiae* 2a.2ae.174.2, ad 3: "cuiusmodi prophetiam habuerunt omnes illi qui numerantur in ordinem Prophetarum," in *Opera omnia*, 10:395. Trans. Blackfriars, 45:77.

102. Aquinas, *De veritate* 12.7, resp., in *Opera omnia*, 22.2:391–92.

103. Aquinas realizes that he disagrees with Augustine on this matter. Augustine held that the highest prophet received both images and understanding; see Aquinas, *Summa theologiae* 2a.2ae.174.2, obj. 1 and ad 1, in *Opera omnia*, 10:394. As Serge-Thomas Bonino notes, Aquinas also disagrees with Maimonides, who held a similar position; see "Le rôle de l'image dans la connaissance prophétique," 539.

104. Aquinas, *De veritate* 12.7, resp., in *Opera omnia*, 22.2:391: "supra naturalem facultatem."

ecy" is because it does not depend on imagination.[105] He inherited from Isidore of Seville a belief that the *pro* in *prophetia* comes from *procul*, or "far," and because intellectual prophecy has the intellect see spiritual substances in a direct rather than hidden manner, it is more than prophecy.[106] Instead, "the prophecy in which there is admixture of the sight of imagination possesses the nature of prophecy more perfectly and more properly, for in this the knowledge of prophetic truth is darkened."[107] What darkens it is imagination, whose images are like "clouds that darken the light of understanding."[108] The prophet who sees through them works hard to gain insight that is mediated and, in a cognitive sense, far away. That occurs in bodily and imaginative prophecy, both of which satisfy Isidore's criterion. Whereas al-Kindī and Avicenna highlight the lifelike quality of imagination's images, then, Aquinas focuses directly on their opacity. For him, disorientation is not a useful side effect of imaginative prophecy but a deliberate goal. The prophet cannot fail to recognize that their insight is partial or to be aware of superior understanding and greater mysteries that lie stubbornly beyond their grasp. Prophecy is revelation that makes you aware that there is much you do not know.

Aquinas's prophet recognizes the transcendent significance of prophecy precisely because imagination obfuscates its content. Embracing one brand of imaginative confusion, however, Aquinas seeks to eliminate others. For instance, he subordinates imagination to the illuminated intellect and gives it an expressly secondary role in prophecy. Imaginative prophecy consists of two stages: "the illumination of the mind and the formation of the species in the imaginative power."[109] In other words, such prophecy requires images—here species—impressed on imagination and a mind illuminated so that it can understand them.[110] The impression is either a new im-

105. Aquinas, *De veritate* 12.7, resp., in *Opera omnia*. 22.2:391: "excedit modum prophetiae." Intellectual prophecy involves imagination only secondarily insofar as it contributes to the understanding of the vision. It presumably also allows the intellect to record the vision.

106. See Aquinas, *De veritate* 12.1, resp., in *Opera omnia*, 22.2:367. On the Isidoran root of Aquinas's etymology, see Torrell, *Recherches sur la théorie de la prophétie*, 212. In Arabic, the word for prophet, *nabīy*, does in fact come from a root that means "far off, distant."

107. Aquinas, *De veritate* 12.12, resp., in *Opera omnia*, 22.2:407: "illa invenitur perfectius rationem prophetiae habere et magis proprie cui imaginaria visio admiscetur; sic enim veritatis propheticae cognitio obumbratur." Trans. McGlynn, *Truth*, 2:167.

108. Aquinas, *De veritate* 12.12, ad 7, in *Opera omnia*, 22.2:406: "nebulae quibus obumbratur intellectuale lumen." Trans. McGlynn, *Truth*, 2:166.

109. Aquinas, *De veritate* 12.8, resp., in *Opera omnia*, 22.2:394: "scilicet mentis illustratio et formatio specierum in imaginativa virtute." Trans. McGlynn, *Truth*, 2:146.

110. On "species" as a specific term for imagination's images, see Michaud-Quantin, *Études sur le vocabulaire philosophique du Moyen Age*, 121.

age imprinted directly, most often by angels, or a rearrangement of species already within imagination into a new shape.[111] Aquinas thus separates the act of interpretation from, and privileges it over, the reception of images in imagination: "he is a prophet whose mind alone is enlightened to pass judgment even on those elements which have been seen by others in imaginative forms."[112] That is why Joseph is honored as a prophet, not Pharaoh. Only the intellect, illuminated by Christ, can make sense of what appears in imagination, which is now relatively passive. However, the defining "farness" of prophecy means that the intellect cannot fully comprehend what it sees in imagination. If prophecy exceeds human understanding, then the intellect must be stymied to a degree when it confronts imagination's images. In this respect, imagination still eludes the intellect's grasp.

Aquinas's effort to contain imagination is also undermined by the resemblance of powerfully imaginative phenomena to one another. For al-Kindī and Avicenna, the prophet might experience images as perceptions, but Aquinas seeks to protect his prophet from the seductive power of imaginary spectacle. The prophet's soul "is not under the control of [imagination's] phantasms, but knows through the prophetic light that the objects that it sees are not things, but likenesses signifying something."[113] Aquinas's prophet sees images for the symbols they are. However, even as Aquinas tries to circumscribe imagination by diminishing its images' power to confuse judgment, he collapses the barrier he erects. On rare occasions, he writes, a prophet might in fact experience images as sensations, a comment that leads him instantly to distinguish such prophets from the possessed and crazy.[114] Whereas the latter suffer "some disordering [*inordinatione*] of nature," prophets do not. However, it is not at all clear that such a prophet,

111. See Aquinas, *De veritate* 12.7, resp., in *Opera omnia*, 22.2:391. He writes that "the formation of species in the imaginative power is part of the work proper to angels" ("specierum formatio in ipsa [imaginativa virtute] ad ministerium proprie pertinet angelorum"), *De veritate* 12.8, resp., in *Opera omnia*, 22.2:394. Trans. McGlynn, *Truth*, 2:146. Albertus Magnus also thought that angels might impress new images; see his *De prophetia* 2.4.147, ed. Torrell, 157. As Bert Roest notes, however, Albertus sometimes seems uncomfortable with this possibility; see "Divinations, Visions, and Prophecy according to Albertus Magnus," 328. Duns Scotus instead believes that angels cannot impress new phantasms or species directly (*Ordinatio* 2.11.1, in *Opera omnia*, ed. Hechich, 8:218).

112. Aquinas, *Summa theologiae* 2a.2ae.173.2, resp., in *Opera omnia*, 10:387: "Erit autem propheta si solummodo intellectus eius illuminetur ad dijudicandum etiam ea quae ab aliis imaginarie visa sunt." Trans. Blackfriars, 45:56.

113. Aquinas, *De veritate* 12.3, resp., in *Opera omnia*, 22.2:377: "illis phantasmatibus non detinetur, sed cognoscit per lumen propheticum ea quae videt non esse res sed similitudines aliquid significantes." Trans. McGlynn, *Truth*, 2:120.

114. Aquinas, *Summa theologiae* 2a.2ae.173.3, resp., in *Opera omnia*, 10:388.

a crazy person, and one possessed by demons would experience their conditions differently. A degree of uncertainty is to be expected from prophecy because it surpasses the individual even while making use of their cognitive faculties. It meets and exceeds human capacity simultaneously. That is why it requires imagination, and perhaps why Aquinas, in spite of his relative skepticism about the faculty, retains it. Because of its fundamental haziness, imagination inspires the awe that Aquinas needs from prophecy.

POSSESSION

When he mentions demonic possession, Aquinas points to a problem that vexed Christian theologians into the early modern period: possession and prophetic revelation resemble each other, in part because of their shared reliance on imagination, but for obvious reasons must be distinguished. Defending the common view that women are especially susceptible to both, William of Auvergne wrote that it is the nature of female souls "to take impressions far more easily than male souls."[115] Where imagination is prone to impression, either revelation or possession might follow, each resembling the other. So thorny was the problem that it motivated a whole genre of religious writing known as the discretion or discernment of spirits.

The centrality of imagination to possession is well known, and in fact figures disproportionately in studies of the faculty.[116] Possession bears further scrutiny because of its similarity to other marvels that similarly require a heightened imaginative power and because it draws on imagination's ability to confuse mental representations with bodies in a particularly illuminating way. A helpful source on this topic is William of Auvergne, once teacher at the University of Paris and eventual bishop of Paris, whose writings on demonic deception were foundational. "The first link in medieval demonology," William drew on newly available Greek and Arabic philosophy to construct a theory of demonic activity that maximized the powers of imagination.[117] The

115. William of Auvergne, *De universo* 2.3.24, in *Opera omnia*, 1:1066bH: "quia longe facilioris impressionis sunt qua [*sic*] animae viriles." (I follow convention in giving the page number, then a lowercase *a* or *b* to designate the right or left column, respectively, and finally the uppercase letter printed in the text that orients the reader vertically.) See also Newman, "What Did it Mean to Say 'I saw'?"

116. For Murray Bundy, demons' use of imagination motivated medieval distrust of the faculty (*Theories of Imagination*, 208–9). In a similar vein, Alastair Minnis lists demonic deception through imagination as one reason for medieval suspicion of it ("Medieval Imagination and Memory," 239–49).

117. Boglioni, "Saints, miracles et hagiographie chez Guillaume d'Auvergne," 334. As Roland Teske notes, he was particularly influenced by Avicenna (*Studies in the Philosophy of William of Auvergne*, 24).

disarming vivacity of its images seduces the possessed person, who cannot distinguish between demon-impressed images and extramental reality. Nor should they: William is clear that such images possess for the mind the reality of perceived bodies. So successfully do the images substitute for such bodies that they alienate the victim from the world around them, enclosing them instead within the alternative reality of their imagination. William likens the process to siege warfare: the external senses are starved so that the inner ones might become disproportionately robust.[118] In other words, the unusual strength of imagination expresses the supernatural force of possession. Similarly, John Duns Scotus holds that angels and demons create visions not by imprinting them directly on the intellect, but by concocting powerful images that distract the intellect from other thoughts. "The highly charged imagination makes the intellect so distracted from thoughts about anything that is actually cognized that the intellect seems to see it intellectually."[119] The intensity of the imagined images overwhelms the intellect so that it cannot direct its attention elsewhere. Once something is powerfully imagined, it might be cognized, and therefore appear in the intellect, but only through the mediation of imagination.

William held that demons use imagination to submit the soul to their will. They have special access to the faculty: "no thinking person today doubts that evil spirits spiritually attack holy men by means of their thoughts and imaginations: how can this be if the spirits do not have access to their souls, and if they do not have the ability to paint thoughts of this sort in their imaginations, and perhaps in their intellective power?"[120] The belief that demons, like angels, can act on imagination was widely held and was based, in part, on the placement of imagination within the sensitive rather than rational soul. Albertus Magnus explains that the internal and external senses "are all under demons according to the grade of nature."[121] As spiritual beings, angels and demons stand above matter and sensa-

118. William of Auvergne, *De universo* 2.3.13, in *Opera omnia*, 1:1042aH.

119. Duns Scotus, *Ordinatio* 2.11.1, in *Opera omnia*, ed. Hechich, 8:215: "intensa imaginatio facit animum ita distractum ab omni alia cogitatione cuiuslibet actualis intellectionis quod videtur ipsum intellectualiter videre."

120. William of Auvergne, *De universo* 2.3.23, in *Opera omnia*, 1:1061bD: "Nullus intelligens hodie dubitat, quin maligni spiritus viros sanctos spiritualiter impugnent cogitationibus & imaginationibus: qualiter autem hoc possunt si non est eis accessus ad animas eorum, & si non est eis facultas pingendi cogitatum huiusmodi in imaginationibus eorum, & forsitan virtute intellectiva ipsorum?" William holds open the possibility that demons can act on the intellect directly, but scholastics more often reject it. See, for instance, Albertus Magnus, *Sent.* 2.8.10, in *Opera omnia*, ed. Borgnet, 27:185; and Aquinas, *Summa contra Gentiles* 3.104, in *Opera omnia*, 14:325–26.

121. Albertus Magnus, *Sent.* 2.8.10, resp., in *Opera omnia*, ed. Borgnet, 27:185, "sunt secundum gradum naturae sub daemone omnes."

tion. Under certain circumstances, then, demons can use imagination as their plaything, creating images from scratch and convincing women that they are witches who fly or participate in evening equestrian outings with Diana.[122] Magical illusions too are often the product of demons. Albertus explains that the magician works from without and presents an object to the senses, while demons work from within to make the individual think that they have seen something else.[123] In all of these situations, demons manipulate imagination directly, using it to make false appearances register as perceived objects or events.

The possessed person not only confuses internal images with perceptions but believes that such images alone are real. Seemingly weighted with the materiality of bodies, they prevent the person from perceiving the world outside their soul, even their own body. William outlines the procedures of possession with a story about an evil spirit who made a man think that he was a wolf.[124] After possessing him, the spirit cast the man in a hidden place and then entered into a wolf himself. In that state, he attacked men and animals so that the townspeople, as well as the possessed man himself, thought he was the wolf tormenting the town. The story came to the attention of a holy man, who apparently knew instinctively that it was false. He guided the townspeople to the man in the hidden place and freed him from his possession.[125] William then offers his analysis:

> Thus you see in this example how the image of the wolf that the evil spirit impressed in his organ of imagination took that man out of himself and put him in the wolf so that he might believe or think nothing of his substance or his being except that he himself was that wolf . . . The deceiving impression . . . was in that man in his organ, namely in his imagination, which impression, due to its strength and intensity, he understood, or rather imagined, not as a sign but as the thing itself, that is, as the very wolf. He was able to understand or think nothing else with

122. Albertus Magnus, *Summa theologiae* 2.30.2, in *Opera omnia*, ed. Borgnet, 32:328.

123. See Albertus Magnus, *De somno et vigilia* 3.1.3, in *Opera omnia*, ed. Borgnet, 9:181. Thomas Aquinas likewise attributed to demons an array of magical deeds; see Thorndike, *A History of Magic and Experimental Science*, 2:602–6. On the role of demons in magic according to William, see Marrone, "William of Auvergne on Magic in Natural Philosophy and Theology."

124. William's comments on werewolves here belong to a larger discussion of the topic in the Latin West. See Bynum, *Metamorphosis and Identity*, 77–112.

125. The story is at *De universo* 2.3.13, in *Opera omnia*, 1:1043bB–C. As Caroline Walker Bynum has shown, scholastics generally resisted the possibility of body hopping or metempsychosis and sought alternative explanations, as William does here. See her *Metamorphosis and Identity*.

> respect to his being, as I've said. Thus he was in an exceedingly fast and deep sleep.[126]

So firmly is the deceiving image fixed on imagination that the man can only conclude that he is the very wolf he imagined. Imagination succumbs and the intellect follows, and with the internal faculties thus possessed, the man loses awareness of his own flesh. His seeming immersion into a wolf's body testifies to imagination's ability to alter one's perception of the world. Alienated from his surroundings, the victim might seem to inhabit others'.

Demons can accomplish such a feat, in William's view, only because imagined experience is not necessarily diminished or lacking relative to experience of the extramental world. The point is made most clearly by his characterization not just of possession but also of revelation, madness, and even postmortem suffering as sleep or a dream (*somnus*).[127] By *somnus* he means a state characterized by heightened imagination that enlivens inner experience at the expense of outer. It is characterized by inversion: inner senses act like outer ones so that dreaming feels like being awake. Sleep, then, becomes the normative state. That is why pleasure can be equally intense in either, a point that William makes with reference to dreamed sex. Similarly, hunger and thirst might be sated in either state: "one who dreams of eating or drinking is no less pleased than one who might eat or drink in truth."[128] Presumably, the pleasure lasts only as long as the dream, but is no less intense within its confines. After telling the story of the man who thought himself a wolf, he writes, "Now therefore it is clear to you what impressions of this sort can do even in healthy people, as you clearly see in dreams, where they move dreamers spiritually *no less than the truth itself moves them.*"[129] For Wil-

126. William of Auvergne, *De universo* 2.3.13, in *Opera omnia*, 1:1043bD–44aE: "Vides igitur in hoc exemplo, qualiter imago lupi, quam in organo imaginationis spiritus ille malignus impresserat, hominem illum a se ipso abstraxerat, & in ipsum lupum sic traxerat, ut nihil de substantia sua, vel esse suo, aliud ipsi credere, vel cogitare licet, nisi quod ipse esset lupus ille . . . impressio vero arriptitia . . . in homo ille erat in organo, scilicet imaginationes ipsius, quam impressionem, non ut signum, propter vehementiam, & profunditatem ipsius, sed ut rem ipsam, hoc est, ut ipsum lupum, apprehendebat, hoc est, imaginabatur, nihil aliud de esse suo, ut dixi, apprehendere, vel cogitare valens. Erat igitur in somno vehementer fixo, & profundo." William also allows for the possibility that the evil spirit entered the man and the wolf's imagination was the one deceived, 1044aE.

127. All but revelation are discussed below. On it, see William of Auvergne, *De universo* 2.3.20, in *Opera omnia*, 1:1057bD.

128. William of Auvergne, *De universo* 2.3.13, in *Opera omnia*, 1:1041bD–42aE: "non minus delectatur, qui somniat se comedere, vel bibere, quam delectaretur, si in veritate comederet, vel biberet."

129. William of Auvergne, *De universo* 2.3.13, in *Opera omnia*, 1:1044aF: "Iam igitur tibi manifestum est, quid possint impressiones huiusmodi etiam in hominibus sanis,

liam, impressions on imagination provoke passions that in turn move the one experiencing them. In this case, they move dreamers' bodies and souls as strongly as passions inspired by waking experiences. As a result, one who suffers possession, like one who suffers madness, is disoriented, losing their hold on reality precisely because imagined events seem real. Imagination readies the soul to experience an alternate reality by loosening its grip on the actual one.

What gives imagined experience special power is not just its replacement of perception but its mimicry of it. Paradoxically, imagination trumps the bodily senses by re-creating their effects. The vividness of its images is not remarkable in itself; people experience vivid sensations all the time. Rather, the particular force of imagination lies in its ability to create the effects of bodily experience in the absence of such experience. Nowhere does William describe that power more arrestingly than in his doctrine of hellfire. Majority opinion favored the idea that hellfire was bodily fire, and at points William appears to agree, but he also endorses the possibility of spiritual hellfire, or at least explains how it could work.[130] It consists in the species of fire imprinted on imagination, a possibility William defends with reference to dreams: "It is clear regarding dreamers that they sometimes dream of themselves burning and being in fire, and they are tormented unbearably as if they were in fact burning. As a result, since the truth and substance of the fire are not in them, but only the species of fire is in their phantasy or imagination, it is clear that they suffer the torment of burning in this case only through the species of fire."[131] Imagination creates the effects of fire without possessing its "truth or substance" and sinners burn without "in fact burning." Such fire is equally potent, however, and even surpasses bodily fire insofar as it lasts forever. William's comments on hellfire cast light on the brand of dream that most interests him, possession. We can now see that one who suffers from spiritual hellfire does not misperceive anything, and likewise that the possessed person is not wrong to respond to an imagined wolf as though it were real. In both cases, an imagined object or event exercises the power of perceived ones.

Possession thus relies on imagination's ability not just to mimic but also

quemadmodum evidenter vides in somniis, ubi non minus movent spiritualiter somniantes quam veritas ipsa moveret." Emphasis mine.

130. On medieval views about hellfire, see Barbezat, "In a Corporeal Flame." On William's views, see Bernstein, "William of Auvergne on the Fires of Hell and Purgatory."

131. William of Auvergne, *De universo* 1.1.55, in *Opera omnia*, 1:682aG: "Manifestum est de somniantibus, quoniam interdum somniant se ardere, & esse in igne, & crucientur intolerabiliter, tanquam in veritate ardeant; quare quoniam veritas, & substantia ignis apud eos non est, sed sola species ignis, vel in fantasia, vel imaginatione eorum est, manifestum est eos cruciatum huiusmodi ardoris a sola specie ignis pati."

to create the effects of bodies. Seemingly exceeding their status as images, they create an alternate reality that seduces the soul. Because they present invented images as experiences, the possessed soul responds to delusion as transportation. It overestimates the meaning of images precisely because those images overreach their expected boundaries. Possession, then, like prophecy, visions, and veridical dreams, depends on imagination to generate both uncertainty and significance. At their most vivid, imagined events replicate those in the external world so closely that the two are hard to distinguish, a situation that lies at the foundation of all the marvels discussed thus far. Where imagination operates at maximal strength, its productions are most ambiguous. Were they no more than that, however, they would not necessarily matter. Confusion is not significant on its own. Mental representations astonish because they not only resemble but also act on the soul and body like perceived objects. They promise that the soul has powers only periodically realized but astonishing in their reach.

This chapter has argued that, in the context of the marvels discussed, the power of imagination's images lies in their ability to confuse the boundary between objects within the soul and those outside it. Images that originate in imagination, whether imagination independently creates them or a demon or angel draws pictures within it, can be more vivid than the images gleaned through perception. That hypervivacity conveys the greater-than-human force of prophecy and creates the immersiveness of possession. As we will see in the next chapter, the strength of imagination's images also helps to explain how supernatural beings might alter bodies. Because imagination's images, as spiritual beings, can exercise dominion over natural ones, they suggest the power of angels and demons to move or otherwise alter bodies.[132] Imagination is powerful not only because its images have outsized effects, but also because it subjects natural beings to spiritual ones in the manner of supernatural creatures. It might be a source of deception, but it also provides some of the soul's most spectacular powers, and that too could generate concerns about it.

132. Finding terms that clearly distinguish representational objects as they exist within the soul from those things that exist in the world outside is tricky. Modern oppositions, such as spirit versus matter, image versus object, the spiritual versus the physical, or the incorporeal versus the corporeal, do not correspond well with medieval concepts. I adopt here Aquinas's language, which distinguishes between things with spiritual being and those with natural being (*esse spirituale* or *naturale*). See, for instance, *De anima* 1.10, in *Opera omnia*, 45.1:50–51. On this quandary, see also King, "Rethinking Representation in the Middle Ages," 87–88.

[CHAPTER 2]

Marvels and the Philosophy of Imagination

Bewitchment, Telekinesis, and the Moving of Mountains

Chapter 1 looked at marvels that use imagination to muddy the barrier between interior and exterior phenomena, and this chapter turns to those that actually cross that barrier. In a case like bewitchment, imagination alters the "real," extramental world. Medieval theories of marvels thus rely on an imagination more powerful than is usually permitted now. While anyone might experience vivid imaginings that feel like perceptions, and imagination's ability to affect one's own body is indisputable—Avicenna illustrates it with the example of the wet dream—imagination is less often credited with the power to move or otherwise change objects at a distance.[1] The medieval imagination, however, is potentially world-altering. The traditional opposition between imagination and reality is inapplicable when imagination can actually reshape, transport, or even create objects in the extramental world. Its power to cross the boundary between the soul and the world beyond was its most startling one because it required the faculty to surpass seemingly natural limitations. What is astonishing about the evil eye, for instance, is not just the act that comes to define it, namely, the maiming of a child through an old woman's envious gaze, but the laws of nature that such an act seems to transgress. The marvel is unsettling precisely because of the realness—the sheer bodiliness—of imaginative effect.

By transgressing the crucial boundary between things that exist within

1. Avicenna cites the wet dream as an example of imagination's "marvelous" influence over matter: *De anima* 4.2, ed. Rahman, 179. Imagination's influence, in his view, is mediated by the spirit.

the soul and those in the world outside, imagination helps to explain how marvels could mean more than the events that constitute them. A marvel like bewitchment signifies as a symbol as much as an event, one that reveals reservoirs of human potency that are usually untapped. In this chapter, I argue that imagination implies powers greater than itself through images that overperform themselves, acting like, and on, foreign bodies, even though they are not bodies themselves. That is a key reason why the faculty is useful to an array of marvels. Far-reaching in its power and apparently exceeding its own rightful limitations, it lends them indeterminacy and undefined, unbounded significance.

MARVELS THROUGH THE MULTIPLICATION OF SPECIES

The previous chapter showed how imagination imitates the effects of perceived bodies, and from there it is no small leap to the concern of this one, namely, imagination's actual influence on such bodies. However, as William of Auvergne shows, one capacity gestures at the other. If imagination's phantasms can generate the same intellectual and bodily responses as perceived objects, then they show that things that exist within the soul can act much like the bodies outside it. It hardly follows that the former can act *on* the latter, but William nonetheless transitions from one to the other, as though minimizing to another degree the difference between internal images and the things they depict. He points to a person's ability to make a camel fall through the sole use of their imagination, as well as a torpedo fish's ability to bind the limbs of a man "either with its imagination or another spiritual passion."[2] At stake in such marvels is not just imagination's power but the general dominion of nonbodily powers—whether the soul or spiritual beings like angels and demons—over bodies. If imaginative images can act, however mediatedly, on external bodies, then spiritual beings can likewise act in the world. Thus demons can gather wax and make a candle in the course of deceiving people.[3] They cannot have sex with women, but they can impregnate them with the transported semen of an animal.[4] Angels too subject bodies to their will. William tells the story of Habakkuk, carried from Judah to Babylon by his hair according to an apocryphal addition to the book of Daniel. William asks how an incorporeal angel might lift Habakkuk and answers that the angel, like the magnet that moves iron,

2. William of Auvergne, *De universo* 2.3.16, in *Opera omnia*, 1:1046bE and 1046bF: "vel imaginatione sua, vel alia passione sua spirituali."

3. William of Auvergne, *De universo* 2.3.24, in *Opera omnia*, 1066aG.

4. On demonic impregnation, see Elliott, *Fallen Bodies*, 56–60 and 153–54. For William's discussion, see *De universo* 2.3, in *Opera omnia*, 1070–73.

suspends the natural weight of its object by a contrary disposition.[5] The angel, in other words, disposes Habakkuk to be light. Spiritual beings and imagination are mutually validating: each shows how bodies submit to nonbodily forces. Placed in such company, imagination appears to possess nearly superhuman power.

As such comments suggest, imagination's ability to alter bodies became its most spectacular one. That ability was qualified, with intermediaries between imagination and the body acted upon, but especially in the Latin West, imagination was the faculty that became most closely identified with such marvels. It was believed capable of affecting people, other animals, or inanimate objects, as well as nature. Its powers included bewitchment, telekinesis, and the ability to alter the weather, although the focus here is on imagination's power over objects at a distance. Action at a distance, that is, the action of one thing on another without being in physical contact with it, was a popular topic in medieval Latin philosophy, in part because philosophers supporting the possibility recognized that they were disagreeing with Aristotle.[6] Now especially familiar from horror movies and television shows, in which evil people regularly move objects without touching them, this power was not initially confined to the wicked, but it did become increasingly associated with them. Not coincidentally, it also became the subject of controversy in the Latin West, figuring into the Paris Condemnations of 1277 and finding opposition among later theologians who thought a too-powerful imagination was an offense to divine omnipotence. As imagination became more closely tied to marvels in the Latin West, there was a countervailing tendency to define its limitations, which led late medieval philosophers to comment more explicitly on imagination's exceptional powers than their predecessors had done.

I begin by describing two different theories that accounted for imagination's ability to alter foreign bodies, one from al-Kindī and the other from Avicenna, and both crucial to theories of marvels in the Latin West.[7] I end with their legacy in the Latin West, and particularly with the efforts of

5. William of Auvergne, *De universo* 2.3.23, in *Opera omnia*, 1:1062aG–63aB.

6. See, for instance, Albertus Magnus, *Commentarii in Sententiarum* 2.7.6, in *Opera omnia*, ed. Borgnet, 27:152; and his *Summa theologiae* 7.29, in *Opera omnia*, ed. Borgnet, 32:317. Matthew Boyd Goldie discusses the importance of the Aristotelian principle to medieval philosophers in *Scribes of Space*, 168–77.

7. Reviewing theories of prophecy in the Latin West, Dag Hasse identifies three that pertain to action at a distance, those of al-Kindī, Avicenna, and Aquinas. He characterizes Aquinas's theory, which allows the soul to act on the medium and thus to act on the external object indirectly, as "more successful" than the others, but I treat it as a variant of al-Kindī's theory. See Hasse, "Influence of Arabic and Islamic Philosophy on the Latin West."

Thomas Bradwardine and Nicole Oresme, writing in the fourteenth century, to determine the boundaries of imagination's power. Their efforts testify to the remarkable abilities imagination was thought to possess, abilities that needed to be limited precisely because they threatened to stretch too far. The writings examined in this chapter show once again how imagination helps to complicate marvels in a way that invites spectators to overestimate their significance. Not only mimicking perception but exercising influence over its objects, imagination pushes marvels beyond normally fixed boundaries in an especially flashy way. Its effects extend into the world and, once seemingly visible, make the potency of marvels similarly apparent. The result is not just that imagination's powers are on display but that its specific capacity, as a faculty of the soul, to transgress the normal boundary between the soul and the world outside it loudly proclaims itself. Behaving so improbably, the faculty adds to the mystery and import of the marvels it helps to create.

The logical starting point for this discussion is again al-Kindī, although this time I focus on his most popular work in the Latin West, the *De radiis*, also known as the *De theoretica artium magicarum*.[8] It had its greatest impact in Latin translation, which preserved the text; the Arabic original does not survive. It presented a mechanism by which the soul could exercise power over foreign bodies that influenced Roger Bacon and remained popular beyond the Middle Ages. That power is rooted in the text's ambitious theory of rays. For al-Kindī, all astral and earthly objects emit invisible rays, which accounts for the effects of the stars on the sublunary world and of sublunary objects on one another. Such rays also account for action at a distance. The cases that he considers are incantations, prayers, the names of God, curses, written symbols, talismans, and animal sacrifice. All depend on a series of conditions in order to be effective: one must imagine a particular outcome, desire it, believe that it will be achieved, and finally perform an act, either uttering words, such as a prayer or a spell, or completing some sort of manual act, such as animal sacrifice or the creation of a talisman.[9] Al-Kindī takes a special interest in imagination, whose power comes not from vivid images of its own or another's invention, as we

8. Daston and Park write that medieval texts were often renamed so that their interest in marvels and wonders would be more apparent (*Wonders and the Order of Nature*, 25). This seems to be the case with the alternative Latin title here. On the text's attribution, see d'Alverny and Hudry, Introduction to "Al-Kindī, *De Radiis*," 149–67.

9. Al-Kindī, *De radiis* 5, ed. d'Alverny and Hudry, 231–33. Al-Kindī holds open the possibility that the verbal or manual act may in rare instances be unnecessary (232). For a French translation of the text, see *De radiis*, trans. Ottaviani; and for an English translation of the first five chapters, see *Philosophical Works of al-Kindī*, trans. Pormann and Adamson, 219–34.

have seen, but rather from objects whose forms have been impressed on it through sense perception.[10] At issue here, then, is the retentive imagination, which stores data from the senses. Informed by objects, imagination can in turn act like, and on, bodies, even those at a distance from the one imagining.

As Claire Fanger notes, scholars often cite al-Kindī's *De radiis* and acknowledge its importance to theories about magic in the Latin West, but they rarely analyze it in detail.[11] Because of its complexity and influence, I describe its theory of rays at some length. It begins with the stars and their dominion over what al-Kindī calls the elemental world, the sublunary world that includes earth and is constituted by the four elements.[12] Each star emits invisible rays in every direction. These rays, shifting their position relative to earth (because they are issued by stars in a rotating sphere), intersect now with some, now with other rays of varying potencies that weaken or strengthen the initial ray's effect. A direct line that creates a clean perpendicular angle with an object is typically the most potent, while "rays are weakened in effect according to their degree of obliqueness, except insofar as they are strengthened by the concurrence of the rays of other stars in the same place."[13] This complex series of movements, as well as the diversity within matter itself, accounts for the diversity found in the elemental world because the confluence of rays and conditions at any two places is hardly ever the same. Anyone with a full understanding of this astral choreography would understand everything about the world below: "whoever had knowledge of the entire condition of the celestial harmony would equally understand past, present, and future things."[14] Likewise, understanding any earthly thing in the fullness of its causes would require comprehension of the whole celestial harmony.

Everything in the elemental world—everything from plants to people to voices—also emits rays and affects other things through those rays: "it is clear that everything in this world, either substance or accident, makes

10. The Latin translation calls them "species." On its synonymy with *forma* in contexts such as this, see Lindberg, *Theories of Vision from al-Kindi to Kepler*, 113–14.

11. Fanger, "Things Done Wisely by a Wise Enchanter," 102.

12. See al-Kindī, *De radiis* 1, ed. d'Alverny and Hudry, 218.

13. Al-Kindī, *De radiis* 2, ed. d'Alverny and Hudry, 219: "secundum proportionem obliquationis in effectu debilitantur, nisi in quantum aliarum stellarum radiis concurrentibus in eisdem locis confortantur."

14. Al-Kindī, *De radiis* 2, ed. d'Alverny and Hudry, 223: "Unde qui totam condicionem celestis armonie notam haberet tam preterita quam presentia quam futura cognosceret."

rays in its way in the manner of the stars."[15] These rays derive their power from the celestial harmony and fill the elemental world, likewise strengthening or weakening each other's effects insofar as matter permits.[16] The elemental rays, like those of the stars, express something of the nature of their progenitor and communicate that nature to foreign objects, and in this lies their potential power over other things.[17]

Imagination's special power resides above all in its ability to reproduce the rays of perceived objects. Appealing to an already familiar notion, al-Kindī calls man a microcosm, or *minor mundus*, who enjoys special status in the world because he is uniquely "proportioned" to it.[18] This leads him to a less common idea: man's special status in the world empowers him to move bodies, much like the *major mundus*, through the rays he produces: "he possesses the power to induce movement in appropriate matter through his deeds just as the world has."[19] He possesses this power principally through his imagination, which operates in the manner of the macrocosm: a person "is and is called *minor mundus* by virtue of his center and the unity of his complexion and the entirety of things contained in the place of his imagination, through which he is similar to the entire world in power and effect."[20] The first two elements, regarding the individual's center and complexion, pertain to the person's special relationship to the celestial harmony; it is the third that is most important here. Because imagination contains so much of what is in the world through the forms imprinted on it, it can exercise something of the macrocosm's power.

It does so by imagining a body, which enables it to send out rays like the object imagined. Al-Kindī explains: "when a man conceives of some corporeal thing with his imagination, that thing assumes actual existence

15. Al-Kindī, *De radiis* 3, ed. d'Alverny and Hudry, 224: "manifestum est quod omnis res huius mundi, sive sit substantia sive accidens, radios facit suo modo ad instar siderum."

16. The variable receptivity of matter to a particular force explains why the same force affects different things differently—thus fire softens lead but hardens brick (al-Kindī, *De radiis* 3, ed. d'Alverny and Hudry, 225).

17. Al-Kindī adds a qualification: it is strictly inaccurate to speak of one earthly object affecting another through its rays. Rather, it is always the celestial harmony that acts, and elemental things are related to it only through concomitance (*De radiis* 4, ed. d'Alverny and Hudry, 228–29).

18. Al-Kindī, *De radiis* 5, ed. d'Alverny and Hudry, 230.

19. Al-Kindī, *De radiis* 5, ed. d'Alverny and Hudry, 230: "recipit potentiam inducendi motus in competenti materia per sua opera sicut habet mundus."

20. Al-Kindī, *De radiis* 9, ed. d'Alverny and Hudry, 256: "minor mundus est et dicitur ratione centri et unitatis complexionate et universitatis rerum in loco ymaginationis contentarum per que mundo universo similis est in virtute et effectu."

according to its species in the imaginary spirit. Whence the same spirit emits rays moving exterior things, like the thing of which it is an image."[21] When imagination forms an image of a body, the imaginary spirit acquires its force and is able to produce rays like it, affecting other bodies accordingly. Along with reason, it is imprinted with the form of things perceived, and as a result, the imaginary spirit has "rays conforming to the rays of the world."[22] Much as stars act on the terrestrial world at a distance through their rays, so the imaginary spirit issues rays that similarly affect objects removed from it. In the previous chapter, we saw that imagination's images can exercise the power of perceived objects by mimicking them persuasively. Here, they behave more fully like the bodies imagined. With their connection to the extramental world thus strengthened, the distinction between mental representations and bodies becomes attenuated. Al-Kindī's conclusion is clear: because imagination is informed by the rays that bodies emit, it can in certain circumstances act on bodies itself.

Al-Kindī's ambitious claims for imagination provoked censure in the Latin West, most directly in the *Errores philosophorum*, a text regularly ascribed to the Augustinian friar and eventual archbishop of Bourges, Giles of Rome. Giles complained that, contrary to Augustine, al-Kindī thought that the soul could create new things, that a "spiritual substance could, through imagination alone, generate real forms."[23] In other words, according to Giles, he believed that imagination could generate a new form by causing a body to become something other than what it was.[24] That one thing could become another was not itself an objectionable proposition, insofar as Aaron's rod, for instance, became a serpent. What Giles objects to is the notion that imagination effects such transformations. In spite of his concerns, however, the belief that imagination alters foreign bodies persisted for many centuries. Influential in that legacy was the Franciscan Roger

21. Al-Kindī, *De radiis* 5, ed. d'Alverny and Hudry, 231: "Preterea cum homo concipit rem aliquam corpoream ymaginatione, illa res recipit actualem existentiam secundum speciem in spiritu ymaginario. Unde idem spiritus emittit radios moventes exteriora, sicut res cuius est ymago."

22. Al-Kindī, *De radiis* 5, ed. d'Alverny and Hudry, 230: "radios conformes radiis mundi."

23. Giles of Rome, *Errores philosophorum* 10.6, ed. Koch, 50: "spiritualem substantiam ex sola imaginatione posse introducere veras formas." Trans. Riedl, same volume, 49.

24. Al-Kindī comes closest to supporting this interpretation when he suggests that, where matter is receptive and conditions allow, the same species might be generated in the mind and in an external object. See *De radiis* 5, ed. d'Alverny and Hudry, 231: "Eodem modo ymago mentalis et realis, quia sunt eiusdem speciei sese consequuntur dummodo utriusque materia ad illius forme susceptionem sit declivis, et alia concurrant accidentia que secundum locum et tempus exiguntur ad rei generationem."

Bacon. Although he did not highlight the work of imagination proper, he did translate al-Kindī's theory of rays into a doctrine, the multiplication of species, that proved both palatable to and durable in the Latin West. Thus David Lindberg, after describing al-Kindī's theory, writes: "this is a natural philosophy that was destined to influence Robert Grosseteste and Roger Bacon and to reappear in their doctrine of the multiplication of species."[25] Grosseteste did not much concern himself with marvels, but Bacon did. For him, the multiplication of species accounted for a slate of marvels, and Bacon's account was rehearsed for generations. Along the way, the doctrine rediscovered al-Kindī's concern with imagination.

The multiplication of species has received a lot of attention, principally from those interested in medieval theories of perception in the Latin West.[26] It is a theory complicated in its details but easily summarized: "the object sends its form through the medium to the perceiver—a form that would come to be known in the Latin translation as 'species.'"[27] Species are invisible representations that convey information about an object across the space between the object and the percipient. They act much like al-Kindī's rays, and in fact Bacon sometimes referred to his signature text on the topic, *De multiplicatione specierum*, as *De radiis*.[28] Bacon thus writes that "every agent creates a power and species from itself in extrinsic matter," species that function like al-Kindī's rays to extend a thing's influence outward, ultimately enabling action at a distance.[29]

It is thanks to the species they emit that the basilisk can slay with its sight alone, that the wolf who first sees a man will render him hoarse, and that a hyena prevents a dog from barking in its shadow.[30] Man, because of the greater dignity of his nature, can accomplish other feats. Bacon points to fascination, which is often treated as synonymous with the "evil eye" but can signify simply bewitchment, usually with a harmful intent.[31] He writes of the Mongols, who bewitch their enemies and defeat them without

25. Lindberg, *Theories of Vision*, 19. For a fuller discussion, see Lindberg, *Roger Bacon's Philosophy of Nature*, xliv–xlvi.

26. On Bacon's theory of the multiplication of species, see Lindberg, *Roger Bacon's Philosophy of Nature*, liii–lxxi; and Tachau, *Vision and Certitude*, 3–26.

27. Smith, "Perception," 337.

28. Lindberg, *Roger Bacon's Philosophy of Nature*, xxvii.

29. Bacon, *De secretis operibus artis et naturae* 3, ed. Brewer, in *Opera quaedam hactenus inedita*, 1:528: "agens omne facit virtutem et speciem a se in materiam extrinsecam."

30. Bacon, *De secretis operibus artis et naturae* 3, ed. Brewer, in *Opera quaedam hactenus inedita*, 1:529.

31. On fascination, see Camille, *The Gothic Idol*, xxxi. Helpful definitions can be found in al-Ghazālī, *Maqāṣid al-falāsifa* 2.5.9, ed. al-Kurdī, 3.73, Latin trans., ed. Muckle, *Algazel's Metaphysics*, 194; Avicenna, *Ishārāt* 2.10, ed. Forget, *Le livre des théorèmes et des avertissements*, 221; William of Auvergne, *De universo* 2.3.16, in *Opera omnia*, 1046aG;

battle, justifying Bacon's deeply held belief that "works of wisdom" (*opera sapientiae*) such as this need to be applied to combat.[32] A people as small and weak as they only "subdued the whole world," minus Egypt and Africa, because of the power of bewitchment.[33] The eyes have special potency, a point that Bacon illustrates with reference to a phenomenon drawn from Aristotle that appears frequently in writings about marvels, that is, a menstruating woman who looks into a new mirror and stains it with a blood-tinged hue.[34] Bacon's theory is that the woman emits species that impress themselves on the mirror, thus replicating something of her physical condition in the object.[35]

In all of these cases, the soul impresses its species on "things external, and especially so when it acts with strong desire, definite purpose, and great confidence," conditions that are familiar from al-Kindī's *De radiis* as well as Avicenna's *De anima*.[36] Although his species-based theory of action at a distance appears indebted to al-Kindī's theory of rays, imagination plays no prominent part in it. Various of his successors, however, restored it.[37] Thus Nicole Oresme (d. 1382), master of theology at Paris, adviser to King Charles V, and eventual bishop of Lisieux, appeals to it directly. Like Bacon, he uses the multiplication of species to explain the staining of the mirror and the basilisk's special power, as well as what became the canonical example of fascination, when an envious old woman disfigures a beautiful child.[38] He cites the last in support of a general principle that the soul

---

and Oresme, *De configurationibus* 2.38, ed. Clagett, *Nicole Oresme and the Medieval Geometry of Qualities and Motions*, 382.

32. Bacon thought that the Antichrist would use such devices against Christians, who were thus obligated to invest heavily in natural philosophy so that they might become adept in the tools themselves. See Bartlett, *The Natural and the Supernatural*, 129–34; and Power, *Roger Bacon and the Defence of Christendom*, 195–208.

33. Bacon, *The Opus majus of Roger Bacon*, ed. Bridges, 1:400: "totam latitudinem mundi prostraverunt." Trans. Burke, 1:416.

34. Aristotle, *On Dreams* 2, 459b27–60a11, trans. Barnes, *The Complete Works of Aristotle*, 1:731; and Bacon, *De secretis operibus artis et naturae* 3, ed. Brewer, in *Opera quaedam hactenus inedita*, 1:529.

35. Implicit here is the belief that a menstruating woman is defined by menstruation more than by other qualities, and also a belief in the special power, often maleficent, of menstrual blood. For more, see McCracken, *Curse of Eve*.

36. Bacon directs his reader to the latter, *Opus majus*, ed. Bridges, 1:396: "res extra; et maxime quam ex forti desiderio et intentione certa et confidentia magna operatur." Trans. Burke, 1:412.

37. Imagination also became integral to the multiplication of species doctrine as various philosophers developed it; see my *Imagination, Meditation and Cognition*, 82–110.

38. See Oresme, *De configurationibus* 2.38, ed. Clagett, *Nicole Oresme and the Medieval Geometry of Qualities and Motions*, 380–84. Stefan Caroti notes that Bacon is the most likely source for Oresme's doctrine of the multiplication of species ("Éléments

"can be the cause of the transmutation of a foreign body . . . by means of a forceful thought or imagination."[39] So firm had the association of imagination with fascination and other marvels become that Oresme can declare that "one ought not to imagine that imagination alone does these things, nor that it has as much power as some people think."[40] The phrase "as some people think" is telling: explaining marvels through imagination had become, from Oresme's perspective, common. He does not disagree, but simply proposes additional causes.

THE SOUL'S POWER OVER MATTER

In his analysis, Oresme draws on al-Kindī and also Avicenna, who provided another highly influential mechanism to explain action at a distance. It appears in his account of motive prophecy, which concerns bodily movement. Characteristically, he begins with the nonprophetic brand of movement, that is, the soul's movement of its own body, as when imagined embarrassment results in a blush. In a colorful example often repeated in the Latin West, Avicenna writes that a tree trunk lying on the ground will be crossed without incident, but once placed as a bridge over deep waters, it inspires fearful and paralyzing illusions. Someone "does not dare to cross over it (except by creeping slowly) because he powerfully imagines the image of falling in his soul, which his nature and the power of his members obey" by refusing to proceed.[41] So compelling is the vividly imagined possibility that it arrests the body. At its furthest nonprophetic extreme, the soul's control over the body enables it to imagine itself into health or illness beyond the capacities of any doctor.[42] Avicenna uses both examples

pour une reconstruction," 97). Regarding Oresme's views on fascination, Bert Hansen writes, "I believe that, for his ideas and perhaps also for his citations, Oresme owes much to Roger Bacon's *Opus maius*" (*Nicole Oresme and the Marvels of Nature*, 313n69).

39. Oresme, *De configurationibus* 2.38, ed. Clagett, *Nicole Oresme and the Medieval Geometry of Qualities and Motions*, 380–82: "Potest . . . esse causa transmutationis corporis alieni . . . per ymaginationem seu cogitationem fortem." Trans. 381–83.

40. Oresme, *De configurationibus* 2.38, ed. Clagett, *Nicole Oresme and the Medieval Geometry of Qualities and Motions*, 384: "Non est ergo ymaginandum quod hec faciat ymaginatio sola, nec quod tantam habeat potentiam ut aliqui putant." Trans. 385.

41. Avicenna, *De anima* 4.4, ed. Rahman, 200: "lam tajsur an yamshiya 'alayhi (dabīban illā bi-l-huwaynā) li-annahu yatakhayyalu fī nafsihi ṣūrata al-suqūṭi takhayyulan qawīyan jiddan fa-tujību ilā dhālika ṭabī'atuhu wa-quwwatu a'ḍā'ihi." Latin trans., ed. Van Riet, 64. The content within parentheses is not in all of the Arabic manuscripts surveyed by Rahman or in the Latin translation edited by Van Riet. Hasse provides a list of references by Latin scholastics to this (289) and other passages from Avicenna's text in *Avicenna's* De anima, 234–314.

42. Avicenna, *De anima* 4.4, ed. Rahman, 199–200.

to illustrate the soul's unmediated power over the body. Notably, both also depend on imagination.

Avicenna allows only prophets to act on foreign bodies at a distance. Although some of the marvels associated with this brand of prophecy came to typify imagination's potency in the writings of Latin scholastics, Avicenna expressly denies that it is rooted in imagination. He instead uses the estimative power to account for the marvels, including the evil eye, what the Latin translation calls "the work of the bewitching eye." Whereas imagination incites desire, the estimative power, an offshoot of Aristotle's *phantasia* that perceives nonsensible attributes like danger, exercises power by inciting the will.[43] As Taneli Kukkonen shows, the estimative power, "an original Avicennian invention," also supports hypothetical thinking and considers what might be naturally possible.[44] Avicenna writes that "the soul often acts on another body as it acts on its own. Such is the work of the bewitching eye and of the estimative power of the agent. For when the soul is steady, noble, and similar to the [higher] principles, matter which is in the world obeys it and undergoes change because of it, and whatever is pictured in the soul will be found in matter."[45] A form held with particular intensity within it can thus alter external bodies. Avicenna here adopts the Neoplatonic conviction that "matter is entirely obedient to the soul" and likens the soul's authority over extrinsic matter to that of the world soul.[46] As Fazlur Rahman explains, Avicenna's doctrine "is based on the essential divinity of the human soul."[47]

Al-Ghazālī supplies an additional example that often accompanied Avicenna's comments on the evil eye, what the Latin translation refers to as

43. On Avicenna's estimative power, see Black, "Estimation (*Wahm*) in Avicenna" and "Imagination and Estimation"; as well as Kukkonen, "Ibn Sīnā and the Early History of Thought Experiments," 443–49. Avicenna locates the estimative power along with the compositive imaginative power in the middle ventricle of the brain. See Hasse, "The Soul's Faculties," 308n9.

44. Kukkonen, "Ibn Sīnā and the Early History of Thought Experiments," 444–47, at 444. Averroes would later argue that there was no need to posit a separate estimative power since its functions are performed by the imaginative power (Hasse, "The Soul's Faculties," 314).

45. Avicenna, *De anima* 4.4, ed. Rahman, 200: "wa-kathīran mā tu'aththiru al-nafsu fī badanin ākhara kamā tu'aththiru fī badani nafsihā ta'thīru al-ʿayni al-ʿāyīni wa-l-wahmi al-ʿāmili, bal al-nafsu idhā kānat qawīyatan sharīfatan shabīhatan bi-l-mabādi'i aṭāʿahā al-ʿunṣuru alladhī fī al-ʿālami wa-infaʿala ʿanhā wa-wajada fī al-ʿunṣuri mā yataṣūwara fīhā." Latin trans., ed. Van Riet, 65. Hasse calls this passage, in its Latin translation, "by far the most popular and well-known passage" in the Latin West from Avicenna's writings about prophecy (*Avicenna's* De anima, 165).

46. Avicenna, *De anima* 4.4, ed. Rahman, 201: al-ʿunṣūru bi-l-jumlati ṭawwaʿa li-l-nafsi." Latin trans., ed. Van Riet, 66.

47. Rahman, *Prophecy in Islam*, 48.

a "proverb" about a camel: upon seeing a camel, someone "regards it as pleasing, and in the same manner [as in other examples] he marvels at it, and it happens that his soul is malicious and envious. He imagines the fall of the camel and the camel, influenced through its estimative power, falls immediately."[48] Wanting to destroy what he cannot have, he infects the estimative power of the camel and causes it to fall. What I translate as "imagines" above is *yatawahhamu*, more literally meaning that he "uses the faculty of estimation" (*wahm*), which the Latin translation renders with *estimat*. Again, emphasis falls on estimation. The prophet's soul can sometimes accomplish even more impressive feats: "it heals the sick and sickens the wicked and makes it so that natures are destroyed (and that natures are fortified) and that elements are changed, so that what is not fire is made fire and what is not earth is made earth."[49] Action at a distance in these cases depends on the soul's superior powers rather than on imaginative forms.

However, the highly potent imagination became affiliated with, and even defined by, such marvels in the Latin West. The estimative power played a more limited role in Latin scholasticism generally, and specifically lost ground to imagination in the context of marvels.[50] As Béatrice Delaurenti notes, passages about the soul's power on foreign bodies and about imagination, not connected directly by Avicenna, were juxtaposed by various scholastics in the Latin West, in a manner that proved highly influential.[51] Albertus Magnus shows how Avicenna's writings might lend themselves to such an interpretation. There are some men, he writes, endowed from birth with the ability to alter foreign bodies: "with their souls they act to change the bodies of the world with the result that they are said to produce miracles."[52] He proceeds to mention bewitchment and then, a few sentences later, cites Avicenna directly: "Avicenna says that imagining

48. Al-Ghazālī, *Maqāṣid al-falāsifa* 2.5.9, ed. al-Kurdī, 3.73: "tasthasinu al-jamala mithlan wa-yataʿajjabu minhu wa-yattafaqu an yakūna nafsuhu khabītha ḥusūdata fa-yatawahhamu suqūṭa al-jamali fa-yanfaʿilu al-jamalu ʿan tawahhumihā wa-yasquṭu fī al-ḥāli." Latin trans., ed. Muckle, *Algazel's Metaphysics*, 194. For more on this passage, see Minnema, "A Hadith Condemned at Paris."

49. Avicenna, *De anima* 4.4, ed. Rahman, 200–201: "tabriʾu al-marḍā wa-tumarriḍa al-ashrāra, wa-yatbaʿuhā an yuhdamu ṭabāʾiʿun (wa-an tuʾakkada ṭabāʾiʿun) wa-an tastaḥīla lahā al-ʿanāṣiru, fa-yaṣīru ghayr al-nāri nāran wa-ghayr al-arḍi arḍan." Latin trans., ed. Van Riet, 65–66.

50. On the relatively limited role of the estimative power in the Latin West, see Black, "Imagination and Estimation," 59.

51. Delaurenti, "Pratiques médiévales de réécriture," 365–74. See also Black, "Imagination and Estimation," on Latin scholastics' departure from their Arabic sources with respect to the two faculties.

52. Albertus Magnus, *De animalibus* 22.1.5, ed. Stadler, 2:1353: "suis animalibus agunt ad corporum mundi transmutationem ita ut miracula facere dicantur."

the color red increases blood flow and motion, and someone with great sadness who fears leprosy will become leprous, and many other things of this sort happen in man."[53] Before arriving at Avicenna, Albertus is vague about the causes of such marvels, but Avicenna, by expressly naming imagination, albeit in a different context, perhaps provided a mechanism that could be applied to more marvels than he associated with it. Thus Oresme writes that "Avicenna . . . posits that the intellectual soul, or the imaginative faculty, is so potent in some people that it moves not only its own body but also foreign bodies, even elements, and can make it rain and so forth."[54] Avicenna's motive prophecy now presupposes a powerful imagination, which Oresme, against Avicenna, tasks with inciting the will. Thomas Bradwardine summarizes Avicenna's belief that a soul can act on foreign bodies, heal the ill, alter the elements, create rain, or perform the evil eye, and he notes that Avicenna "seems to intimate that the soul does such deeds out of the strength and firmity of the form of the thing impressed on it and of the imagination of it, and Algazel agrees about such imaginary work . . . as do certain other moderns."[55] Note that Avicenna "seems to intimate" such a position: Bradwardine is aware that Avicenna does not overtly attribute the marvels to imagination. Rather, Bradwardine assimilates Avicenna's views to those of al-Ghazālī and unspecified "moderns." He suggests that belief in imagination's role in such marvels was widely held in his own day.

On the specific topic of the camel, William of Auvergne writes of a man "who, by imagining the fall of a camel, caused it to fall only through such imagining."[56] This example of telekinetic power became so familiar that it made its way into the Condemnations of 1277, although without specifically targeting imagination. Article 112 condemns the belief "that superior intelligences create impressions on inferior ones, just as one soul makes an impression on another and even on the sensitive soul, and through such an

53. Albertus Magnus, *De animalibus* 22.1.5, ed. Stadler, 2:1353: "dicit Avicenna quod ymaginans colores rubeos auget sanguinis motum et fluxum: et multum tristis et timens lepram erit aliquando leprosus: et cetera multa in homine contingunt huiusmodi."

54. Oresme, *De causis mirabilium* 4.4, ed. Hansen, *Nicole Oresme and the Marvels of Nature*, 354: "Avicenna . . . ponit quod anima intellectiva seu ymaginativa virtus in aliquibus hominibus est ita potens quod non solum proprium corpus movet sed et aliena ymo et elementa et potest facere pluere et cetera." Trans. Hansen, 355. He links imagination to the evil eye at *De configurationibus* 2.38, ed. Clagett, *Nicole Oresme and the Medieval Geometry of Qualities and Motions*, 382.

55. Bradwardine, *De causa Dei* 1.1.32, ed. Savile, 44: "videtur innuere animam facere talia opera, ex fortitudine & firmitate formae rei sibi impressae & imaginationis de illa, cuius & imaginariae fictioni consentit Algazel . . . & quidam alii modernorum." See also *De causa Dei* 1.1.32, ed. Savile, 46.

56. William of Auvergne, *De universo* 2.3.16, in *Opera omnia* 1:1046bE: "illo, qui imaginando casum cameli, sola imaginatione huiusmodi dejecit illum."

impression some sorcerer casts a camel into a ditch with his sight alone."[57] Returning the focus to imagination, Giles of Rome rebukes al-Ghazālī for "holding that the soul through the imagination operates in other bodies," and then provides the examples of fascination and the fallen camel.[58] He joins an array of Latin scholastics, including Aquinas and Albertus Magnus, in making imagination at least partly responsible for the power of the evil eye.[59]

DEBATING IMAGINATION'S ROLE IN MARVELS: BRADWARDINE AND ORESME

So conventional did imagination's association with marvels become that late medieval philosophers in the Latin West addressed it explicitly and at length, although there has been little scholarship on it. I focus here on Bradwardine and Oresme because both tried to clarify the scope of the faculty's power and the mechanisms it employed explicitly. They returned repeatedly to imagination's potential to influence objects at a distance, and thus to transgress the normally inviolable barrier between the soul and bodies in the external world. They make it clear that imagination's spectacular power invited ambitious, even overly ambitious claims about it, as though its ability to influence foreign objects might qualify it to perform actions appropriate only to God and spiritual beings like angels and demons. Such oversized claims especially surrounded perceptible marvels, presumably because they were improbable and yet displayed themselves in the light of day, or at least were reported to do so. So spectacular were they that they could easily be mistaken for miracles. What made them easy to misunderstand was what made imagination, operating within them, easy to overestimate: both seemed to accomplish more than unaided nature permits. The boundary of nature itself is therefore at issue in the work of both philosophers. They ask what imagination cannot do as a means of posing a more basic question: where do a person's natural capacities end? Even as they seek to delimit imagination's powers, however, they show why it resists their efforts.

57. *Chartularium Universitatis Parisiensis*, ed. Denifle and Châtelain, 1:549: "Quod intelligentia superiores imprimunt in inferiores, sicut anima una imprimit in aliam, et etiam in animam sensitivam; et per talem impressionem incantator aliquis prohicit camelum in foveam solo visu." Oresme presumably has this article in mind when he writes that Avicenna's belief that imagination can act on foreign bodies was condemned at Paris (*De causis mirabilium*, ed. Hansen, *Nicole Oresme and the Marvels of Nature*, 313n69). See Minnema, "A Hadith Condemned at Paris."

58. Giles of Rome, *Errores philosophorum* 9.16, ed. Koch: "ponens animam per imaginationem operari in corpore alieno." Trans. Riedl, same volume, 45.

59. On Aquinas and Albertus, see Hasse, *Avicenna's* De anima, 167–68.

The fourteenth-century pilgrim William of Boldensele writes aphoristically, "where nature suffices there is no need to turn to miracles."[60] The sentence could serve as a motto for what is usually called the naturalism of the late Middle Ages.[61] Leah DeVun defines naturalism as "the systemic study of nature through disciplines such as natural philosophy, astronomy/astrology, medicine, and alchemy."[62] More narrowly, it characterizes the efforts of philosophers to consider natural causes for supposedly supernatural phenomena, that is, miracles. Oresme and Bradwardine were on opposite sides of this issue. Bradwardine, the "Oxford calculator" who was briefly archbishop of Canterbury, seeks to protect miracles from the encroachment of naturalizing, reclassifying explanations. In that vein, he seeks to limit the role of imagination in a variety of marvels and miracles in his magnum opus, the *De causa Dei*. A theologically conservative work, it rejects what Heiko Oberman calls the "defamation of divine sovereignty," that is, constraints on divine power.[63] In Bradwardine's view, marvels and miracles are often misunderstood in a way that affronts God. He disdains overconfident philosophers who presume to understand their operations fully: "blush, oh philosopher who takes pride in knowledge. You scorn God by keeping him so small that small you with your small mind might scrutinize the whole of him, might lay bare all his secrets, might grasp and know him completely."[64] It is clear from the text that Bradwardine has natural philosophers in mind. He accuses them of casting God in their image and confining his power to the boundaries of their capacity. They impose on God their own limitations when they presume to explain naturally phenomena that are beyond their ken.

Bradwardine takes particular offense at the notion that miracles are merely natural, and he opposes what he presents as the common belief that imagination accounts for many of them. He retains imagination when describing certain marvels that require the multiplication of species, offering the familiar examples of the menstruating woman, the basilisk, and fascination to argue that certain people can, through the species they emit, "infect

60. William of Boldensele, *Liber de quibusdam ultramarinis partibus* 7, ed. Deluz, 263: "ubi natura sufficit non est ad miraculum recurrendum."

61. See, for instance, Shank, "Naturalist Tendencies in Medieval Science."

62. DeVun, *Prophecy, Alchemy, and the End of Time*, 165n5.

63. Oberman, *Archbishop Thomas Bradwardine*, 30. On the text, see also Leff, *Bradwardine and the Pelagians*, 11–20; and Dolnikowski, *Thomas Bradwardine*, 165–72.

64. Bradwardine, *De causa Dei* 1.1.32, ed. Savile, 27: "Imo erubesce Philosophe, & scientia superbiens, dedignare tam parvum Deum habere, ut tu parvus, per parvam mentem tuam totum ipsum scruteris, omnia eius secreta rimeris, capias & cognoscas plenarie ipsum totum."

the medium" and act on objects at a distance.[65] His priority, however, is to shrink imagination's purview in order to maximize divine power. Some of his arguments are based in logic. If imagination could heal someone far away, it would also need to heal everyone in the medium, which does not happen. It should exercise proportionate powers: if it can accomplish great miracles, it should be capable of lesser ones, and that is not always the case. He also circumscribes its powers directly. Although capable of certain wonders at short distances, such as bewitchment, it can face obstacles in the form of an unwilling patient or unfavorable weather because imagination's species are unable to penetrate especially dense air.[66] He concludes that the human imagination, however potent, is not nearly as potent as Christ, who suffered no such limitations. He asks "how the soul by wishing or imagining could resuscitate the dead and summon souls from heaven or hell?"[67] He continues, "Whose imagination so unexpectedly, so powerfully, and so miraculously converted the Jew Saul who was so expert in law, so passionate about the law, and such a committed persecutor of the Christian faith?"[68] It was Christ and nobody's imagination that led Saul to confound Jews and convert Greek philosophers.

Positioning Christ and the human imagination as alternative explanations, Bradwardine elevates the faculty even as he seeks to restrict it. He invites us to consider what the two have in common and how one might be mistaken for the other. Both accomplish action at a distance, which is why they offer alternative explanations for unusual events. Imagination, even Bradwardine's scaled-back version of it, appears to be one of a person's greatest powers. Its actions can easily be confused with miracles, and since miracles are, by definition, supernatural, they cannot be explained solely through natural means. As a result, the mechanisms of miracles cannot be understood fully by humans, and Bradwardine relies instead on divine omnipotence in order to account for them. Natural explanations for seeming miracles are attractive, in part, because they make them knowable, which

65. He insists that the multiplication of species works only at short distances. See Bradwardine, *De causa Dei* 1.1.32, ed. Savile, 46, "inficiunt medium."

66. Bradwardine, *De causa Dei* 1.1.32, ed. Savile, 44–45: "Possit ergo esse tanta distantia inter illam & aegrum, vel in parva distantia medium ita indispositum per densitatem aut aliam qualitatem, quod ipsum sanare non possit."

67. Bradwardine, *De causa Dei* 1.1.32, ed. Savile, 45B: "quomodo etiam potest anima volendo aut imaginando mortuos suscitare, & animas a Coelo vel Inferno ad corpora revocare"?

68. Bradwardine, *De causa Dei* 1.1.32, ed. Savile, 45D: "Cuius etiam imaginatio Saulum Iudaeum tam peritum in lege, tam ferventem in lege, tam vehementer persecutorem fidei Christianae, tam inopinabiliter, tam potenter, tam mirabiliter convertebat?"

is why Bradwardine complains about the hubris of natural philosophers. They pretend that they can account for phenomena they do not truly understand. Willing to rule out divine causation, philosophers turn instead to natural causes, among them imagination.

Bradwardine analyzes an array of miracle stories with the express goal of denying imagination a role in them. I summarize two before turning to Bradwardine's arguments. The first comes from an early fourteenth-century geography of Asia, the *Flos historiarum terra Orientis*, written by an Armenian monk, Hayton of Corycus.[69] According to the story, which Bradwardine says he can personally verify, the province of Hanissen in Georgia is always dark, a punishment for its former, idol-worshipping ruler, Sanoreus. In times past, he commanded that all the inhabitants of Asia gather to adore a certain idol. Pious Christians refused and fled, seeking refuge in Greece. "That most wicked son of iniquity," Sanoreus, pursued them with his army and encountered them in Hanissen.[70] He ordered the Christians killed, they prayed, darkness fell on the area, and the Christians escaped. The wicked (*iniqui*) still live in that "valley of darkness" and will live there until the end of time.[71]

The next story comes from Marco Polo, the famous Italian explorer and writer, and takes place in Samarkand, a city governed by Mongols and directly overseen by the Khan's brother, Prince Cygatay, but inhabited by Muslims and Christians as well.[72] In a clear case of Christian wish-fulfillment, Marco Polo reports that the prince studied Christian doctrine, converted, and received baptism. Insofar as Marco Polo has the Mongols divided between Muslims and Christians, he gestures at concerted efforts by both groups to bring the Mongols to their side. Cygatay gave the Christians permission to build a church in the city in honor of John the Baptist. A marvel of architectural ingenuity, the church was supported by a sole marble column placed at its center. Its base was crafted from a stone that the Christians procured from local Muslims, but the Muslims, inevitably loathing the Christians, gathered in protest. "It was made so that the Prince died," a construction so passive that one wonders whether the Muslims

69. Glenn Burger has edited a fifteenth-century English translation of the text under the title *A Lytell Cronycle*.

70. Bradwardine, *De causa Dei* 1.1.32, ed. Savile, 43: "ille pessimus iniquitatis filius."

71. Bradwardine, *De causa Dei* 1.1.32, ed. Savile, 43: "illa tenebrositatis valle."

72. The Mongols conquered Samarkand in 1220 and held it throughout Marco Polo's lifetime, but although Bradwardine identifies the Mongol Khan as its ruler, he focuses not on the Mongol but on the Muslim inhabitants, the "Sarraceni" who "worship Muḥammad" ("Mahometum adorant"); *De causa Dei* 1.1.32, ed. Savile, 43. His decision is part of a larger pattern whereby medieval Christians tend to vilify Muslims more than Mongols.

used black magic or some other brand of unnarratable evil to kill him, and the Muslims, now with the aid of Cygatay's Muslim son, demanded the return of their stone.[73] The Christians offered a great sum to keep it, but the Muslims refused, eager to see the church collapse. The Christians began tearfully to call on John the Baptist, and on the day when the stone was to be removed, the column began to float the span of three hands over the base all on its own, and there it stands, we read, to the present day, unsupported by any human props.

Bradwardine insists that natural causes do not account for such wonders, first ruling out astrological causation before turning to the human spirit and then to imagination. On the topic of the miracle stories, he writes, "I wonder whose imagination might hinder such an army and enclose such a land in shadows, as were touched on above."[74] Focusing on Hanissen, he writes that it was not the imagination of the Christians, who surely thought of fleeing, not of darkness or their enemies. As for the idolatrous locals, "they, it would seem, did not imagine themselves surrounded by such darkness but rather imagined themselves pursuing the Christians."[75] Continuous darkness requires a continuous cause, "but who persists in thus imagining continuously? Whose imagination supported the aforementioned column with its base removed?"[76] The Muslims were more likely imagining the church's destruction, and the Christians were more likely hoping to be delivered from the Muslims or to keep the base in its current position than contemplating so unlikely a miracle. Bradwardine then asks, wouldn't the people imagining the miracle at some point need to sleep, and wouldn't they eventually die? His objections are strikingly pragmatic. He does not directly deny that imagination has the capacity to support the church or immerse a land in perpetual darkness. Rather, he rests his objections on logic and logistics: unattributed claims for a miracle-performing imagination are inconsistent and impractical. Because they lack the explanatory power they aspire to, one should instead place faith in God. Such is Bradwardine's method: because miracles do not submit to natural explanations, one cannot compare their methods with other, natural alternatives. He therefore looks for flaws in those natural explanations themselves. Where

73. Bradwardine, *De causa Dei* 1.1.32, ed. Savile, 43: "Factum est autem ut moreretur Princeps."

74. Bradwardine, *De causa Dei* 1.1.32, ed. Savile, 45: "Cuius etiam quaeso imaginatio inclusit tantum exercitium, & tantam patriam tenebris, sicut superius tangebatur?"

75. Bradwardine, *De causa Dei* 1.1.32, ed. Savile, 45: "ipsi enim (ut videtur) non imaginabantur se comprehendi tali caligine, sed persequi Christianos."

76. Bradwardine, *De causa Dei* 1.1.32, ed. Savile, 45: "quis sic imaginando continue perseverat? Cuius imaginatio sustentaverit columnam praedictam base subtracta?"

nature fails to explain a phenomenon, he argues, one should attribute it to God. Again, he positions imagination and direct divine action as alternative, mutually exclusive causes. To accept one is to reject the other.

Bradwardine is clear that imagination's potential power over foreign bodies creates misunderstanding, and he responds by confining the faculty's dominion, at least in one respect, to the soul. Drawing on another of Marco Polo's stories, this one about a mountain that was relocated, he asks whose imagination was capable of transferring it. He adds an illuminating apostrophe to Avicenna: "Oh *magnanime* Avicenna, having a great [*magnam*] soul [*animam*], move this little mountain with your imagination, or at least a small piece of it, and I will give you a golden mountain to keep."[77] His mention of a golden mountain is not casual. In medieval philosophy, it is the stock example that defines the compositive imagination, which creates a new image out of two things, here gold and a mountain, that the senses have separately perceived.[78] The point of the golden mountain is that it exists only in imagination. Bradwardine's challenge could be rephrased as follows: if Avicenna can move an earthly mountain with his imagination, then Bradwardine will make one of his own imaginative constructs, the golden mountain, equally real. Not only real, it will be transportable, even across time. Temporal and geographical boundaries would thus dissolve along with that between imagined and real objects.

Bradwardine's purpose in comparing the two mountains is to better distinguish them, with the golden one belonging to the soul and the real mountain to the world outside. Suggesting that Avicenna failed to recognize the difference, he implicitly charges him with subjecting bodies to imagination's authority. He attempts to reel in imagination's power by denying it dominion over nature proper. However, his concession elsewhere that it sometimes acts on objects in the world, as in the case of fascination, means that he cannot restrict it to the soul absolutely. His own failure clearly to demarcate its boundaries points to its slipperiness. As we have seen, its influence on external bodies proves its potency and invites people to confuse its powers with those of God. But the error is not easily remedied. Once its influence is allowed to extend into the world and thus to exceed the confines of the soul, it is hard to settle on any boundary that might conclusively contain it.

Like Bradwardine, Oresme sought to distinguish genuine miracles

77. Bradwardine, *De causa Dei* 1.1.32, ed. Savile, 45: "O Avicenna magnanime, animam magnam habens, transfer per imaginationem tuam istum monticulum, aut minimam glebam eius, & dabo tibi montem aureum possidendum."

78. Serge-Thomas Bonino rightly observes that "the example is repeated endlessly" ("Le rôle de l'image dans la connaissance prophétique," 550).

from only supposed ones. However, whereas Bradwardine worried that too many miracles had been deemed natural, Oresme thought that natural explanations should be applied more broadly.[79] As Joel Kaye writes, "his intellectual program was to expand the sphere of the natural and the licit in the realm of knowledge at the expense of magic, superstition, and false belief."[80] To that end, he sometimes appealed to imagination. For instance, magical acts like fascination "are produced not by a demon but most often by imagination."[81] Many of his declarations smack of skeptical rationality: people too easily assign significance to coincidences, they notice one correct prophecy more than the thousands that are proven wrong, and they create marvels and miracles through their misapprehensions. But he still credits, and seeks to account for, spectacular marvels. He describes monsters, for instance, as resulting from the natural process of generation gone awry: "there is no other cause of monstrosity than the failing of something needed" for proper generation.[82] Hardly the beacon of rationality that he is sometimes supposed to be, he is willing to accept a wide array of possibilities.

Although dubious about some of the claims made for imagination, Oresme believed that its powers were vast. Most spectacularly, perhaps, he thought an individual could on rare occasions alter their body's own color and shape through imagination. A pregnant woman could likewise alter such qualities in her fetus.[83] As indicated above, Oresme both associates imagination with the multiplication of species and uses the doctrine to explain various marvels, perhaps rehabilitating it in the process.[84] To illus-

79. Bert Hansen notes that, while many scholastic philosophers pointed to natural causes for marvels, Oresme appears to have been the only one to have devoted an entire work expressly to this topic (*Nicole Oresme and the Marvels of Nature*, 10).

80. Kaye, "Law, Magic, and Science," 229. See also Quillet, "Enchantements et désenchantements de la nature selon Nicole Oresme."

81. Oresme, *De configurationibus* 2.28, ed. Clagett, *Nicole Oresme and the Medieval Geometry of Qualities and Motions*, 344: "Non igitur fiunt a demone sed ut plurimum ymaginatione." Trans. Clagett, 345.

82. Oresme, *De causis mirabilium* 3, ed. Hansen, *Nicole Oresme and the Marvels of Nature*, 230: "Monstruositas ergo non est causa alia quam defectus alicuius requisiti." Trans. Hansen, 231.

83. Oresme introduces the topic in *De causis mirabilium* 4 (ed. Hansen, *Nicole Oresme and the Marvels of Nature*, 346 and 353), and cites Augustine and Avicenna in his defense in the *Tabula problemata*, q. 203 (same edition, 388). Augustine had referred to the pregnant woman's will rather than imagination (*De Trinitate* 11.2.5, ed. Mountain and Glorie, 50:339). For scholarship on the maternal imagination, see Daston and Park, *Wonders and the Order of Nature*, 415n97.

84. Stefan Caroti argues that Oresme redeemed the doctrine in the aftermath of Ockham's criticisms ("Éléments pour une réconstruction de la philosophie de la nature," 95–96).

trate his claim that "the soul can sometimes act through a forceful imagination or thought on an alien body," he offers the case of the evil eye:[85]

> if there is some old woman who, out of the evilness of the complexion of her brain, envies beauty or is inclined to bring about the shriveling or corruption of the most tender flesh of a particular infant, then it is possible that, with regard to an infant present before her, she might so strongly imagine and shape her desire with such difformity and without any art that the eyes of this old woman will subsequently be infected and contract a certain maleficent quality through which the infant to whom the old woman directs her gaze and who is readily susceptible to a foreign impression of this sort will be infected.[86]

Oresme here relies on his theory of difformity, which he introduces in the *De configurationibus*.[87] It uses the internal configuration of entities, especially their "difformity" as opposed to conformity, to explain their effects. As Marshall Clagett explains, configuration accounts for the different effects produced by bodies composed of the same elements in the same quantities.[88] Oresme uses it to describe how some people more effectively realize their goals than others: "if someone imagines or thinks about revenge with feeling, and the difformity of his cogitation or imagination is duly figured, then he will duly perform the intended acts and will be as one particularly fortunate in carrying out or executing his intention."[89] As goes

85. Oresme, *De configurationibus* 2.38, ed. Clagett, *Nicole Oresme and the Medieval Geometry of Qualities and Motions*, 382: "agit anima per ymaginationem seu cogitationem fortem quandoque in corpore alieno." Trans. 383.

86. Oresme, *De configurationibus* 2.38, ed. Clagett, *Nicole Oresme and the Medieval Geometry of Qualities and Motions*, 384: "si fuerit aliqua vetula que ex malitia complexionis cerebri invideat pulchritudinem vel sit inclinata ad affectandum compressionem et corruptionem tenerrime carnis unius infantis, tunc possibile est quod circa infantem presentem ita fortiter ymaginetur et affectionem suam tali difformitate figuret absque aliqua arte quod oculi proprii illius vetule ex hoc inficientur et contrahent quandam maleficam qualitatem per quam inficietur infantulus ad quem ipsa vetula diriget visum et qui infans est huiusmodi peregrine impressionis faciliter susceptivus." Trans. 385.

87. The *De causis* makes no reference to this theory, meaning that Oresme probably abandoned it before writing the *De causis* or came up with it afterward. On the difficulty of dating the two texts, see Hansen, *Nicole Oresme and the Marvels of Nature*, 11 and 46–48.

88. Clagett, *Nicole Oresme and the Medieval Geometry of Qualities and Motions*, 15. Matthew Boyd Goldie discusses Oresme's notion of difformity in *Scribes of Space*, 174–84.

89. Oresme, *De configurationibus* 2.37, ed. Clagett, *Nicole Oresme and the Medieval Geometry of Qualities and Motions*, 378: "si quis cum affectione ymaginetur aut cogitet de vindicta et istius cogitationis vel ymaginationis difformitas fuerit debite figurata, tunc

revenge, so goes javelin-throwing: one's internal state influences the body's performance and can make the weaker person the better thrower. In the case of the evil eye, imagination shapes desire, whose difformity infects the eye and transmits species to a child who then receives their impression. However, the soul moves an external body only rarely, at short distances, and when the recipient of the action is properly disposed.[90]

Oresme attempts to deepen the philosophical discussion of marvels, and to that end he seeks to contextualize and better define imagination's actions within them.[91] He addresses the faculty as it participates in both approaches to marvels analyzed in this chapter, one based in the multiplication of species and the other in the basic dominion of the soul over bodies. Citing Avicenna and al-Ghazālī directly, he says that the matter of the world obeys a noble soul "without another, intermediate alteration."[92] As a result, elements might be altered, weather changed, sterility and death effected. He appeals to imagination, but expressly disagrees with al-Ghazālī, who relied too heavily on the faculty in his efforts to explain such marvels, in Oresme's view. Again eager to temper overly ambitious claims for it, he appeals to his theory of difformity. Discussing the same slate of marvels, he writes: "one could still reduce such action to the intention of imagination combined with a certain figuration of it specifically requisite for this kind of action."[93] Thought or imagination is itself insufficient to produce such results, and it is in this respect that Avicenna and al-Ghazālī were wrong. They failed to recognize the joint necessity for a certain configuration of qualities. What is perhaps most striking in the efforts of both Bradwardine and Oresme to rein in theories about imagination's powers is how powerful the faculty remains. They preserve its ability to influence foreign bodies and, in Oresme's philosophy, even nature itself, but their concessions complicate their project. As they suggest, imagination's influence over objects at a distance is what had most encouraged philosophers to overestimate its potency. It transgresses the boundary that should limit it. Excessiveness

---

ipse actus imp[e]ratos exercebit debite et erit in prosecutione seu executione intentionis seu quasi bene fortunatus." Trans. 379.

90. Oresme, *De configurationibus* 2.38, ed. Clagett, *Nicole Oresme and the Medieval Geometry of Qualities and Motions*, 384–86.

91. On Oresme's approach to marvels and his commitment to natural philosophy, see Grant, "Scientific Thought in Fourteenth-Century Paris," 111–16.

92. Oresme, *De configurationibus* 2.38, ed. Clagett, *Nicole Oresme and the Medieval Geometry of Qualities and Motions*, 382: "absque alia intermedia alteratione."

93. Oresme, *De configurationibus* 2.38, ed. Clagett, *Nicole Oresme and the Medieval Geometry of Qualities and Motions*, 382: "si ita esset adhuc illud posset reduci ad intentionem ymaginationis cum quadam figuratione eiusdem ad hoc specialiter requisita." Trans. 383. On al-Ghazālī, see 2.35, ed. Clagett, 374.

thus defines the unusually potent imagination, and for that reason it is hard to moderate the claims made for it. Its seeming unboundedness is much of its essence.

Oresme's and Bradwardine's caution about imagination is nonetheless noteworthy. Koen Vermeir writes that attitudes toward the marvel-performing imagination became more negative during the early modern period, and the same trajectory is visible in the medieval discussion.[94] Al-Kindī honors the faculty and those who use its maximal powers, while various philosophers, including Avicenna and Roger Bacon, allow only the truly special to move foreign objects, but such relatively positive attitudes become harder to find toward the end of the Middle Ages.[95] The point is effectively made by Oresme, who confusedly assigns marvels—both their generation and their reception—to an imagination at once debilitated and strengthened. "Imagination or affection can be so heightened" that one might cure one's own illness, or bewitch someone else.[96] Imagination's powers are here augmented, but old women who bewitch infants have diseased imaginations: "Some old woman whose imaginative power has been vitiated and corrupted as the result of a poor cerebral complexion and has become excessively attached to certain things is prone to carry out certain nefarious magical acts."[97] The strong imaginations of old women are now the product of corruption. Those who are susceptible to magic likewise possess imaginations at once powerful and compromised. Old women, children, the ill, and the crazy often share a "strong imagination," but also have a "defect of the interior sense organs."[98] For them, it is often the case that "magical results take place in the imagination and not in reality."[99] A

94. Vermeir, "The 'Physical Prophet' and the Powers of the Imagination," 561.

95. As Delaurenti notes, Avicenna thought that a soul exceptionally pure or exceptionally wicked had greater power to move foreign objects and bewitch others, although it is only the exceptionally pure soul that can alter the elements ("Pratiques médiévales de réécriture," 353, 355).

96. Oresme, *De configurationibus* 2.38, ed. Clagett, *Nicole Oresme and the Medieval Geometry of Qualities and Motions,* 382: "ymaginatio vel affectio potest tantum intendi."

97. Oresme, *De configurationibus* 2.28, ed. Clagett, *Nicole Oresme and the Medieval Geometry of Qualities and Motions,* 344: "Ad quedam namque maleficia magica peragenda sunt apte vetule quedam quarum virtus ymaginativa ex malicia complexionis cerebri viciata est et corrupta et aliquibus rebus nimis affixa." Trans. Clagett, 345.

98. Oresme, *De configurationibus* 2.26, ed. Clagett, *Nicole Oresme and the Medieval Geometry of Qualities and Motions,* 338: "ymaginationem fortem"; and 2.29, 346: "vitio organorum sensuum interiorum."

99. Oresme, *De configurationibus* 2.28, ed. Clagett, *Nicole Oresme and the Medieval Geometry of Qualities and Motions,* 342: "maxime ille qui nundum dederunt ymaginationem suam et cogitationes voluptatibus carnis . . . ista igitur fiunt in ymaginatione non in re." Trans. Clagett, 343.

strong imagination thus empowers people to create magic even as it makes them vulnerable to its effects. The faculty cannot be precisely delimited, which makes it either marvelous or deceptive, depending on one's perspective. Oresme has it both ways at once, and thus identifies one more way in which uncertainty attaches to it.

Implicit throughout these first two chapters is a claim that imagination not only contributed to the complexity and resonance of marvels but also helped them to produce the wonder that in large part defined them. The point is worth making overtly because it challenges a familiar, even clichéd understanding of marvels, which is that they feed off ignorance. Wonder dissipates as understanding increases because, as scores of medieval sources declare, wonder is the response to something whose causes are unknown.[100] Thomas Aquinas thus explains that "the desire to understand the causes of the things they see is in all men by nature, whence men first began to philosophize because they wondered at the things they saw whose causes they did not know, but discovering the cause, they rested."[101] Understanding resolves wonder. Similarly, Matelda tells Dante in *Purgatorio*, "I will explain how what you marvel at proceeds from its cause, and I will purge the fog that strikes you."[102] The notion is common in Arabic sources as well, hence al-Qazwīnī: "the marvel appears confusing to someone because they lack knowledge about something's cause or about the nature of its effect."[103] If wonder and understanding are inversely proportionate, then insofar as imagination contributes to understanding, it would seem to counteract wonder. Certainly, the naturalistic study of marvels in the Middle Ages has been seen as deflating wonder, or as a "de-wondering" that "tended to naturalize and flatten the phenomena explained."[104] Since imagination participates in such efforts, it might appear to neutralize wonder, but as Bynum notes, interest in marvels only intensified as philosophers endeavored to explain them. My explanation

100. Bert Hansen provides a long list of examples in *Nicole Oresme and the Marvels of Nature*, 64–69.

101. Aquinas, *Summa contra Gentiles* 3.25, in *Opera omnia* 14:67: "Naturaliter inest omnibus hominibus desiderium cognoscendi causas eorum quae videntur: unde propter admirationem eorum quae videbantur, quorum causae latebant, homines primo philosophari coeperunt, invenientes autem causam quiescebant."

102. Dante, *Purgatorio* 28.88–89, ed. Durling: "Io dicerò come procede / per sua cagion ciò ch'ammirar ti face, / e purgherò la nebbia che ti fiede."

103. Al-Qazwīnī, *'Ajā'ib al-makhlūqāt*, Introduction, ed. Sa'd, 31: "al-ajabu ḥayrata ta'ruḍu li-l-insāni li-quṣūrihi 'an ma'arifati sababi al-shay'i aw 'an ma'arifati kayfīyat ta'thīrihi fīhi."

104. Bynum, "Miracles and Marvels," 802. As she notes, she draws "de-wondering" from a paper delivered by Katharine Park.

is that imagination did not explain away wonder but rather helped to produce it.

In the theories considered here, imagination functions less to foreclose inquiry than to redirect it. Investigating the faculty's role in marvels, philosophers often take up basic questions about the soul's potency, cognitive certitude, the relationship of the natural to the supernatural, and of course the susceptibility of bodies to the powers of the soul. Imagination leads them to harder and harder questions. Insofar as it helps to explain how marvels work, it by no means simplifies them. Marvels do many things: they confuse judgment, suggest their own great significance, and resist containment. In other words, part of understanding marvels is understanding why they are so hard to understand. Scrutinizing imagination helped philosophers to accomplish that task. It did not leave them with easy answers or inert marvels. Rather, it helped them to decipher and protect marvels' very inscrutability.

These first two chapters have analyzed the role of imagination in the production of various marvels in order to explain what they were thought to do and how they were thought to do it. The operations of the faculty cast light on the defining indeterminacy and apparent meaningfulness of the marvels that it generates and perceives. In other words, marvels invite scrutiny because they are hard to classify and because, as apparently meaningful phenomena, they promise to reward inquiry. Imagination invests them with those qualities. They have the status of imagined events or objects, and that means that their precise boundaries are hard to set. They might be real, meaning bodily, or they might simply seem to be. They might exist, whether solely within the soul or also outside of it. In either event, they resist easy answers. The following chapter focuses on another sense in which marvels are imaginative: their creativity. It turns attention to nature more than to the individual, but the similarities are striking. As marvels showcase a person's inventiveness, so they call attention to nature's own, and as they realize the outer limits of an individual's power, so they make use of nature's greatest resources. Creativity itself cannot be reduced to truth or falsehood, the real or the make-believe. Marvels, as expressions of creativity, resist those same binaries.

[CHAPTER 3]

Philosophers' Fables

Chapters 1 and 2 have shown that imagination powered marvels of different sorts during the late Middle Ages, but without the implication that they were false or merely notional. For marvels, to be imaginative was to be productively indeterminate. With effects possibly confined to the soul, possibly not, imagination created uncertain boundaries for the marvels in its ambit. This chapter continues to explore late medieval natural philosophy and its theories of marvels, but instead of marvels created by or directed at people, it turns to marvels involving other animals as well as stones and the earth itself. It looks specifically at moments where philosophers compare natural marvels to those of literature. Literary references within medieval natural philosophy have received scant scholarly attention, but because they often appear where the topic is marvels, they deserve some attention.[1] My assumption is that the methods philosophers use to explain marvels provide insight into their understanding of them. The fact that they call on expressly invented marvels in order to explain naturally occurring ones (or potentially naturally occurring ones) shows that they approached marvels not according to any facile opposition between truth and falsehood, but rather as creative possibilities. This bears stressing: if invented, poetic marvels can illuminate natural ones, then marvels' own truth or falseness is not essential to their definition. And if such an opposition did not structure their thinking about marvels, then it should not determine our analysis of them. This chapter argues instead that marvels signify as imaginative possibilities, or more accurately as nonimpossibilities, that represent nature's highest creative potential.

Both philosophers and theologians connect the disciplines. For instance, when Albertus Magnus writes that the stone gagatronica has power

1. Kellie Robertson analyzes the representation of nature in late medieval literature in a generalized philosophical context, but does not look for references between them; see *Nature Speaks*, especially 1–90. The scarcity of scholarship on such references is why this chapter relies more heavily than the others on primary sources.

to bring its wearer victory, he offers the example of Hercules.[2] If it is not clear from the outset that Albertus recognizes Hercules's fictiveness, the examples that follow will make the point directly. Once we exclude the possibility that he thought that a man named Hercules existed and a certain stone accounted for his powers, we are left to wonder what he gains by likening a natural phenomenon to a fabulous one. By way of explanation, I will argue that marvels represent the outer limit of nature's creative potential. They are possibilities that seem impossible, natural things that seem unnatural, comprehensible things that seem incomprehensible, and potentially real things that seem invented. They play at the margins of categories in a way that pushes those margins outward, to the point where nature might find its limitations. Its most inventive creations, whether actual or potential, invite comparison with people when they are at their most creative, in the writing of poetry, and the two follow similar rules.

Philosophers' allusions to poetry focus attention on nature's creativity when it produces marvels, ones that might rival and even surpass those of poets. That nature is sometimes likened to a poet in the Middle Ages is well known, but the comparison is not just a trite metaphor.[3] Both nature and poets invent what had not existed, and both seek to inspire wonder through their designs. The ingenuity evident in existing things also shows what nature can accomplish and suggests that it might have further wonders in store. The categories of true and false are largely irrelevant to creative expressions, and so it is with marvels that might or might not exist, but that in either case suggest nature's maximum creative potential. The previous chapters have shown that marvels create wonder in part by making one thing look like another, an attribute that is especially visible here where they resonate across genres to create likeness among unlike things. Because marvels live somewhere between things and notions, they can signify broadly, embodying the improbable inventiveness of the created world itself.

2. Albertus Magnus, *Mineralium* 2.2.7, in *Opera omnia*, ed. Borgnet, 5:37: "Gagatronica est lapis diversii coloris sicut pellis capriolae, cuius virtutem Avicennam dicit esse, quod victores reddat se gestantes. Expertum autem dicunt esse in Alcide principe quodam, quod quoties hunc lapidem secum habuit, semper vicit in terra et mari: quoties autem caruit, fertur hostibus succubuisse." (Gagatronica is a stone of diverse colors, like the skin of deer, whose power is, according to Avicenna, to make victorious those who wear it. They say that this is shown by a certain prince Alcides [patronymic for Hercules], and whenever he had this stone with him, he always conquered, both on land and in sea, but when he was without it, he is said to have succumbed to his enemies.) Trans. Wyckoff, *Book of Minerals*, 94.

3. Barbara Newman shows the richness of nature's creative work in *God and the Goddesses*, 51–137.

MARVELS AS NONIMPOSSIBILITIES

The point that marvels are possibilities requires some elaboration. For medieval philosophers, nature is limited to what is logically possible as a proper subset is related to a set. In other words, the category of the logically possible is the larger one, and nature will not realize nearly every logical possibility. As natural phenomena, marvels too must be logically possible, and philosophers often evaluate them from that perspective. A colorful portrait of nature's relationship to logic appears in Alain of Lille's twelfth-century *Sermo de sphaera intelligibili*, when Logic attends the wedding of Nature with her own son, who is her form in the sensible world. The kiss between them produces three daughters: possibility, essence, and truth. Together, as Peter Dronke explains, they represent all that exists or can exist in the natural world.[4] In other words, Nature joins herself to the sensible world and produces what is or might be within it. What is worth noting is the relationship between Nature and Logic that Alain depicts. It is Logic who plays the music at this allegorical wedding: "Logic, who declares the truth of natural things, attends as herald and plays the lute for these nuptials with organs of prepositions and terms."[5] With characteristic allegorical density, Alain has Logic impose the boundaries that contain Nature's activity. Notice that prepositions and terms are not the music he produces but the very organs he uses to make it. The point is that art is regulated by logic, and so Nature can only dance to the music that Logic plays for her with instruments that are his and his alone. Even God was thought to be bounded at the furthest extreme by logic, doing nothing that would constitute a logical contradiction.[6] Confined to the realm of the logically possible, nature confronted more limitations, which marvels too had to respect. Still, logical possibility is a capacious category that left marvels enough room for a tango.

Alain shows that nature, as a concept, includes what might be as well as what is. Nature, in other words, is not confined to the real, but also encompasses endless possibilities. From an Augustinian perspective, all that might exist is contained within the natural world in the form of *rationes seminales*, or seminal forms that are embedded in creation. They are, in Vincent of Beauvais's words, "the hidden seeds of things" that God planted

4. Dronke, *Fabula*, 149.

5. Alain of Lille, *Sermo de sphaera intelligibili*, in *Alain de Lille: Textes inédits*, ed. d'Alverny, 300: "His nuptiis Logica veritatis naturalium declarativa suo assistens preconio, propositionum terminorumque organis citarizat."

6. On divine omnipotence and its limitation by the principle of noncontradiction, see Courtenay, *Capacity and Volition*, 25–55.

"in the visible elements of this world."[7] Augustine explains that "as mothers are pregnant with their young, so the world itself is pregnant with the causes of things to be born," which, "tucked away and held in the secret bosom of nature, might break forth in some way and be outwardly created by the unfurling of the measures and numbers and weights that they have received in secret."[8] From them comes everything that is and that might be. William of Auvergne credits the remnants of creative light in the world with a host of marvels, many of which are yet to be discovered, and Albertus turns to them to explain how Pharaoh, like Moses, transformed a rod into a serpent.[9] With the power to give rise to new things and transmute existing ones, these *rationes* promise infinite, unknowable possibilities.

The belief that nature submits to logic bears on marvels and their status as nonimpossibilities. Regarding such marvels as the reported ability to survive without food for twenty years, Oresme writes, "the causes of such particulars are unknown to us and it is enough for me that it not be concluded to be impossible."[10] His claim is not that such a marvel is true, but that it is not impossible, which is a much lower standard. Insofar as it is not impossible, it might also be explained. Scholars have written extensively about the tendency of natural philosophers in the Latin West to reason *secundum imaginationem*, that is, as Hans Thijssen defines it, to reason "in all imaginable ways within the realm of the logically possible."[11] In other words, they do not limit themselves to what was known to be true of nature, or what Aristotle had written about nature, but instead entertain hypotheticals, often stemming from suppositions about God's absolute power.[12] This method of analysis is distinctive to natural philosophers, and

7. Vincent of Beauvais, *Speculum naturale* 2.104, in *Speculum quadruplex* 1:146B: "occulta rerum semina visibilibus huius mundi elementis originaliter indidit."

8. Augustine, *De Trinitate* 3.8, ed. Mountain and Glorie, *CCSL* 50:143: "nam sicut matres grauidae sunt fetibus, sic ipse mundus gravidus est causis nascentium . . . secreto naturae sinu abdita continentur erumpant quodam modo et foris creentur explicando mensuras et numeros et pondera sua quae in occulto acceperunt."

9. William of Auvergne, *De universo* 2.3.21, in *Opera omnia*, 1:1058F; and Albertus Magnus, *Summa theologiae* 7.304, in *Opera omnia*, ed Borgnet, 31.1:322.

10. Oresme, *De causis mirabilium*, 3.4, ed. Hansen, *Nicole Oresme and the Marvels of Nature*, 220: "Talium specialium cause sunt ignore nobis et sufficit mihi quod non concludatur esse impossibile." Trans. 221.

11. Thijssen, "Late-Medieval Natural Philosophy," 173. For more on reasoning "secundum imaginationem," see Dewender, "Imaginary Experiments"; and Murdoch, "From Social into Intellectual Factors."

12. This is distinct from "the *positio impossibilis* tradition of medieval disputation," which begins with an impossibility and then considers what would follow from it, but both speak to medieval philosophers' interest in reasoning beyond the bounds of what was known to be true (Kukkonen, "Ibn Sīnā and the Early History of Thought Experiments," 450).

it creates generous boundaries for their speculations, which might range well beyond the real or demonstrable.

This is, perhaps, why experimentation was not a central component of medieval science. The question why medieval philosophers did not systematically set out to test their hypotheses, including many that were easily testable, is a question that has long engaged critics. The most persuasive answer, I think, comes from Joel Kaye, who writes, "with few exceptions, philosophers believed that the certainty required of science was to be found through the application and test of technical logic rather than through direct observation of the contingent object world."[13] Some experimentation was conducted, but the behavior of an individual just was not thought to provide as much useful information as a rigorous process of reasoning that relied on logic. The replicability crisis that has recently risen to the fore in the sciences might not surprise them. The discovery that the results of many, if not most, scientific studies cannot be replicated calls into question the assumption that one set of discrete objects, unless suitably large, will act like another. Insofar as they direct their attention to marvels, medieval natural philosophers thus work to establish their nonimpossibility from a logical perspective. As Oresme writes on several occasions, nobody knows the upper limits of divine potential. The "highest limit" in natural matters—how big a man might be, for instance—"is not known or knowable except by God."[14] Nature varies wildly at the level of the particular. That is why declaring a marvel to be impossible might smack of hubris. As al-Qazwīnī writes, "Nothing should be deemed too great for the power of the Creator or the cunning of creation and everything therein."[15]

The ninth-century philosopher al-Jāḥiẓ is explicit. In his prodigious study of animals, he counsels his reader to approach marvels with an inclination to examine rather than reject them out of hand. So self-evident is this point that he uses irony to express it: "What a terrible thing is the disposition toward acceptance and confirmation."[16] He elaborates: "The truth that God commanded us to seek out, made us want, and pushed us towards requires us to reject two pitfalls with respect to information: one of them consists of what is contradictory and absurd, and the other con-

13. Kaye, *Economy and Nature in the Fourteenth Century*, 164.

14. Oresme, *De causis mirabilium* 4.6, ed. Hansen, *Nicole Oresme and the Marvels of Nature*, 288: "non scitur nec scibilis est nisi a Deo maximus terminus." Oresme gives the example of a man's size at 4.3, 276.

15. Al-Qazwīnī, *'Ajā'ib al-makhlūqāt*, ed. Sa'd, 29. Translated in Zadeh, "Wiles of Creation," 32: "lā yusta'zhamu shay'u ma'a qudrati al-khāliqi wa-ḥīlati al-makhlūqi wa-jamī'a mā fīhi."

16. Al-Jāḥiẓ, *Kitāb al-ḥayawān*, ed. Hārūn, 3:238: "bi'sa al-shay'u 'ādatun al-iqrāri wa-l-qabūli." French trans. Souami, *Le cadi et la mouche*, 73.

sists of what is impossible in nature, which exceeds people's abilities."[17] Al-Jāḥiẓ, in other words, encourages inquiry into the world's oddities (*gharā'ib al-dunyā*) insofar as one avoids logical contradictions and natural impossibilities. They are the boundaries that contain the quest for knowledge, and particularly knowledge about marvels. In the same spirit, the prolific traveler al-Masʿūdī writes of intensely bright fish that are supposedly able to calm turbulent waters. He writes that no mariner in the area contests the report and concludes, "I do not say that this is possible or impossible, or that it is necessarily the case, since it is possible that God the all-powerful might rescue his followers from destruction."[18] He assumes a skeptical reader who might need to be reminded that God sometimes protects people who are in harm's way. He encourages a willingness to ponder the possibility of marvels without accepting or rejecting them out of hand.

Philosophers and theologians were willing to grant that there might be only a grain of truth to marvels, or even that marvels were claims that simply had yet to be disproven. At the beginning of his *Liber de natura rerum*, Thomas of Cantimpré explains that he sometimes includes in his book "opinions of the vulgar not universally refuted," opinions "not openly dissonant with the truth."[19] Such opinions are worthy of inclusion until they are unanimously rejected as false or proven to be impossible. Thomas explains that the reader should not approach his claims as fictitious (*ficticium*) for that reason.[20] Rather, they should consider them possibilities, for instance by noting that various of the marvels he describes occur in the East, where nature operates differently than it does in the West. Natural philosophers often surmise that marvels could not become widely known without some basis in truth, but that requirement is easily met. In defense of the existence of prophetic dreams, for instance, Bradwardine writes, "it is impossible that something well known be false in its entirety."[21] Similarly, Albertus Magnus, commenting on the sapphire's supposed ability to cure abscesses, writes that "this is a widespread belief; and it is impossible that

17. Al-Jāḥiẓ, *Kitāb al-ḥayawān*, ed. Hārūn, 3:238: "wa-l-ḥaqqu alladhī amara allāhu taʿālā bihi wa-raghghaba fīhi wa-ḥaththa ʿalayhi an nankara min al-khabari ḍarra bayna: aḥaduhumā mā tanāqaḍa wa-istiḥāla, al-ākharu mā imtanaʿa fī al-ṭabīʿati, wa-kharaja min ṭāqati al-khilqati." French trans. Souami, *Le cadi et la mouche*, 73.

18. Al-Masʿūdī, *Kitāb murūdj adh-dhahab* 16, ed. and French trans. de Meynard and de Courteille, 1:345: "wa-mā dhakarnāhu ʿanhum fa-mumkinu ghayru mumtaniʿin wa-lā wājiba idh kāna jāʾizan fī maqdūri al-bārī ʿazza wa-jalla khalāṣu ʿabādihi min al-halāki."

19. Thomas of Cantimpré, *Liber de natura rerum*, Prologue, ed. Boese, 4: "vulgi opiniones non per omnia refutandas," "aperte non sit dissona veritati."

20. Thomas of Cantimpré, *Liber de natura rerum*, Prologue, ed. Boese, 5.

21. Bradwardine, *De causa Dei* 1.1, coroll. 32, ed. Savile, 32C: "Impossibile enim est ut famosum sit falsum secundum totum."

there should not be truth in the whole or in a part of what is commonly said by all."[22] Sharing what appears to have been a piece of common knowledge about common knowledge, neither makes any claim for the literal truth of the well-known marvel in its entirety. Perhaps someone who was cured of an abscess happened to wear a sapphire, and perhaps that is all the truth that is required. At a minimum, marvels are nonimpossibilities sometimes just shy of outright falsehood, sometimes simply awaiting conclusive refutation, that have at least a toehold on the ledge of logical possibility. Some are far more certain, but this is their least common denominator.

In the beginning of his far-ranging, thirteenth-century cosmology, al-Qazwīnī describes his criteria for including marvels in his text: "marvels made by the Creator" are not subject to doubt, but regarding "elegant tales ascribed to transmitters," he writes, "I take no responsibility for those." Finally, he describes "strange oddities for which a lifetime would not be enough to test them. It does not make sense to ignore all of them just because there is doubt about some of them."[23] Distinguishing categories of marvels based on their trustworthiness, he expressly rejects responsibility for their truth. Those created by God are beyond doubt—"there can be no doubt or imperfection concerning them"—but he does not stand behind the others.[24] Still, those that elicit doubt should not prejudice anyone against the whole lot. Like al-Jāḥiẓ, he worries more about reflexive dismissal of marvels than about credulous acceptance. Writing early in the eleventh century about the different calendars and chronological systems used in different nations, the astronomer al-Bīrūnī acknowledges the challenge posed by written records that are not always reliable "on account of the numerous lies that are mixed up with all historical records and traditions. And those lies do not all on the face of it appear to be impossibilities, so that they might be easily distinguished and eliminated. However, that which is within the limits of possibility has been treated as true, as long as other evidence has not proven it to be false."[25] Nonimpossibilities are pre-

22. Albertus Magnus, *Mineralium* 2.1.1, in *Opera omnia*, ed. Borgnet, 5:24: "Hoc etiam ab omnibus vulgatum est, et non potest esse quin in toto vel in parte sit verum quod ab omnibus communiter est dictum." Trans. Wyckoff, *Book of Minerals*, 56.

23. Al-Qazwīnī, *'Ajā'ib al-makhlūqāt*, ed. Sa'd, 29. Translated in Zadeh, "Wiles of Creation," 32: "'ajā'ibu ṣan'i al-bārī ta'ālā," "ḥikāyatun ẓarīfatun mansūbatun ilā ruwātihā lā nāqatun lī fīhā," "khuwāṣṣun gharībatun wa-dhālika mimmā lā yafī al-'umru bi-tajribatihā wa-lā ma'nā li-tarki kullihā li-ajli al-mayli fī ba'ḍihā."

24. Al-Qazwīnī, *'Ajā'ib al-makhlūqāt*, ed. Sa'd, 29. Translated in Zadeh, "Wiles of Creation," 32: "lā mayla fīhā wa-lā khalala."

25. Al-Bīrūnī, *Al-āthār al-baqīya 'an al-qurūn al-khāliya*, Preface, in *Chronologie orientalischer Völker*, ed. Sachau, 5: "li-kathrati al-abāṭīli allatī tadkhulu jumala al-akhbāri wa-l-aḥādīthi wa-laysat kulluhā dākhilatan fī ḥaddi al-imtinā'i fa-tumayyaza

sented as true, while open impossibilities are excluded. Granting that lies sometimes seem possible, he allows that some have crept into his considerations. Unable to identify them, he errs on the side of inclusivity. A similar attitude informed philosophers' writings about marvels.

Such philosophers encourage an accepting attitude toward marvels based on their recognition that nature has its surprises. God can accomplish through nature far more than we can understand, and so, as Taneli Kukkonen writes with respect to al-Ghazālī, "an open mind is best kept with regard to the way nature works: our view of the potentialities inherent in things may not correspond to the reality of things, and God's freedom is so wide as to seem limitless in our eyes."[26] People may misjudge what is possible for nature, but the field of possibilities is so great that they should not limit it, and for that reason, it is better to entertain even unlikely possibilities than dismiss them through ignorance. Roger Bacon writes that after witnessing the powers of the magnet, with its improbable ability to move iron without being in physical contact with it, "nothing is difficult for me to believe."[27] It is a gateway marvel that, once pondered, facilitates belief in greater marvels, and Bacon was not the only one who thought so.[28]

In a fascinating letter that, like al-Bīrūnī's comparative study of timetelling systems, was not known in the Latin West, Avicenna considers what sort of existence marvels, and specifically nonexisting marvels, have within the soul. He takes as his example the *'anqā' mughrib*, an enormous, "fabulous bird approximating to the phoenix."[29] Avicenna explicitly ranks the bird among the mind's "impossible images" (*al-ṣuwar al-muḥālat*), impossible in the sense that the objects depicted never have existed and never will exist, as Deborah Black explains.[30] Avicenna, then, acknowledges the non-

---

wa-tuhadhdhaba lakinna mā kāna minhā fī ḥaddi al-imkāni jarā majrā al-khabari al-ḥaqqi idhā lam yashhad bi-buṭlānihi shawāhidu ākharu." Trans. Sachau, *The Chronology of Ancient Nations*, 3.

26. Kukkonen, "Plenitude, Possibility, and the Limits of Reason," 555.

27. Bacon, *De secretis operibus et de nullitate magiae* 6, ed. Brewer, *Opera quaedam hactenus inedita*, 1:537.

28. Gervase of Tilbury begins a discussion of marvels with the magnet, *Otia imperialia* 3.1, ed. Banks and Binns, 562. See also *De mirabilibus mundi*, attributed to Albertus Magnus, in *Il* De mirabilibus mundi *tra tradizione magica e filosofia naturale*, ed. Sannino, 104–5; and Avicenna, "Risāla fī al-fi'l wa-l-infi'āl," 9–10.

29. Charles Pellat, *'anḳā'*, *Encyclopaedia of Islam*, 2nd ed. The *'anqā'* became a standard example of a nonexisting thing in classical Arabic philosophy (Kukkonen, "Ibn Sīnā and the Early History of Thought Experiments," 445n48). See also Mikkelson, "Flights of Imagination," 36–47.

30. Black, "Avicenna on the Ontological and Epistemic Status of Fictional Beings," 431. See Avicenna, "Rasālat fi-l-nafs li-l-Shaykh al-Ra'īs," in "'L'épître sur la disparition des formes intelligibles vaines après la mort' d'Avicenne," ed. Michot, 155.

existence of the bird, which is perhaps worth stressing, since it exemplifies a sort of discrimination that medieval philosophers are typically thought to lack. His interest lies not in the bird's nonexistence but in its status, specifically as a nonexisting thing, as an image within the soul.[31] His ultimate purpose is to determine whether fantastic creatures like it are thinkable by the intellect after death. In other words, is it possible for someone in heaven to imagine a unicorn? He answers no because such creatures live in the imagination, and as a faculty of the senses, imagination does not survive death.[32] All sensory faculties depend on the body and die with it. In heaven, then, one does not have to worry whether a given thinkable object exists, because the intellect can only conceive of existing things. The nonavailability of such forms is the clearest indication of their ontological status. In this life, however, such marvels enjoy a conceptual existence that makes them thinkable to the intellect.[33] The *'anqā'* is, in other words, comprehensible as a species of animal with qualities like size and color. As Avicenna describes it, the wayfarer's intellect is not especially well equipped to differentiate between the species of existing and nonexisting things. Marvels seem to capitalize on that cognitive disposition.

Avicenna acknowledges the belief (*i'tiqād*) of some people that the *'anqā'* is real, and he accounts for their error.[34] Crucial is its status as a creature of imagination. As he writes, "if imagination does not act as intermediary, absolutely no image contrary to reality will come to be in the intellect."[35] Only through imagination can the intellect form a concept of a nonexisting thing, and the intellect must return to imagination each time it wants to think about the bird. In Black's words, "every time the rational soul thinks about unreal forms, it must turn anew to the imagination," and when the intellect can no longer turn to imagination for such images, it loses access

31. Augustine too asks how the soul distinguishes between the true figure ("vera figuram") that accurately represents a thing in the intellect and the imaginary one, made up by "cogitation, which the Greeks call *phantasia* or *phantasma*" ("eam quam sibi fingit cogitatio, quae graece sive phantasia sive phantasma dicitur"), but does not delve as deeply into the question (*Soliloquiorum* 2.20.34–36, ed. Hörmann, 93–98). On cogitation as a name for imagination, see my "Medieval Latin Rhetoric and the Internal Senses."

32. According to Christian theologians, it returns with the resurrected body.

33. This position poses some philosophical challenges, which Deborah Black describes and seeks to resolve in "Avicenna on the Ontological and Epistemic Status of Fictional Beings."

34. Avicenna, "Rasālat fi-l-nafs li-l-Shaykh al-Ra'īs," ed. Michot, "L'épître sur la disparition des formes intelligibles vaines," 155.

35. Avicenna, "Rasālat fi-l-nafs li-l-Shaykh al-Ra'īs," ed. Michot, "L'épître sur la disparition des formes intelligibles vaines," 157: "fa-idhā lam yatawassaṭ al-takhayyulu lam taḥṣul al-battata ṣūratun mukhālafatun li-l-ḥaqqi fi-l-'aquli."

to them.[36] Marvels, whether they are real or not, would seem to exist in the soul in a similar way. The disappearance of some of them from the intellect after death will settle the question of their reality, and until then, people can think about them much as they think about things that certainly exist.

The precarious status of marvels as things that might be entertained until definitively proven not to exist is reflected in the language used to discuss them. In the *De civitate Dei*, Augustine comments on several present-day marvels, such as a fountain cold by day and hot by night, or apple trees in Sodom whose fruit is filled with ash, and writes, "since these marvels are not nonexisting [*non . . . non sunt*] just because human reason and discourse falter with respect to such works of God, so it is not the case that those other marvels [such as heaven and hell] will not be [*non . . . non erunt*] just because either sort of marvel cannot be comprehended by men."[37] The present-day marvels are both evidence that people believe in things they do not understand and a goad to the impious to believe in future marvels that are similarly beyond their grasp. Even though Augustine writes that he does not doubt the existence of the marvelous trees of Sodom, so authoritative are the sources that testify to them, he still describes them and like marvels as "not nonexisting." We will see similarly contorted language from other writers below. It shows that marvels have a fragile form of existence, which is why the very category of marvel is an unstable one that threatens to dissolve under scrutiny. Because they signify an opening of possibilities and a widening of the range of what might be, their definition must remain flexible.

NATURE'S IMAGINATION

The marvels discussed in previous chapters were imaginative in the sense that they involved the human faculty of imagination. The natural marvels addressed in this chapter are still expressions of imagination, but not in quite so direct a sense. They perhaps appeal to the human faculty of imagination, but they do not emerge from it. If any imagination accounts for them, it is nature's own. Consider, for instance, the *De naturis rerum* by the English abbot Alexander Neckham. In a section devoted to the oddities of fish (*de monstruosis piscibus*), he lingers on marvels, as on the torpedo fish that paralyzes anyone it looks at. With respect to the creation of fish,

36. Black, "Avicenna on the Ontological and Epistemic Status of Fictional Beings," 433.

37. Augustine, *De civitate Dei* 21.5, ed. Dombart and Kalb, 2:766: "cum in talibus operibus Dei deficiat ratio cordis et sermonis humani, sicut ista non ideo non sunt, sic non ideo etiam illa non erunt, quoniam ratio de utrisque ab homine non potest reddi."

nature was playful; "nature is seen to play in them," he writes.[38] With their different sizes, shapes, and colors, and their unusual powers, they advertise the plenty of nature so effectively that Neckham assumes that nature herself had a good time creating them. Insofar as he thinks that fish and other sea creatures showcase nature's creativity especially well, he is not alone. Thomas of Cantimpré likewise writes that sea creatures, or *monstra marina*, were created to inspire wonder (*ammirationem*); "in hardly any other things under the heavens did God work so marvelously, except in human nature."[39] Both their variety and their potential hugeness impress.

According to Pliny, the sea contains all that is on earth and more: "according to popular opinion, whatever is generated in any part of nature is in the sea, and also many things that are not seen elsewhere. One finds there likenesses of all sorts of things, and not only of animals. One who looks can discern a grape, a sword, a saw, and a cucumber, similar in color and odor to those on land."[40] The idea persisted into the Middle Ages, with Gervase of Tilbury, for instance, pointing to the monkfish and kingfish to support his claim that there is nothing on dry land that is not duplicated in the sea.[41] Likewise, in the *Thousand and One Nights*, the sea princess Jullanar tells the Persian king, "In the sea there are people of all types and creatures of all kinds, just as there are on land, and more."[42] These include not just natural but also artificial forms. As al-Dimashqī writes, "there is also a fish that resembles a man in battle, with a small sword in one hand, a round shield in the other, and a helmet with a visor on its head. Each of those is part only of the animal proper, of the living body proper. The sword is a member of its body, and the shield is a member of its body, and the helmet is a member its body. It is called the executioner of the sea, and it is mostly found in the sea off of Sardinia and Barcelona."[43] Artificial and natural objects are similarly represented in the sea.

38. Alexander Neckham, *De naturis rerum* 2.25, ed. Wright, 144: "in quibus natura ludere visa est."

39. Thomas of Cantimpré, *Liber de natura rerum* 6.1, ed. Boese, 232: "vix in aliquibus rebus sub celo ita mirabiliter operatus sit deus, excepta humana natura."

40. Pliny, *Natural History* 9.1, ed. and trans. Rackham, 164–65: "ut fiat vulgi opinio quicquid nascatur in parte naturae ulla et in mari esse, praeterque multa quae nusquam alibi. Rerum quidem, non solum animalium, simulacra inesse licet intellegere intuentibus uvam, gladium, serram, cucumin vero et colore et odore similem."

41. Gervase of Tilbury, *Otia imperialia* 3.63, ed. Banks and Binns, 678.

42. *Thousand and One Nights*, 237th night, ed. Muhsin Mahdi, 489: "fī al-baḥri ṭawāīfun (ṭawā'ifun) wa-ashkālun min sāiri (sā'iri) al-ajnāsi kamā fī al-barri wa-aktharu." Trans. Haddawy, *Arabian Nights*, 473.

43. Al-Dimashqī, *Nukhbat al-dahr* 4.4, ed. Mehren, 144: "wa-samakatun ayḍan kaṣūrati rajulin muḥāribin, bi-yaddihi sayfun qaṣīrun wa-bi-l-ukhrā tursun mudawwarun wa-ʿalā ra'sihi bayḍatun bi-rafrafin. Wa-dhālika kulluhu qiṭʿatu wāḥidatu ḥayawānin

In sea creatures, nature displays not just her playfulness but her creativity, even acting as a creative artist. Neckham writes, "if you wish to understand thoughts by fish, you will find in them strange expressions of imagination. For wonderful figments of thought surpass the audacity of paintings and poets, about which it is said [by Horace], 'painters and poets have always had license to dare anything.' The painter is the mind, but she does not just paint. No, she fashions forms that the power of nature is not fit to bring to light."[44] Fish symbolize thoughts even more creative than those expressed through poetry and painting. They are like thoughts that have no constraint, that live only in the mind and cannot be expressed in the world. Nature, then, is like the artistic human mind, but she exceeds even her own constraints. Paradoxically, these fish that represent thoughts that could never be translated into objects because they exceed nature's own power do exist. It as though nature surpasses herself in their creation. With his fish that are real and yet also objects of thought, Neckham could hardly explain more clearly that marvels are not like normal things in the world. Even as objects, they represent more than objects. They are thoughts at their most creative, seemingly self-vivifying in their potency, and confined only to the limitations of nature's imagination.[45]

Alexander suggests that marvels be read as products of nature's creative imagination. Unlike classical Arabic literature, which considers the creative imagination at length, writers in the Latin West rarely address it, but it should be noted that they sometimes do. Neckham assumes its existence in his comments above, but in his *De divisione philosophiae*, the well-known translator Dominicus Gundissalinus is more explicit. He writes, "It is the property of poetry to make the hearer imagine [*ymaginari*] through its words something beautiful or ugly that does not exist, so that the hearer might believe it [*credat*] and either hate or desire it. Although we are certain that it is not so in reality, nevertheless our souls are drawn to hate or

---

wāḥidin, jismin ḥayyin wāḥidin, al-sayfu 'uḍū wa-l-tursu 'uḍū wa-l-khūdhatu 'uḍū. Yusammī sayyafa al-baḥri, wa-aktharuhā yūjadu bi-baḥri sardāniyati wa-barshalūnati." French trans. Mehren, *Cosmographie*, 189.

44. Neckham, *De naturis rerum* 2.25, ed. Wright, 144: "si per pisces accipere velis cogitationes, reperies in eis monstruosas imaginationum notas. Cogitationum namque figmenta prodigiosa audaciam pictorum et poetarum excedunt, de quibus dicitur: 'pictoribus atque poetis / Quidlibet audendi semper fuit aequa potestas.' Pictor tamen est animus, sed nec solum depingit, immo et fingit formas, quas nec naturae potentia dignaretur in lucem proferre."

45. Which would, in light of the earlier discussion, seem only to extend as far as the logically possible.

desire what we imagine."[46] Poetry uses imagination to provoke the sensitive appetite and inspire desire or disgust toward objects that the intellect knows not to exist. Such inventions have being only within the work of art, whereas nature, according to Neckham, can make its imaginative creations real. The previous chapter has shown that the human imagination might act similarly in the case of certain marvels, although Neckham does not acknowledge such a possibility here; he focuses only on the human imagination insofar as it expresses itself in works of art. Still, the similarity between artistic creativity and marvel-making creativity is crucial to understanding why poetry figures into philosophers' analysis of marvels. The idea that natural marvels are products of nature's creative imagination helps to explain why they bring marvels of literature to mind. In both cases, marvels are artfully crafted, unlikely creatures that take shape in the imagination when it exercises its maximal powers.

CROSS-DISCIPLINARY MARVELS

Although medieval learning does not conform to strict disciplinary boundaries, marvels are interdisciplinary in a particularly deliberate way. Thus Pliny, whose weighty *Historia naturalia* was foundational to writings on nature in the Latin West, alternates among poetic, historical, and scientific sources without, typically, calling much attention to the difference. He pretends to exclude "marvelous events" from his work, but the "sterile material" he offers instead is hardly so bland.[47] The "twenty thousand noteworthy things" that he shares with his reader constitute an idiosyncratic assortment that includes a host of improbable tales and draws material from variously authoritative sources.[48] Not just telling his reader where unicorns come from (India) or the mythical *eale* (Ethiopia), Pliny recounts fanciful tales, as of an elephant that competed with Aristophanes for the

46. Gundissalinus, *De divisione philosophiae*, ed. Baur, 74: "Proprium est poetice sermonibus suis facere ymaginari aliquid pulchrum vel fedum, quod non est, ita, ut auditor credat et aliquando abhorreat vel appetat: quamvis enim certi sumus, quod non est ita in veritate, tamen eriguntur animi nostri ad abhorrendum vel appetendum quod ymaginatur nobis." It is entirely possible that Gundissalinus depended on Arabic philosophers for his understanding of the creative imagination, as claimed, for instance, by Päivi Mehtonen, "Poetics, Narration, and Imitation," 299–302. See also Kemal, *The Philosophical Poetics of Alfarabi, Avicenna, and Averroes.*

47. Pliny, *Natural History*, Preface, ed. and trans. Rackham et al., 1:9: "casus mirabiles," "sterilis materia."

48. Pliny, *Natural History*, Preface, ed. and trans. Rackham et al., 1:12: "viginta milia rerum dignarum cura."

love of a young woman.[49] Pulling from different sources and stitching them together, he also mixes areas of expertise, allowing poets, for instance, to comment authoritatively on geography and botany. When Pliny describes the division of Ethiopia into two regions, he accordingly calls on Homer, "who relates that the Ethiopians are divided in two directions, toward the East and West."[50] Along with Aeschylus, Orpheus, and Hesiod, Homer also lays the foundations for botanical science.[51] Pliny credits him with knowing that plants are the source of Circe's bewitching powers. According to Pliny, she lived in an area rich in herbs, and her descendants live there still, using them to charm snakes.

Insofar as he groups fabulous matters like the sorceress Circe with factual ones like Ethiopian politics, Pliny is hardly alone. Such open disregard for disciplinary or ontological distinctions survives him by centuries. To take an especially famous example, Dante assigned people he knew personally to the same fate as mythical heroes and collapsed the distinction between them. Poets inhabit the afterlife along with their characters, and so Virgil tells Statius that Antigone, Hypsipyle, and other characters from the *Thebaid* are in hell.[52] He describes them to Statius as "your own people," created by him and now with souls like his.[53] Neither Pliny nor Dante failed to appreciate the difference in kind between fact and fiction, but each opted to de-emphasize the distinction. As we saw in the introduction, Umberto Eco comments on medieval writers' disinclination to cordon off fact from fiction, which does not mean that medieval writers were unconcerned with credibility. Pliny, for instance, accuses the Greeks of excessive credulity in response to werewolf stories.[54] He also recognizes a difference between the opinions of the learned and unlearned, as with respect to the roundness of the earth.[55] He cares about accuracy and flags claims that he deems incredible or incorrect, but he does not pretend to tell only true stories. His chronicle of natural oddities instead betrays an inclusive attitude that seeks out similarities across sources more than differences. Marvels again function within it to reveal the breadth of possibilities within the natural world.

49. On the unicorn, see Pliny, *Natural History* 8.31, ed. and trans. Rackham et al., 3:56. On the *eale*, see 8.30, 3:54. On the elephant suitor, see 8.5, 3:12.

50. Pliny, *Natural History* 5.8, ed. and trans. Rackham et al., 2:250: "verissima opinione eorum qui desertis Africae duas Aethiopias superponunt, et ante omnis Homeri qui bipertitos tradit Aethiopas, ad orientem occasumque versos." The reference is to Homer's *Odyssey* 1.21–25.

51. Pliny, *Natural History* 25.5, ed. and trans. Rackham et al., 7:142–44.

52. Dante, *Purgatorio* 22.109–14, ed. and trans. Durling.

53. Dante, *Purgatorio* 22.109, ed. and trans. Durling, "le genti tue."

54. Pliny, *Natural History* 8.34, ed. and trans. Rackham et al., 3:60.

55. Pliny, *Natural History* 2.65, ed. and trans. Rackham et al., 1:296–300.

Within medieval natural philosophy, marvels regularly find themselves studied with respect to a range of sources. As Alexander Neckham writes, "it should be known that marvels are found in every discipline," and philosophers appeal to many disciplines when attempting to explain them.[56] A brief example from Albertus Magnus makes the point. In the midst of explaining monstrous births, he compares monsters to the Minotaur. He writes, "Due to a power that is acting in opposition, a human birth might have the head of a ram or a bull, as is said of the Minotaur in the tales [*fabulis*] of the poets."[57] Albertus's purpose is to account for the generation of monsters, and because his principal explanation is that they come from the copulation of animals of different species, and the Minotaur is the offspring of a human woman and a bull, it is arguably relevant. He expressly recognizes that the Minotaur is an invention of the poets, a fable, which might lead one to ask what purpose the reference serves. Explaining an unlikely phenomenon by comparing it to a purely fictive one would be an odd tactic if one's aim were to persuade one's reader that the phenomenon operated as described. While the Minotaur illustrates what is, for Albertus, a possible truth about monsters' hybridity, and perhaps suggests that a favored explanation for monsters has trickled into poetry, it is not particularly effective as a piece of evidence. The principal function of the reference, I propose, is to highlight the nearly poetic creativity of nature. Monstrosity is a natural phenomenon so striking that it resembles mythology, a marvel that borders on make-believe. At the same time, by appealing to poetry in a work of natural philosophy, Albertus uses generic hybridity to comment on the species hybridity of monsters. As monsters and the Minotaur are produced by parents from different species, so marvels generally are the offspring of poetry and philosophy, among other disciplines. This is not euhemerism, since the Minotaur is not supposed to have existed. Rather, it is a testament to the ingenuity of nature, which, at its most spectacular, possesses the character of poetry. Through its marvels, it captures something of the force of purely invented creatures.

BRADWARDINE AND THE PARTING OF THE RED SEA

A fascinating passage from Thomas Bradwardine shows further how marvels bridge different genres and showcase nature's creativity. In it, he col-

56. Neckham, *De naturis rerum* 2.173, ed. Wright, 301: "Sciendum igitur quod in omni disciplina mira reperiuntur." He means that each of the seven liberal arts has its marvels.

57. Albertus Magnus, *De animalibus* 18.1.6, ed. Borgnet, in *Opera omnia*, 12:252: "Ex virtute enim in oppositum agente partus hominis forte habebit caput arietis aut tauri, sicut dicitur de Minotauro in fabulis poetarum." Trans. Resnick and Kitchell, *On Animals*, 2:1304.

lects a dozen stories borrowed from different disciplines that tell, in more or less opaque ways, versions of the miracle of the parting of the Red Sea. His sources range from Ovid to Josephus, from Aristotle to Alexander romances, from historical chronicles to philosophy, and from theology to mythology. Although the anthology of sorts is focused upon a miracle rather than a marvel, the miracle retells itself in the marvels. They evoke it as, in Bradwardine's view, non-Christians testify to Christian truths. He exhorts his reader as he begins: "if you do not believe the histories of Christians about miracles done among them, believe the histories of philosophers, poets, chroniclers, Gentiles, and others who never received the faith of Christ."[58] His sources are eclectic by design in order to show that miracles echo across the world and marvels represent them indirectly and in diluted form. The following chapter offers further examples of this phenomenon, with present-day marvels constellating around the sites of biblical miracles and presenting less powerful versions of them, amplifying the miracle at their literal and thematic center.

As the stories begin, Bradwardine makes no mention of the parting of the Red Sea. He starts with a story about an earthquake that sends lava flowing down Mount Etna, splitting in two so that it does not harm a group of men carrying their aged parents on their backs. The lava, like the Red Sea, parts to protect God's chosen ones. Bradwardine anticipates the connection by likening the lava to a river: "it poured from the mountain like a river over the earth," and when it reached the dutiful children, "the river of fire and flame was also divided."[59] Equally suggestive, he writes that the earthquake, "along with very strong rains and raging winds, in certain places replaced the sea with dry land, and dry land with the sea."[60] The phrasing calls to mind the biblical story, with its repeated emphasis on the "dry land" (*siccum*) that the Israelites walked as they crossed the sea.[61] Perhaps because he is thinking about Sicily, perhaps because it is in the same chapter of one of his sources, Solinus's *De mirabilia mundi*, Bradwardine

58. Bradwardine, *De causa Dei* 1.1, coroll. 32, ed. Savile, 39B: "si historiis Christianorum de miraculis apud ipsos factis non credis, crede historiis philosophorum, poetarum, chronographorum, Gentilium, et illorum qui nunquam receperant fidem Christi."

59. Bradwardine, *De causa Dei* 1.1, coroll. 32, ed. Savile, 39B: "ferebatur in modum fluminis super terram" and "ignis divisum est flumen incendii quoque." Especially in the second quotation, he stays close to the wording of *De mundo* 6, ed. Lorimer and Minio-Panuello, 23: "factus fluvius divisus est; divisum autem est ignei hoc quidem huc, hoc vero illuc, et servavit illesos simul parentibus iuvenes."

60. Bradwardine, *De causa Dei* 1.1, coroll. 32, ed. Savile, 39B: "atque cum imbribus maximis rabieque ventorum, in quibusdam locis mare convertit in aridam, et aridam in mare."

61. See Ex 14:16, 21, 22, and 29.

then writes of Sicilians making sacrifices at a pagan altar on Vulcan's Hill, laying young green twigs before it.[62] If their sacrifice is pleasing, the twigs improbably burn, producing a fire that, although acrobatic—Bradwardine tells us that its flame "flails about with tremendous contortions"—does not harm the people.[63] God again appears to intervene, taming nature in order to protect virtuous pagans.

Bradwardine proceeds with Pliny's story of the Hirpi who, when they make their sacrifices on Mount Soracte, walk on fire without harm. They complete an unlikely journey, albeit across burning ground rather than a seabed. The stories reveal the two organizing themes of Bradwardine's collection: the four elements and passageways, whether marvelously impeded or unimpeded. The story of the Hirpi features both, as fire rather than water imperils the pagans, and they cross without injury. Their success signals their virtue. In each example, nature proclaims its purposefulness by acting against its inclinations. Fire burns young twigs while protecting those who leave them; lava divides itself to the benefit of youngsters who love their parents; burning coals leave feet unburned. The fact that it discriminates, burning where it typically would not and not burning where it typically would, implies the oversight of the Christian God, who alters nature's normal operations.

As Bradwardine continues, he writes that Alexander the Great enclosed the ten lost tribes of Israel, whom he equates with the people of Gog and Magog, in the Caspian mountains, a feat he only achieved after calling on the "God of Israel" for help.[64] Alexander closed off a narrow pathway through the mountains in order to contain them. Here, God blocks a path, using earth rather than water to contain the unfavored tribes. In this way, Bradwardine seems to remind his reader that the parting of the Red Sea was followed by the flooding of Israel's enemies. God opens and he closes. That the Israelites are the object of both actions, first allowed to cross over to the Holy Land and then stuck on a mountain, makes their own trajectory part of his point about unobstructed divine power. God awards and withholds his favor as he wishes, and so the Israelites were the chosen ones before they were not.

62. Solinus, *De mirabilia mundi* 5, in *Collectanea rerum memorabilium*, ed. Mommsen, 51.

63. Bradwardine, *De causa Dei*, 1.1, coroll. 32, ed. Savile, 39C: "flamma, quae flexuosis excessibus vagabunda."

64. Bradwardine, *De causa Dei* 1.1, coroll. 32, ed. Savile, 40A. Alexander the Great was sometimes credited by medieval Christian theologians with being Christian. See, for instance, Petrus Comestor, *Historia scholastica*, *PL* 198:1498A. Showing a similar instinct to claim him as their own, Islamic sources sometimes characterize him as an ancient Persian king (Zadeh, *Wonders and Rarities*, chap. 8).

Also on the topic of famed, non-Christian conquerors who were aided by God, Bradwardine later retells at length the story of Genghis Khan crossing the mountain Burkhan Khaldun according to instructions he received in a vision. It was God's will that he make so difficult a crossing, Bradwardine explains. He is aware that Genghis's victory enabled him to march westward and reconquer lands then in the possession of Muslims, completing a journey into a different sort of promised land. As Alexander hemmed in the Israelites, so Genghis weakened the Muslims, each acting as God wished. In fact, Christians often sought, and sometimes received, help from the Mongols in their battles against Muslims; they wanted more Mongols to act as Genghis is made to act here. The attention to pathways in both stories reflects on the reader's own situation, proceeding from one story to another without transition, moving along the route that Bradwardine clears for them. The implication is that God's providence is visible in any number of sources, all intended to resonate with one another. Their very heterogeneity suggests the cohesiveness of God's power: it is the one thing that unifies so disparate a collection and makes it coherent.

By the time he gets to the biblical miracle, Bradwardine has already told five stories, and after naming it, he quickly moves past it without further mention. The reader is left to infer that the stories surrounding it figuratively reenact it and to apply this lesson retrospectively. In an intermission from the tales, he writes that Hermogenes, Avicenna, al-Ghazālī, and Abū Maʿshar, none Christian, all believed in miracles, with the clear implication that everyone should therefore do so. He proceeds, and I quote at length in order to illustrate his method:

> Also Josephus, at the end of the second book of the *Antiquities*, refers to Israel's crossing by means of the Red Sea and offers it as evidence of faith. Let nobody disbelieve reports of miracles if the path of salvation, namely across the sea, was followed by virtuous men in ancient times, whether by the will of God or according to revelation. Likewise, the Sea of Pamphilia was divided for those who fought with Alexander the King of Macedonia long ago, since there was no other path, and it offered passage to them, whether through the will of God or sudden revelation, so that they could together destroy the head of the Persians, and all who wrote the deeds of Alexander are agreed on this. Also, the *Historia Scholastica*, where it relates what happened to Esther according to Josephus, says that Alexander the Great, by praying to the God of Israel that they might enclose the ten tribes within the Caspian mountains, reached by turns the mountains that had been blocked off and passed through an impassable place. Also, Valerius Maximus, Book 8 chapter 1, writes that a

certain vestal virgin suspected of corruption, unharmed with respect to the token of her integrity [i.e., with her hymen intact], by praying to the goddess Vesta beforehand, carried a sieve full of water from the Tiber to her Temple without spilling any of it.[65]

Bradwardine stitches together a series of stories from different sources, often staying close to the language of the original text. The insistent parataxis recalls medieval chronicles, which likewise leave the reader to make connections after depositing a pile of information before them. One reference to Alexander the Great introduces another, and one story about a virgin generates another, indicating that Bradwardine's method is associative and idiosyncratic. Each of these stories implicitly suggests the others. With such bare transitions and so little commentary, the reader is invited to identify on their own the logic that binds them.

Bradwardine's method becomes his very argument. The cumulative diversity of the stories seems designed to reveal a surprisingly consistent focus: marvels reflect the creativity of nature and its creator by resonating across genres and disciplines. His account is reminiscent of exegetical *catenae* and *distinctiones* that group together different meanings of a word. He collects an array of stories that the parting of the Red Sea might evoke, varying his sources so spectacularly that he makes their seeming dissimilarity his very subject, and then presents them for inspection. Recall that he had asked his readers to "believe the histories of philosophers, poets, chroniclers, Gentiles, and others who never received the faith of Christ." After he quotes Ovid's story of Claudia Quinta, he introduces historical and theological sources "lest," he writes, "I appear to base myself only on the suspect pronouncements of poets."[66] He regularly cites his sources, calling attention to how scattered they are. He is aware of the different genres and

65. Bradwardine, *De causa Dei* 1.1, coroll. 32, ed. Savile, 39E–40A: "Item Josephus 2 Antiquit. ultimo, referens transitum Israel per medium maris rubri, in argumentum fidei haec subjungit. Nullus vero discredat verbi miraculum, si antiquis hominibus & malitia privatis, via salutis, licet per mare, sit facta, sive voluntate Dei, sive sponte revelata, dum & eis qui cum Alexandro Rege Macedoniae fuerunt olim & antiquitus resistentibus Pamphylicum mare divisum fit, & cum aliud non esset iter, transitum praebuit eis, volente Deo per eum destruere Persarum principatum, & hoc consitentur omnes qui Actus Alexandri, conscripserunt. Historia atque Scholastica, ubi actum est de Hester recitat a Josepho memorato, quod Alexandro magno orante Deum Israel, ut intra montes Caspios includeret 10 Tribus, praerupta montium accesserunt ad invicem & locum immeabilem perfecerunt. Refert quoque Valerius Maximus lib. 8. 1. quod Virgo quaedam vestalis de corruptione suspecta, in argumentum suae integritatis illaese, oratione Deae Vestae praemissa, cribrum plenum aqua de Tyberi in eius Templum integerrime deferebat."

66. Bradwardine, *De causa Dei* 1.1, coroll. 32, ed. Savile, 41A: "ne indictis suspectis Poetarum tantummodo videar me fundare."

categories he draws from, as Albertus Magnus was when he mentioned the Minotaur. For Bradwardine, the variety reveals the singleness of God's plan.

Returning to the stories themselves, we see that water, predictably, is the subject of several. Following the lead of Josephus, Bradwardine explicitly compares the crossing of the Red Sea to Alexander the Great's crossing of the Sea of Pamphylia. More remarkable are two stories of pagan, virginal virtue. First, Bradwardine tells Valerius Maximus's story of a vestal virgin, Tuccia, who proved her chastity by transporting water from the Tiber to the Temple of Vesta in a sieve, as we saw above: "she carried a sieve full of water from the Tiber to her Temple without spilling any of it." The unlikely soundness of the sieve proves the virgin's chastity: herself whole, she makes an object designed to release liquids contain them. Her walk of nonshame is the parting of the Red Sea abstracted. Tuccia's journey is here defined, then, by the marvelous containment of water that would normally flow. As the parting of the Red Sea exalts those left dry, so Tuccia, untouched by water that does not spill, untouched by a lover, stands apart. Rewarded for her devotion to a pagan goddess, she becomes a fitting representation of divine providence, even though she is pagan. Chastity often goes proxy for religious virtue in such contexts, as wholeness suggests holiness. Finally, the journey from river to temple is like the crossing of the Red Sea insofar as Tuccia travels home, with the sieve acting as the marvel that enables her to do so. It is an emblem of external aid, a sign of a greater power that protects her.

Bradwardine proceeds with a thirty-eight-line quotation from Ovid's *Fasti* that tells the story of Claudia Quinta, one familiar from various "histories and poems."[67] He mentions Livy, Solinus, and Augustine as supplemental sources. Another virgin suspected of impurity, Claudia Quinta proved her chastity through a prayer to Cybele, successfully asking that a ship stuck in the mud, carrying a statue of the goddess, be released. In this story, the water flows, but it is improbably traversable. The boat, so familiar a Christian symbol, acts like the Israelites who cross the water, carrying not the ark but a statue of a pagan goddess. As in the case of the parting of the Red Sea, it is the purity of faith that protects one who would cross threatening waters, even if it is the wrong faith. By using Claudia Quinta to represent the Israelites, Bradwardine again insists that pagan devotion can symbolize Judeo-Christian devotion.

Particularly in these stories of virginal virtue, Bradwardine seems to relish the unlikeliness of his parallels. The stories of Claudia Quinta and Tuccia do not intuitively suggest the parting of the Red Sea, and that seems

67. Bradwardine, *De causa Dei* 1.1, coroll. 32, ed. Savile, 40B–E.

to be much of his point. By making a seeming hodge-podge of references coherent, he celebrates the creativity that connects them and ascribes it to God. He is the one who has planted such allusions in sources scattered far and wide, composed in different languages for people of different faiths. All are to be led to the Bible, presumably, and through it to Christianity.

It is worthwhile to note the oddity of drawing on marvels when Bradwardine's point is specifically that the parting of the Red Sea was not a marvel as traditionally understood, that is, not an event that can be explained through nature alone. He arrives at the topic of the Red Sea through defense of other biblical miracles, first prophecy and then the eclipse that, according to the synoptic gospels, coincided with Jesus's crucifixion. In each case, he attempts to discount natural explanations and rely instead on God. He proceeds, then, not by distinguishing miracle from marvel, but by showing that both miracles and marvels proclaim God's power. In other words, according to Bradwardine, even marvels depend on direct divine intervention in the world.

His method of analysis makes a point that will be echoed in the remaining chapters, which is that marvels often exert a centripetal force. Philosophers bring other marvels and stories into their orbit, making surprising connections across them. Marvels are, by definition, unexpected, and those that become routine tend to stop inspiring wonder, like the making of glass from sand.[68] Bradwardine heightens their element of surprise, using the marvel to direct wonder toward God. Recall that inspiring such wonder is a principal purpose of marvels, often cited by medieval writers and expressed in a wide array of texts. In the *sīrat Sayf ibn Dhī Yazan*, the title character is therefore taken on a tour of "the world and all its marvels."[69] The quest for marvels counts as a spiritual journey that also encourages personal growth. As Travis Zadeh writes of al-Qazwīnī's cosmology, "contemplating creation is a pious activity designed to affirm God's majesty and to appreciate the interconnected beauty and strangeness of existence."[70] Similarly, *Piers Plowman*'s protagonist "Wente wide in this world wondres to here," learning how best to serve God by surveying creation.[71] In the thirteenth-century *Llibre de meravalles* by Ramón Llull, the protagonist's

68. In the *Squire's Tale*, Chaucer writes that such glass is a marvel that no longer inspires wonder because people "han yknowen it so fern" (l. 256, ed. Benson, *The Riverside Chaucer*).

69. *Sīrat Fāris al-Yaman al-Malik Sayf ibn Dhī Yazan*, 1:100: "al-dunyā wa-mā fīhā min al-ʿajāʾibi." Trans. Jayyusi, *The Adventures of Sayf ben Dhi Yazan*, 69. The genre of the *sīra* will be discussed further in chapter 5.

70. Zadeh, *Wonders and Rarities*, chap. 5.

71. Langland, *Piers Plowman*, Pro. 4, ed. Kane and Donaldson.

father instructs him, "'See the world, and marvel at men, because they no longer love, know, and honor God.'"[72] The entire book recounts Félix's efforts to amend their collective error, to marvel at marvels that are meant to be marveled at precisely in order to inspire love and reverence for God. The notion that the marvels of creation provoke wonder and devotion was so familiar as to be clichéd in both Christian and Islamic thought.

The creativity that Bradwardine displays in pasting together an unlikely set of sources mirrors the creativity of the created world, which retells a biblical miracle in myriad forms. Seeing how one story might be refigured in another is a particular talent often on display in medieval biblical commentary as well as theology. In the case of marvels, the quest for inventive parallels is unimpeded by the distinction between fact and fiction, as imagination proper is unimpeded by it. As a marvel itself, creation seems to invite clever connections of the sort that Bradwardine and Albertus make. Neither author was unaware of the difference between genres or their different claims to truth, but such differences were inducements rather than impediments. Both saw that real things can be as improbable as fabricated ones, and linking the two only heightens their productive capacity to surprise.

In his preface, Bradwardine likens himself to various figures who, like him, faced daunting tasks. Aiming to defend divine omniscience without nearly possessing it, he compares his project to that of heroes and philosophers: "here the infinite Chaos of Anaxagoras, here the inescapable labyrinth of Daedalus, here the monstrous miracle of the Hydra, and yet a more monstrous thing than Hydra. For in her case three heads were immediately restored when one was cut off, but as both experience and Athena confirm, innumerable doubts are reborn when one is excised."[73] His comparison of himself to classical heroes who overcame seemingly impossible obstacles is not unusual in itself. Alexander Neckham, for instance, compares himself to Phaeton, Icarus, and Atlas in the preface of his *De naturis rerum*.[74] But Bradwardine intends no self-aggrandizement. Rather, he suggests that he, Anaxagoras, Theseus, and Hercules all needed help to contain an outsized enemy. The pre-Socratic philosopher Anaxagoras stands out because he

72. Llull, *Llibre de meravelles*, Prologue, ed. Badia et al., *Nova Edició de les obres de Ramón Llull*, 10:82: "Ve por le mon e maravella-t dels homens per que sessen a amar e conexer e a loar Deu." Modern Castilian trans. Gimferrer, *Obra escogida*, 27.

73. Bradwardine, *De causa Dei*, Preface, ed. Savile, b3r: "Hic igitur Chaos Anaxagorae infinitum, hic inextricabilis Daedali Labyrinthus, hic Hydrae miraculum monstruosum: imo et monstruosior res quam Hydra. In ipsa namque, uno capite amputato tria continuo recreverunt: hic autem et experientia et Pallade attestante, una dubitatione succisa innumerabiles aliae renascuntur."

74. Neckham, *De naturis rerum*, Preface, ed. Wright, 2.

was a philosopher who existed, not a literary character. He was well known for his belief that the cosmos was initially a chaotic mixture of components, later set in order by an intellect (*nous*). It was a theory that accorded nicely with Genesis's account of God taming primordial chaos, and Bradwardine appeals to it as an example of divine intervention. Only God could bring order to chaos, as heroes, presumably, relied on more than their own powers when they slew monsters. Mythology, philosophy, and theology meet at the precipice of the unknown, where immense forces are glimpsed but cannot be controlled or apprehended without help. "Both experience and Athena confirm" the challenges that he faces, not because experience and Athena are similarly real, but because his is no normal quest. It requires him to test the outer limits of his natural capacity, as marvels test theirs. In Bradwardine's view, each requires superhuman aid in order to exceed his normal limitations. That is as true of characters from poetry as of philosophers from history.

ST. PATRICK'S PURGATORY AND THE *AENEID*'S SIBYL

The methods of Bradwardine and Albertus Magnus are shared by other philosophers and theologians, particularly when their focus is marvels. Oresme, for instance, appeals to sources far and wide when he seeks to explain how noxious vapors that are released from deep in the earth cause hallucination and other forms of mental disorder. In a short chapter devoted to the topic, he cites Palladius's fourth-century *De agricultura*, Galen's medical works, the *Epitoma historiarum Philippicarum* of the third-century Roman historian Marcus Junianus Justinus, Lucan's *Pharsalia*, Virgil's *Aeneid*, the story of St. Patrick's Purgatory, Augustine's *De divinatione daemonum*, Gratian's *Decretum*, and the biblical book of Isaiah.[75] Similarly willing to cross disciplinary boundaries, he assumes that all shed light on marvels. In the course of his argument, he proposes that Owen's vision when he visited purgatory was not actually a vision but a hallucination, which, as a hallucination, pretended to be a perception. We have seen how different categories of marvels can be confused with one another when their mechanisms overlap. Oresme takes advantage of the similarity of visions to delusions to recategorize the former as the latter. Owen did not deliberately deceive others, but was misled by the subterranean vapors he inhaled into thinking that the apparitions before him were real. Oresme likens his mental disorientation to that of the Cumaean Sibyl when she spoke to Aeneas.

75. Oresme, *De configurationibus* 2.32, ed. Clagett, *Nicole Oresme and the Medieval Geometry of Qualities and Motions*, 360–64.

Similarly altered by subterranean vapors, she was no prophet even though she spoke the truth. Turning to examples from poetry, and linking them to chronicles, natural philosophy, canon law, and the Bible, he insists that marvels resonate broadly in a way that unites different disciplines.[76]

The story of St. Patrick's Purgatory sat at the intersection of different disciplines—hagiography, poetry, chronicle—long before Oresme wrote about it. Described by Henry of Saltrey, Roger of Wendover, Jacobus de Voragine, and Marie de France, among others, it was a place in Ireland that people visited, and it is still a tourist site. The different sorts of testimony did not bother Oresme. What interested him was Owen's entrance into Purgatory through "a hole in the side of a well."[77] Citing Palladius's work on agriculture, Oresme explains that wells sometimes contain noxious vapors that cause madness or hallucinations.[78] He therefore finds Owen's journey to purgatory *through a well* to be suspicious. He was likely in a stupor (*in stuporem*), deceived (*deceptus*), and altered in his mind (*in mente mutatus*), hallucinating a journey to Purgatory rather than actually experiencing one.[79] He does not deny that Owen thought he visited Purgatory or that the protagonist deserves to be called a saint. He disputes only the fact of the journey. What most calls its veracity into question for Oresme is its similarity to poetry. The author recounts "many marvels that are not very credible nor consonant with the statements of saints but that are quite similar or comparable to the things that Virgil narrates [*fabulatur*] about Aeneas."[80] In other words, the description of Owen's experiences resembles epic poetry more than saints' lives, and that makes it suspect. The result of mind-altering vapors, his hallucinations constitute not a sacred vision but a secular marvel. In the course of his analysis, Oresme implies that hallucination resembles poetry more than religious literature because,

76. Note that Oresme credits Patrick with the journey to Purgatory rather than the knight Owen, who actually makes the journey in the source texts. I replace his references to Patrick with Owen in my discussion here.

77. Oresme, *De configurationibus* 2.32, ed. Clagett, *Nicole Oresme and the Medieval Geometry of Qualities and Motions*, 364: "foramen in lateram cuiusdam putei." The Latin *puteus* can mean "well" or "pit," even "pit of hell," but it makes more sense to enter through the side of a well than of a pit. Marie de France's version consistently uses "fosse," which has the same range.

78. Oresme, *De configurationibus* 2.32, ed. Clagett, *Nicole Oresme and the Medieval Geometry of Qualities and Motions*, 360.

79. Oresme, *De configurationibus* 2.32, ed. Clagett, *Nicole Oresme and the Medieval Geometry of Qualities and Motions*, 364.

80. Oresme, *De configurationibus* 2.32, ed. Clagett, *Nicole Oresme and the Medieval Geometry of Qualities and Motions*, 364: "multa mirabilia que non sunt bene credibilia nec dictis sanctorum consona, sed quasi similia vel proportionalia eis que Vergilius de Enea fabulatur." Trans. Clagett, 365.

although Owen's account is not willfully concocted, the two share the language of make-believe.

Oresme reads the *Aeneid*, like the story of St. Patrick's Purgatory, as mischaracterizing a marvel and giving it undue authority. In this case, a secular marvel masquerades as prophecy. Located in a vast underground cavern filled with deceiving winds, the Cumaean Sibyl too experienced the mind-altering effects of terrestrial vapors. She joins Owen, Lucan's Oracle of Delphi, and others in support of Oresme's claim about their distortive powers. That is why, Oresme tells us, Virgil writes of the Sibyl, "'Apollo plies the spurs beneath her breast,' and immediately following, 'As soon as the frenzy ceased and the raving lips were still.'"[81] On Oresme's reading, Virgil tells us to interpret the Sibyl as crazed, even though the content of her rantings is true. She "wraps true things in obscure ones," according to Virgil, but she is not a prophet.[82] To underscore the point, Oresme contrasts her words with those of God, who boasts in Isaiah that he "turns soothsayers to madness."[83] Her frenzied raving indicts her. Both she and Owen attribute a natural phenomenon to supernatural forces, inflating and misjudging their experiences because of their vapor-clouded imaginations. As we have seen, imagination often makes matters seem more impressive than they are.

The key point is that Oresme applies the same method of analysis to poetry and to natural philosophy, as he assigns their marvels a common cause. That is not because he fails to recognize the difference between them; in fact he insists on distinguishing them. Rather, as unusual, imaginative phenomena that are characterized by unusual vividness, marvels share the same characteristics in both. Recall Albertus Magnus pointing to Hercules when listing the special powers of the stone gagatronica. He does not hesitate to interpret a matter in poetry as though it were real. If Hercules really did conquer his foes when he bore the stone, the stone would be the cause. Such scenes might seem to show that these philosophers misunderstood literature by treating its events as true. They show instead, I argue, that by applying the same analytical techniques to literary and natural marvels, they dismiss the question of truth altogether. The marvels in literature are

81. Oresme, *De configurationibus* 2.32, ed. Clagett, *Nicole Oresme and the Medieval Geometry of Qualities and Motions*, 362: "'stimulos sub pectore vertit Apollo,' et statim sequitur, 'ut primum [cessit] furor et rabida ora quierunt.'" Trans. Clagett, 363. The lines are from the *Aeneid* 6.101–2.

82. Virgil, *Aeneid* 6.100, trans. Fairclough, *Eclogues, Georgics, and Aeneid 1–6*: "obscuris vera involvens."

83. Oresme, *De configurationibus* 2.32, ed. Clagett, *Nicole Oresme and the Medieval Geometry of Qualities and Motions*, 362: "ariolos in furorem vertens." The reference is to Is. 44:25.

as provisional as those in philosophy. Both are part of the same thought experiment: if such marvels are real, how would they work? In this case, the answer lies in subterranean vapors.

CRABS, MEDUSA, AND FOSSILS

A final example from Avicenna and Albertus Magnus shows powerfully how marvels bring natural objects into proximity with fictive ones. In his *Mineralium*, Albertus writes that "it seems wonderful to everyone" that fossils sometimes contain imprints of animal bodies inside them.[84] He begins, then, with an acknowledged marvel, a source of wonder, which he tries to explain with the aid of Avicenna: "Avicenna says that the cause of this is that animals, just as they are, are sometimes changed into stones."[85] The metamorphosis explains why the imprints of bodies and their organs remain visible inside stones after the bodies have decayed. Albertus elaborates on Avicenna's theory for a few sentences, explaining how, in the presence of a "petrifying power" (*vis . . . lapidificativa*), animals might revert to their base elements, namely, earth and water, and then transform into stones, which consist of the same elements.[86] Indeed, in the Latin translation of the relevant text, Avicenna writes, "certain vegetation and animals are turned into stones by a certain petrifying mineral power, and this happens in stony places."[87] The Arabic text is less conclusive: "if what is reported about the petrification of animals and vegetation is true, then it is because of the powerful strengthening of mineral petrification that happens in some stony places."[88] We see once again that medieval philosophers are game for considering the mechanisms of marvels without presupposing their truth.

84. Albertus Magnus, *Mineralium* 1.2.8, in *Opera omnia*, ed. Borgnet, 5:21: "Admirabile omnibus videtur."

85. Albertus Magnus, *Mineralium* 1.2.8, in *Opera omnia*, ed. Borgnet, 5:21: "hujus causam dicit Avicenna esse, quod animalia secundum se tota aliquando mutantur in lapides." Trans. Wyckoff, *Book of Minerals*, 52.

86. Albertus Magnus, *Mineralium* 1.2.8, in *Opera omnia*, ed. Borgnet, 5:21. Vincent of Beauvais also writes about a "virtute quadam minerali lapidificativa" and also depends on Avicenna (*Speculum naturale* 7.80, in *Speculum quadruplex*, 1:476A). On Vincent's sources for the passage, see Moureau, "Les sources alchimiques de Vincent de Beauvais," 86.

87. Avicenna, *De mineralibus*, in *De congelatione et conglutinatione lapidum*, ed. Holmyard and Mandeville, 46: "quedam vegetabilia et quedam animalia vertuntur in lapides virtute quadam minerali lapidificativa et fit in loco lapidoso."

88. Avicenna, *Kitāb al-shifā'*, in *De congelatione et conglutinatione lapidum*, ed. Holmyard and Mandeville, 74: "wa-in kāna mā yuḥkā min tuḥajjira ḥayawānun wa-nabātun ṣaḥīḥan, fa-l-sababu fīhi shaddatu quwwati maʿdinīyati maḥjirati yaḥdathu fi baʿḍi al-baqāʿi al-ḥajarīyati."

Both Albertus and Avicenna expand their focus, more or less overtly, beyond philosophy. In a famous tenth-century piece of travel literature, written nearly fifty years before Avicenna's birth and likely known by him, al-Masʿūdī tells a "well-known story" (*amruhu mustafīḍu*) about a species of crab: "if they leave the water with rapid movement and happen to reach land, they will become stones. No longer animals, they become stones instead."[89] Perhaps it is the sort of story that Avicenna has in mind, although he cites no source. Albertus is more specific. After describing the mechanism by which animals become stones, he writes, "attesting to this is the story [*fabula*] of Gorgon, who is said to have converted into stone those who looked upon her. They called a strong mineralizing power Gorgon, and with respect to her, they call Gorgon the disposition of the bodily humors toward the petrifying power [*virtutem lapidificativam*]. These, then, are all the statements that seem necessary about stones in general."[90] The first book of the treatise ends here, without further comment.

Gorgon is the family name of the three snake-haired daughters of Phorcus, Medusa among them. As the most famous sister, she became simply "Gorgon," whose power to transform her spectators into stone was a matter of common knowledge. A popular image in art and literature, she appealed to sculptors who carved her face into corbels and pillars, no doubt relishing the irony of turning stone into her head. She transformed not just people but natural objects into stone, and often into coral. Ovid, for instance, writes that Perseus "softens the ground with leaves, spreads twigs that float beneath the sea's surface, and then lays the head of Medusa, daughter of Phorcus, upon it."[91] The blood of the head hardens the twigs, and sea-nymphs replicate the marvel, scattering coral across the seas. Pliny writes that "Gorgonia is nothing but coral," which is soft in the sea but hard on land, and Solinus adds that "Metrodorus calls [coral] Gorgon."[92] Her association with coral, an animal typically included in medieval Latin lapi-

89. Al-Masʿūdī, *Kitāb murūdj adh-dhahab* 16, in *Les prairies d'or*, ed. de Meynard and de Courteille, 1:345: "fa-idhā abānu ʿan al-māʾi bi-surʿati ḥarakati wa-ṣāra ʿalā al-barri, ṣārat ḥijāratan, wa-zāla ʿanhā al-ḥayawāniyatu wa-yudakhkhilu tilka al-ḥijāratu."

90. Albertus Magnus, *Mineralium* 1.2.8, in *Opera omnia*, ed. Borgnet, 5:21: "Hoc autem testatur fabula Gorgonis, quae ad se respicientes dicitur convertisse in lapides. Gorgon virtutem fortem mineralium vocaverunt: respectum autem ad eam vocant dispositionem humorum corporum ad virtutem lapidificativam. Haec igitur sunt quae de lapidibus in communi videbantur dicenda." Trans. Wyckoff, *Book of Minerals*, 53.

91. Ovid, *Metamorphoses* 4.742–43, ed. Henderson, trans. Miller and Goold: "mollit humum foliis natasque sub aequore virgas / sternit et inponit Phorcynidos ora Medusae."

92. Pliny, *Historia naturalia* 37.59, in *Natural History*, ed. Eichholz, 10:296: "Gorgonia nihil aliud est quam curalium." Solinus, *Collectanea rerum memorabilium* 2.43, ed. Mommsen, 45: "Metrodorus gorgiam nominat."

daries, might influence Albertus's decision to include her in his discussion of minerals and stones.

It is worth noting that marvelous objects tend to have marvelous backstories. Often, stones that are created in exceptional ways exercise exceptional powers. Al-Masʿūdī tells us that the crabs that become stone, for instance, can be used for medicinal purposes, especially for ocular ailments. Coral is credited with protecting sailors, driving away insects, repelling enchantment, counteracting poison, and many other feats. Albertus, calling on Medusa, intensifies the marvelousness of the fossil.

Albertus calls the story of Gorgon a *fabula*, and yet her story witnesses (*testatur*) to the validity of Avicenna's account of fossils. But myth does not function as evidence, precisely. Rather, his interest lies in the similarity between philosophy and poetry. In the same way that Bradwardine gathers stories that might be thematically related to the parting of the Red Sea, so Albertus gathers those relating to the transformation of animals into stone. Also like Bradwardine, Albertus seems eager to locate parallels that cross generic and ontological boundaries. He shows that nature and poetry share a propensity to create unusual creatures, and their inventiveness is reflected in the creativity of Albertus's unintuitive comparison. Further, he writes that, as Gorgon turned people into stone, so Gorgon is also a stone-making power or the humoral disposition toward it. In other words, the petrifying power Gorgon is presumably strong in animals that turn into stone, which have an internal power that exerts a Gorgon-like force on them. The fossil is drawn into the realms of myth and metaphor because fossils resemble Gorgon as much as Gorgon resembles them. Naming nature's operations for her accentuates the similarity, as though Gorgon is nature's proclivity personified.

A related example shows how nature displays poetic power and creativity. The constellation Perseus contains a star called Gorgon's Head or *caput Gorgonis*, also known as Algol, probably from Arabic *al-ghūl*, the source of English "ghoul."[93] Being born under its sign was typically considered to be a bad omen. Albertus, for instance, elsewhere writes that when the stars rise "in Aries toward Gorgon's head . . . what is born will both be a man and not have the shape of a human body."[94] In other words, what is born will be a monster. The star does not turn people into stone, but it does make them

93. Algol can refer to the whole star cluster or, more often, to the key star, representing Medusa's eye. John Gower, for instance, calls the singular star "Algol" (*Confessio amantis* 7.1329, ed. Peck), and astronomers still refer to it by that name.

94. Albertus Magnus, *Problemata determinata* 35, ed. Weisheipl, 349–50: "in Ariete versus capud [*sic*] Gorgonis . . . natus et homo erit et figuram corporis humani non habebit."

misshapen. The powers that a mythological monster exercises become the powers that nature itself—its stones or its stars—exercises. Nature, then, is cast in Gorgon's role, with the power to make monsters, and with powers that are themselves monstrous, in its etymological sense. She displays her potency in these marvels.

Marvels thrive where boundaries are crossed and sources proliferate. In the fossil example, Albertus appeals to philosophy and mythology, geology and astronomy, Greeks and Muslims. He calls attention to the marvel's breadth of meanings and sources explicitly. The status of the created world as a marvel invites such diffuse references, as the unintuitive connections themselves reflect back on its marvelousness. Part of marvels' power to produce wonder, as we have seen many times, lies in their ability to make different kinds of things resemble each other. They are born of intersections, existing where one thing looks like something else, in spite of the barriers that would separate them. The philosophers who appeal to poetry's marvels make surprising comparisons deliberately, not because they fail to understand categorical differences, but because they are more interested in unlikely similarities. They suggest that there is order in the multiplicity of nature's creations and intention in its poetic spectacles.

[CHAPTER 4]

Imaginative Geography

The remaining chapters focus on marvels within medieval literature, beginning with travel literature.[1] Plentiful though they are in the genre, however, they are not alone. The most fabulous claims, like those about women who grow on trees and animals that rise from the dead, unapologetically sit alongside accurate descriptions of pilgrimage routes and topography.[2] The relatively staid material about geography, cultural customs, and history functions to keep marvels in a state of suspension, possibly real and possibly not. The deictics of travel literature—something of import happened on this rock, in this place, beneath this building, not far from here—insist on the accessibility and tangibility of the events they describe. They suggest that the whole of the text's content is equally visible. Strictly mundane or *mundus*-oriented topics serve to make the marvels they accompany more plausible, as spectacular marvels make geography more wonderful. As we have seen, everything in creation can be called marvelous, and travel literature takes advantage of the narrow definition to support the broad one: the most startling marvels show that creation as a whole is marvelous. In this respect, travel literature best typifies the reciprocal realism that I described in the introduction: the "real" is enlivened by imagined people and places as strongly as imaginative creations are fortified by real things.

The combination of stories about dragons and cyclopes with precise geographies and heartfelt calls for crusade has created an obstacle for schol-

1. The phrase "imaginative geography," used as the title of this chapter, has received a good deal of scholarly attention, with competing interpretations. Suzanne Akbari discusses its meaning for Edward Said and Michel Foucault before offering her own view, which reads imaginative geography not as "a universally accepted 'truth,' but rather [as] a discourse that is continually in the process of being articulated and thus creating, as it were, its own truth" (*Idols in the East*, 14). I here focus literally on the imaginative quality of medieval travel literature and its indebtedness to the faculty of imagination.

2. Throughout this chapter, I use "travel narrative," "travel literature" and related phrases interchangeably. For efforts to define and distinguish among them, see Legassie, *Medieval Invention of Travel*, 16–18; and Phillips, *Before Orientalism*, 51–52.

ars trying to pinpoint the genre of travel literature.[3] It also raises questions about the response of readers: was such information equally believable?[4] On one end of the spectrum, a text like *Mandeville's Travels* might be understood as "realistic prose fiction," or as expressing travel literature's "unavoidable kinship with fiction."[5] From this general perspective, travel literature, or at least some of it, is fiction or proto-fiction that anticipates the novel and science fiction.[6] On the other end, and more popular now, is the opinion that a text like the *Devisement* "was accepted for its facts; it was perceived as an account of actual events."[7] Thus the readers of Johannes Witte de Hese's *Itinerarius* "accepted it as a source of generally factual information."[8] This is a version of the medieval age of faith thesis, which holds that people in the medieval Latin West accepted claims more credulously than their successors.[9]

There is a great deal of room for intermediate positions and some effort to claim them, as when Mary Campbell locates the monsters of travel literature "somewhere *between* the symbolic and the actual."[10] As the quotation suggests, marvels tend to be the real focus of scholarly comments about credibility. What inspires doubt is less whether India is where a writer says it is than whether Pygmies or griffins live there. Each conditions our response to the other, and each merits investigation. In other words, how Pygmies color our response to geographical information about India is just as good a question as the inverse. My position is that travel literature deliberately places easily believable claims alongside those that are harder

3. For example, Tamarah Kohanski and David Benson write that *Mandeville's Travels* possesses "a generic complexity that makes it difficult to define or categorize (it is not genuine history or anthropology, of course, but not really literature or theology in the usual sense)"; *The Book of John Mandeville*, 2.

4. On this question, specifically with respect to *Mandeville's Travels*, see Higgins, *Writing East*, 8–14. On the believability of eyewitness claims in medieval travel literature, see Frisch, *The Invention of the Eyewitness*, 41–60.

5. Campbell, *The Witness and the Other World*, 123; and Zumthor, "Dire le voyage au Moyen Âge," 86.

6. Zumthor sees science fiction as a distant relative of travel literature ("Dire le voyage au Moyen Âge," 93). See also Frye, *Secular Scripture*, 5.

7. Yeager, "The World Translated," 159. Kim Phillips distinguishes between English readers of the *Devisement*, who "seem to have treated the book as a serious factual account with moral value," and others (*Before Orientalism*, 37). She bases this claim on the work's inclusion in manuscripts that contain philosophical works and histories, but as this book shows, marvels often cross from philosophy and history to romance and back again without needing to be true.

8. Westrem, *Broader Horizons*, 11. Cited in Phillips, *Before Orientalism*, 46.

9. On the perduring myth of the medieval age of faith, see Justice, "Did the Middle Ages Believe in Their Miracles?"

10. Campbell, *The Witness and the Other World*, 79, original emphasis.

to believe. Such hybridity had long been a feature of geographies and histories in the West, dating back to Pliny, Strabo, Ctesias, and Herodotus. Classical teratological writings (from Greek *téras*, "portent" or "marvel") are a common source for both traditions.[11] The texts cobble together an assortment of what might now appear to be unlike things and compress them into a whole, and I would argue that their components are not so much mismatched as productively heterogeneous. They help to mark out the range of what is possible for nature, allowing its most spectacular features to resonate in its most mundane ones. We have seen that medieval writers tended not to distinguish categorically between facts and legends, which means that the marvels of literature and those of natural philosophy were able to coexist alongside one another. A possible consequence is that readers did not worry overmuch about filing content into one category or the other. They might even have enjoyed not knowing with certainty where the line between the real and the invented ought to be placed.[12]

This chapter draws both on Arabic travel narratives, or geographies as they are more often called, and on Latin ones, though they seem not to have shared many readers. One Arabic geography is known to have been translated into Castilian, the *Kitāb al-jaghʿrāfīya* from the twelfth-century Andalusian geographer al-Zuhrī. Only one manuscript of the translation survives, from the fifteenth century.[13] There is more evidence that Arabic geography in the narrow sense, sometimes referred to as mathematical geography, influenced writers in the Latin West.[14] No Arabic translation of travel literature from the Latin West is known to exist. Indeed, apart from Orosius's *Histories*, some translations of the Psalms, and a handful of other texts from al-Andalus, Latin works seem not to have been translated into Arabic during the Middle Ages.[15]

There is a decent chance that an expatriate and polyglot like Marco Polo might have encountered some Arabic travel literature, but its value does not depend on its presence in the hands of Christians. The similarities between the two bodies of literature are overwhelming, including their joint fascination with distant places, their preoccupation with marvels, and

11. See, for instance, Tornesello, "From Reality to Legend," which focuses on Persian sources.

12. For a fuller discussion of this reading, see my "Possibilities of Medieval Fiction."

13. See Bramon, *El mundo en el siglo XII*, for a modern Castilian translation of the Arabic text as well as an edition of the sole surviving Castilian manuscript. I thank Travis Zadeh for pointing me to this text.

14. There is a good deal of debate on this issue. A balanced account is provided by Dalché, "Géographie arabe et géographie latine."

15. Burnett, "The Translating Activity in Medieval Spain," 1037. See also Sahner, "From Augustine to Islam."

the similarity of the techniques they use to analyze them.[16] To study both together is inevitably to raise the topics of Orientalism and (post)colonialism, which often focus on travel literature when they are taken up by medievalists.[17] It is not possible simply to reverse perspectives and study Muslim, Jewish, or other perspectives on Christians alongside Christian perspectives on them. As Martin Jacobs notes, no piece of Hebrew travel literature in the period describes Christian Europe, and with the exception of al-Andalus, that is often the case with travel literature from Islamic communities as well.[18] One medieval map produced in eleventh-century Cairo shows England (called *Inqilṭirra*), the earliest surviving map to designate England with that name, but Western Europe was not their focus.[19]

Those who are familiar with Arabic travel literature only from Ibn Baṭṭūṭa's fourteenth-century *Travels* might mistake an exception for the rule. He takes some interest in marvels, but more consistently focuses on his own experiences and the stories he hears about various noteworthy people. The text is anecdotal and conversational, whereas the genre more often focuses on geography and assorted oddities in the world, much like the travel literature of the Latin West. Arabic travel literature blossomed following the Umayyad expansion of the Islamic empire, which opened up routes between Europe and China for the first time since the fall of the Roman empire. Travelers like Sallām and Ibn Faḍlān were able to take advantage of the new accessibility of distant lands. For the Latin West, travel literature grew most markedly following the rise of the Mongolian empire in the thirteenth century. The *pax mongolica* similarly opened up paths for trade and diplomatic missions, as the Mongols came to oversee the whole of the silk road. Merchants like Marco Polo and Christian missionaries like William of Rubruck and John of Plano Carpini traveled east to sell their wares, suss out potential enemies to Christendom, identify weaknesses

16. Several scholars have called for Arabic works to be included more often in studies of medieval travel literature produced in the Latin West; see, for example, Kinoshita, "Reorientations," 40–41. On the need for medievalists to work across languages more broadly, see Gaunt, "Can the Middle Ages Be Postcolonial?"

17. The scholarship on this topic is considerable. One might begin with Akbari, *Idols in the East*, 5–11; Phillips, *Before Orientalism*, 4–27; Cohen, ed., *The Postcolonial Middle Ages*; and Lampert-Weissig, ed., *Medieval Literature and Postcolonial Studies.*

18. Jacobs, *Reorienting the East*, 4. Chinese travel literature is similarly focused; see Campany, *Strange Writing.*

19. Rapoport and Savage-Smith, *Lost Maps of the Caliphs*, 23. The fact that this first appearance of England is written in Arabic bears stressing, since it rightly signals the authority and learnedness of Islamic cultures in the period. The map is part of a work that was only rediscovered in 2000. An edition of the manuscript, with English translation, has been edited by Rapoport and Savage-Smith, *An Eleventh-Century Egyptian Guide to the Universe.*

they might exploit, or try to convert Mongols to their side.[20] When they wrote about their travels, they included tales about marvels they heard or saw.

That the stories were not usually translated in either direction is to be expected. They are partisan and self-promoting, and translation would have been inconvenient to the purpose of either.[21] Each portrays the world as full of messages for its people uniquely, committed to its own religion's specialness. Christian authors write about balm, for instance, as a nearly magical substance thought capable of healing and preserving bodies, but only cultivatable by them.[22] Similarly, as we saw in Bradwardine's *De causa Dei*, Christian writers claim that Genghis Khan received a vision from God with instructions that allowed him to conquer western lands then held by Muslims.[23] They cast Genghis as a Christian proxy, wresting lands away from Christians' great enemies and keeping alive the hope of eventual Mongol conversion to Christianity. Indeed, such texts have Mongols predict their own eventual conquest and conversion.[24] They subscribe to the notion of a Christian manifest destiny, as though Christian expansion is not just right but ordained. History is skewed in the favor of Christians, and nature will deliver its bounty to them.[25]

An alternative manifest destiny expresses itself in stories such as the following by Ibn Khurdādbih: when the Arabs conquered Spain and entered

20. Shirin Khanmohamadi notes that this period of exploration was brought to an end by the fall of Acre (1291), the conversion of Persian Mongols to Islam (starting in 1316), and the Ming conquest of the Mongols of China (1368); Khanmohamadi, *In Light of Another's Word*, 113.

21. A good deal of recent scholarship has emphasized the "cosmopolitan" or relatively open-minded perspective of travel literature from the Latin West. See, for instance, Khanmohamadi, *In Light of Another's Word*; Heng, *Medieval Invention of Race*, 287–416; Lochrie, "Provincializing Medieval Europe"; Akbari, *Idols in the East*; and Ganim and Legassie, eds., *Cosmopolitanism and the Middle Ages*. It is occasionally open-minded, and often not. It is, however, regularly partisan.

22. See Truitt, "The Virtues of Balm in Late Medieval Literature." For the claim that Christians alone can cultivate it, see Jacques de Vitry, *Historia orientalis* 86, ed. Donnadieu, 346; and *Mandeville's Travels* 7, ed. Deluz, 153.

23. See, for example, Hayton of Corycus, *Flos historiarum* 3.6, ed. Dulaurier et al., 152; and *Mandeville's Travels* 24, ed. Deluz, 383. According to the scribe's note at the end of the text, Hayton dictated the *Flos* in French and it was then translated into Latin (*Flos historiarum*, 253). I therefore cite the French text, but the Latin translation has the same book and chapter divisions.

24. John of Plano Carpini says that they know they will be conquered, but not by whom (*Historia Mongolorum* 5.19, ed. Menestò, *Storia dei Mongoli*, 264). *Mandeville's Travels* also mentions their future conversion, cap. 26, ed. Deluz, 409.

25. That is, if they prove worthy. For the common idea that Christians' sins were the impediment that kept them from claiming the Holy Land, see Jacques de Vitry, *Historia orientalis* 1, ed. Donnadieu, 96; and *Mandeville's Travels* 15, ed. Deluz, 279.

Toledo, they found two marvelous buildings, one of which had been sealed with twenty-four locks. It was supposed to remain closed, its contents unknown, but the conquerors learned that the last Christian king of Spain opened it in spite of his bishops' warnings. Inside, he found images of Arabs on horseback, "with their turbans and sandals, their bows and arrows."[26] Ibn Khurdādbih points to features that identify the conquerors as both Arabs (turbans and sandals) and warriors (bows and arrows), so that his readers might reach the same conclusion. Because "this happened in the same year as the invasion of the country by the Arabs," Ibn Khurdādbih suggests that the king's incursion caused the invasion and Spanish defeat.[27] Making the greedy king responsible for his own loss, the marvel of the locked building shows that the land belonged to the Arabs even before their victory. History resolves in favor of Arab domination, making the Islamic conquest of Iberia merely one step in the unfolding of God's plan.

Likewise, in his cosmography, the thirteenth-century Syrian geographer al-Dimashqī describes a type of fish in the waters near Constantinople that bears an inscription: "on their back is written in Arabic, 'there is no god but God,' and between their gills in the rear is written, 'Muḥammad is the messenger of God.'"[28] Tattooed with the *shahāda,* this species of fish testifies to the future conquest of Constantinople, which was under periodic attack by Ottomans and others at the time when al-Dimashqī wrote the text, but was still in the hands of Christians. With his recognizably Muslim fish, inscribed with Arabic text, al-Dimashqī suggests that the area is destined to become part of their empire. It is a literal message meant for Constantinople's future conquerors, the people who will be able to read it. He continues with another species of fish in the vicinity whose appearance is a good omen. "Fishermen are blessed by them," and for that reason they release them back into the sea if they catch them.[29] Good fortune and freedom will prevail here. Marvels as well as nature itself call for the expansion of the empire, as though they are biased toward it.

26. Ibn Khurdādbih, *Kitāb al-masālik wa-'l-mamālik,* ed. de Goeje and Sezgin, 157: "bi-ʿamā'imihum wa-niʿālihum wa-qassiyahum wa-nablihum." French trans., 118.

27. Ibn Khurdādbih, *Kitāb al-masālik wa-'l-mamālik,* ed. de Goeje and Sezgin, 157: "fa-dakhalat al-ʿarabu baladahum fī al-sanati allatī fatḥun fīhā dhālika al-bābi." French trans., 118.

28. Al-Dimashqī, *Nukhbat al-dahr fī ʿajā'ib al-barr wa-l-baḥr* 5.4, ed. Mehren, 144: "maktūbun ʿalā ẓahrihā bi-l-ʿarabīyati, lā ilaha illā allāhu, wa-maktūbun bayna udhnaynihā min khalfin, muḥammadun rasūlu allāhi." French trans. Mehren, *Cosmographie,* 190. Arabic was sometimes considered to be the lingua franca of all species; Ouyang, "Solomon's Ring," 457.

29. Al-Dimashqī, *Nukhbat al-dahr* 5.4, ed. Mehren, 144: "wa-yatabāraku bi-hā al-ṣayyādūna." French trans. Mehren, *Cosmographie,* 190.

Muslims and Christians were aware of the competing traditions. Ibn Baṭṭūṭa writes that, according to Christians, the destroyers of a church in Damascus would be stricken with madness, but no harm came to the Muslims who converted it into a mosque, and so "God gave the lie to the assertion of the Greeks."[30] A story meant to confirm Christian authority ends up undermining it. Similarly, also in the fourteenth century, William of Boldensele rejects a story that the corpse of Muḥammad hung suspended in the air "through the power of the rock that draws iron, as is falsely claimed."[31] Not susceptible to the power of magnets, he was rather elevated by perfectly mundane means, through the aid of other men. We saw in the previous chapter that the magnet was often used to make other marvels more believable. In the report that William rejects, it literally supports a more ambitious marvel, what is from his perspective simple subterfuge. Even without the translation of such texts across cultures, we find efforts to disprove each other's claims. Presumably there was no appetite to rebut more of them.

MARVELS AND THE QUESTION OF CONVICTION

Marvels are a fixed feature of medieval travel literature, a fact so well-known that it finds itself tucked into subordinate clauses, as when Geraldine Heng refers casually to the "fantastical marvels expected of travel literature."[32] Authors advertise in their opening leaves the marvels to come. For example, the Franciscan Odoric of Pordenone, whose fourteenth-century account of his trip to visit the Mongol Khan survives in more than one hundred manuscripts, introduces his text with the promise, "I can truly rehearse many great things and marvels."[33] Likewise, the prologue to Marco Polo and Rustichello of Pisa's *Devisement du monde* declares that Marco thought "it would be too great an evil if he did not cause all the marvels that he saw to be written down."[34] These authors are hardly distinctive in this respect. Travel was thought to reveal marvels; that was

30. Ibn Baṭṭūṭa, *Riḥla*, ed. Defrémery and Sanguinetti, *Voyages*, 1.199: "wa-akdhaba allāhu zaʿma al-rūmi." French trans. on same page.

31. William of Boldensele, *Liber de quibusdam ultramarinis partibus* 3, ed. Deluz, 218: "per virtutem petre que ferrum trahit ut false divulgatum est." This remains an understudied text, even though it is an important source for *Mandeville's Travels*.

32. Heng, *Invention of Race*, 351.

33. Odoric of Pordenone, *Relatio* 1, ed. van den Wyngaert, 413: "multa magna et mirabilia . . . possum veraciter enarrare." Trans. Yule, *The Travels of Friar Odoric*, 63.

34. Marco Polo and Rustichello of Pisa, *Devisement* 1, ed. Ronchi, *Milione*, 306: "tropo seroit grant maus se il ne feist metre en ecriture toutes les granç mervoilles qu'il vit." I treat Marco Polo and his scribe Rustichello as co-authors, as is now scholarly conven-

one of its great benefits. So firmly wedded are the two that Jacques de Vitry, in his chronicle of the Holy Land that also served as a source text for later travel literature, modeled himself after the marvel-witnessing traveler. As bishop of Acre from 1216 to 1225, Jacques was intimately familiar with parts of the Holy Land, and he adopts the role of guide when he introduces readers to its marvels. He defends his decision to include them by appealing to St. Brendan, the sixth-century Irish saint who spent seven years seeking the promised land of the saints and found no shortage of marvels along the way. As Brendan traveled "in order that he might see *the marvels of God in the deep*," so Jacques will tell his reader about an assortment of marvels, including such phenomena as earthquakes, special stones and plants, and monstrous peoples.[35] By taking Brendan as his model, he makes reading equivalent to a sort of exploration. To encounter the world abroad, whether through travel or through reading, meant encountering marvels, and travelers were expected to return with tales. The Sultan in Chaucer's *Man of Law's Tale* is therefore eager to talk to merchants after they travel abroad "for to leere / The wondres that they mighte seen or heere."[36]

We have seen that natural philosophers were rarely dogmatic about the marvels they examined, and the same is often true of the writers of travel literature. Jacques de Vitry recognizes the implausibility of various marvels, such as the trees of the sun and the moon that prophesy to Alexander the Great. First drawing a parallel with Balaam's speaking ass, which shows that human speech sometimes comes from an unlikely source, Jacques then offers his opinion that the trees are inhabited by demons. Still, he insists on humility: "we are ignorant and unable to comment in this work on the most precious medicinal and aromatic trees which God placed from the beginning in the garden of pleasure, in the most distant, elevated, and temperate parts of the orient."[37] Alexander, in other words, might have visited the earthly paradise, or something like it, and who is Jacques to say what sorts of trees might grow there?[38] Notice how reluctant he is to

---

tion. I cite the Franco-Italian version of the text, which is widely thought to be the earliest. The English translation is based on Moule and Pelliot, *Description of the World*, 1:73.

35. Jacques de Vitry, *Historia orientalis* 83, ed. Donnadieu, 336: "ut videret *mirabilia Deo in profundo*." The quotation is from Ps 106:24.

36. Chaucer, *The Man of Law's Tale*, 181–82, ed. Benson, *Riverside Chaucer*.

37. Jacques de Vitry, *Historia orientalis* 87, ed. Donnadieu, 350: "Illas autem preciossisimas medicinales et aromaticas arbores, quas Dominus in extremis et excelsis et termperantissimis orientis partibus ab initio plantavit in horto voluptatis, presenti opusculo tanquam ignotas inferere non valemus."

38. Gervase of Tilbury likewise speaks of the trees of the sun and moon in the context of the tree of life (*Otia imperialia* 1.15, ed. Banks and Binns, 82–84).

discount the story outright, explaining how, through demons, it might be true, and giving a biblical precedent for nonhuman speech. He relays the marvel without making a judgment about it, but like al-Jāḥiẓ and al-Mas'ūdī, who were cited in the previous chapter, he encourages a willingness to believe. Jacques later punctuates a list of monstrous races with the stipulation: "if they perhaps seem incredible to anyone, we compel nobody to believe them; everyone is well-supplied with their own sense. We think there is no danger in believing those things that are not contrary to faith or good conduct."[39] He recalls Augustine, writing that there is a "sort of text that is not to be read as though one is required to believe it, but rather the reader has freedom of judgment."[40] What they describe is not Coleridge's willing suspension of disbelief, but a weaker willingness to entertain possibilities. Jacques recognizes that such willingness is chosen, contingent, and revocable. The contrast with belief as it pertains to matters of faith is explicit: in the case of marvels, a lower grade of assent is not just allowed but incumbent on the reader.[41] The stakes are lower.

The prolific writer and traveler al-Mas'ūdī provides another example. After surveying different stories about dragons—perhaps they are the result of winds that, ascending from the depths of the water into the air, curl in on themselves, or perhaps one particular dragon is an actual creature, exiled to the land of Gog and Magog, providing sustenance for inhabitants there—he returns to an earlier discussion of tides.[42] They might be explained, he writes, by an angel who steps into the far reaches of the Sea of China, thereby creating high tide, and then retracts their foot, making the water ebb.[43] Immediately afterward, he writes, "The things we have described are neither impossible nor necessarily so, but rather belong to the category of that which is possible and admissible, because they are transmitted by individuals and are attested only by them. They are not found

39. Jacques de Vitry, *Historia orientalis* 92, ed. Donnadieu, 406: "si forte alicui incredibilia videantur, nos neminem compellimus ad credendum, unusquisque in suo sensu abundet. Ea tamen credere contra fidem non sunt vel bonos mores, nullum periculum estimamus."

40. Augustine, *Contra Faustum* 11.5, in *De utilitate credendi*, ed. Zycha, 320: "genus litterarum non cum credendi necessitate, sed cum iudicandi libertate legendum est." Vincent of Beauvais cites this passage in *Speculum naturale*, Pro.11, in *Speculum quadruplex*, 1:9D.

41. Jacques contrasts the two in *Historia orientalis* 92, ed. Donnadieu, 406.

42. Al-Mas'ūdī, *Kitāb murūdj adh-dhahab* 14, ed. de Meynard and de Courteille, with French trans., 1:266–68.

43. Al-Mas'ūdī, *Kitāb murūdj adh-dhahab* 14, ed. and trans. de Meynard and de Courteille, 1:270.

within the accounts transmitted through uninterrupted chains with authoritative and well-dispersed sources."[44] In other words, these are one-off reports, and for that reason they stand in contrast to well-attested sayings passed down according to an uninterrupted chain of transmitters, or *isnād*. Such sayings are not dismissible; one is required to believe the knowledge they transmit (*al-akhbār al-mūjabat al-ʿilm*).[45] A practice derived from Jewish scholars and begun in Islamic communities in the seventh century, the building of *isnād* from the most authoritative sources became a standard feature of Arabic writings. Anyone who spends time with classical Arabic texts quickly becomes familiar with the "according to z, according to y, according to x" chains, ideally ending with Muḥammad, that introduce authoritative statements.[46] In this passage, al-Masʿūdī expressly contrasts tales of dragons and the angel-based theory of the tides with the writings of sharia, or legal texts.[47] It is a stark distinction between what must be believed and what can harmlessly be entertained. Again we see that the stakes are low when it comes to marvels. Insofar as they encourage one to marvel at creation, they serve a useful purpose, but they are not meant to be matters of firm conviction.

Jacques de Vitry's and al-Masʿūdī's inclination to give marvels the benefit of the doubt is based above all on the conviction that creation is marvelous, as we have seen, and their unwillingness to foreclose possibilities should not be mistaken for certainty. Al-Masʿūdī provides further evidence that he thought the angel-based theory of tides simply impossible to evaluate. He earlier surveyed several theories about the tides at some length.[48] The tides had attracted considerable philosophical attention in the preceding century, most notably in Abū Maʿshar's *Kitāb al-mudkhal al-kabīr*, an introduction to astronomy that was translated into Latin twice during the Middle Ages. As Pierre Duhem writes, "one could say that, from this book, all the Latin Middle Ages learned the laws of the ebb and flow of the sea,"

44. Al-Masʿūdī, *Kitāb murūdj adh-dhahab* 14, ed. and trans. de Meynard and de Courteille, 1:270–71: "wa-mā dhakarnā fa-ghayru mumtaniʿi kunuhu wa-lā wājibu, wa-huwa dākhilun fī hayyizi al-mumkini wa-l-jāʾizi, li-anna ṭarīqahā fī-l-naqli ṭarīqu al-afrādi wa-l-āḥādi wa-lam yarid min khabari majīʾi al-mutawātrīna min al-makhbarīna wa-l-istafāḍati."

45. Al-Masʿūdī, *Kitāb murūdj adh-dhahab* 14, ed. and trans. de Meynard and de Courteille, 1:271.

46. On the development of *isnād*, see Touati, *Islam et voyage au Moyen Âge*, 44–53.

47. Al-Masʿūdī, *Kitāb murūdj adh-dhahab* 14, ed. and trans. de Meynard and de Courteille, 1:271.

48. See al-Masʿūdī, *Kitāb murūdj adh-dhahab* 11, ed. and trans. de Meynard and de Courteille, 1:244–55.

especially insofar as they focused on the moon.[49] However, al-Mas'ūdī's focused treatment of the tides does not include the possibility of angelic intervention. He instead isolates that possibility and places it in the context of a separate discussion of unknowables. The theological character of the theory might have provided further motivation for the distinction. As the Andalusian al-Gharnāṭī wrote, "the prophet . . . asked God about the ebb and flow of the sea, and he answered . . . 'There is an angel in the depths of the sea and when he puts his foot in it, the sea rises, and when he lifts it, the sea falls.' God knows best."[50] The final sentence is al-Gharnāṭī's stock disclaimer, easy to find in al-Qazwīnī's *'Ajā'ib* and other texts as well, affirming humility when making any debatable claim. Al-Mas'ūdī wrote centuries before him, but he might well have shared al-Gharnāṭī's belief that this is a theological question better suited to divine rather than human understanding. It is a possibility that cannot be investigated or substantiated, and so al-Mas'ūdī leaves the reader to their own judgment.

MARVELS IN THE HOLY LAND

One of the features of marvels that comes across more clearly in literature than philosophy is their mercurial nature. They are shape-shifters, subject to revisions major or minor by the authors who reinterpret them. I begin with a marvel rooted in biblical history that shows both how marvels can be repurposed and how they keep biblical history alive. In both respects, the literal truth of the marvel is relatively unimportant. It has a symbolic, interpretive relationship to the biblical past that keeps it vivid in the present. As we saw in Bradwardine's *De causa Dei*, miracles often act as a foundation for marvels, though here in a geographical as well as a thematic sense. Land with biblical significance has almost mythical power that expresses itself through the marvels that endure. As Katharine Park has noted, travel writers tend to assume that certain marvels are only possible in certain places. In this respect, they agree with natural philosophers who thought that the particular constellation of astrological and other influences in one place

49. Duhem, *Le système du monde*, 2:369. See also Lemay, *Abu Ma'shar and Latin Aristotelianism.*

50. Abū Ḥāmid al-Gharnāṭī, *Al-mu'rib* 3.1, ed. Bejarano, 17: "wa-qad su'ilu rasūlun allāha . . . 'an al-maddi wa-l-jazari, fa-qāla . . . malikun 'alā qāmūsi al-baḥri idhā qaḍa'a rijlahu fīhi, fāḍa, wa-idhā rafa'ahu, ghāḍa, wa-allāhu ā'lamu." Castilian translation in same edition, 70. Al-Gharnāṭī seems more confident than Mas'ūdī regarding the transmission of this idea from the time of Muḥammad. An anonymous Arabic text that survives in a twelfth-century manuscript, *The Book of the Ebb and the Flow*, contains a similar passage. See Martínez Martín, "Teorías sobre las mareas según un manuscrito arabe del siglo XII," 180.

was different from that in another, with the result that marvels were often not transportable, and perhaps also explaining why the "cabinet of wonders" or "curiosities" phenomenon was not a medieval one.[51] In the case of biblical miracles, place is doubly important, since the land on which they occurred pulses with residual force, powering marvels that are allusive and interpretive. Through their reworkability, they suggest that the land retains special, if diminished, dynamism and vitality.

This section and the next privilege *Mandeville's Travels*, a text written in the mid-fourteenth century and seemingly composed in Anglo-Norman by someone who may or may not have been named Mandeville.[52] Although the attribution of authorship is a live question, I will refer to the author as Mandeville for convenience. The text presents in many ways the clearest example of supposed subterfuge by a writer of travel literature. For Iain Higgins, for instance, *Mandeville's Travels* is one of "many medieval texts that violate the good faith" of readers "by presenting as true what is only partly so, or not even so."[53] He adds, "It must be admitted that the text engages in much deception."[54] "Deception" suggests that Mandeville willfully and culpably misled his reader, as though the immense popularity of the text—it survives in more than three hundred manuscripts—was unfairly won.[55] The unusually emotional language that scholars direct at Mandeville suggests the seriousness of his apparent fraud. The consummate armchair traveler, he cobbled together sources for material that he presents as eyewitness reports. As a result, the difference between what *Mandeville's Travels* actually is (a compilation and amplification of the work of other writers) and what it claims to be (a faithful account of the author's own travels) is stark. It presents an extreme case of the medieval tendency to write imaginatively about geography, and for that reason, it merits special attention. An argument that accounts for it can potentially account for less exceptional cases as well.

Many travel writers and chroniclers share marvels connected to the Dead Sea, which is no surprise, given its biblical significance and the unusual properties its high salinity gives it. It is alternately associated with life and death. According to Jacques de Vitry, for instance, "no living thing

51. Park, "Meanings of Natural Diversity," 140–43. Al-Kindī's theory of rays explains the unique conditions in any given place, as I discuss in chapter 2. See particularly his *De radiis* 2, ed. D'Alverny and Hudry, 219. On marvels and collecting, see Bynum, "Wonder."

52. A thorough overview is provided by Deluz, *Le livre de Jehan de Mandeville*, 1–72. For a more recent discussion, see Higgins, *Book of John Mandeville*, ix–xxiii.

53. Higgins, *Writing East*, 75.

54. Higgins, *Writing East*, 75.

55. Referring to the Middle English versions, Ralph Hanna calls the text "the most popular piece of nonreligious Middle English prose" ("Mandeville," 221).

can be generated in it, and nothing having life can be submerged in it."[56] It can neither give life nor take it. According to Mandeville, it is called dead because "neither man nor beast possessing life can die in this sea, and this has been proven many times when men who deserved death were thrown into it and remained in it for three or four days, but they could not die because it retains nothing that has life in it."[57] Note that its preservation of life is not benevolent or just—men who *deserved death* were unable to die in it—but rather, it rejects life as though life were inassimilable to it. Odoric of Pordenone has the sea more or less swallow the living, writing: "if anyone walks near its shore and falls into the water, he will never be found."[58] Burchard of Mount Sion likens it to the mouth of hell.[59] They all imagine the Dead Sea as an abyss not so much protecting life as rejecting it, whether by refusing to kill those who enter into it or by killing them instantly. The sea's antagonism toward life even extends to its shores, which produce fruit trees whose fruit is filled with ash.[60] The water from the sea hydrates trees whose fruit cannot be eaten, sustenance that cannot sustain life, in another way showing animus toward the living. Burchard will not allow that anything grows around it, not even grass, not even up in the mountains, because its fumes are noxious.[61] The flexibility in the details shows that the marvel is itself a living thing, reinterpretable and therefore renewable, but all of the accounts are thematically linked.

All four authors identify the ultimate cause of such unusual behavior: the sins of Sodom and Gomorrah. Immediately after describing the ashen fruit, Jacques writes, "God rained down fire and sulfur over Sodom and Gomorrah and three other cities."[62] For Jacques, because the Dead Sea is close to the five destroyed cities, its marvels are closely linked to their sins.

56. Jacques de Vitry, *Historia orientalis* 53, ed. Donnadieu, 224: "nihil vivum in eo generatur nec aliquid habens in eo submergi valet."

57. Mandeville, *Le livre des merveilles du monde* 12, ed. Deluz, 226: "ne homme ne beste qe ad en luy vie ne poroit morir en cel mer, et ceo ad esté prové mointe foiz qe home jectoit dedeinz gentz qe avoient deservy mort et demor roient III jours ou IIII, mes ils ne poaient morir qar elle ne retient nulle chose qe ait en luy vie." Trans. Higgins, *Book of John Mandeville*, 61.

58. Odoric of Pordenone, *Relatio* 14.3, ed. van den Wyngaert, 449: "si aliquis iuxta ipsius ripam vadit et cadit in aquam, nunquam talis ille invenitur." Trans. Yule, *Travels of Friar Odoric*, 109.

59. Burchard of Mount Sion, *Descriptio terrae sanctae* 6, ed. Laurent, 59.

60. Jacques de Vitry, *Historia orientalis* 53, ed. Donnadieu, 224; and Mandeville, *Le livre des merveilles du monde* 12, ed. Deluz, 226. Trans. Higgins, *Book of John Mandeville*, 61.

61. Burchard of Mount Sion, *Descriptio terrae sanctae* 6, ed. Laurent, 59–60.

62. Jacques de Vitry, *Historia orientalis* 53, ed. Donnadieu, 224: "Dominus enim ignem et sulphur pluit super Sodomam et Gomorram et alias tres civitates."

Physical proximity is made conceptual, in other words, through these marvels. Burchard of Mount Sion is explicit: the barrenness around the sea "is certainly a dreadful judgment of God, who has punished the sins of the people of Sodom for so many centuries that even the land itself has been paying the price."[63] The land suffers guilt by association and speaks back through its marvels, making a monument to its own injury. That the men of Sodom are specifically represented by trees that cannot support life and a sea that is hostile to it is both meaningful and homophobic. Both authors read homosexuality as corrupting the instinct for generation and use it to account for marvels that pervert nature. Mandeville adds the detail that the fruits are "very beautiful and their color is beautiful to see and they seem fully ripe."[64] They seduce but disappoint those who succumb and take a bite. Forbidden fruits, they are reminiscent of original sin, and so they represent not only desire that has escaped its bounds but also disobedience.

Various details, as regarding the Dead Sea's stillness and innocuousness, hark back to biblical miracle. Mandeville tells us that the Dead Sea is called dead because "it does not run."[65] This likely alludes to the Israelites' crossing into the Promised Land, as the book of Joshua describes it. When the priests bearing the ark touched the river Jordan with their feet, it temporarily stopping flowing, and specifically stopped flowing into the Dead Sea (Jo 3:16).[66] This miracle helped to protect the Israelites from drowning, which likely accounts for the claim that nobody can drown in the Dead Sea even in the present. The Sodomites reverse the value of the initial miracle, making the sea not so much respectful of life as antagonistic toward it. Mandeville adds the detail that feathers sink and iron floats in the Dead Sea, acting contrary to their natures and marking the sea's power as inversion.[67] The Sodomites sinned "against nature" (*contre nature*) and were, according to Jacques, "enemies of nature" (*hostes naturae*), so nature, through these reversals, condemns them.[68] Mandeville amplifies and inter-

63. Burchard of Mount Sion, *Descriptio terrae sanctae* 6, ed. Laurent, 59–60: "Et est tremendum pro certo Dei iudicium, qui per tot secula annorum peccatum adeo persequitur Sodomorum, quod eciam terra ipsa penas soluit." Trans. Pringle, *Description of the Holy Land*, 283.

64. Mandeville, *Le livre des merveilles du monde* 12, ed. Deluz, 226: "pommes très beles et de bele color a regarder et toutes maures par semblant."

65. Mandeville, *Le livre des merveilles du monde* 12, ed. Deluz, 226: "elle ne court point."

66. As Shayne Legassie notes, Burchard insists specifically that the Jordan flows into the Dead Sea (*Medieval Invention of Travel*, 149).

67. Mandeville, *Le livre des merveilles du monde* 12, ed. Deluz, 226.

68. Mandeville, *Le livre des merveilles du monde* 12, ed. Deluz, 226; and Jacques de Vitry, *Historia orientalis* 53, ed. Donnadieu, 224.

prets the biblical miracle through such marvels, which assure the reader that the land does not forget.

Some of the same techniques appear in Mandeville's account of a well in Samaria. Jacques de Vitry describes it at the beginning of his section on marvelous bodies of water: a well both "wonderful and pleasing" to see changes color four times each year, alternately green, blood-red, cloudy, or mixed (*pulverulentum seu turbidum*), and clear.[69] Mandeville repeats the information almost exactly, but he ties it to Samaria's different religious populations: Christian, Muslim, Jewish, and pagan.[70] The members of each group wear a differently colored head wrap, whether red, white, blue, or yellow. His account of the head wraps might come from William of Boldensele, whose content and wording are similar.[71] The colors do not match, but Mandeville invites the reader to find a connection between juxtaposed claims. Their mismatch might also reflect the depths of the people's confusion, the misalignment of their identities. The scene offers an example of Mandeville's methods, showing how he copies and pastes from his sources, giving passages new meanings because they are hitched together.

The well would seem to represent the Samaritans and their multiple allegiances. The key piece of information that Mandeville gives his readers in order to guide their interpretation is that the Samaritans were "converted and baptized by the Apostles, but they have not kept their teaching well."[72] These are a people as changeable as the well, not Christians and not Jews. According to the Hebrew Bible, after their conquest in the eighth century, the Assyrians forced the Jews of Samaria out of the city and imported settlers into it.[73] The community that resulted was necessarily divided, and as Mandeville writes, the Samaritans identified themselves as neither Christians nor Jews. Samaria, now in the West Bank, is therefore a city of foreigners unnaturally brought together. Mandeville removes Jacques's observation that the well is pleasing to see and instead has it reflect poorly on the city's religious divisions. Now the marvel suggests that the people are not in their natural state, themselves constituting a marvel that bodes ill. The well

69. Jacques de Vitry, *Historia orientalis* 85, ed. Donnadieu, 338: "mira et grata." Before Jacques, the marvel is described by Isidore of Seville, *Etymologiarum* 13.13.25, ed. Lindsay, vol. 2 (no pagination); and Geoffrey of Monmouth, *Vita Merlini*, ed. Clarke, 118. Geoffrey draws a great deal of material from Isidore.

70. Mandeville, *Le livre des merveilles du monde* 12, ed. Deluz, 234–35.

71. See William of Boldensele, *Liber quibusdam ultramarinis partibus* 9, ed. Deluz, 278.

72. Mandeville, *Le livre des merveilles du monde* 12, ed. Deluz, 234: "convertyz et baptizez et par les Apostres, mes ils n'ount mie bien temuz lour doctrine. Trans. Higgins, *Book of John Mandeville*, 66.

73. See 2 Kgs 17:3–6.

and the Dead Sea, so interpreted, define the present as a passing, symbolic moment that lies between a more vivid past and a prescripted future, when the lands will be folded into the Christian empire. They function as both an echo and a warning. Through his reinterpretation of the well-attested marvels, Mandeville does not prioritize fidelity to his sources, sources that themselves vary. Rather, he uses marvels to put the land in thoughtful dialogue with its past, and to keep the past visible in an ever shifting present.

MANDEVILLE'S IMAGINATIVE MARVELS

Travel literature contains many sorts of marvels, including monstrous and otherwise unusual people (troglodytes, Pygmies, Siamese twins), unusual animals (unicorns, *rukh*s, sea monsters), unusual plants (balm, a tree that grows baby lambs, another that produces women who are biologically whole), and unusual bodies of water (the Dead Sea, the Black Sea).[74] All demonstrate the marvelousness of nature, and all resonate with the natural philosophy of the period. I focus here on marvels that rely, expressly or only conventionally, on imagination in order to show how they are imaginative in a medieval as well as a modern sense. Mandeville's reinterpretation of familiar marvels showcases his own imagination, as he reinterprets received tales and projects them onto geographical space. At the same time, the marvels retain the character of the faculty of imagination insofar as they are potentially real or illusory. Their indeterminacy gives them a special power to enliven imagination even as they depend on it. Composed of vivid images whose reality remains unclear, they pique imagination because they speak its language.

One scene involves magicians "who perform plenty of wonders" at the Khan's court.[75] They make the sun and moon seem to appear and disappear, and "they make the most beautiful young women in the world dance, as it seems to the people, and then they make other young women appear carrying golden cups full of mare's milk, and this they give to the lords and the ladies to drink. And they make knights jousting in their arms appear . . . And they make hunts in pursuit of stags and boars appear along with running dogs."[76] The detail about magically transported cups full of drink,

74. On the trees that grow women, the trees of *wāq al-wāq*, see Toorawa, "Wâq al-wâq," 393–96. The description of the island recalls the Amazons, and as Toorawa notes, the Amazons were explicitly placed there in fifteenth- and sixteenth-century texts (396).

75. Mandeville, *Le livre des merveilles du monde* 25, ed. Deluz, 394: "qe font trop de mervailles."

76. Mandeville, *Le livre des merveilles du monde* 25, ed. Deluz, 394–95: "font venur daunces des plus beals damoiseals du mounde, ceo semble as gentz. Et puis font venir

whether wine or milk, is likely drawn from Mandeville's frequent source, Odoric of Pordenone.[77] It also appears in Marco Polo and Rustichello's *Devisement*, although it is not clear whether Mandeville was familiar with the text.[78]

This scene presents us with an example of the sort of amplification common in travel literature, as one piece of information finds its way to others, from other sources, that might resemble it. To the core detail about cups magically transported across the room he adds illusory ladies dancing and serving, as well as men jousting and hunting. Mandeville draws the surrounding stories from any number of possible sources. Pre-Christian, initially oral traditions have beautiful women gathering in fields at night and troops of armed men jousting and hunting.[79] The scenes are often characterized as illusions or as products of magic, but the people seen might also be identified as corpses inhabited by demons or souls stuck in purgatory.[80] As is to be expected with legends of this sort, the history of their development is self-contradictory and nonlinear. Nonetheless, the specific marvels that Mandeville includes had already arranged themselves into a trio before he adopted them. Identifying the figures involved as illusions rather than demons or souls from beyond the grave, Mandeville appeals to their popular representation. By introducing them into a scene he adopted, he treats them as creative representations, expressions of an author's imagination and a provocation to the reader's.

The grouping of the separate legends about dancing ladies, knights jousting, and men hunting has precedent within natural philosophy, literature, and visual art, although the pattern has not received critical attention. In *Sir Orfeo*, the poet tells us that the eponymous king often sees a series of scenes on hot afternoons, as he wallows in the woods. He describes three: first, the fairy king and his men hunt; second, an army of knights appears; and third, knights and ladies dance.[81] The first two disappear as quickly as they arrive, and the third likewise passes by him. They might be illusions, and they might not. But the *Orfeo* poet, like Mandeville, adds one unfamil-

---

des autres damoiselles portantz des coupes d'or pleine de lait des jumentz, et donent a boire as seignurs et as dames. Et puis font venir des chivalers joustantz en lour armes . . . Et puis font venir chaces des cerfs et des cenglers et des chiens currantz." Trans. Higgins, *Book of John Mandeville*, 142.

77. Odoric of Pordenone, *Relatio* 30, ed. van den Wyngaert, 482.

78. Marco Polo and Rustichello of Pisa, *Devisement* 75, ed. Ronchi, *Milione*, 403.

79. Lecouteux, *Chasses fantastiques*, 8; for more on the distinct legends, see 13–25, 45–52, and 81–124. On the wild hunt, see also Green, *Elf Queens and Holy Friars*, 172–78.

80. Green, *Elf Queens and Holy Friars*, 177–78.

81. *Sir Orfeo*, 283–302, ed. Bliss. Neil Cartlidge considers analogues for *Orfeo*'s wild hunt and wild horde in "Sir Orfeo in the Otherworld," 201–9.

iar scene to the familiar trio. Rather than magically moving cups, *Orfeo* has women hawking, and among them Herodis. He uses the already familiar visions to call attention to his innovation, as though the opening set of visions is well known to his readers.[82]

The example best known to medievalists in English departments is surely Chaucer's *Franklin's Tale*, in the scene where the cleric displays his considerable powers to Aurelius and his brother, and concocts images of knights jousting, of a gruesomely detailed hunt, and of a beautiful woman (here Dorigen) dancing.[83] The scene plays into the tale's interest in the power of illusions of various sorts. Dorigen, worried that her husband abroad will not be able to return home safely, obsesses over black rocks that might cause his ship to falter. She stares from the cliffs near her house, pondering the rocks, thinking of death: "ther wolde she sitte and thynke / And caste hir eyen dounward fro the brynke" watching the "grisly rokkes blake" that make "hir herte quake" (857–58, 859, 860). Thinking, looking down from a high cliff, fearing her husband's death and presumably contemplating her own, she develops an obsession in real time, under the reader's eye. Her fixation on one sort of illusion, the fatal rocks, is matched by Aurelius's with her, and both are mirrored in the cleric's magic show. Its illusions show the power of imagination given free rein, of the obsessed person's susceptibility to images. Dorigen and Aurelius stand in decided contrast to Dorigen's husband, Arveragus, who is not vulnerable to such mental tricks because he is not "ymaginatyf" (1094).

Chaucer, like Mandeville, is clear that these are mere illusions, as fleeting as Dorigen's thoughts about rocks should be. But they threaten to be made real through the power of Dorigen's fear and Aurelius's desire. Although the magician makes the rocks merely seem to disappear, adding one more illusion to his quiver of tricks, the magic act turns her hypothetical promise to Aurelius, and Aurelius's to the clerk, into firm commitments. That illusions create the threat of unwanted sex and of financial ruin shows their particular power, especially to those in delicate mental states. The lovelorn and "ymaginatyf" are especially vulnerable to them. Chaucer shares with Mandeville a belief in the world-altering power of illusions, but Mandeville imports them to a different end. Uninterested in the power they might exercise over susceptible minds, he locates them inside the Mongolian empire and treats them as the prodigious feats of wise and powerful sorcerers. Prestige marvels that advertise the learnedness of the people and cultures

82. I discuss *Sir Orfeo* and this additional scene at greater length in chapter 6.

83. Chaucer, *The Franklin's Tale*, 1189–1201, ed. Benson, *Riverside Chaucer*. All future references to Chaucer's works are to this edition. Robert Cook notes the similarity between the two scenes in "Chaucer's Franklin's Tale and *Sir Orfeo*."

that produce them, they can be created only by the most masterful magicians. At the same time, they advertise the process by which Mandeville groups and distributes marvels in the world through the work of his own imagination.

Fantastic marvels were often associated with foreign lands. William of Auvergne writes that "fantasies of illusions abound to the greatest degree now" in Egypt, and Odoric of Pordenone writes of India that, "in the whole world, there are not such and so many marvels as there are in this region."[84] While marvels involving monstrous peoples and fantastic beasts can come from any region that is, from the author's perspective, far-off and unfamiliar, marvels produced by enchanters or magicians tend to come from peoples deemed sophisticated, such as Egyptians, Indians, Greeks, Chinese, and Persians.[85] Expertise in illusion-making and related acts of magic was thought to be the product of advanced learning.[86] Mandeville makes use of the association of imaginative marvels with foreign lands, giving a well-attested set of marvels a specific location when he assigns it to Mongol enchanters. By allowing them to create sophisticated illusions, he also places the Mongols alongside the most learned medieval cultures. As Geraldine Heng notes, early Christian visitors to the Mongols sometimes painted them as backward or as savages, while later visitors more often saw them as civilized, the inheritors of Chinese cultural authority who were led by a great ruler.[87] By attributing the wild hunt and other legends to them, Mandeville defines Mongols as philosophical prodigies. Allowing them to perform highly skilled feats, he makes theirs a first-tier civilization. Further, when he takes a detail he inherited about magically moving cups and nestles it into a well-known canon of masterful illusions, he extends the Mongols' history. Perhaps such illusions are now thought to originate with them, with their culture projected back in time, or perhaps the Mongols have inherited ancient knowledge through the Chinese or others. Either way, they are part of ancient learned traditions.

84. William of Auvergne, *De universo* 2.3.23, 1:1065aA: "In Aegypto . . . ludificationum fantasiae maxime abundant nunc." Odoric of Pordenone, *Relatio* 18, ed. van den Wyngaert, 457: "in toto mundo non sunt tot et tanta mirabilia quot sunt in isto regno." Marco Polo and Rustichello write that Indians are especially skilled in the diabolical arts and enchantments. See *Devisement* 74, ed. Ronchi, *Milione*, 94.

85. Houari Touati writes that, from the perspective of the writers of Arabic travel literature, "only the Greeks, the Persians, and the Hindus had wisdom to transmit to them" (*Islam et voyage*, 14). In the *Kitāb tabaqāt al-umam*, Ṣāʿid al-Andalusī surveys different peoples and their contributions to knowledge. In his view, only the Indians, Persians, Chaldeans, Greeks, Romans, Egyptians, Arabs, and Jews have contributed significantly.

86. Kieckhefer, *Magic in the Middle Ages*, 100–101.

87. Heng, *Invention of Race*, 290, 359.

When Mandeville takes a prearranged collection of marvels and places it on a map, he projects imaginative content onto geographical space in a remarkably literal way. Of course, geography had long been imaginative, organized according to theological, literary, or moral principles rather than strictly cartographical ones.[88] What is distinctive about Mandeville is his decision to plot marvels, realizing the double meaning of the word "plot" when he creates a map that follows the contours of a preestablished narrative. The particular marvels that he commits to the Mongols make the imaginative component of his geography all the more salient because they were thought to originate in the imagination.

William of Auvergne addresses two of the illusions at issue here—the dancing ladies and knights in battle—and roots them expressly in the faculty of imagination. He sets out to determine what sort of being the objects seen might possess. Are the knights real, are they riding real horses, and are they bearing real arms?[89] His favored interpretation is that they are not. Demons instead make images of them appear, whether to tempt deluded people into serving them, or to act as agents of God and inspire penitence for sin. He writes: "all that seems to be there or be done there is only there and done through a vision or an illusion or a phantasm."[90] The illusions are, in other words, one of three sorts of imaginative phenomena; the distinction here involves little difference. William refers his reader to his earlier explanation of how such illusions can be created, to a discussion of demons' power with respect to human imagination.[91]

It bears stressing, then, that these illusions emerge from imagination. Whether or not Mandeville was familiar with the well-established link between the illusions and the faculty of imagination, as Chaucer appears to have been, his additions are striking insofar as they also subject the illusions to his own creative imagination. In other words, as products of imagination, they lend themselves to imaginative reworking. They are at once spectral and witnessed, tied to a geographical location that gives them a sort of realness, but placed there at Mandeville's whim. Easily repurposable, they can be deployed as he wishes and elaborated at will. This example shows with special clarity how marvels play with the possibility of their own realness, with the different layers of play creating a puzzle that is

88. See, for instance, Sobecki, "New World Discovery."

89. See William of Auvergne, *De universo* 2.3.24, in *Opera omnia* 1:1065–67.

90. William of Auvergne, *De universo* 2.3.24, in *Opera omnia* 1:1066aF: "totum, quod ibi vel esse, vel agi videtur, in visione, sive illusoria, sive fantastica solummodo est, & agitur." William broaches demons at 1:1066aG. He touches on souls in purgatory briefly at 2.324, 1:1067aC–D.

91. William of Auvergne, *De universo* 2.3.24, in *Opera omnia* 1:1066aG.

not meant to be solved. Whether to believe them is a question they raise, not one that they answer. We see too how natural philosophy and travel literature engage in a shared conversation about marvels. Again, the same marvels are the shared property of different disciplines.

Mandeville's use of another familiar marvel shows in a different way how he adapts marvels imaginatively and organizes them on the map. It is the marvel of women who have two pupils in a single eye. Mandeville might have drawn the report from any number of sources, although he does so with a twist. The usual claim is that a certain group of people, usually women (Pliny includes men) from Scythia, known as Bithiae, have double pupils (*pupillas geminas*) in one eye, which gives them the power to kill or bewitch others. Such is the report of Ovid, Pliny, Solinus, Roger Bacon, John of Salisbury, and Vincent of Beauvais, among others.[92] Mandeville instead claims that women with "precious stones in their eyes" kill people by looking at them, just "as the basilisk does."[93] In this case, Mandeville appears to have read *pupillas geminas*, or twin pupils in one eye, as *pupillas gemmas*, or pupils that are gems. It is an easy error to make based on the words' minims, one of the strokes used by Latin scribes. The words "*ge*mi*nas*" and "*ge*mm*as*," each with six consecutive downward strokes in their center, would look the same in the absence of strong ligatures. The error is perhaps original to Mandeville; I have found it nowhere else. I think it is clear that he intended to include a well-attested marvel rather than to invent a new one.

Mandeville imports the marvel of the double-pupiled and now be-gemmed women into the domain of travel literature. Its wide-ranging sources—poetic, philosophical, and historical—make it hard either to dismiss as a complete fabrication or to accept as a fact. That Mandeville compares the women to the mythical basilisk makes his reference most similar to that of Bacon, who begins the relevant discussion by sketching his doctrine of the multiplication of species. As discussed in chapter 2, he appears to adopt from al-Kindī the idea that all things, animate and inanimate, celestial and terrestrial, send off invisible images of themselves, or species, through which they affect other things, as the magnet does when it attracts iron. This is how "the basilisk kills with its sight alone" and how, a few sentences later, "in Scythia there is a region where women 'have two

92. See Ovid, *Amores* 1.8.15, ed. Henderson, 348; Pliny, *Natural History* 7.2, ed. Henderson, 2:516; Solinus, *Collectanea rerum mirabilium*, ed. Mommsen, 95; John of Salisbury, *Polycraticus* 15, ed. Migne, *PL* 199:575D; and Vincent of Beauvais, *Speculum historiale* 1.93, in *Speculum quadruplex*, 4:12v. The reference by Bacon is discussed below.

93. Mandeville, *Le livre des merveilles du monde* 31, ed. Deluz, 449: "pierres precioses dedeinz les oilz," "si come fait le basilisk."

pupils in one eye'" and have the power to kill men by looking at them.[94] They can exercise such power when enraged, and in fact it is often the case with marvels of this sort that strong emotion is necessary for the imagined harm to take effect.

Bacon's aim in grouping the two marvels is to comment on the particular powers of the soul, which can express themselves through the eye. When the double-pupiled women enact the harm they envision, they turn images within the soul into physical realities. As he adapts the marvel, Mandeville suggests more strongly than Bacon that the women are imaginative constructions. He places them not in Scythia but on an island seemingly near India and surrounds them with similarly unusual women on nearby islands. The women with gems for eyes are followed by a description of an island where men fear that women have serpents in their vaginas, and so they pay other men to take their wives' virginity. After that comes a story about women who mourn childbirth and celebrate the death of their children.[95] The catalog of weird women is one of several instances where Mandeville uses thematic connections to determine geographical ones. The stories of the women are grouped not just in the text but also in the world, with all proximate and located in the "Ocean Sea." They remind the reader that *topos*, or place, is the root of "topic": stories are arranged on a map, and their thematic similarities are represented through their physical proximity. The text acts like a rhetorical exercise, grouping like ideas and keeping them together on the map, projecting mental content out onto the world with its synapses intact.[96] So powerful are mental images in this text that they determine supposed physical realities.

The variously odd women also illustrate another common tactic in travel literature, which is to reverse Western customs. What should occasion sadness brings joy and vice versa. What should be desired, like a virgin wife, is feared. The marvels' significance depends on their counterintuitiveness, or their departure from Christian European norms. As Jacques Le Goff writes, "in the medieval West, *mirabilia* tended to create a sort of inverted world" where scarce things were plentiful and taboo things were accepted.[97] Travel literature presents cities where men tend to newborns, where

94. Bacon, *De secretis operibus artis et naturae* 3, ed. Brewer, *Opera quaedam hactenus inedita*, 529: "basilicus interficit solo visu . . . in Scythia regione sunt mulieres geminas pupillas habentes in uno oculo." Bacon quotes Solinus. In the following sentence, he paraphrases Ovid's description of the same marvel.

95. See Mandeville, *Le livre des merveilles du monde* 31, ed. Deluz, 449–51.

96. Mary Carruthers's emphasis on memory and its division into discrete places is relevant here (*Book of Memory*, 153–94). See likewise Rita Copeland on topics as places of invention (*Rhetoric, Hermeneutics, and Translation*, 151–78).

97. Le Goff, *L'imaginaire médiéval*, 24.

wood sinks and fire cools, where virginity is shameful and gold is cheaper than wool. The strangeness contributes to the sense that the marvels mean something, as the author of *Mandeville's Travels* expressly states. After describing fish that cast themselves onto the shore, he writes, "this thing seems to me a greater wonder than any I have seen."[98] "It is entirely against nature," he explains, "that the fish . . . should come to give themselves up . . . Therefore I am certain that it cannot be without great significance."[99] The unnaturalness of the behavior marks its import. *Mandeville's Travels* thus lingers on Constantinople because, in the order of his text, "it is the first country varying from and disagreeing with our country over here in faith and writing."[100] The unexpected or unfamiliar helps to make marvels marvelous. It organizes the world according to a comforting opposition between familiarity and difference, even as it emphasizes the creativity of both author and nature.

Stories about marvels lend themselves to reconfiguration, whether or not travelers have seen them directly. Even when their own experience should have discounted them, travel writers often include them. As Sebastian Sobecki notes, in such moments "preferment [is] given to texts . . . over experience," and literary history takes precedence over perception.[101] It is in the nature of marvels to be passed along and adapted from one text to another. Sometimes they are invented from scratch, but far more often they are retold. Using the example of *Mandeville's Travels*, Anthony Bale characterizes such changeability as a meme, which he defines as "a shared cultural representation that prospers through being copied and adapted, rather than through its relationship or likeness to an original."[102] Bale's argument helpfully shifts attention away from the issue of fidelity, which is not to say that medieval readers were indifferent to it, but that marvel sto-

98. Mandeville, *Le livre des merveilles du monde* 21, ed. Deluz, 348: "Ceste chose me semble a plus grant mervaille qe nulle chose qe jeo veisse unques." Trans. Higgins, *The Book of John Mandeville*, 119.

99. Mandeville, *Le livre des merveilles du monde* 21, ed. Deluz, 348: "est de tout contre nature qe ly pesshouns . . . se viegnent prendre a la mort de lour propre volunté . . . Et pur ceo suy jeo certein qe ceo ne poet estre sanz grant significacioun." Trans. Higgins, *The Book of John Mandeville*, 119.

100. Mandeville, *Le livre des merveilles du monde* 4, ed. Deluz, 115: "ceo est la primer païs variant et descordant en foi et en lettres de nostre païs de cea." Trans. Higgins, *The Book of John Mandeville*, 15.

101. Sobecki, "New World Discovery." Dorothee Metlitzki makes a similar point: "the factual knowledge of countries and cultures did not . . . supplant traditions and conventions associated with them in literary treatment" (*Matter of Araby*, 136). Legassie offers a different opinion (*Medieval Invention of Travel*, 63).

102. Bale, "'Ut legi,'" 208. Helen Cooper earlier used the meme to describe the transmission of romance (*The English Romance in Time*, 4).

ries were not beholden to it. As he notes, "the meme has the capacity to be at once idea *and* thing, image *and* place."[103] Its value depends not on the recovery of an original or on measuring the distance of a given representation from it. Insofar as travel writers reimagine the marvels in their sources, they acknowledge the creativity that those marvels embody.

CREDIBILITY AND THE TRAVEL WRITER

If, as I contend, marvels in travel literature function as imaginary creations, lending wonder to the mundane world as they borrow solidity from it, then what are we to make of the fact that authors often insist on the credibility of their accounts? The issue has to be addressed because travel writers themselves bring it to the fore. While some, like al-Mas'ūdī and Jacques de Vitry, presented their reports with qualifications, stressing that the most unlikely marvels do not need to be believed, others were more assertive. While it is easy enough to distinguish marvels from scripture or legal texts, it is harder to explain why authors often ask their readers to view them as trustworthy. Does this merely enrich the game, calling into further question what can be believed in these texts? Perhaps for some authors, like Mandeville, but not for others. John of Plano Carpini, for instance, writes, "If for the attention of our readers we write anything that is not known in your parts, you ought not on that account to call us liars, for we are reporting for you things we ourselves have seen or have heard from others whom we believe to be worthy of credence."[104] It certainly reads like an earnest appeal. Travel writers regularly write that they share what they witnessed or heard from authoritative sources. According to Rustichello's prologue, the *Devisement* contains "some things which [Marco Polo] did not see, but he heard them from trustworthy men."[105] Odoric of Pordenone concludes, "All these things written above I either beheld with my own eyes or heard from trustworthy men. As for those things that I did not see myself, the common talk of those countries bears witness to their truth."[106]

103. Bale, "'Ut legi,'" 210, his emphasis.

104. John of Plano Carpini, *Historia Mongolorum*, Preface, ed. Menestò, *Storia dei Mongoli*, 228: "Sed si aliqua scribimus propter notitiam legentium, que in vestris partibus nesciuntur, non debetis propter hoc nos appellare mendaces, quia vobis referimus illa que ipsi vidimus vel ab aliis pro certo audivimus." Ed. Dawson, *Mission to Asia*, 4.

105. Marco Polo and Rustichello of Pisa, *Devisement* 1, ed. Ronchi, *Milione*, 305: "auques hi n'i a qu'il ne vit pas, mes il l'entendi da homes citables et de verité." Trans. Moule and Pelliot, *Description of the World*, 1:73.

106. Odoric of Pordenone, *Relatio* 38.6, ed. van den Wyngaert, 494: "hec omnia que superius scripta sunt, aut propriis oculis ego vidi aut ab hominibus fide dignis audivi. Comunis autem locutio illarum contratarum illa que non vidi testatur esse vera." Trans.

Some authors explain that they have pulled the trustworthy wheat from the untrustworthy chaff. Al-Gharnāṭī writes that, when he returned from his travels, learned people asked him about the marvels (*ʿajāʾib*) that he encountered "and about which of the trustworthy reports I considered to be authentic among the many that circulate."[107] Apparently the air was thick with accounts about marvels, and he was not the only one to wonder which ones merited belief. Even the trustworthy reports (*al-akhbār al-thiqat*) needed to be sorted, sound (*ṣaḥḥa*) from unsound. As a genre based more on repetition and reconfiguration than outright invention, marvel stories inevitably passed hands. There is no particular reason to doubt that, in many cases, these authors in fact heard or read about the marvels that they did not personally witness or that they considered their sources trustworthy. That does not mean they vouched for the truth of each story or thought their judgment with respect to a source's credibility was infallible. Nor does it mean that they refrained from exercising poetic license.

Even in their ancient origins, travel narratives fell on a continuum between more and less credible accounts, a continuum that was drawn by the writers themselves. Authors like Herodotus criticized those like Ctesias for being insufficiently rigorous. They are echoed in later years by al-Masʿūdī's criticisms of his overly permissive forebears. He cites al-Jāḥiẓ, who writes that a rhinoceros fetus gestates for seven years, at which point only the head of the animal will exit the birth canal, and that only periodically, in order to graze. Al-Masʿūdī asked locals and merchants about the matter, all of whom disagreed with al-Jāḥiẓ, and so he concludes, "I do not know how this story made its way to al-Jāḥiẓ, whether he copied it from a book or got it from someone."[108] In either case, he suggests, al-Jāḥiẓ was not as discriminating as he might have been with his sources. Ibn Ḥawqal explains that he would ask learned men to tell him about other places and would then measure their accounts against others' and finally against his own experience, which led him to realize that most of what they told him was false.[109] In the same style, albeit without the same diligence, Mandeville tells his reader not to believe the accounts of those claiming to have scaled Mount Ararat

---

Yule, *The Travels of Friar Odoric*, 160. See also Christine de Pizan, *Le chemin de longue étude*, 1490–96, ed. Tarnowski.

107. Al-Gharnāṭī, *Al-muʿrib*, Prologue, ed. Bejarano, 8: "wa-mā ṣaḥḥa ʿindī bi-ṭarīqi al-istifāḍatī min nuqlati al-akhbāri al-thiqati [reading *thiqat* for *thiqāat*]." Spanish trans., 56.

108. Al-Masʿūdī, *Kitāb murūdj adh-dhahab* 16, ed. de Meynard and de Courteille, 1:387–88: "lastu udrā kayfa waqaʿat hādhihi al-ḥikāyatu li-l-jāḥiẓi a-min kitābin naqalahā am makhbarun ukhbirahu ʿanhā bihā."

109. Ibn Ḥawqal, *Kitāb ṣūrat al-arḍ*, 329. French trans. Kramers and Wiet, *Configuration de la Terre*, 1:322.

because only one man, with God's aid, did so.[110] He claims authority for himself in part by encouraging skepticism toward others, distancing himself from the tellers of tall tales. All are aware that travel chronicles sometimes stretch credibility, or veer into outright falsehood. Shayne Legassie shows convincingly that readers in the Latin West were often skeptical about the claims of travel literature, a skepticism that inspired the anxious plea of John of Plano Carpini, quoted above, and other writers' frequent, sometimes perfunctory vows that they really and truly saw this or that.[111]

Undeniably, travel writers claim to have seen marvels that they did not see. So often does the *Devisement* promise that Marco Polo personally witnessed any number of far-fetched marvels that the claims come across as rote. Ibn Baṭṭūṭa too "simultaneously pillages other texts and claims eyewitness authority."[112] Indeed, such claims of trustworthiness—Shayne Legassie calls them "authenticating gambits"—are a well-known feature of medieval travel texts.[113] As Mary Campbell writes, with some exaggeration, "the anxious, even florid, claim to veracity and reliability is a conventional feature of any premodern, first-person narrative of travel."[114] They are sometimes identifiably misleading, as when Mandeville writes that he never took a particular route to Jerusalem, "which is why I cannot describe it well," implying that he has taken the other routes and therefore describes them reliably.[115] His disavowal works to shore up his credibility as it satisfies a generic expectation, one that led redactors and editors to multiply claims of direct witnessing.[116]

One of the perplexing features of these eyewitness claims is that they are sometimes excerpted along with the stories they accompany. Bradwardine borrows from Hayton of Corycus a story about a city miraculously

110. Mandeville, *Le livre des merveilles* 16, ed. Deluz, 293. Mandeville seems to draw the story of the one man from Simon de Saint-Quentin, *Histoire des Tartares* 31.97, ed. Richard, 59–60. It was customary to describe Mount Ararat as unscalable. See, for instance, Hayton of Corycus, *Flos historiarum* 1.9, ed. Dulaurier et al., 128; and William of Rubruck, *Itinerarium* 38, ed. van den Wyngaert, 323.

111. Legassie, *Medieval Invention of Travel*, 59–93. Christine Chism notes that Ibn Baṭṭūṭa also found a skeptical readership ("Memory, Wonder, and Desire," 32).

112. Chism, "Memory, Wonder, and Desire," 32.

113. Legassie, *Medieval Invention of Travel*, 47. Discussing *Mandeville's Travels* in particular, Geraldine Heng comments on its "aura of authoritative verisimilitude" (*Invention of Race*, 349).

114. Campbell, *The Witness and the Other World*, 141.

115. Mandeville, *Le livre des merveilles* 14, ed. Deluz, 267: "pur quoy jeo ne le porroy bien deviser." Trans. Higgins, *The Book of John Mandeville*, 81.

116. Kohanski and Benson note, for instance, that some of the redactors of *Mandeville's Travels* added testimonials along the lines of "I, John Mandeville, say this is true" (Introduction to *The Book of John Mandeville*, 3).

submerged in darkness, described in chapter 2, and Hayton affirms, "I was there and I saw it."[117] When Bradwardine, who was not a traveler, shares the story, without referencing his source, he also writes, "I was personally there, and in faith I saw hidden things."[118] The complexity of eyewitness claims is well known, and they can be manufactured as easily as any other type of claim.[119] The distance between them and wholly invented accounts is often small. Christian de Pizan, for instance, has her main character survey the world's wonders and conclude, "I saw so many strange things that I could not relate them all in a hundred years, were I to live so long. Whoever does not believe me ought to travel the same path that I followed without flagging."[120] Hitching the claim that she saw the world's marvels to her defensive challenge that the skeptical reader do the same, she shows that the promise to have seen a marvel can be mimicked as easily as the appeal for belief.

In the case of travel literature, the ventriloquized testimony is not necessarily surprising. Borrowing someone else's first-person voice simply keeps the source intact, and the absence of attribution is unremarkable in the context of medieval texts, which regularly exclude them. Such borrowings, I suggest, are no more or less believable than the initial author's claim that a spectacular marvel exists, and perhaps those who repeated them recognized as much. In both cases, the reader might be wary, and might assume that the avowal is false or that the reported marvel is made up, but they would not have a reliable rubric to tell them which to discard and which to entertain. Authors sometimes play with this uncertainty explicitly, as we will also see in the following chapters on romance. They are aware that readers might respond to their accounts with a raised eyebrow, and they reassure them either in earnest or in jest even as they keep that uncertainty alive.

Travel writers often seek to establish a baseline credibility with tactics that are recognizable as tactics. For instance, Marco Polo and Rustichello celebrate their own reasonableness when they pause over a familiar marvel, the salamander and its supposed invulnerability to fire.[121] The *Devise-*

117. Hayton of Corycus, *Flos historiarum* 1.10, ed. Dulaurier et al., 129: "je fu là e la vi."

118. Bradwardine, *De causa Dei* 1.1, coroll. 32, ed. Savile, 43: "ibi personaliter fui, & fide vidi etiam occulata."

119. Jamie Taylor places such testimony "between the historical and the imagined" (*Fictions of Evidence*, 8). See also Frisch, *The Invention of the Eyewitness*; and Pagden, *European Encounters with the New World*, 51–88.

120. Christine de Pizan, *Le chemin de longue étude*, 1491–96, ed. and trans. Tarnowski: "tant y vi d'estrangetez / Que n'en seroit le fait comptez / En cent ans, se je tant vivoie; / Et qui nel croira, si le voye / Par le chemin que je le vi, / Que sans lasseté j'assouvi."

121. See, for instance, Bacon, *Opus majus*, trans. Burke, 2:629; and Gervase of Tilbury, *Otia imperialia*, Pref. to Book 3, ed. Banks and Binns, 558–60.

ment unravels the marvel by distinguishing the animal called salamander from the substance we call asbestos: "Because people did not know the truth about the salamander, they said and still say that the salamander is a beast, but it is not true. I shall tell you the truth now."[122] The authors cast themselves as truth-tellers who clear the table of earlier misconceptions, using their predecessors as al-Masʿūdī uses al-Jāḥiẓ. A modicum of credibility is purchased at the expense of those who erred and can be shown to have erred. Similarly, the *Devisement* tells its audience that griffins "are not made at all as people on this side believe."[123] Arbiters of truth who weed out and correct falsehoods, its authors ask half-seriously for the reader's trust. Such corrective gestures are themselves conventional in the genre, and they satisfy a need to keep the audience guessing. Sometimes, they seem wholly earnest. Regarding Prester John, the fabled Christian ruler of India and/or other lands in the East, the Franciscan William of Rubruck declares, "less than a tenth of what they say about this is true."[124] William does not doubt the existence of Prester John, but his skepticism about the claims he has heard seems to be more than a posture. Whether such discriminating gestures are heartfelt or cynical, they keep marvels in a provisional state that defies conviction.

There are other ways in which authors acknowledge readerly skepticism. For those who might ask why marvels cannot be brought home, where they might be inspected in the local marketplace, writers explain their nontransportability. Al-Gharnāṭī, for instance, writes that the water of the Black Sea is black, but the moment you remove it, it instantly becomes clear.[125] Any samples brought home would look like normal water. In other instances, the marvel self-destructs in some way. Ibn Baṭṭūṭa writes of an alchemist who could turn copper into gold, but immediately afterward he renounced the art, never performing the marvel again.[126] Impossible to replicate or relocate, such marvels also ensure that the writer's claims are both unverifiable and irrefutable.

As we have seen, all of these writers stipulate that marvels might defy belief. Marco Polo, for instance, writes that the enchantments of the people of Kashmir are so amazing that "there is no one who did not see them who

122. Marco Polo and Rustichello of Pisa, *Devisement* 60, ed. Ronchi, *Milione*, 376: "por ce que les jens ne savoient la certance de la salamandre le disoient en la mainere qu'il dien encore que salamandre soit beste, mes il ne est pas verité. Mes je le voç dirai orendroit."

123. Marco Polo and Rustichello of Pisa, *Devisement* 191, ed. Ronchi, *Milione*, 594–95.

124. William of Rubruck, *Itinerarium* 17.2, ed. van den Wyngaert, 206: "plus dicebant de ipso in decuplo quam veritas esset." Trans. Jackson, *The Mission of Friar William*, 122.

125. Al-Gharnāṭī, *Al-muʿrib* 3.1, ed. Bejarano, 17.

126. Ibn Baṭṭūṭa, *Riḥla*, ed. Defremery and Sanguinetti, *Voyages*, 1:137.

could believe them."[127] It is a logical puzzle: do I believe you when you tell me that I cannot believe you? Sometimes, marvels beggar belief so entirely that the authors say they must leave them undescribed. Although Tibetan astrologers perform "the greatest marvels," the *Devisement* leaves them unnarrated: "they should not be described in our book because people would be too amazed."[128] Tempting the reader with the prospect of marvels too spectacular not just to be believed but even to be described, the *Devisement* suggests that part of its purpose is to entice. The marvels that remain are, by contrast, barely believable, and that is their purpose: to exceed understanding and capture something of the marvelousness of creation.

Travel writers recognize that marvels in particular elicit doubt, but even those most eager to be believed retain them. John of Plano Carpini still writes about men who have no joints in their legs, a land where the sunrise is so loud that it kills Mongol invaders, and the Mongol use of fat gathered from human victims as fuel to burn the houses of their enemies.[129] Al-Masʿūdī still tells the story (without endorsing it) of a man who rode a dragon into paradise in order to find the source of the Nile, and he states as fact that the rhinoceros horn, when split open, contains an image of a man or peacock or other animal in black relief against the white background.[130] Improbable marvels might be expunged by authors eager to shore up their credibility. They might relinquish far-fetched claims that they know will sound unbelievable. That they keep them anyway shows that credibility is not their primary concern. Rather, they celebrate the mystery of marvels and of nature. More marvels are likely to be proven false, but as al-Qazwīnī often writes, "there is no reason to abandon all the reports [about marvels] just because there is doubt about some of them."[131] The goal is not to separate those that will pass muster from those that will not, but to present the full, heterogeneous assortment for the reader's scrutiny and enjoyment.

We have seen that writers use marvels that are easy to accept, like the magnet, in order to encourage an open mind toward others. Based on certain premises—namely, that creation is marvelous, that marvels like

127. Marco Polo and Rustichello of Pisa, *Devisement* 49, ed. Ronchi, *Milione*, 363: "ne est nulz que ne le vist qui le poust croire." Trans. Moule and Pelliot, *Description of the World*, 1:140.

128. Marco Polo and Rustichello of Pisa, *Devisement* 116, ed. Ronchi, *Milione*, 465: "ne est pas buen a contere en nostre livre por ce que trop se mervelieront les jens." Trans. Moule and Pelliot, *Description of the World*, 1:272.

129. John of Plano Carpini, *Historia Mongolorum* 5.6, 5.16, and 6.15, ed. Menestò, *Storia dei Mongoli*, 254, 262–63, and 282, respectively.

130. Al-Masʿūdī, *Kitāb murūdj adh-dhahab* 14 and 16, ed. de Meynard and de Courteille, 1:268–69 and 386, respectively.

131. See, for instance, chap. 3, note 23, above.

magnets do undeniably exist, and that it would be hubristic to dismiss the wonders of creation preemptively—readers might be willing to entertain unlikely phenomena as possibilities. The authenticating gestures I have surveyed serve a similar function. They ask their audience to consider as possible even things that are almost certainly false. Some authors make the request more teasingly than others, and it would be a fool's errand to try to distinguish in each case the one from the other. That, I think, is much of the point: if the line between the real and the false, the possible and the impossible cannot be drawn, or if there is little interest in drawing it, then any of the stories might be pondered. If the travel writer who really saw a marvel is hard to distinguish from the one who only swears to have done so, maybe that makes travel literature as a whole more entertaining. For their part, the writers discussed here expected their audience to question marvels and invited them to scrutinize them, but not to decide which were true and which false. Instead, they invited them to marvel at a world pregnant with possibilities and to enjoy accounts that captured its imaginative richness.

Chapter 3 argued that nature's creativity in the making of marvels is poetic, and it follows that literature could embellish it further. From that perspective, Mandeville's inventiveness might supplement nature's own, and even the most outlandish marvels or fabricated tales might reflect productively on the wonders of creation. I have argued that nature as a concept includes not just what is but what might be, and that it elicits wonder not just from the marvels it has created but from those it has not revealed and yet might have the capacity to create. Perhaps, then, there was little need to impose a firm boundary between nature's actual feats and imaginative extensions of them. Of course, natural philosophy and travel literature are different genres with different aims and methods, but it is easy to see how certain conventions in the philosophers' discussions of marvels, such as the common definition of marvels as natural possibilities or the notion that marvels define nature at its most creative, might invite imaginative elaborations and sometimes playful reinterpretations. The final two chapters, on romance and other purely fictive genres, will take those instincts to their limit.

[CHAPTER 5]

Marvelous Trials

Travel literature and romance are interrelated and overlapping categories, as anyone who has read Alexander the Great romances knows. The heroes of romance often travel to mythical or semimythical places like Gorre and Babylon in pursuit of adventure or damsels in distress, and their authors often link real to imaginary places in the manner of much travel literature. For instance, by the conclusion of the Castilian *Flores y Blancaflor*, Flores rules both the fictional emirate of Almería and the historical emirate of Córdoba. The Arabic *sīra*, properly designated not as romance but as historical epic, figures into this and the following chapter because, like romance, it places marvels in unmistakably invented settings, even if they sit alongside historical or pseudo-historical ones. For instance, the hero of the *sīrat Sayf ibn Dhī Yazan*, who is based on the sixth-century ruler of Yemen, pauses his martial and romantic exploits to visit the magical Garden of Delights.[1] Flying over it with the aid of his adoptive sister, a *jinnīya* (female genie or fairy) who has the capacity for flight, he insists that they stop. If he were to get so close and not visit, he says, he would disappoint his friends, "and if I do not describe it, they will ridicule me. Nor would it be right to lie, for lying dishonors men."[2] This is the discourse of travel literature, with its appeal to fidelity and its conviction that the marvels of other lands ought to be experienced and described. In the garden, Sayf finds sophisticated women who "have acquired the nature of birds," one of whom will become his favored wife.[3] His goals are conquest and love, but his approach to travel resembles that of al-Masʿūdī or al-Idrīsī, who enjoy travel for its own sake.

1. An attentive reader will notice that *sīrat* sometimes has a *t* on the end. That happens when it is part of a genitive construct (*iḍāfa*).

2. *Sīrat Fāris al-Yaman al-Malik Sayf ibn Dhī Yazan*, 1:285–86: "fa-in lam aṣifhu hum yaḍḥakūna ʿalayya wa-lā yujawwizu lī an akdhiba fa-inna al-kidhbu yashīnu al-rijāla." Trans. Jayyusi, *The Adventures of Sayf ben Dhi Yazan*, 168.

3. *Sīrat Fāris al-Yaman al-Malik Sayf ibn Dhī Yazan*, 1:292: "mutaṭabbaʿūna biṭabāʾiʿi al-ṭuyūri." Trans. Jayyusi, *The Adventures of Sayf ben Dhi Yazan*, 175.

It might be tempting to place them at different points on a continuum between fact and fiction, but as we have seen, such judgments are inevitably fraught, in part because marvels expressly undermine them.

Although there are clear similarities between the texts that we designate separately as travel literature and as romance or, in the Arabic tradition, as epic, romance in particular has often been held apart from other bodies of medieval literature and applauded for its relatively sophisticated understanding of marvels. Certainly no other genre is as closely linked to them. Its very mention likely brings to mind magical rings and enchanted towers, genies trapped in bottles, and knights on praiseworthy quests. As Douglas Kelly writes, "marvels are indeed the primordial stuff—the hyle, as it were—of romance."[4] Romance without marvels would be form without matter, and as any Aristotelian knows, matter rarely (if ever) subsists without form. Other scholars take such claims further, past romance to fiction entire. Francis Dubost, for instance, writes that "the marvel is in the same class as [*assimilée à*] fiction, forming the ambiguous mode of representation between being and non-being, of phantasms, of words without things, of images without substance [*consistance*]."[5] From this view, marvels are emblems of fiction that help to define its uniqueness.

If marvels are integral to romance, and if fiction takes root in them, then romance must be the origin of fiction. Thus Northrop Frye writes that "romance is the structural core of all fiction" that, in John Ganim's words, provides us with "our very idea of literariness."[6] Tying these different claims together, we see that romance is the seed of fiction at least in part because of its marvels. Karen Sullivan writes that "it is in the capacity of authors like Augustine, Gerald, and Wace to entertain the possibility of marvels, like dragons, giants, and prophecies, without affirming or denying that of which they speak, that we can find a major source of the fictionality of medieval romance."[7] By Sullivan's formulation, a capacity to withhold judgment about marvels, at least as old as Augustine, flourishes in medieval romance, and that agnosticism elevates the genre. If marvels can be fictional or proto-fictional constructs distinctly in romance, then romance itself can be the source of secular fiction.

As Julie Orlemanski rightly notes, the typical story that scholars tell about the rise of fiction is simultaneously a story about the secularization of literature, as though literature comes of age once it no longer seems to

4. Kelly, "The Domestication of the Marvelous in the Melusine Romances," 45.
5. Dubost, "Merveilleux et fantastique au moyen âge," 19.
6. Frye, *Secular Scripture*, 15; and Ganim, "Myth of Medieval Romance," 163.
7. Sullivan, *The Danger of Romance*, 93.

solicit belief.[8] The notion that romance is skeptical toward its marvels suits that narrative well. However, although the marvels within romance are distinct in some ways from those in other genres and disciplines, they are not distinct for the reasons usually proposed. Decades ago, scholars argued that marvels within romance set themselves apart from those in history because they do not aim to be true. Matilda Bruckner, building on Douglas Kelly's work, writes that "the marvelous became the focal point for romance and the truth it signified superseded claims for historical veracity."[9] In other words, while medieval history and romance are similarly interested in marvels, that likeness conceals a more significant difference. The marvels in romance signify in a self-contained way, without referring to history or accepting its brand of truth.[10] Bruckner responds not just to Kelly, but also to scholars like Eugene Vance and Tony Hunt, who argue that romance calls attention to logic in order to undermine it.[11] According to Vance, "logicality is a precondition of the *merveilleux*" in *Yvain* "and perhaps in other romances as well," in the sense that logic sets the conditions of the probable that marvels, as the improbable, disrupt.[12] Because its marvels are not bounded by logic or the need to be factually accurate, romance carves out an independent space for literature.

If marvels were accepted as truths when they appeared outside of romance, only to be viewed with skepticism when they appeared within it, then they might well support the claim that romance presents fictive creations in a new way. The marvels of natural philosophy or travel literature would constitute a sort of reality that romance would refashion, but without the claim to realness.[13] Even if such marvels did not chart a path out of the so-called age of faith, they would still serve a postmedieval, teleological narrative that favors realism over fantasy.[14] However, the premise of the arguments above, that historians and philosophers were committed to the literal truth of marvels, is a position that I argue against in the first three chapters of this book. They do make logicality a condition of marvels, but only in the sense that they must be logically possible, and, as I noted, logi-

8. Orlemanski, "Who Has Fiction?" 150–51.

9. Bruckner, *Shaping Romance*, 116. She cites Kelly, "*Matiere* and *genera dicendi* in Medieval Romance."

10. Gabrielle Spiegel's "Forging the Past" is essential reading on the vexed nature of historical truth in the period.

11. Vance, *From Topic to Tale*, especially 21–27 and 46–52; and Hunt, "Aristotle, Dialectic, and Courtly Literature."

12. Vance, *From Topic to Tale*, 46.

13. However, on the traditional opposition between romance and realism, see Fradenburg, "Simply Marvelous."

14. See, for instance, Gallagher, "The Rise of Fictionality."

cal possibility is a large tent. Even the marvels of romance are rarely logically impossible. That would require, for instance, two things to be in the same place at the same time, or the same thing both to be and not to be in a single instant. Everything that happens in the world is logically possible, as are miracles, and many other things besides.

Although the marvels of natural philosophy and chronicles are not truths or supposed truths that set the marvels of romance in relief, there are still important differences between the two. Whereas marvels in philosophy and history are viewed as nonimpossibilities, or simply phenomena that have yet to be conclusively debunked, there is no parallel presumption in romance. True, it was thought possible that some of its marvels might have existed, including unusual stones and herbs. Figures like Orpheus, Merlin, and the Sibyl are marvel-making prophets in literature but were also supposed to have lived.[15] Orpheus was credited with works on charms, herbs, and stones, as well as with songs and poems, while of course also featuring within romance.[16] He was even made into a marvel himself, since his head was said to have prophesied after his death on the island of Lesbos.[17] Separating the "real" from the "fictional" Orpheus or Sibyl was not a project that garnered much interest in the period. Rather, the interconnectedness of philosophical and literary accounts of marvels shows an interest in merging discourses rather than separating them. Orpheus's supposed expertise in natural philosophy qualified him to travel to hell and to prophesy. His historical persona fed his literary one, and vice versa. Still, in spite of the cross-disciplinary resonance of many of its marvels, romance does not need its marvels to be true or possibly true. Authors often treat them as possible, or certain, but that discourse of possibility differs from philosophers' talk of nonimpossibility.

Dubost's claim that marvels are much like fictive beings because words and images are divorced from things in the extramental world bears further scrutiny. He specifically likens them to "phantasms," which is interesting since, as I have argued, imagination—which produces phantasms—is often involved in their production. A marvel like bewitchment consists in phantasms, and to that extent I agree with Dubost, except that we part ways on the meaning of the word. By "phantasm," he means to describe an inert image that exists only within the mind and has no power within the extra-

15. There were ten different sibyls according to Lactantius. His list, drawn from Varro, "became canonical" in the Latin West (Smoller, "'*Teste Albumasare cum Sibylla*,'" 78). See also McGinn, "'*Teste David cum Sibylla*.'"

16. See Hernández, "Literatura mágica y pseudocientífica atribuida a Orfeo."

17. See Álvarez, "La muerte de Orfeo y la cabeza profética," 128–34. On Orpheus in medieval Christendom, see Friedman, *Orpheus in the Middle Ages*.

mental world. In the philosophical sources, however, phantasms are *not* divorced from things in the world, or at least not necessarily. They can cause a camel to fall or a plague to strike, as we have seen. In my reading, the specter of the philosophers' phantasm, with powers that extend beyond one's soul, colors the marvels of romance. That is not to say that literary objects might exercise world-altering powers, but that dominant and well-known philosophical theories about marvels gave imagination's images substantial powers that resonate in romance and the *sīra*. When their authors insist on the believability of marvels that are wholly invented, they silently allude to such theories and play with a possibility that no longer holds.

It is often claimed that romance or its marvels anticipated fiction or set its foundations more than other genres or literary objects.[18] One could argue just as convincingly, I think, that dream visions, with their self-referentiality and experimentalism, show a sophisticated literary self-consciousness, or that religious meditations maximize the powers of the creative imagination in a way that Chaucer, for instance, does not.[19] Either genre could be seen to presage later developments. Romance is elevated in histories of fiction in part because it complements the priorities of those who have written them. Associated with skepticism and nascent realism, it is a prequel written after the fact, once fiction has been defined through the realist novel.[20] My interest instead lies in romance's marvels insofar as they illuminate features of medieval fiction that are unique to it, as I explained in the introduction, rather than tilting forward. They depend on the general indistinction between what is real and what is invented, and they make use of the resemblance between spectacular inventions and spectacular natural events.

This chapter focuses on marvels' reception within romance and outside it. It shows that marvels in romance retain their defining indeterminacy and play with the uncertainty of their own existence. Whether they are real or not is a live and energizing question within the texts discussed below. As objects that are other than they seem, they are easily misrecognized, and for that reason they work well to test faith in matters that cannot be conclusively proven. In contrast to the common notion of medieval enchantment, marvels might even train a reader *not* to be overly credulous. In that vein, the prologue to the *Thousand and One Nights* advertises the text as a means to temper susceptibility—but before proceeding, I ought to comment on the role of the text, along with that of the *sīra*, in these final chapters.

18. As noted by Ashe, *Early Fiction in England*, xvii.

19. For Chaucer, imagination typically dominates the weak, whether the melancholic (Troilus), fearful (Dorigen), or irrational (Januarie).

20. On the constructedness of realism and fictionality as they relate to the novel, see Freedgood, *Worlds Enough*, ix–33.

Insofar as Arabic literature and romance from the Latin West are discussed together, the topic is usually lyric. For centuries, scholars have argued that Arabic love poetry influenced Provençal and early Castilian love poetry, either its themes or form.[21] Samuel Stern breathed new life into the so-called Arab thesis when he demonstrated, in the 1940s, that the final refrain, or *kharja*, of a small percentage of surviving Hebrew and Arabic poems known as *muwashshaḥāt* consisted partly or entirely of Andalusi Romance that was written in Arabic or Hebrew script.[22] Deciphering those final lines, he was able to identify linguistic assimilation in the specific context of poetry. Still, there is no single Arabic lyric known to have been translated into a romance language, nor any known allusion within all of Provençal poetry to an Arabic author, and that limits the claims that can be made for influence.[23] Scholars have also proposed Arabic influence on notions of courtly love or, more specifically, on such conventions as the martyr for love, often with special attention to Ibn Ḥazm's *Ṭawq al-Ḥamāma*, or *Ring of the Dove*.[24] Another thread of scholarship interests itself in the possibly Byzantine or Arabic sources for various works that circulated in the Latin West—including *Aucassin et Nicolette* and *Flores y Blancaflor*—and in poems that might imitate such literature, such as Chaucer's *Squire's Tale*.[25] Provocative though such possibilities are, there is still insufficient information about routes of transmission to make them conclusive.[26]

21. See, for instance, Menocal, *The Arabic Role in Medieval Literary History*, 80–88; and Bezzola, *Les origines et la formation de la littérature courtoise*, 1:183–96. For Menocal's own argument for influence, see her *Shards of Love*. The precedence of the strophe has attracted particular attention, with Cynthia Robinson concluding that "recent studies have convincingly demonstrated the chronological precedence of the Arabic strophic form over the Romance one," though without proving the influence of the former over the latter (Robinson, *In Praise of Song*, 275).

22. Stern, *Les vers en espagnol dans les muwaššah hispano-hébraïques* (1948); Menocal, *The Arabic Role in Medieval Literary History*, 83–85. As Heather Bamford notes, about 10 percent of the surviving *muwashshaḥāt* have *kharajāt* at least partly in Andalusi Romance ("A Romance *Kharja* in Context," 169).

23. Robinson, *In Praise of Song*, 279; Bezzola, *Les origines et la formation de la littérature courtoise*, 1:188.

24. See Giffen, *Theory of Profane Love among the Arabs*, 99–115; and Menocal, *The Arabic Role in Medieval Literary History*, 71–90.

25. These connections are more often asserted than proven. See, for example, Bezzola, *Les origines et la formation de la littérature courtoise*, 1:198–99. More of an argument is available for the *Squire's Tale*: see Lynch, "East Meets West"; Metlitzki, *The Matter of Araby*, 75–80; and Norris, "Sayf bin Ḏī Yazan and the Book of the History of the Nile," 132–34 and 143.

26. That is to say that clear sources and analogues have not been identified, although the very short story of Ni'ma and Nu'm in the *Thousand and One Nights* is similar in plot to *Flores y Blancaflor*. The suggestions of influence and imitation are compelling, and I find the possibility that Chaucer, for instance, had some knowledge of the *sīra* hard to

Both the *Thousand and One Nights* and the Arabic *sīra* have been called romance, in the way that scholars in America and Western Europe often assimilate foreign literatures to the categories—generic, temporal, or other—that apply most accurately to local productions.[27] Because the Arabic texts place marvels in settings that are mostly invented, and because they sit alongside rich philosophical and geographical traditions concerning marvels, they merit study alongside romance, but there are significant differences as well. Love tends not to be the primary concern of the *sīra*, for instance, and marvels are not as integral to it. Still, it thematizes marvels in some similar ways and it is worth considering, however briefly, in these final chapters. Though often discussed in tandem with the *sīra*, the *Thousand and One Nights* is typically classified with *ʿajāʾib* literature, or the literature of marvels, which is mostly cosmological or otherwise philosophical in nature.[28] *Siyar* (plural of *sīra*), in contrast, are typically long, heroic narratives. Usually linked to historical events and places, they constitute what Lyons calls "myth-history."[29] They are united by "their shared emphasis on heroes and heroic deeds of battle, their pseudo-historical tone, and their indefatigable drive toward cyclical expansion."[30] In these respects, they are similar to Alexander the Great romances, and indeed one includes Alexander. They normally consist of prose, rhymed verse, and poems, and they often include love plots, if not in the foreground of the narrative. They also draw often on supernatural and magical elements, including marvels, though typically not with the same frequency as romance. The earliest references to the genre date to the twelfth century, with the earliest manuscripts dating to the fifteenth.[31] The *sīra* is most similar to the long, narrative romances of the Latin West, though it is important not to pretend that they constitute a single genre. There is no evidence that the *sīra* influenced such romance, nor has there been a concerted effort to look for it.[32]

The *Thousand and One Nights* is discussed more in the next chapter than this one, but it makes senses to introduce it here, alongside the *sīra*. It is

---

resist, given how closely the *Squire's Tale* matches its setting, plot, tone, and techniques, but there is as yet no firm evidence about how he might have learned about it.

27. Some who focus on such texts also discuss them as romance. See, for instance, Heath, "Romance as Genre in *The Thousand and One Nights*."

28. For different views, see von Hees, "The Astonishing: A Critique and Re-reading of ʿAǧāʾib Literature"; and Zadeh, "Wiles of Creation," 21–26. On the *Nights* with respect to other framed narratives, see Wacks, *Framing Iberia*.

29. Lyons, *The Arabic Epic*, 1:134. Lyons points to *Sayf al-Tījān* as an unusual *sīra* insofar as it has a wholly imaginary setting (1:12).

30. Heath, *The Thirsty Sword*, xvi.

31. Heath, *The Thirsty Sword*, xv–xvi.

32. As Heath notes in *The Thirsty Sword*, xvii.

possible that the work or parts of it circulated in the Latin West during the Middle Ages, though that has not yet been demonstrated.[33] Its textual history has received a great deal of critical attention, and is sometimes made out to be more complicated than it was, at least in the Middle Ages.[34] A short fragment from the Arabic text—just a title page and sixteen lines of text—survives from the ninth century. In the tenth, the author of the famous book catalog *Kitāb al-fihrist*, al-Nadīm, describes a Persian text called *One Thousand Stories*. He names Shahrāzād and summarizes the frame narrative, leaving no doubt that he describes a version of the story collection now familiar.[35] Also in the tenth century, al-Masʿūdī refers to the Persian collection and adds that the popular Arabic translation is called *Alf layla*, or *One Thousand Nights*.[36] The oldest substantial manuscript of the text dates to the fourteenth century, and its tales form the basis of later expansions. I refer in this book only to tales from that manuscript, which is typically called the Syrian manuscript.[37] Whereas the *sīra* shares some similarities with historical romances in the Latin West, the *Thousand and One Nights* is closer to the nonhistorical romances that are set in purely fantastic locations.

Returning, then, to the prologue of the *Thousand and One Nights*, we find the author writing that it "includes great deeds [*siyar jalīlat*] that teach the reader discernment [*al-firāsata*] so that they will not fall under its [the book's] power, and it will bring delight and diversion from the ills of the world at times of trouble."[38] In line with a classical standard, the text aims to entertain as well as instruct. It teaches the art of discourse (*kalām*) and educates "people of high status" with "edifying histories and excellent lessons."[39] Most noteworthy is the claim that it teaches discretion or dis-

33. Kathryn Lynch considers whether Chaucer in particular might have known the work; see Lynch, "East Meets West," 532–34.

34. For helpful studies of that history, see Mallette, *European Modernity*, 1–33; and al-Musawi, *Scheherazade in England*; as well as Pinault, *Story-telling Techniques*, 4–12; and Mahdi, *Thousand and One Nights*, 3:2–10.

35. See Mallette, *European Modernity*, 204.

36. Al-Masʿūdī, *Kitāb murudj dh-dhahab*, ed. de Meynard and de Courteille, 4:90–91. The title was expanded to *Alf layla wa-layla*, or *One Thousand and One Nights*, at least by the twelfth century. See Pinault, *Story-telling Techniques*, 5.

37. Pinault, *Story-telling Techniques*, 7–9. Mahdi notes that the "Syrian branch" is itself quite stable, and writes that "all manuscripts of this group contain the stories with which other manuscripts begin" (*Thousand and One Nights*, 3:141).

38. *Thousand and One Nights*, ed. Mahdi, 3:56: "wa-yataḍammanuhu ayḍān siyarun jalīlatun yataʿallamu sāmiʿahā al-firāsata minhā ḥatta lā yadkhula ʿalayhi ḥaylahu, wa-yuṣīra lahu al-tanazzuhu wa-l-surūru awqāta al-kadari min aḥwāli al-zamāni al-mufattanihi bi-l-shurūri." Trans. Haddawy, 3.

39. *Thousand and One Nights*, ed. Mahdi, 3:56: "siyaru kathīratu al-adabi wa-maʿānī fāīqa li-ahli al-rutabi." Trans. Haddawy, 3.

cernment that protects the reader from the power (*ḥayl*) of the book. In other words, it encourages a degree of skepticism about great deeds, *siyar*, the same plural term that names the body of historical heroic narratives, the *sīra*. The sorts of claims made in such stories are like the fantastic tales of the *Nights*, and the reader is not to give in to them uncritically. Far from asking for gullibility, they train the reader to exercise good judgment so as *not* to be gullible. Readers ought to be self-conscious and self-reflective about the marvels, which continue to pique imagination because they are not easily classifiable.

BELIEF IN FAIRIES: THE CASE OF MÉLUSINE

Like travel literature, romance often raises the topic of its own veracity. Marie de France shares, she writes, "stories that I know to be true," and the speaker of the *Quest of the Holy Grail* assures his reader, "it seems to me that this is true in every detail."[40] Romance often assumes a skeptical reader, as when the speaker of Chrétien's *Cligés* notes that the story's source "is very old, and therefore it is more worthy of belief"; when the speaker of *Perceval* promises, "I am not lying about the bed"; and when the speaker of *Bevis of Hampton*, after telling a story about dragons, writes, "who that nel nought leve [whoever will not believe] me, / Wite at [Learn from] pilgrimes that there hath be."[41] These works treat the stories they tell and the marvels they describe as truths so improbable that the reader will doubt them. Thus the speaker of *Amadas and Ydoine* writes that Amadas ran so far that "it would seem marvelous if anyone were to tell the truth about it."[42] And they assure their readers that they write in good faith, as when Chrétien's speaker writes, "I do not wish to make you believe something that does not seem true."[43] These are complicated assertions, intended to be complicated and not easily dismissed. Perhaps surprisingly, the authors

40. Marie de France, *Guigemar*, in *Les lais de Marie de France*, ed. Rychner, 19: "Les contes ke jo sai verrais." Trans. Burgess and Busby, *The Lais of Marie de France*, 43. *La queste del Saint Graal*, 86, ed. Pauphilet: "ce est voirs de toutes choses." Trans. Shoaf, *The Quest of the Holy Grail*, 150.

41. Chrétien de Troyes, *Cligés*, 24–26, ed. Poirion and Walter: "Li livres est molt ancïens / Qui tesmoigne l'estoire a voire / Por ce fet ele mialz a croire." Trans. Kibler, *Arthurian Romances*, 123. Chrétien de Troyes, *Perceval*, 7696, ed. Poirion: "nule fable ne faz." Trans. Kibler, 475. *Bevis of Hampton*, 2651–52, ed. Herzman et al., *Four Romances*.

42. *Amadas and Ydoine*, 2536–37, ed. Reinhard: "Qu'a mervelles seroit tenu, / Qui la verité en diroit." Trans. Arthur, 58.

43. Chrétien de Troyes, *Erec and Enide*, 6915–16, ed. Poirion and Dembowski: "ne vos voel pas feire acroite, / Chose qui ne sanble trop voire." Trans. Carroll, *Arthurian Romances*, 122.

of romance, like some travel writers, insist far more strongly on the truth of their marvels than natural philosophers do.[44] This is our first clue that something more complex than wholehearted enchantment is at issue.

A discourse of possibility characterizes the marvels of medieval romance. Their authors ask their audiences to believe them and insist that the events described can actually occur. One of the more striking examples of this tendency, and one that can provide insight into it, appears in the prologue to the late fourteenth-century *Roman de Mélusine*. There, Jean d'Arras writes, "I believe that the marvels which occur on earth and throughout all of creation are the most true, including those things that are said to be the work of fairies."[45] He suggests that the fairy element of his story is the most likely to inspire doubt—"comme les choses dictes faees," as if to say "even the stuff about fairies"—and he focuses his reader's attention on it, doubling down where doubt is most likely to creep up. He makes the confident declaration early in his prologue, after explaining why he started to write the romance and how he based it on the "true chronicles" in the library of his patron, Jean, duc de Berry.[46] The romance is set in the context of the Hundred Years' War and ultimately works to shore up Jean de Berry's claims to Lusignan lands.[47] It is a story about fairies that is also deeply implicated in political and historical affairs. This perhaps makes Jean d'Arras's comments in his prologue more difficult to interpret. Where does belief in fairies fit into a political argument made to benefit a patron?

As Richard Firth Green writes, "fairy beliefs were very far from being a fringe phenomenon in the Middle Ages."[48] Nonetheless, the prologue's bald claims about belief in fairies seem to express something other than straightforward belief in fairies. The author does not simply write that he believes Mélusine is real or that the Lusignan dynasty rightly traces its existence back to her, although he does say both. He writes that fairy stories are "the most true" (*les plus vrayes*), those things that are least subject to doubt. The exaggeration in the phrasing hints at the playful distortion at work here, as Jean blows out of proportion the case for fairies' realness. He couches such comments in references to King David, St. Paul, and Aristotle, which together help to illuminate his intentions. He cites David

44. As we saw in chapter 4, however, some travel writers instead insist that the marvels they describe do not need to be believed.

45. Jean d'Arras, *Mélusine*, ed. Vincensini, 112: "croy que les merveilles qui sont par universel terre et monde sont les plus vrayes, comme les choses dictes faees." Trans. Maddox and Sturm-Maddox, 19–20.

46. Jean d'Arras, *Mélusine*, ed. Vincensini, 110: "vrayes coroniquez."

47. See Harf-Lancner, "Littérature et politique."

48. Green, *Elf Queens and Holy Friars*, 41.

to show that the works of God exceed our understanding: "The prophet David says that the judgments and punishments of God are like a boundless, bottomless abyss, and that he is unwise who attempts to understand them through his intellect."[49] Paul and Aristotle both speak to the reality of invisible things. Jean points to Romans, presumably Romans 1:20, and its promise that invisible things might be seen through visible ones.[50] Tying both themes together, he writes, "I believe that no man save Adam has ever had perfect knowledge of God's invisible works."[51] Such claims are perfectly mainstream, supported as they are by unimpeachable authorities. The question is whether Jean applies them to the case of Mélusine in earnest. He tells a popular story, built on a legend about a fairy of Lusignan, as Laurence Harf-Lancner has shown.[52] Like the writers of travel literature, he does not simply repeat what he has read; he combines, selects, and elaborates at will. The final story about Mélusine's sister Melior, for instance, is drawn from *Mandeville's Travels*, one of the books in Jean de Berry's collection that Jean d'Arras says he consulted when writing.[53] He is aware of his own interventions and amplifications, and surely recognizes both that his story is nothing like scripture and that belief in its fairies is nothing like religious faith. However, his tone does not read as wholly ironic, either.

It is worth noting that Jean d'Arras does not directly argue for the realness of fairies but rather asserts it. In his closing comments, as in his prologue, he declares that his story is true—"I maintain that this story and the chronicles are true, as well as the things concerning fairies"—and repeats his introductory comments about the inscrutability of God's works, but the latter does not prove the former.[54] God *can* make fairies, but that does not prove that he *did*. That God can do nearly anything (short of creating a logical contradiction) does not in any way suggest that he *does* do nearly everything. Jean, in other words, argues for open-mindedness and persuadability, detached from the particular claim he wishes to persuade his reader to believe. His tone has something in common with that of the speaker in Chaucer's General Prologue, when he apologizes in advance for

49. Jean d'Arras, *Mélusine*, ed. Vincensini, 112: "David le prophete dit que les jugemens et punicions de Dieu sont comme abysme sans rive et sans fons et n'est pas saige qui les cuide comprendre en son engin." Trans. Maddox and Sturm-Maddox, 19–20.

50. Jean d'Arras, *Mélusine*, ed. Vincensini, 114.

51. Jean d'Arras, *Mélusine*, ed. Vincensini, 114: "je cuide qu'onques homme, se Adam non, n'ot parfaicte congnoissance des euvres invisibles de Dieu." Trans. Maddox and Sturm-Maddox, 20.

52. Harf-Lancner, *Les fées au Moyen Âge*, 85–117.

53. Harf-Lancner, "Littérature et politique," 170.

54. Jean d'Arras, *Mélusine*, ed. Vincensini, 816: "je repute ceste histoire et la cronique a estre vraye, et les choses faees." Trans. Maddox and Sturm-Maddox, 229.

speaking "pleynly" and reporting the tales of his pilgrims accurately, lest he tell a "tale untrewe" (727, 735). He illustrates a species of *licentia*, or license, as "when we say that we fear how the audience may take something that we know they will hear willingly, yet that the truth moves us to say it nonetheless."[55] In other words, he uses a well-established rhetorical device. To it, the speaker adds, "Crist spak hymself ful brode [openly] in hooly write," as though he and Jesus were fellow truth-tellers, and the *Canterbury Tales* resembled scripture (739). He turns to Plato, who "seith . . . The wordes moote be cosyn to the dede" (741–42). It would be hard to disagree with Christ or Plato in these respects, but their authority and the legitimacy of the points they defend hardly speak to the decision of Chaucer's speaker to record wicked tales faithfully. Even if Chaucer were recording rather than inventing the tales, fidelity in the one respect is not like fidelity in the others. Similarly, Jean calls upon authorities who are unimpeachable in themselves, making claims that are hard to gainsay, but who still fail to support the conclusion at hand. As the rhetorical sophistication of their comments reveals, neither argues in earnest.

The conundrum of the prologue is resolved, I think, by its resemblance to the arguments natural philosophers make about marvels. Insofar as Jean d'Arras ties a marvel like fairies to divine possibility, he sounds surprisingly like them. In chapter 3, I discussed natural philosophers' fondness for reasoning *secundum imaginationem*, or entertaining hypothetical scenarios that were consistent with God's absolute power. They took up marvels, I argued, in that spirit: because they were not logically impossible, they fell under the category of ponderables. Their mechanisms might be worked out without any firm presumption that they existed. Jean d'Arras presents us with a similar argument, though applied to a different conclusion and placed in a context that alters its significance. Note that he directs attention explicitly to the scope of God's power, warning his readers away from presuming to impose limitations on it, precisely in the fashion of philosophers discussing divine possibility and concluding that no marvel should be declared impossible for God. Jean differs insofar as he draws a stronger conclusion, for realness rather than nonimpossibility. Because God can make fairies, he suggests, he does make fairies, and specifically the fairy Mélusine, whose life is such as his text describes. Since it is impossible to state with certainty that Mélusine does not exist, he makes the logical error of concluding that she does. He applies to his romance, then, a common method of defending belief in marvels, and retools it. In this gesture, we see

55. *Rhetorica ad Herennium* 4.37.49, ed. and trans. Caplan, 352–53: "dicimus nos timere quomodo accipiant, sed tamen veritate commoveri ut nihilosetius dicamus."

a playful extension of serious arguments beyond the bounds of their own earnestness. The logical flaw marks the game, one that he might well have expected his reader to recognize, given how often natural philosophers argue for the possibility of marvels on the basis of God's absolute power.

Jean d'Arras alludes directly to the philosophical study of marvels, referring to Aristotle and others, to shore up his claims about the reality of fairies. He promises the reader that he has studied "ancient authors" along with "other authors and philosophers."[56] As he characterizes it, his is a scholarly approach to marvels, consistent with that of the philosophers, and not to be dismissed. That marvels are and have been studied by serious people licenses the reader to consider the possibility of a real Mélusine. In the same spirit, Jean reads the willingness to believe marvels as a sign not of credulity but of sophistication. The "more uncultivated" will be least inclined to believe him, whereas the "more refined in wit and learned in natural science will rather be inclined to find such a thing possible."[57] Such flattery—itself common in philosophical accounts of marvels, as we have seen—aims to woo the reader, to position marvels with science, and to attribute them to the learned. He attempts to buoy his credibility further by likening his text to travel literature which, in his view, teaches one the truth of marvels: "It is only by frequenting a variety of countries and lands and nations, and by reading and understanding the ancient books, that one comes to know what is real and true concerning things that seem incredible."[58] Reminiscent of Chaucer's appeal to books as substitutes for personal experience, his claims establish his text's authority.[59] It is as good as seeing the things described oneself. Aggressively asserting the truth of the story and appealing to the most authoritative authorities, the prologue is less a testament to belief in fairies than a recognizably imperfect imitation of arguments testifying to their possibility.

Avowals like that of Jean d'Arras can be vexing for modern readers, who might well wonder whether he actually believes in fairies or in the historicity of Mélusine. They were surely complicated for medieval readers as well. We have every reason, however, to assume that they were educated

56. Jean d'Arras, *Mélusine*, ed. Vincensini, 814–16: "anciens autteurs . . . autres anciens autteurs et philosophes." Trans. Maddox and Sturm-Maddox, 229.

57. Jean d'Arras, *Mélusine*, ed. Vincensini, 816: "plus . . . grossiere . . . plus sera deliee de engin et de science naturelle et plustost y aura affection que ce soit chose faisable." Trans. Maddox and Sturm-Maddox, 229.

58. Jean d'Arras, *Mélusine*, ed. Vincensini, 818: "par hanter les diverses contrees et païs et nacions, et par lire les anciens livres et les entendre, congnoist on le vif et le vray des choses semblans increables." Trans. Maddox and Sturm-Maddox, 229.

59. See, for instance, Chaucer, *Legend of Good Women*, 1–39, ed. Benson, *Riverside Chaucer*.

consumers of marvels and equal to the challenge that Jean offered them. The terms that philosophers applied to marvels were ripe for reworking by those who might take advantage of the fact that very little is logically impossible. It is in the nature of possibility to have wide boundaries: distant possibilities sit alongside near ones, and outlandish spectacles can be kept afloat because they cannot be conclusively disproven. Recognizing that the discourse of marvels revolves around possibility, Jean pretends that the marvels he invents qualify. It is hard to prove even invented stories to be logically impossible, and so Jean reasons with a wink that we might as well call them true.

FAIRIES AND ENCHANTERS

In chapter 1, I described marvels, in part, as phenomena or objects that are other than they seem. Bewitchment seems unnatural but is not; a flying horse seems impossible but is not; imaginings seem like perceptions but are not. The same quality belongs to marvels in romance, and characters of romance are often confused in their presence. Confusion is a standard response to wonder as medieval philosophers defined it, as is the fear that often accompanied it. Marvel-makers like the prophet Merlin and the fairy Mélusine elicit both, due primarily to the uncertainty surrounding the source of their powers—demonic or divine. Mélusine, for instance, recognizes the discomfort she inspires and repeatedly assures others that she is no demonic or fantastic creature. When she first meets the man who will become her husband, she tells him accurately about recent events in his life, ones that she did not witness, and says, "I know well that you believe I am an illusion or diabolical creation based on my words and deeds, but I assure you that I am on God's side and believe everything a true Catholic must believe."[60] Her avowal acknowledges uncertainty about fairies' precise classification, whether demonic or divine. She is in this very respect, and perhaps paradoxically, a comprehensible fairy, one who is legible within an intellectual context that granted both benevolent and malevolent creatures the power she possesses. She follows the rules that govern unusual behavior.

Although Mélusine is bound to inspire doubt as a prophet, Jean d'Arras intensifies it, partly at the hands of her mother.[61] According to the mother's

60. Jean d'Arras, *Mélusine*, ed. Vincensini, 165: "je sçay bien que tu cuides que ce soit fantosme ou euvre dyabolique de mon fait et de mes paroles, mais je te certiffie que je suiz de par Dieu et croy en tout quanque vraye catholique doit croire." Trans. Maddox and Sturm-Maddox, 33.

61. As Gabrielle Spiegel notes, the Mélusine character in the source texts is unable to attend church or touch holy water, and so is more aligned with wickedness, whereas

decree, Mélusine becomes a serpent "from the navel down" every Saturday, a transformation that is bound to make her appear more demonic.[62] Because her lower body is transformed, there is the further suggestion that her genitals are somehow diseased, especially since she bears eight children with unusual physical features, like a single eye or an enormous tooth, as well as one with three eyes who is evil from birth and kills two of his wet nurses. It is not clear whether her last two children bear such anomalies.[63] As we have seen, medieval medical theories often made mothers responsible for their children's deformities, a power usually vested in their imaginations. In some circumstances, it was thought that images seen by the mother might imprint themselves on the child, in the way that Jacob's sheep, shown a striped branch while they were mating, produced streaked or spotted offspring (Gen. 30:37–40).[64] While Jean d'Arras nowhere suggests that Mélusine wishes such changes on her children—she clearly aspires for herself and for them to be fully human—their physical anomalies might express something of her nature or imagination against her will. At a minimum, they cast further doubt on her.

The questions about Mélusine's true nature persist, and indeed cannot be resolved. Her uncharacterizability is essential to her character. Her husband Raymondin connects all of her unusual powers together after one of their sons dies at the hands of another, railing against her: "Deceitful serpent! By God, what you are and what you do are nothing but phantasms. None of the children you have borne will come to good in the end."[65] When he calls her a serpent, he defines the whole of her through a form that she only partly and temporarily assumes. By calling her a deceitful (*tresfaulse*) serpent, he makes that intermittent external affliction internal and essential: she now has the nature of a serpent. His attention to her shape-shifting suggests that her physical changeability itself makes her untrustworthy. Extending his attack and describing her actions as phantasms, he sug-

Jean d'Arras balances her good and evil features ("Maternity and Monstrosity," 101–2).

62. Jean d'Arras, *Mélusine*, ed. Vincensini, 134: "du nombril en aval."

63. Douglas Kelly argues that the absence of explicit oddities in their form indicates that Mélusine is becoming more human ("The Domestication of the Marvelous in the Melusine Romances," 34).

64. The late thirteenth-century *Quodlibeta* of Pseudo-Rigauld moves, for example, from Jacob's sheep to the human mother whose unwholesome imagining malforms her fetus, resulting in a hideous (*turpissimum*) child. He attributes both to the faculty of imagination. See his *Quodlibeta* 2.11, ed. Delaurenti, "Les franciscains et le pouvoir du regard," 181–82.

65. Jean d'Arras, *Mélusine*, ed. Vincensini, 692: "tresfaulse serpente, par Dieu, ne toy ne tes fais ne sont que fantosme ne ja hoir que te ayes porté ne vendra a bon chief en la fin." Trans. Maddox and Sturm-Maddox, 191.

gests that they are only appearances and illusions, as unstable as she herself is. According to Raymondin, she might not even exist in reality, and is in any event unfaithful to the nature she would claim for herself. Matilda Bruckner calls attention to the fact that Raymondin, after first spying on Mélusine, describes her as a "precious unicorn" and himself as a serpent spewing venom.[66] As she notes, Raymondin at first takes responsibility for his transgression in spying on Mélusine by assuming her form, if only metaphorically. At the same times, he likens her to a unicorn, symbol of Christ, unusual in its shape but in a good way. That she leaves her footprint as a trace in her final departure from the castle—"the form of her footprint remains"—furthers her resemblance to Christ.[67] But when he calls her a child-ruining serpent, he shows how easily she can be reshaped and how susceptible she is to negative reinterpretation. Her weekly metamorphosis becomes a metaphor for the way that others perceive her as a divided and therefore suspect creature, difficult to categorize and therefore easy to vilify. When she becomes a full-fledged dragon after Raymondin's betrayal, she is left unredeemed, consigned to "dark penance" until Judgment Day and no longer allowed to be on "God's side."[68] Raymondin makes her what he feared she was, although her nature remains unchanged. As she transforms, she tells him about her family history, as though to insist that all mysteries regarding her will now be resolved. She becomes transparent as she leaves the stage, relinquishing her power along with the hybridity and mystery that had supported them.

By intensifying the doubts that Mélusine's powers elicit, then, Jean intensifies a natural feature of marvels. As we saw in the first chapter, prophecy and demonic deception typically depend on imagination in a way that potentially makes the one difficult to distinguish from the other. Merlin, for instance, inspired suspicion in those who thought him not a prophet but a victim of demonic deception.[69] Jean dramatizes that uncertainty. The powers themselves are not debatable within the story, since Mélusine does accurately prophesy about past and future, and she does become half-serpent every Saturday. What is up for debate is their source and, relatedly, the true nature of Mélusine. In spite of her good deeds and her assurances about her piety, she is ultimately unknowable, as marvels are typically unknow-

66. Jean d'Arras, *Mélusine*, ed. Vincensini, 664: "la licorne precieuse." Bruckner, "Natural and Unnatural Woman," 25–26.

67. Jean d'Arras, *Mélusine*, ed. Vincensini, 704: "la fourme du pié toute escripte." Trans. Maddox and Sturm-Maddox, 194. On late medieval representations of Christ's footprints on the Mount of Olives, see Bynum, *Dissimilar Similitudes*, 227–51.

68. Jean d'Arras, *Mélusine*, ed. Vincensini, 696: "la penance obscure."

69. Sullivan, *The Danger of Romance*, 64.

able, even as they spur efforts to discover their root causes. They motivate inquiry, but rarely yield to it fully, and the mystery that remains around them is reflected in the suspicion that Mélusine cannot dispel. Insofar as he doubts Mélusine's goodness, spies on her, and then assails her, driving her away, Raymondin also shows that too much scrutiny can destroy marvels. At least as far as he is concerned, Mélusine's physical hybridity does not survive it. Further, once she assumes dragon form, she no longer aids her loved ones through prophecy or manages the expansion of her dynasty. One she is revealed, she is effectively inert as far as the action of the romance is concerned. Mélusine asks Raymondin to read her correctly, but he fails, and fails culpably. Her uncertain origins pose a question that can only be answered through faith, and by requiring certainty that it is not in the nature of marvels to provide, he proves himself unworthy of her love.

Mélusine is similar in these respects to Melior in *Partonopeu de Blois*, a twelfth-century French romance that was subsequently translated into Middle English and several other languages.[70] Melior, queen of Byzantium and trained enchantress, lures young Partonopeu to her home in Chef d'Oire, after scouts have determined that he is the most desirable potential mate for her. Delivered by an enchanted boat, he arrives to find a city surrounded by a checkered wall made of white and red marble, along with sculptures of lions and dragons, "and images of other shapes that seemed naturally alive."[71] The unusual ornament in the form of the wall and the expert craftsmanship that makes artificial things appear natural, along with the spectacular decoration of Melior's palace, lead him to "consider all of it a phantasm."[72] That is, he thinks these are illusions, the products of someone else's imagination or misrepresentations created by his own. He finds in the palace a table laden with food, and invisible servants who serve him, and "he marveled so much that he thought everything was enchanted. He was so amazed and so filled with wonder that he did not know whether he was sleeping or awake, and he did not know what to make of it, whether it

70. I refer here to the earlier and shorter French version of the romance, often referred to as the Arsenal text, as edited by Georges Crapelet, as well as the Middle English translation that is based on it, edited by Adam Bødtker. On the different surviving editions of the romance, as well as the relationship between the English and French texts, see Rikharðsdottir, *Medieval Translations and Cultural Discourse*, 113–21.

71. *Partonopeus de Blois*, 843–44, ed. Crapelet: "Et ymages d'autre figure / Qui samblent vives par nature." I have consulted the modern French translation by Collet and Joris, *Le roman de Partonopeu de Blois*, which has the same line numbers unless otherwise indicated.

72. *Partonopeus de Blois*, 880, ed. Crapelet: "A por fantosme tot tenu." Similarly, in the Middle English translation, he concludes that all "was but fantasye" or "fantayne" (*The Middle English Versions of Partonope of Blois*, 943 and 1061, ed. Bødtker).

were true or a lie."[73] The food, servants, and ornament are real things that seem like illusions that are designed to seem real. "He considered all of it to be make-believe and the work of the devil," not surprisingly disoriented by the seeming impossibility of invisible servants.[74] As Sarah Kay notes, "there are indications that this empty city is the realm of the dead," uninhabited, it seems, by any living creature aside from Partonopeu.[75] When he mistakes reality for the mere appearance of it, he misperceives marvels that ask to be misperceived; such is the nature of objects that are other than they seem.

Like Mélusine, Melior has special powers, though in Melior's case they are learned, not innate. In a charming scene of fairy formation, Melior explains that, as the only daughter of the Emperor of Constantinople, she received an excellent education, first in the liberal arts, then medicine, then religion, and finally in necromancy and enchantment.[76] As we would expect, her instruction in curative herbs, illusions, and the manipulation of the elements proceeded directly from conventional learning, the two differing more in degree than kind. She recounts creating for her father familiar illusions in which knights or animals fight, as well as creating illusions of other sorts, like making a room seem larger or smaller than it is. With that last skill, she has the power that the Miller tauntingly ascribes to the clerks in the *Reeve's Tale*, "Myn hous is streit [small], but ye han lerned art,/ Ye konne by argumentes make a place/ A myle brood of twenty foot of space" (4122–24). Hers is a talent so closely linked to learned magic that learnedness itself can be mocked with it. Melior can also create light in the dark and conceal whomever she chooses, hence the invisible servants who give Partonopeu dinner. She is expert, then, in optical illusions and light. Her different abilities are thematically consistent with one another, since all manipulate vision. They specifically undermine someone's ability to trust that what they see is real. That her powers have to do with sight underscores their association with perception and judgment. Her marvels preview the sort of work that Partonopeu will be called upon to perform, to exercise good judgment and deprioritize the evidence of his senses. Like Raymondin, he will be asked to recognize Melior's virtue in spite of temptations to do otherwise.

As a mistress of appearances, Melior is not surprisingly an object of sus-

73. *Partonopeus de Blois*, 905–10, ed. Crapelet: "Tant s'est li enfes merveliés / Qu'i cuide molt estre engeniés. / Tant s'esbahist, tant s'esmervelle / Qu'il ne set s'il dort u il velle, / Ne il ne set se ço est songe, / Se ço est voirs u c'est mençonge."

74. *Partonopeus de Blois*, 983–84, ed. Crapelet: "tot tient à fable / Et à ovraigne de diable."

75. Kay, *Courtly Contradictions*, 276.

76. *Partonopeus de Blois*, 4579–96, ed. Crapelet.

picion. Partonopeu doubts her piety, much as Raymondin suspects Mélusine's, and finally concludes that "she is not a demon" when he hears her swear on the Virgin Mary.[77] Melior does not prophesy, but her proficiency in illusions raises similar questions. Is hers an innocuous sort of diversion, or is it evidence of her unholiness, of her allegiance with dark powers? As with prophets like Merlin, so sorcerers, enchanters, and fairies who create powerful illusions inevitably raise questions about the source of their abilities, whether demonic or not. That is because such powers can arise from different sources, even though they are similarly unseeable and unprovable. It is the nature of such marvels to both motivate inquiry and complicate it. Romances like *Mélusine* and *Partonopeu de Blois* can therefore use marvels to test the devotion of men to women who, like the marvels they create, invite multiple, starkly different interpretations.

If belief is here a matter of faith, it is not the simplistic sort associated with credibility. Rather, to remain faithful to Mélusine and Melior is to resist superficial explanations and to exercise discretion. It is specifically not to be gullible. As Melior repeatedly tells Partonopeu, he need only respect her command that he not see her for more than a year in order to live happily ever after, but his initial concerns—when she first approaches him, invisible, he worries that she is a "living demon"—are not entirely allayed.[78] He continues to struggle when it comes to trusting what he cannot see, and his mother fuels his doubts. Worrying that "he has been deceived and mocked by the devil," she solicits the aid of a bishop to release her son from Melior's influence.[79] Part of what makes her concerns powerful is their plausibility. Melior tells Partonopeu, "your mother thinks and believes that I am someone who makes phantasms," and of course she does make phantasms.[80] That is a true belief, and it poses a challenge throughout the poem: until she loses or sacrifices her powers, Melior *can* deceive whomever she chooses. Her precise talent is that she can make things seem other than they are.

With Melior at its center, the romance not surprisingly focuses on the difficulty of distinguishing between similar scenarios and identifying those that are trustworthy. Partonopeu is asked, along with the reader, to see how similar situations are crucially different. Marvels' power to make one thing resemble another drives the poem, which creates sets of superficially similar scenes. The discretion required of one who inspects marvels is required

77. *Partonopeus de Blois*, 1158, ed. Crapelet: "maufés n'est ce mie."

78. *Partonopeus de Blois*, 1120, ed. Crapelet: "vif maufé."

79. *Partonopeus de Blois*, 3925–26, ed. Crapelet: "si traïs / Et par diable escarnis."

80. *Partonopeus de Blois*, 4253–54, ed. Crapelet: "vostre mère cuide et croit / Que quanques fac fantosme soit."

of the reader as well. The speaker suggests as much as the poem begins, when he reminds his reader that a wise person "carefully inspects every word" in order to understand its sense, and then takes to heart those words that encourage good behavior and discards the bad.[81] He asks the reader to make distinctions of the sort that Partonopeu fails to make. His failure in this respect lies at the heart of one of the romance's best known scenes, when he, brought unwittingly to the same bed in which an invisible Melior lies, rapes her.[82] She assures him that she would have fought him off if she had been able: "Had I had the strength, I assure you that I would have broken all your fingers," or, in the Middle English, "Had I had strengthe or ells myghte, / I dar welle say in all þys fflyghte / Ye shulde not have had þat now ye have."[83] She wanted him to come to her palace and lie in her bed, but she did not want him to rape her. The scene undermines the conventions of noble courtship in a way that makes it more disorienting. Melior had worried, she says, that Partonopeu would think she was promiscuous by bringing him to her, and he is too young to be presented to the court as her mate, but by the end of the scene, the question of her virtue has given way to the question of his.[84] She had seemed to compel him to come to her, but in the end *he* compels *her*. Partonopeu here fails in an extreme way to read Melior's marvels properly. By refusing to respect the difference between his desire and hers, he realizes the negative potential of marvels to provoke rash judgments, and he shows just how dangerous the failure to consider a marvel carefully can be.

The poem invites us to read this scene in conjunction with another courtship that, although not physically violent, is decidedly unchivalrous. Partonopeu's mother, with the consultation of her brother, the king of France, seeks to reroute his affections. She gets him drunk with wine that, in the Arsenal text, is not explicitly spiked, though there are some hints that it might be. When Partonopeu returns to Melior and confesses his misdeed, she warns him not to let the devil deceive him into seeing her "either with drinks or with poisons."[85] Drinks and poisons are closely linked here,

81. *Partonopeus de Blois*, 125, ed. Crapelet: "porgart cascune parole."

82. On the appropriateness of the term "rape" here, see Vines, *Women's Power in Late Medieval Romance*, 93–99. Rikharðsdottir helpfully compares the French, English, and Old Norse versions of the scene in *Medieval Translations and Cultural Discourse*, 132–43.

83. *Partonopeus de Blois*, 1309–10, ed. Crapelet: "Se force eüsce, par mes lois, / Ja vos froissasce tos ces dois." *The Middle English Versions of Partonope of Blois*, 1584–86, ed. Bødtker.

84. Partonopeu is thirteen years old in the Arsenal text and eighteen in its Middle English translation.

85. *Partonopeus de Blois*, 4183, ed. Crapelet: "U par boires u par puisons."

in a way that suggests the mother's wine has special properties. The Middle English is more explicit, calling the wine a "craft," "enchawntenment," and "charmynge."[86] Once Partonopeu drinks it, he is filled with passion toward the king's niece, presumably Partonopeu's cousin, and he agrees to marry her, only coming to his senses once the niece boasts about how she has made Partonopeu relinquish his former love. In order to steer his affections away from Melior, then, Partonopeu's mother uses tactics of the sort that she wrongly accuses Melior of using. Assuming that Melior has bewitched him, she uses magic or simple liquor to make him love. She responds to an imagined sort of love potion, in other words, with a better functioning one, manipulating Partonopeu's desires in a way that Melior does not. One woman encourages love through magic that steers Partonopeu toward her, while the other manipulates his affections against his wishes. One uses magic to aid love and the other uses magic, or simple intoxication, to compel it. The poem invites its reader to compare these two superficially similar scenes and understand the crucial differences between them, just as Partonopeu is supposed to recognize that Melior is more trustworthy than his mother. As marvels make different sorts of phenomena resemble one another, so the plot produces similar confusion regarding the women who produce such marvels, requiring their beloveds and the reader to distinguish carefully between them. Notice that Melior reassigns the part of the villain in her warning to Partonopeu: it is his mother who is the demon, not her. As Sarah Kay writes, "a series of parallels and contrasts" connects the two women, "as though each were the anamorphic distortion of the other."[87] Melior asks Partonopeu to distinguish them properly, and pressures the reader to do so as well, using superficially similar situations to place a premium on scrutiny and discretion.

Like Raymondin, Partonopeu exposes his beloved against her wishes, and just as Raymondin's exposure of Mélusine exposes his unfaithfulness, so Partonopeu's exposure of Melior reveals his fickleness, not hers. After her effort to reroute Partonopeu's affection fails, his mother devises another plan that underscores the poem's indebtedness to the Cupid and Psyche myth.[88] She gives her son a lantern that is, again, explicitly enchanted in the Middle English text—Partonopeu says that "the crafte of Nygromansy" made it—but not in the Arsenal. He is to use it to inspect Melior because,

86. *The Middle English Versions of Partonope of Blois*, 5126, 5446, 5308, and 5333, ed. Bødtker.

87. Kay, *Courtly Contradictions*, 282.

88. Rikharðsdottir, *Medieval Translations and Cultural Discourse*, 113–14.

his mother explains, "demons are ugly."[89] Partonopeu uses it and concludes "that he had never seen a more beautiful woman," which resolves all his doubts.[90] He learns that she has nothing to hide, but only by violating his repeated promises to her. He hides the lantern under the covers, signaling his infidelity to Melior as he not only breaks his many promises to her but replaces her in their bed. That he conceals a lantern shows how perverse his behavior is: lanterns are made to illuminate, not to be hidden. By exposing her nakedness against her wishes, he again pursues his desire at the expense of hers, and also seems eager to co-opt her powers. Melior's special ability, as we have seen, is to play with appearances, creating illusions and making people invisible. Through the lantern, Partonopeu not only appropriates that power for himself but deprives Melior of it. Indeed, once he exposes her, she loses her powers, as she had warned. It is not clear what this loss consists of—whether the powers are relinquished, for instance, or somehow destroyed—but it is to be expected that, once Melior is no longer mysterious, she will no longer be marvelous. As transparency flattens Mélusine, so Melior becomes less exceptional once she poses no puzzle.

Spying and shining bright lights are antithetical to marvels, which, as we have seen, thrive on indeterminacy and collapse without it. That is what makes them effective as devices to test a lover's devotion and faith. Features of marvels that are by now familiar—including their openness to competing interpretations, their ability to inspire confusion and disorientation, and their inscrutability—make them well suited to proving devotion that should not require evidence. Marvels like these require the lover to recognize his beloved's virtue even when circumstances invite him not to. They require him not to be misled by appearances. However, believing in the benevolence of Mélusine or Melior, when they produce the sorts of marvels that demons might also produce, turns out to be too big a challenge for either lover. By failing to honor their requests not to be spied upon or seen, Raymondin and Partonopeu instead show how easy it is to doubt the makers of marvels. When they peek behind the curtain, they expose marvels at the cost of the marvels themselves. In addition, Raymondin loses Mélusine forever, while Partonopeu has to embark on an elaborate and lengthy quest to regain Melior's affections. Neither reads marvels or their makers properly. Each has experienced his beloved's benevolence on many occasions,

89. *The Middle English Versions of Partonope of Blois*, 5850, ed. Bødtker; *Partonopeus de Blois*, 4462, ed. Crapelet: "lais ert li maufés."

90. *Partonopeus de Blois*, 4516, ed. Crapelet: "Qu'ainc ne vit mais tant bele rien." In the Middle English version, she is "þe ffeyrest shape creature / That ever was formed þorow nature": *The Middle English Versions of Partonope of Blois*, 5864–65, ed. Bødtker.

but they both worry that the women are unfaithful to their appearances, a temptation that is all the more powerful because of the mysteries lying under the surface of the marvels they generate. It is the nature of marvels to raise doubts, not to quash them. Only when interpretation is no longer required, when the nature of the women has been fully revealed, do the two men recognize their errors, but at that point they have failed their tests. To know with certainty that the women are benevolent is already to have betrayed them.

Fairies like Melior and Mélusine recall the jinn of the *sīra*, which likewise claim different allegiances and create confusion.[91] In the Quran, they describe themselves: "some among us submit and some among us are unjust," and those who are unjust are "kindling for hell" (72:14–15). They "could at anytime shift toward goodness or toward evil."[92] With roots in pre-Islamic paganism, they feature in the Quran as supernatural creatures, born of fire rather than earth, sometime servants of Solomon. Residents of the sublunary world, they are created to serve God alongside humans.[93] Muḥammad converted jinn as well as people, and literary characters like Sayf ibn Dhī Yazan conquer the world of jinn as they conquer other nations. The jinn might also marry humans, as in the *sīrat Sayf al-Tījān*. Particularly common is the marriage of a human man to a *jinnīya*; women joined to male jinn are more often compelled. Like fairies, jinn attracted serious scholarly attention. The fourteenth-century jurist al-Shiblī, for instance, considers the possible mechanisms of human-jinn procreation, describes the nature of jinn bodies, and debates (inconclusively) whether marriage with them is permissible.[94] William of Auvergne, as we shall see, wondered whether Merlin or the Huns were demon progeny, as al-Shiblī pondered human-jinn procreation and reported that the queen of Sheba, Bilqīs, had a jinn mother.[95] Because they are changeable, they have no single, true nature, and so the *Thousand and One Nights* tells the story of two evil *jinnāni* who are inspired by the beauty of two young lovers and devote themselves to helping them.[96] The jinn often elicit confusion—the question "are you

91. As Amira El-Zein notes, "The term jinn in Arabic refers to all invisible spiritual entities," including jinn, demons, and angels, especially in pre-Islamic and early Islamic times (*Islam, Arabs, and the Intelligent World of the Jinn*, 34).

92. El-Zein, *Islam, Arabs, and the Intelligent World of the Jinn*, xi.

93. Blatherwick, *Prophets, Gods, and Kings*, 24.

94. See al-Shiblī, *Ākām al-marjān fī aḥkām al-jānn*, ed. Badeen. See also Leemhuis, "Can You Marry a Djinni?"

95. Al-Shiblī, *Ākām al-marjān fī aḥkām al-jānn*, 70–71; Leemhuis, "Can You Marry a Djinni?" 225. For more on the development of legends around the queen of Sheba, see Lassner, *Demonizing the Queen of Sheba*.

96. *Thousand and One Nights*, 78th–83rd nights, ed. Mahdi, 241–52.

human or jinn?" appears often in the *sīra*—and they have special powers, but they tend not to elicit the same sort of suspicion as fairies. Their true nature, even when it alters, becomes manifest, and is not the subject of recurring doubt. In *Mélusine* and *Partonopeu de Blois*, good deeds do not prove a fairy's benevolence, which is why belief in the sorceresses becomes the test of a lover's devotion. Because she also creates illusions, she places further pressure on the distinction between how things seem and how they are. The mysteriousness of marvels becomes a tool to demand a lover's, as well as a reader's, careful attention and good judgment.

CLIGÉS AND THE PERCEPTION OF LOVE

As we have seen, marvels allow for competing explanations and raise the prospect of deception in ways that invite suspicion and therefore test devotion. They also highlight the uncertainties that define love. Emotions can be vexing, of course, hard to identify correctly in oneself and harder to do so in others. Even apart from the possibility of misidentifying it, love is potentially confounding because it can produce feelings that conflict with reality. For instance, in the *Cligés* of Chrétien de Troyes, Cligés's father Alexander stages a conversation with himself, as characters within Chrétien's poems are wont to do, and responds skeptically to his own claim that the God of Love has wounded him with an arrow: "How could he have pierced your body when no wound is visible from the outside?"[97] How do you know that you are wounded if you cannot see the wound? By dividing Alexander into two characters, Chrétien makes him his own outside observer, dubious about the nature of his own pain. The difference between sensation and perceptible fact fractures his subjectivity, alienating the person who feels pierced from the one who sees no wound. Rather than "oafish literal-mindedness," the scene stages perplexity, a device that Chrétien often uses where love is the poem's subject because love, as he represents it, is a crisis of perception.[98] The arrow of love, he says, is the image of his beloved, Soredamors, which enters through the eye but without harming it, as sunlight streams through a pane of glass without injuring it. What Chrétien describes is what scholastic philosophers came to call the sensible species, the image of the object that enters the soul through the senses. An apple cannot enter the sense organs, but a representation or species of it can, and the same is true of Soredamors. Alexander misperceives the nature of

97. Chrétien de Troyes, *Cligés*, 693–94, in *Oeuvres complètes*, ed. and trans. Poirion and Walter: "Comant le t'a donc trait el cors, / Quant la plaie ne pert de fors?"

98. Gaunt, *Love and Death in Medieval French and Occitan Courtly Literature*, 130.

the injury as well as the image he apprehends. Although his heart detected welcome (*bele chiere*) in the image of Soredamors, it was deceived (*traïst*), and so he is doubly misled.[99] The arrow that hurt him was only an immaterial image, and the image itself wrongly showed him a well-disposed Soredamors. The fact that Soredamors *was* well-disposed toward him only deepens the confusion.

This is a highly complicated, would-be technical, and not exactly earnest way to explain the process of falling in love. It speaks to Chrétien's interest in logical and perceptual quandaries. As Eugene Vance writes, "Chrétien often fictionalizes, through his heroes, dilemmas of perception and judgment that were also matters of concern to the logicians of his time."[100] Such quandaries are by nature difficult to resolve. From the perspective of the poem, what Alexander feels (as though he is being struck with an arrow) and what he experiences cognitively (an image of Soredamors has reached the heart, which is a faculty of the will, and it has deemed Soredamors appealing) are confused, but not because Alexander's feelings are incorrect. In fact, the feeling is the more vivid and even the truer state. This is easier to see in a later scene, after the speaker has described Cligés as giving his heart to his beloved, Fenice: "it is not true, nor does it seem to be true, that two hearts can reside in the same body."[101] In both cases, the speaker confuses emotional states with physical ones, and then shows that the two are incommensurate: one body cannot actually have two hearts, and the arrow of love is not actually a physical arrow. At the same time, that confusion accurately captures the feeling of love, which has the force of a physical body in spite of its immateriality. It acts much like the marvels discussed in the early chapters that blur the boundary between the soul and the extra-animate world. The evil eye, for instance, is a gaze that physically transforms its object, as with the camel that falls. Powerful feelings can exercise the force of bodies, and love is more accurately characterized by them, by arrows and transplanted hearts, than by mere images.

True love proves itself through the special, bodily force it exercises, as is clear through contrast with the illusory quality of weaker emotions and through the marvels that characterize both. The feebleness of weaker

99. Chrétien de Troyes, *Cligés*, 740, 742, in *Oeuvres complètes*, ed. and trans. Poirion and Walter.

100. Vance, *From Topic to Tale*, 20. On Chrétien's interest in contraries and contradictions, see also Hunt, "Aristotle, Dialectic, and Courtly Literature," with a discussion of *Cligés* at 109–19.

101. Chrétien de Troyes, *Cligés*, 2807–8, in *Oeuvres complètes*, ed. and trans. Poirion and Walter: "n'est voirs, n'estre ne le sanble / Qu'an un cors ait deus cuers ansanble." Trans. Kibler, *Arthurian Romances*, 157.

affection is shown through the relationship of Fenice and Alis. Alexander's brother, Alis, forces Fenice to marry him against her wishes. Already in love with Cligés, Fenice enlists the help of her nurse, Thessala, to concoct a potion that will prevent Alis from having sex with her. When Alis sleeps, he will dream of having sex with her and will mistake "the dream for truth."[102] As Partonopeu, when served dinner by invisible servants, did not know whether he was awake or asleep, so Alis is led to confuse the one state for the other. The vividness of the dreamed images suggests perceptions and leads him to form false conclusions about their realness. They are, in fact, remarkably detailed and realistic. In his sleep, he tries to seduce her, while "she took pains to resist him and defended her virginity. He implored her and very sweetly called her his sweet friend. He thought he possessed her but did not possess anything."[103] Not only does he think that he has sex with her, but he thinks he conquers her. He lives out a fantasy of chaste feminine resistance and successful male persuasion. That he imagines himself the victor in this scenario makes his deception all the more powerful. These dreams are wish-fulfillments, seducing Alis because they present him with scenarios that he would *like* to be true. Rather than emotions that act with physical force, they are illusions that are twice removed from reality.

The poem continues: "he took his pleasure in nothing, for he possessed nothing, and he kissed nothing. He held nothing, he spoke to nothing, he saw nothing, and he embraced nothing. He struggled with nothing; he wrestled with nothing."[104] Brutal in its repetition, the poem exposes the self-deception that is Alis's supposed prowess. He appears to be almost willfully deceived, captive to an illusion he wishes were true. Again and again, night after night, he is deluded, and deserves to be deluded. As fabliaux often punish a man who is foolish in his expectations, so is Alis punished. He was not supposed to marry. Assuming power only when he wrongly thought that his brother Alexander, Cligés's father, had died, he was allowed to hold onto the throne because he promised Alexander that he would not produce an heir and would leave Cligés to rule after him. The agreement made him a puppet emperor: "both great and small affairs were

102. Chrétien de Troyes, *Cligés*, 3328, in *Oeuvres complètes*, ed. and trans. Poirion and Walter: "le songe a voir."

103. Chrétien de Troyes, *Cligés*, 3336–40, in *Oeuvres complètes*, ed. and trans. Poirion and Walter: "ele li fesoit dongier, / Et se desfant come pucele, / Et cil la prie et si l'apele / Molt dolcement sa dolce amie; / Tenir la cuide n'an tient mie." Trans. Kibler, *Arthurian Romances*, 163.

104. Chrétien de Troyes, *Cligés*, 3341–46, in *Oeuvres complètes*, ed. and trans. Poiron and Walter: "de neant est a grant eise, / Car neant tient, et neant beise, / Neant tient, a neant parole / Neant voit et neant acole, / A neant tance, a neant luite." Trans. Kibler, *Arthurian Romances*, 163.

presented to Alexander: whatever he commanded and said was done, and little was done without his approval. Alis had only the name of emperor."[105] He is an emperor superficially, and a husband wrongfully. With weak claims to both positions, he is aptly punished by illusions that render him impotent. Depriving him of access to Fenice's body, they also deprive him of the heir he ought not to produce. The illusions are alluring because they appear to give him what he wants, but instead they give him what he deserves: seeming reality that is instead pretense.

The situation that Alis finds himself in is a perversion of Alexander's when he searches his body for arrow-inflicted wounds or Cligés's when he feels he has lost his heart to Fenice. Alexander and Cligés feel love so powerfully that they think it manifests itself physically, while Alis's sexual liaisons involve no bodily contact at all. Surrounded by poor imitations and perversions, love elevates itself. It is all the more genuine for being positioned amid corruptions. It is, in Aranye Fradenburg's terms, "the foreverstunning Real" that is always sought, and sought all the more assiduously because it is elusive.[106] For all three men, what seems real is not, but the difference is crucial: Alexander's and Cligés's love is *as though* a physical force, so powerful is it, while Alis's is so feeble that it has no connection to bodies, even when it seems to. For Alexander and Cligés, emotion is so strong that it feels physical, but for Alis, physical contact consists only of illusions. The potion immerses him in his fantasies and destroys his ability to recognize them as such. It reflects an affection that is, compared to the world-altering passion of Alexander or Cligés, less vivid and less real. In other words, ignoble love is mere illusion. True love has the force of physical things.

Thessala's drugging of Alis is closely linked to her later drugging of Fenice, although in this case the drug proves love to be true rather than false. Eager to run away with Cligés but afraid to resemble Isolde, whom she mentions obsessively, Fenice decides that her wisest course is to appear to die, and then live secretly with her beloved.[107] The option is appropriate to a character named after the phoenix. Fenice feigns illness and then swallows a potion concocted by Thessala so that she appears dead. All are convinced except for three doctors from Salerno who happen to be passing through town. Convinced that she only pretends to be dead, they

105. Chrétien de Troyes, *Cligés*, 2568–73, in *Oeuvres complètes*, ed. and trans. Poiron and Walter: "Mes devant Alixandre vienent / Li grant afeire et li petit; / Fet est ce qu'Alixandres dit, / Et po fet an se por lui non. / Alys n'i a fors que le non, / Qui empereres est clamez." Trans. Kibler, *Arthurian Romances*, 154.

106. Fradenburg, "Simply Marvelous," 11.

107. On Tristan and *Cligés*, see Gaunt, *Love and Death*, 128–36.

torture her in increasingly vicious ways, stripping her, beating her, whipping her, and then pouring boiling lead onto her palms that "burned right through them," all without reviving her.[108] The potion makes her insensible to pain—under its power, "she would feel neither good nor bad"—but the disfigurement that her body undergoes, as well as the pain she feels when the potion wears off, qualifies her as "a saintly woman."[109]

When Cligés asks Alis for permission to go to England and prove himself a knight before King Arthur, he tells his uncle that "gold is rubbed against the touchstone so that its purity can be known."[110] Here, the Salernitan doctors are the touchstone that proves the purity of Fenice's love for Cligés. They nearly martyr (*martire*) her while they seek to expose her treachery (6007). That they pour lead through her palms makes her Christlike, her hands pierced by molten rather than molded lead. Her seeming death recalls Christ's death and resurrection, with each eventually ascending, restored. In Fenice's case, she rises not to heaven but to its likeness on earth, a tower built by the master craftsman Jehan, replete with an edenic garden outdoors where she can enjoy her beloved unhindered. These parallels mark Fenice's death as a real, even epic sacrifice. While Thessala's first potion reveals the emptiness at the heart of Alis's affection, the second one proves the heartiness of Fenice's.

The skeptical doctors are right that Fenice is alive and that she seeks to deceive her husband, but we see that their knowledge is inadequate to the circumstances. Salerno was a renowned center of medical learning, and it stands in contrast to Thessaly, for which Thessala is named, "where enchantments are taught and well-established."[111] Such literal-minded doctors are ill equipped to appreciate how Fenice sacrifices herself for love, and so in a true sense dies. The crucifixion imagery reflects poorly on them. They are as unsympathetic as Christ's crucifiers, unfaithful in this case because they fail to rank Fenice's devotion to Cligés above her trickery with respect to Alis. Her fake death represents, in other words, the true faith, while

108. Chrétien de Troyes, *Cligés*, 5990–91, in *Oeuvres complètes*, ed. and trans. Poiron and Walter: "est passez / Par mi les paumes d'outre en outre." Trans. Kibler, *Arthurian Romances*, 196.,

109. Chrétien de Troyes, *Cligés*, 5447, 6079, in *Oeuvres complètes*, ed. and trans. Poiron and Walter: "Ne bien ne mal ne sentira"; "molt sainte chose." Trans. Kibler, *Arthurian Romances*, 189, 197.

110. Chrétien de Troyes, *Cligés*, 4232–33, in *Oeuvres complètes*, ed. and trans. Poiron and Walter: "Por ce toche an l'or a l'essai / Que l'an conoisse s'il est fins." Trans. Kibler, *Arthurian Romances*, 174.

111. Chrétien de Troyes, *Cligés*, 2989–90, in *Oeuvres complètes*, ed. and trans. Poiron and Walter: "Ou sont feites les deablies, / Anseigniees et establies." Trans. Kibler, *Arthurian Romances*, 159.

medically correct doubt signifies as stubborn Jewishness, as blindness and betrayal. The doctors' irrationality is most visible in their paradoxical disregard for Fenice's death. Although doctors, they are the ones who nearly kill her, and would have done so if not for a group of women who attacked them just as "they were about to stretch her over the fire to be roasted and grilled."[112] They set out to prove that she lived, and the fact that they nearly kill her while attempting to expose life shows how profoundly they pervert the situation. Their obsession with exposing her treachery is the distorted image of the passion that leads Fenice to sacrifice herself. Instead of devotion, they detect fakery. Once again, we confront a rupture between appearances and realities, and again the literal explanation is the less accurate one. In the topsy-turvy world that the scene presents, the marvel renders judgments about true and false, about the real and imaginary unstable. Whereas Alis is deceived by what merely seems true, Fenice is best understood through appearances. The fact that she fakes her death in order to cheat on her husband is not the truth of her situation. The marvel makes her an actual martyr to love, its power reflecting the power of love to determine its own reality. As Sarah Kay writes, "love is an inverted order of reality, where the prevailing logic of the world is suspended," and the marvel helps to provide that alternative logic.[113] In this case, Fenice's love makes her sacrifice real.

Love proves itself in the context of illusions and deceptions, and marvels contribute in both respects, whether by creating illusions or by introducing the possibility of deception. They create an environment where love can display its unique power and lovers can prove their devotion. Marvels, like love, resist certitude; neither is easily proven. Aside from helping to advance the plot, they also create interpretive flexibility by presenting situations that can be explained in different ways and by complicating judgments regarding truth and falsehood. They call for sound judgment from those who can scrutinize appearances and recognize that truth might be found in illusions and feelings more than in actions. They also raise the possibility that power might reside outside of its traditional settings so that immaterial things, for instance, are stronger than material ones, and supernatural causes supplant natural ones. The prologue to *Mélusine* serves as an important reminder that this attitude toward marvels, and toward love, is

112. Chrétien de Troyes, *Cligés*, 5998–99, in *Oeuvres complètes*, ed. and trans. Poiron and Walter: "Ja la voloient el feu metre / Por rostir et por graïllier." Trans. Kibler, *Arthurian Romances*, 196. I thank Matilda Bruckner for her insights about the doctors and the implication that they represent New Testament Jews.

113. Kay, *Courtly Contradictions*, 248.

not necessarily earnest, even when it pretends to be. Marvels are useful in that capacity as well, since they constitute mysteries that might, ultimately, be based in nothing.

PROPHECY, GEOMANCY, AND OTHER REVELATIONS

I have stressed that marvels are not truth claims, and for that reason marvels whose purpose is to reveal truth, such as prophecy and related practices like soothsaying, divination, lot-casting, and sand-reading or geomancy, deserve special attention. We have encountered prophets, like Mélusine, who prophesy accurately, but this section is devoted to the forecasts, not the forecasters. Where the prophecies themselves are the focus of attention, they tend to confound as often as clarify. They are typical marvels insofar as they signify in unconventional and surprising ways, but they are unusually self-conscious ones because their legitimacy and meaningfulness are explicit concerns. Difficult to interpret and prone to competing interpretations, they often require external authentication of some sort in order to become legible, and even then they maintain their complexity. Such marvels are, again, mercurial and unstable objects and events that challenge the reliability of appearances and defy easy categorization. Rather than providing easy answers, they create situations in which judgments of truth and falsehood might be fluid, or might resolve in unusual ways. They retain, in other words, many of the characteristics they possess in other disciplines.

Apart from its uncertain source, discussed above, prophecy is prone to manipulation. In *Amadas and Ydoine*, for instance, an Anglo-Norman romance from the late twelfth or early thirteenth century, visions are concocted much like Thessala's potion in order to protect the virtue of the heroine. Ydoine loves a seneschal's son, but while he is off becoming worthy of her, she is forced to accept a count's marriage proposal. She enlists the help of three witches who visit the count and pretend to be the Fates. They tell him that, if he consummates his relationship with Ydoine, he will die, and he believes them. A manufactured vision protects her chastity. What is most remarkable about the scene is Ydoine's later elaboration of it. When she tries to extricate herself from their celibate marriage, she tells her husband that she had a vision while in Rome in which St. Peter and the three Fates appeared to her, telling her that he would die if he had sex with her, and that they had already told him so. She asks the count to confirm whether he has received such a vision, and he replies, "I know very well that you have not lied to me at all. What you have said to me is not an invention, for you have shown me perfect signs."[114] The "perfect signs" are presumably the similarities between her supposed vision and his. He confirms that he was warned not to consummate their marriage, and so he validates Ydoine's lie because it corresponds perfectly with her earlier lie. In the poem, prophecy constitutes its own discourse, both self-referential and self-authenticating. Because it relies on unconventional signs, it signifies differently than normal speech. However, its internal consistency in this case normalizes and validates it. The unexpectedly stable system of reference creates an aura of truth.

There is another reason why the count might believe the vision that Ydoine reports. When she describes it, before he responds with the words quoted above, Ydoine tells him, "When you marry another woman, you will have joy and comfort from her forever."[115] Less than one hundred lines later, the reader learns for the first time that the count too is in love with someone else, the daughter of the count of Poitiers. Whether knowingly or not, Ydoine promises the count the fulfillment of his deepest wish. "He would have gladly separated from Ydoine and married the other woman" earlier had he not feared the response of Ydoine's father, but her prophecy gives him the opportunity he sought.[116] Ydoine too gets what she wanted: the count releases her from their marriage, and she is freed to marry now-worthy Amadas. The meaning of such prophecies is hardly straightforward. They are literally false but speak in something like the optative mood, made true enough by being wished true. They create an alternative reality that all of the main characters prefer to the actual one, and so they agree to accept it. Such visions have all the provisionality and complexity of wishes that are finally realized.

Prophecies present themselves as authoritative, but as *Amadas and Ydoine* shows, they are susceptible to fakery, and they complicate judgments about their truth or falsity. Even when not deliberately manufactured, they might suffer from distortion as they pass through human hands. They typically require interpretation, and interpretation is necessarily unstable, especially when it is based on opaque procedures, such as reading sands or deciphering the behavior of birds. The content of prophecy, vision, or divination is hard to assess on its own, and so the best option for

114. *Amadas et Ydoine*, 7253–56, ed. Reinhard: "'Certes je le sai mult tresbien / Que menti ne m'avés de rien; / N'est pas controeve que me dites: / Enseignies m'ent mostrés parfites.'" Trans. Arthur, *Amadas and Ydoine*, 125.

115. *Amadas et Ydoine*, 7227–28, ed. Reinhard: "De cele que vous puis prendrois / Joie et confort tous jors avrois." Trans. Arthur, *Amadas and Ydoine*, 125.

116. *Amadas et Ydoine*, 7336–38, ed. Reinhard: "D'Ydoine fust mult volentiers / Partis . . . / Car l'autre tantost esposast." Trans. Arthur, *Amadas and Ydoine*, 126.

those who want to sound it out is to scrutinize the signs within it or the context that surrounds it, as the count does. In *Sayf ibn Dhī Yazan*, the manipulation of signs that the wizards see shows how provisional and equivocal they are. A *sīra* that reached its popular form no earlier than the fourteenth century, *Sayf ibn Dhī Yazan* is particularly dense with marvels.[117] As Lena Jayyusi writes, "nowhere in *sīra* literature is the magical and demonic given such a high profile in the plot."[118] The tale features a sorceress named ʿĀqila who, in the course of Sayf's rise to power, undermines those signs directly. In order to protect the work's eponymous hero, she confounds the local wizards she supervises by feeding them implausible revelations. Sayf arrives in the city of Qaymar in order to capture the Book of the History of the Nile, an object invested with magical powers and worshipped as a god by the locals. Aware of a prophecy that says he will steal the book and will go on to rule the lands of Ethiopia and Sudan, the people of Qaymar guard against him, but ʿĀqila circumvents their spells by catapulting him into the city. The people know through sorcery that he has arrived, and the anxious king commands a group of wizards to determine his location, but ʿĀqila, "the mother of wizards,"[119] thwarts their efforts. She stages three scenes that she knows the wizards will be able to see when they cast their sands, scenes that place Sayf in circumstances so ridiculous that they will discredit the wizards who describe them.[120]

First, ʿĀqila places the lower part of Sayf's body inside a fish and the upper part inside a large, semimythical bird and then lowers him into a well so that he is half-submerged. The wizards, reluctant to describe the scene, ask the king to guarantee their safety before proceeding. They divine that Sayf entered the city in a wooden chest and then a fish swallowed him and a bird swooped down to eat him from above, the two creatures seemingly fighting for the morsel that is Sayf. The vision is so implausible that nobody believes it, and the king dismisses the wizards in disgust. When the wizards are to meet a second time, ʿĀqila attaches eagle wings to the back of a gazelle and places Sayf beneath its body. The wizards see not just a hybrid creature with Sayf beneath it but the "joints of rope and iron" that attach

117. On the date of the *sīra*, see Blatherwick, *Prophets, Gods and Kings*, 18. As she notes, the variants of individual *siyar* vary so markedly that it is hard to speak of a single text, but the version studied here is the one usually studied in scholarship (12).

118. Jayyusi, Introduction to *The Adventures of Sayf Ben Dhi Yazan*, xvi.

119. *Sīrat Fāris al-Yaman al-Malik Sayf ibn Dhī Yazan*, 1:83: "umma al-ḥukamāʾi." Trans. Jayyusi, *The Adventures of Sayf ben Dhi Yazan*, 49.

120. On geomancy and Islamic views toward it, see Fahd, *La divination arabe*, 196–204; and Savage-Smith and Smith, "Islamic Geomancy and a Thirteenth-Century Divinatory Device."

the wings, as well as the piece of wood that supports Sayf's weight.[121] The king responds by killing six wizards. Finally, ʿĀqila places Sayf, hands atop his head, on an inverted gold mortar in the middle of a brass dish filled with blood, itself placed inside a larger dish filled with milk. The wizards think he sits on a golden mountain surrounded by a sea of blood and a river of milk. They too are incredulous in the face of such unlikely revelations—they tell ʿĀqila, "This enemy has amazed our minds and bereft us of reason, for what we see before us is beyond any sound mind to understand, astounding whoever hears it"—but they proceed all the same, and the king, again contemptuous, kills three more of them.[122] They are false wizards, he says, "pretending to true arts," offering "words to cloud the mind."[123]

The genius of ʿĀqila's plan is that it makes truth look manufactured. Her name means "wise" or "rational," and indeed her cleverness is her defining feature. Because she knows "secret sciences" and the wizards' art, she can anticipate their method of interpretation and manipulate it.[124] As she tells the king, "each casting will produce its own signs and patterns," and she thwarts the wizards by planting signs that look like signs.[125] They look, in other words, like raw data, symbols that are not fully interpreted. All of the scenes that the wizards see in the sands are unlikely, beginning with the first: a flight in a wooden chest, and then a human-eating fish and bird fighting over Sayf, still alive, in a dark place. ʿĀqila skinned the fish before placing it around Sayf's body, and when the wizards declare that "a fish has swallowed him," we see them interpreting the scene in order to make some sense of it, as people do when they confront perplexing signs, linguistic and otherwise.[126] Assuming that they see Sayf's state clearly, and the scene suggests that they do, they must overlook the fact that the fish is dead and skinned in order to tell a more plausible story. At the same time, they imagine a past for the scene, with a fish first swallowing Sayf and then the *rukh* descending from above. They are like any reader who, presented with dis-

121. *Sīrat Fāris al-Yaman al-Malik Sayf ibn Dhī Yazan*, 1:80: "awṣālu min al-ḥibāli wa-ḥadīdu." Trans. Jayyusi, *The Adventures of Sayf ben Dhi Yazan*, 46.

122. *Sīrat Fāris al-Yaman al-Malik Sayf ibn Dhī Yazan*, 1:83: "hādhā al-gharīmu adhhala ʿuqūlanā wa-adhhaba maʿqūlanā fa-inna alladhī narāhu fī al-takhti mā yadkhulu ʿaqla ʿāqilin wa-lladhī yasmaʿuhu yuṣbiḥa dhāhilun." Trans. Jayyusi, *The Adventures of Sayf ben Dhi Yazan*, 48.

123. *Sīrat Fāris al-Yaman al-Malik Sayf ibn Dhī Yazan*, 1:83: "munāfiqūna . . . hādhā al-qawlu yuḥayyiru al-afkāra." Trans. Jayyusi, *The Adventures of Sayf ben Dhi Yazan*, 49.

124. *Sīrat Fāris al-Yaman al-Malik Sayf ibn Dhī Yazan*, 1:75: "ʿulūmi al-aqlāmi." Trans. Jayyusi, *The Adventures of Sayf ben Dhi Yazan*, 40.

125. *Sīrat Fāris al-Yaman al-Malik Sayf ibn Dhī Yazan*, 1:80: "kullu takhtin lahu ashkālun wa-awzānun." Trans. Jayyusi, *The Adventures of Sayf ben Dhi Yazan*, 46.

126. *Sīrat Fāris al-Yaman al-Malik Sayf ibn Dhī Yazan*, 1:78: "ibtalaʿahu [reading *hāʾ* for *tāʾ marbūṭa*] samakatu." Trans. Jayyusi, *The Adventures of Sayf ben Dhi Yazan*, 43.

crete pieces of data, seeks to connect them. However, the story they piece together still looks like a story, an invention composed of mismatched parts. They conclude, "And so he remains in that trap," caught between two creatures trying to nab him as prey.[127] It is an implausibly static scene, as though time has been paused at the most unlikely of moments. It looks staged, and it is staged, though in such a way as to discredit the wizards who feel honor-bound to report their insights accurately. It appears to reveal their incompetence rather than ʿĀqila's prodigious scheming.

As is often the case, the primary marvel, the casting of sands, is not the source of wonder here, but rather the narrative surrounding it. The wizards' art is not the problem, and so the blame falls on the wizards themselves. ʿĀqila accuses them of eating the wrong foods, which have clouded their judgment so that they misperceive the "signs and patterns" that the sands present, failing to find order within them. She further undermines the wizards in the second scene, which even more clearly advertises its constructedness. The wizards see Sayf in the grasp of a flying, four-legged beast, with wings that "have joints of rope and iron to the right and left, and he himself is laid on a piece of wood."[128] ʿĀqila plants red herrings within the tableau so that it looks like an elaborate construction. It is as though the wizards are the ones joining images together with rope and iron pegs, concocting a scene that, in line with ʿĀqila's comments on the wizards' diet, itself seems undigested. With its crudely hitched-together images, it paints the wizards as flat-footed or unskilled readers who fail to understand the symbolism of the sands.

The first two tableaux call to mind the many hybrid creatures from travel literature and chronicles. In other words, they are recognizable as marvels, and by the conventions of the genres, they belong to distant, even imagined lands. They are inconsistent with what the king knows to be true, which is that Sayf is within the kingdom and that he threatens it, and the inconsistency makes them even less believable. In response to the second divination, for instance, the king asks his people whether any of them has seen such a creature snatch a man and fly away with him, and when they say no, they make the point that spectacular marvels like these can only be believed at a distance. If they are supposed to be local, then the people will know that they do not exist.

The third scene likewise borrows the imagery of distant places, not their

127. *Sīrat Fāris al-Yaman al-Malik Sayf ibn Dhī Yazan*, 1:78: "huwa bāqin ʿalā dhālika al-ḥamālu." Trans. Jayyusi, *The Adventures of Sayf ben Dhi Yazan*, 44.

128. *Sīrat Fāris al-Yaman al-Malik Sayf ibn Dhī Yazan*, 1:80: "awṣālu min al-ḥibāli wa-ḥadīdu dhātu al-yamīni wa-dhātu al-shimāli wa-huwa ʿalā khashabin maṭrūḥa yataḥarraku." Trans. Jayyusi, *The Adventures of Sayf ben Dhi Yazan*, 46.

fantastic creatures but their fantastic landscapes. The golden mortar at the center of the scene suggests a mountain, and the side of the outer brass dish a wall, with a sea of blood and a river of milk between them. The wizards again engage in a degree of interpretation, turning the dishes and liquids into a natural terrain, but one that cannot be local. The king asks, "Where in our city can we find a mountain of gold, a sea of blood, a wall of brass, and a river of milk?" and the answer of course is nowhere.[129] Such features are characteristic of foreign or imagined lands. Roger Bacon, for instance, writes that there are places where it rains milk or blood.[130] As I mentioned in chapter 2, the golden mountain is the standard example of imagination's procedure for invention: it takes two familiar images, gold and a mountain, and combines them into something never before seen. Finding Sayf positioned atop such a mountain, the wizards seem to have placed him in an imaginary construct, and in fact the setting is a product of imagination, though of 'Āqila's rather than theirs. She boasts, "I have brought their work to nought, confounding their arts and turning the tables on them," giving them signs that are not signs.[131] What is literally true looks fanciful, and that is what protects 'Āqila's secret.

In the manner of marvels, the hybrid creatures and fantastic landscape signify as enigmas, but in this context, they beggar belief. The force of the marvels lies ultimately in the fact that they are mostly true. The hybrid animals are not alive, and the supposed landscape is made of a mortar and other dishes, but the wizards see them correctly. They simply misinterpret the data that their arts present to them. Although the marvels seem impossible, they defy expectations by being what they seem to the wizards to be. A gazelle really is yoked to eagle wings with rope, and Sayf really is suspended on a plank beneath. The marvels are products of 'Āqila's machinations, but they capture the mis-seeming nature of marvels perfectly. The text cleverly plays with their conventions, since marvels typically present enigmas that are not as they seem, and here the surprise is that they are almost exactly as they seem. Another layer of complexity comes in the fact that the wizards' reports play differently to the king and his people than to the audience. The wizards cannot believe what they see, and the king and

129. *Sīrat Fāris al-Yaman al-Malik Sayf ibn Dhī Yazan*, 1:83: "naḥnu fī madīnatinā min ayna fīhā jabalun min dhahabin wa-baḥrun min al-damin wa-sūrun min nuḥāsin wa-nahrun min labanin." Trans. Jayyusi, *The Adventures of Sayf ben Dhi Yazan*, 49.

130. Bacon's edition of the *Secretum secretorum*, ed. Steele, *Opera hactenus inedita Rogeri Baconi*, 5:11.

131. *Sīrat Fāris al-Yaman al-Malik Sayf ibn Dhī Yazan*, 1:81–82: "anā afsadtu 'alayhim 'amalahum wa-ḥīrathum fī umūrihim wa-radadtu 'alayhim tadbīrahum." Trans. Jayyusi, *The Adventures of Sayf ben Dhi Yazan*, 47.

his people are equally incredulous, but the reader knows that the visions are close to the truth. Again, marvels call for critical readers who can separate what seems to be the case from what actually is the case in scenes that deliberately complicate judgments about truth and falsehood. The artistry of the author and the challenge to the audience are equally perceptible, and both contribute to the pleasures of the text.

A well-known example from the life of Merlin makes similar points with respect to prophecies that seem impossible but, in Merlin's case, are publicly proven true. In Geoffrey of Monmouth's *Vita Merlini*, Merlin reveals that his sister, Ganieda the queen, has committed adultery, and she responds by trying to discredit him.[132] She asks him to predict the death of a young man nearby, and Merlin prophesies that the boy will be killed by falling from a high rock. Ganieda sends the boy off, has his hair cut and his clothes changed, and then bids him return. Presenting him as another person, Ganieda asks the same question. Merlin says that he will die a violent death in a tree. Ganieda then has the boy dress as a girl, and when he returns, Merlin predicts that he will die in a river. Confident that she has fooled Merlin into prophesying three different deaths for the same person, Ganieda rejoices, and her husband clears her of blame. The people "thought he had lied about the boy's death, in speaking of three deaths when he ought to have spoken of only one," and so they continue to think for years, until the boy becomes a man.[133] While hunting, his horse goes over a precipice, and the man falls toward a river. One of his feet, however, catches in a tree so that his lower body is submerged in the stream while his upper body hangs from the tree. "By his triple death he proved the prophet true."[134]

The account of the triple death appears as well in Robert de Boron's influential story of Merlin.[135] There, Merlin is tested by one of the king's barons who envies Merlin's high standing with the king. The baron asks Merlin to tell him how he will die, appearing in three different guises to do so, and

132. The *Vita Merlini* is distinct from the *Prophetiae Merlini* that Geoffrey included as the seventh chapter in his *Historia regum Brittaniae*. As Julia Crick notes, the *Vita* was "not widely influential"; it survives in only one complete manuscript, edited by Basil Clarke (Crick, "Geoffrey of Monmouth, Prophecy and History," 359).

133. Geoffrey of Monmouth, *Vita Merlini*, 391–92, ed. and trans. Clarke: "Mentitumque tamen pueri de morte putebant / quam dixit ternam cum dicere debuit unam."

134. Geoffrey of Monmouth, *Vita Merlini*, 415, ed. and trans. Clarke: "fecit vatem per terna pericula verum."

135. As James Wade notes, Robert de Boron's *Merlin* was the key source for the Merlin of the Vulgate Cycle (*Fairies in Medieval Romance*, 11). Paul Zumthor makes a stronger claim: "the romance Merlin is derived entirely from Robert de Boron" ("Merlin: Prophet and Magician," 133).

Merlin responds that the questioner will break his neck, hang, and drown. The king withholds judgment and has to wait only a short while before the baron dies as forecasted: he falls from his horse, breaks his neck, and then tumbles into the river, but his leg catches on a bridge.[136] The puzzle of Merlin's prophecy is that it is implausible on its face, discrediting him when he presents it, and validating his powers when it comes true. He secures his credentials as a prophet and silences his skeptics by foreseeing so unlikely an event. Had Sayf been discovered as described in *Sayf bin Dhī Yazan*, the wizards would have been similarly vindicated. Although the outcomes of the stories differ, the prophet and the geomancer both reveal truths that seem impossible, distinguishing what is believable from what is real. Even when confirmed, the truths revealed remain complex. How unlikely is it that Merlin would be asked to predict the death of someone who dies in such an unusual way? Prophetic marvels are as puzzling as any we have seen, generating wonder and engaging their readers through their sheer complexity. In that respect, they retain their character as marvels.

By way of conclusion, I turn to Marie de France's *Lanval*, which returns us to the topic of fairies, in this case a fairy who is publicly shown to be real. While away from court one day, Lanval is approached by an almost impossibly beautiful and rich woman who knows all about his circumstances before he says a word, offers herself to him, and promises to visit him whenever he imagines a meeting place for them. She will be invisible to all other men—"no man save you will see me or hear my voice," she tells him—and she delivers gifts imperceptibly.[137] She is, in other words, a fairy, a status confirmed by the fact that Lanval, doubting (*dotaunt*) his memories of their encounter, does not know what to make of her: "He was at a loss to know what to think, for he could not believe it [*s'aventure*] was true."[138] Fairies often inspire such uncertainty, as we have seen. Of course she commands Lanval not to reveal her existence, and of course he does so anyway, telling Queen Guenevere that he has a lover much more beautiful than her. Arthur summons a panel of barons to determine whether Lanval's beloved in fact surpasses Guenevere or whether he spoke only "out of scorn [*pur vilté*]," with the intent to hurt the queen.[139] As the barons deliberate, the beloved's four attendants arrive

136. Robert de Boron, *Merlin*, in *Le roman du graal*, ed. Cerquiglini, 148–51. Trans. Bryant, *Merlin and the Grail*, 86–88.

137. Marie de France, *Lanval*, 169–70, in *Les lais de Marie de France*, ed. Rychner: "Nuls hom fors vus ne me verra / Ne ma parole nen orra." Trans. Burgess and Busby, *The Lais of Marie de France*, 75.

138. Marie de France, *Lanval*, 198, 199–200, in *Les lais de Marie de France*, ed. Rychner: "Esbaïz est, ne seit que creire, / Il ne la quide mie a veire." Trans. Burgess and Busby, *The Lais of Marie de France*, 75.

139. Marie de France, *Lanval*, 456, in *Les lais de Marie de France*, ed. Rychner.

and then the lady herself. She is his *guarant*, or witness, the proof needed to show that he spoke truly.[140] Before the king and his barons, she "let her cloak fall so that they could see her better."[141] There is no subtlety about the fact that her realness resolves the story. Brought before a panel of judges, she is the sole piece of evidence Lanval produces and the only one he needs.

The question that Lanval's fairy beloved answers is less "Did Lanval speak out of spite?" than "Are fairies real?" We know he spoke out of spite; the poem says so. Her arrival is the real revelation. On top of the fact that Lanval is only half-convinced of his good fortune when he meets her, he repeatedly tells the court that his beloved will not appear, even as four of her attendants pass before them. Lanval broke his promise to her, and she was clear that he would never see her again if he did. It becomes conventional in romance for such promises to be broken, and even if such a convention existed when Marie wrote the lai, such transgressions are not always forgiven, as *Mélusine* testifies. The surprise of the fairy's appearance before the court is also the surprise that such a creature might exist. She is like an improbable prophecy that nonetheless comes true, and she suggests that an open question underlying many marvels is whether they might be seen. In Arthur's court, before a panel of judges, she defends her very realness.

It might fairly be noted that marvels were part of actual trials, not just imagined ones as in *Lanval*.[142] Condemnation of sorcery, of divination, of belief in sylvans and the like were hardly everyday affairs, but neither were they insignificant.[143] Richard Firth Green notes, "One might argue that it was precisely the contested nature of fairy belief that guaranteed its narrative potency for medieval people."[144] Fairies and other marvels that were subjected to legal scrutiny might well have been more vivid or exciting in a narrative framework as a result. Perhaps that also contributed to the uncertainty that characterizes them and the scrutiny they elicit. Potions and feelings might in fact exercise more power than emperors and arrows, so one must read them carefully. Marvels are not enchanting because they stupefy their spectators, then, but because they compel attention and raise questions. They invite readers to puzzle over them, not to accept them credulously. They are hard to believe and hard to understand, and that is much of what makes them enchanting.

140. Marie de France, *Lanval*, 451, in *Les lais de Marie de France*, ed. Rychner.

141. Marie de France, *Lanval*, 605, in *Les lais de Marie de France*, ed. Rychner: "Sun mantel ad laissié cheeir, / Que mieuz la peüssent veeir."

142. See Green, *Elf Queens and Holy Friars*, 42–75.

143. See, for instance, Bailey, *Fearful Spirits, Reasoned Follies*; and Veenstra, *Magic and Divination at the Courts of Burgundy and France*.

144. Green, *Elf Queens and Holy Friars*, 72.

[CHAPTER 6]

Mutatis Mirabilibus

A structuring assumption in scholarship on marvels in medieval romance is that contemporary readers were susceptible to their power in a way that modern readers are not. As Patty Ingham puts it, "if readers of medieval romance found plenty of ways to be enchanted, medievalists have as often been wary of the enchanting aspects of medieval texts."[1] As a result, the modern reader who studies premodern texts might be alienated from their medieval, wonder-prone audience, unmoved by the very qualities that most impressed them. Helen Cooper reads such disenchantment backward, into the authors of medieval English romance themselves. She famously argues that it is "rare for any romance not to leave a sense of disappointment about its marvels," which are "often boring, disappointing, predictable."[2] "Sophisticated authors," seemingly jaded, recognized as much and deactivated their marvels so that the complexity and depth of their literary characters might be enhanced.[3] Since, in her view, marvels give the genre of romance its coherence, a lot rides on their function or failure. As Aranye Fradenburg explains, "Romance is a kind of entertainment whose job is to deliver 'wonders' (things or occurrences that astonish), and thus to deliver us from feeling 'weary,'" and it cannot fill its brief if its marvels fail to impress.[4] Whether its authors were immune to the enchanting power of marvels, or whether modern readers alone are, we are left with the same image of a relatively simplistic, easily impressed medieval audience.

The common belief that medieval people were entranced by marvels

1. Ingham, "Little Nothings," 58n16. John Ganim likewise writes of the "disenchantment of romance current in modern criticism of medieval romance" ("Myth of Medieval Romance," 163), and Daniel Poirion writes that medieval readers responded to marvels differently than modern readers do (*Le merveilleux dans la littérature française du Moyen Age*, 4).

2. Cooper, *English Romance in Time*, 137.

3. Cooper, *English Romance in Time*, 152.

4. Fradenburg, "Simply Marvelous," 21.

is tied to the familiar characterization of the Middle Ages as enchanted. For instance, "if there was an age when anything was considered possible, it was the Middle Ages," and that is why, according to Claude Lecouteux, people in the period embraced marvels.[5] This image of medieval people, mouths agape, credulously accepting both miracles and marvels, is still dominant. Most often associated with Max Weber but not original to him, the belief that medieval people were rapt by what seemed a magical world depends on an opposition to a disenchanted, more rigorously rational modernity.[6] Scholars have disputed both claims, but in recent years they have devoted more energy to rehabilitating enchantment than distancing the period from it.[7] In *Affective Medievalism*, Tom Prendergast and Stephanie Trigg argue not for enchanted but rather for emotionally invested modern readers. Even if they do not share medieval readers' affection for such spectacles as marvels, they still have an affective connection to the period's creations. The two build on Nicholas Watson's argument that the pastness of old objects makes them resonant in a way that links us affectively to them.[8] Modern readers might not believe that relics, for instance, possess special powers, but they might still be moved by them. The inclination to invest meaning in objects beyond what they strictly deserve persists, they note, and it offers a connection to the past that transcends any given relic.[9]

Their point is well taken. One might turn to Anne Lester, who writes of a basilisk-shaped clasp on a thirteenth-century coffret, one that seems designed, as she notes, to warn away anyone who would tamper with the charters it contained.[10] One does not need to believe that the basilisk kills with its sight alone in order to be charmed by the clasp. That does not necessarily entail the same sort of affective response that medieval readers were thought to have, but it places affect on both sides of the historical divide. Insofar as Prendergast and Trigg assume a historical shift in affective response, they share a fundamental assumption with Sianne Ngai, who studies the rise of what she calls "weak or trivial aesthetic categories," as opposed to the hefty ones of former days, namely, the sublime, though in

5. Lecouteux, "Introduction à l'étude du merveilleux médiéval," 273.

6. Orlemanski, "Who Has Fiction?" 150–51. As Eric Weiskott writes, "the Middle Ages . . . is the negative image of the ideological territory claimed for modernity" ("English Political Prophecy," 9).

7. See, for instance, Saler, "Modernity and Enchantment"; and Bennett, *The Enchantment of Modern Life*.

8. Prendergast and Trigg, *Affective Medievalism*, 106–11. They focus especially on Watson, "Desire for the Past."

9. Prendergast and Trigg, *Affective Medievalism*, 65–66.

10. Lester, "The Coffret of John of Montmirail."

many respects her argument could be extended to wonder as well.[11] They agree that readers do not instinctively respond to literature of the past with the same affective intensity that their past readers did, whether because of modern skepticism about marvels or because modern readers no longer give literature the power to inspire so dramatic a response as wonder. Prendergast and Trigg seek to redress the rupture, in part, by reorienting the perspective of modern readers.

Jeffrey Cohen offers a different approach. Building on the work of Jane Bennett, he argues that medieval enchantment should serve as a model for modern engagement with the natural world. Medieval attitudes toward nature, as he interprets them, are useful "for the challenge they pose to those who would disenchant the world."[12] Medieval writings about stones, in particular, with their attention to both marvelous and mundane qualities, present a form of enchantment that enlivens matter, that celebrates "inorganic agency" and "objectal agency."[13] Such an attitude ought to be cultivated, he argues, in the present. Whereas Prendergast and Trigg try to minimize the difference between past and present by pointing to the affective appeal of objects in both periods, then, Cohen seeks to revive a form of medieval enchantment in the present.

My focus instead is on the character of medieval enchantment, which is not as stupefying as it is sometimes taken to be. In my reading, enchantment is a brand of wonder specific to literature that stimulates imagination, which makes it both affectively and intellectually enlivening.[14] I make a distinction, then, between the enchantment that befalls characters within texts and that which applies to their readers. This chapter reads marvels within romances not as shiny objects that forestall thought but as complicated objects directed at informed readers who still might be described as enchanted. Assuming that medieval readers/hearers responded to marvels with the astonishment sometimes experienced by characters within the texts strikes me as a flawed approach. There is no denying that such paralyzing wonder does often strike characters in medieval works, or that wonder in general can be an undignified state. We might consider King Arthur's knights who, asked by the Green Knight if he might speak with Arthur, stare back at him, mute: "al studied þat þer stod, and stalked hym nerre / Wyth al þe wonder of þe world what he worch [work] schulde"

11. Ngai, *Our Aesthetic Categories*, 21.

12. Cohen, *Stone*, 9.

13. Cohen, *Stone*, 235 and 177.

14. On medieval definitions of wonder, see my "Wonder, Marvels, and Metaphor in the *Squire's Tale*," 463–66; and Harb, *Arabic Poetics*, 6–12.

(Everyone who stood there watched the knight and moved cautiously about him, wondering with all their hearts what he would do). Suspecting phantasms or magic of some sort, they stand "stonstil"—stone still, literally petrified—in response to the knight's prodding. It is an unheroic response to the marvel. Their open fear contrasts with Arthur's decision to save face: "Þaȝ Arþer þe hende kyng at hert hade wonder, / He let no semblaunt be sene" (Although Arthur the noble king felt wonder in his heart, he let no trace of it be seen).[15] He conceals his amazement, as though recognizing that it demeans him. Dante too writes in *Purgatorio* that stupor is quickly blunted in high hearts, and the author of *Sayf ibn Dhī Yazan* insists that wonder is dishonorable in the context of battle. Regarding Sayf, he writes, "Arab passion and pride seized him" as he bore into the battle, while "the coward was lost in amazement, and the base man fled, stupefied."[16] Still, there is no reason to assume that readers would be as incapacitated as such cowards, or as inwardly unsettled as Arthur or Sayf, when hearing or reading the texts. I can think of no example where the act of reading about marvels, as it is represented *within* medieval texts, overwhelms the reader with paralyzing amazement.

The common understanding of enchantment obscures the discerning, puzzling, or simply analytical response asked of readers, and all of those responses, I propose, ought to be included in the meaning of the term. My argument here is that authors use marvels strategically by altering them thoughtfully and showcasing their mutability. Marvels, in other words, are both changeable and representative of change. Authors manipulate them to highlight their alterations to source texts and to play with readerly expectations. They assume readers who are fluent in marvels and who might appreciate the skillful crafting and repurposing of them. Whereas chapter 5 focused on marvels as puzzles that test and otherwise challenge their spectators, whether characters within the text or its audience, this one reads marvels as emblems of change, and on several levels. Through sorcery, bewitchment, or otherwise, they can act on foreign objects, changing something's color or shape, but they symbolize changeability as well. They might represent a character's fickleness, for instance, or a king's impetuosity. The stories told about them are likewise subject to change in the manner of scripts that invite revision. As both enigmas and shape-shifters, marvels

15. *Sir Gawain and the Green Knight*, 1.237–38, 242, 467–68, ed. Tolkien et al.

16. Dante, *Purg.* 26.71; *Sīrat Fāris al-Yaman al-Malik Sayf ibn Dhī Yazan*, 1:327, 328: "fa-akhadhathu al-ḥamīyatu wa-l-nakhwatu al-ʿarabīyatu"; "wa-laḥiqa al-jabānu al-inbihāru wa-l-nadhlu wallā wa-ḥāru [ḥā'iru]." Trans. Jayyusi, *The Adventures of Sayf Ben Dhī Yazan*, 201, 202.

continue to be imaginative, creative, indeterminate, and significant in the ways that the early chapters of this book have described, but with features particularly suited to purely fictional settings.

ROMANCE AND THE REWRITING OF MARVELS

That romance and natural philosophy shared an interest in marvels was well known to people living in the Middle Ages, including poets.[17] Chaucer's *Squire's Tale* is explicit. Four gifts, delivered by an Arab ambassador to a Mongol "king" on his birthday, elicit varying degrees of astonishment from a gathered crowd. They are a bronze horse that flies, a mirror that foresees treachery, a sword that can pierce any armor and heal any wound it inflicts, and a ring that confers the ability to comprehend and speak in any avian tongue as well as knowledge of medicinal herbs. The people who gather to stare ("gauren") at them struggle to make sense of them, and they enlist analogs from both literature and philosophy (190). They turn to "olde poetries," comparing the bronze horse to both Pegasus and the Trojan Horse, but they think that it might also be "an apparence ymaad by som magyk" (206, 218). The spear suggests the spear of Achilles and how it healed King Telephus, but it also leads the people to "speken of sondry hardyng of [different ways of hardening] metal, / And speke of medicynes therwithal, / And how and whanne it sholde yharded be" (243–45). It brings to mind chronicle and poetry, as well as magic and what we would now call the science of metallurgy. In responding to the mirror, the people describe the marvelous mirror of Virgil and then "speken of Alocen [al-Haytham, Latinized as Alhazen] and Vitulon [Witelo], / And Aristotle, that writen in hir lyves / Of queynte [clever] mirours and of perspectives" (232–34). They respond to the marvels before them with literary allusions as well as references to natural philosophy and optics, references that show impressive geographical and disciplinary range. The alternation between literary characters and stories, on the one hand, and philosophers' names and methods, on the other, situates marvels within both discourses. Even the "lewed peple" of the tale are aware that there are two sorts of authorities on marvels: poets and philosophers (221). With the tale's setting in distant Sarai, capital of the Golden Horde, as well as its location in the past—the Mongols "werreyed," or warred, against "Russye" in the thirteenth century—it also nods to travel writers and chroniclers (10).

17. The treatment of marvels in romance is often contrasted with that in philosophy because of romance's "favoring of wonder over explanation" (Crane, "Chivalry and the Pre/Postmodern," 79). See also Bynum, "Wonder," 7n23.

On rare occasions, philosophers address the marvels in romance. William of Auvergne, for instance, declares it possible that Merlin had the power of prophecy. He broaches the topic in his *De universo*, in the context of a discussion of demon-human procreation that includes Merlin because his father was reportedly an incubus. Maaike van der Lugt calls him "the most famous son of an incubus in the Middle Ages."[18] As is well known, scholastic philosophers and court clerics like Walter Map and Gervase of Tilbury pondered at some length the possibility of such procreation and its mechanisms. Caroline Walker Bynum, for instance, comments on their "near obsession with fairy-human or demon-human sex."[19] They debated whether demons could produce sperm, whether they harvested it from people or animals, and whether the Huns and Cypriots were demon spawn.[20] William of Auvergne traces the hybrid species back to the Nephilim, parented by the "sons of God" and "daughters of men" (Gn. 6:2). In his view, they warrant belief in demon-human procreation as a rare but not strikingly unusual affair. He helpfully explains that the children of such unions can be identified by their propensity to cry often and breastfeed insatiably.[21] He then turns to Merlin: "From all these things, you can probably gather that a story famous among the common people, a certain case involving one in Britain who is said to be the son of a demon incubus, is not impossible."[22]

Merlin's prophetic powers are often credited to his demon father, and they were sometimes classified as demonic deceptions instead.[23] William's priority is to defend the possibility that Merlin might have received his prophetic gift from his demon father. He calls the possibility "not undeservedly believable," providing another example of the contorted phrasing

18. Van der Lugt, *Le ver, le démon et la vierge*, 193.

19. Bynum, "Metamorphosis," 1000.

20. For more on these issues, see van der Lugt, *Le ver, le démon et la vierge*, 342–45.

21. William of Auvergne, *De universo* 2.3.25, 1072bH–73aA. Walter Map instead tells the story of one demon offspring who led a prosperous life, and deliberately offers the anecdote as a story that goes against expectations (*De nugis curialium* 2.12, ed. and trans. James et al., 158).

22. William of Auvergne, *De universo* 2.3.25, 1072aH: "Ex his igitur omnibus colligere potes non improbabiliter, sermonem famosum, opinione vulgatum, de quodam, qui in majori Britannia filius daemonis incubi fuisse dicitur, non esse impossibilem."

23. Robert de Boron instead divides the powers and gives them separate sources: "the child inherited knowledge of things past from the Enemy, and knowledge of things to come was bequeathed to him by God. It was up to him which way he inclined." (*Merlin*, in *Le roman du graal*, ed. Cerquiglini, 91–92: "sot cil les couses dites et faites et alées, qui il les tient de l'anemi, et le sorplus que il set des coses qui sont a venir volt nostre Sire que il seüst por endroit de l'autre partie. Or se tort a la quele que il volra.") Trans. Bryant, *Merlin and the Grail*, 55.

common to discussions of marvels, as we have seen.[24] Predictable too is his emphasis on the nonimpossibility of the marvel (*non esse impossibilem*). Nearly impossible, nearly unbelievable, such a marvel is rightly characterized by negative and passive verbs. Leaving Merlin himself unnamed, William also assumes a reader well versed in marvels and gestures at their elusive, as well as allusive, quality.

It is worth stressing that William does not conclude that Merlin was, in fact, a prophet. Rather, he affirms that the son of an incubus might have prophetic power. Citing William's reference to Merlin, van der Lugt writes that, at moments like this, theologians "reinforce the veracity of Arthurian legend" in a way that requires explanation.[25] In other words, William might seem to confer personhood on a fictional character. However, "Was Merlin real?" is not the question that concerns William. Rather, he asks whether it is possible that the son of an incubus would have the power to prophesy. His answering yes to that question, or rather responding with the weaker "it is not impossible," does not mean that he fails to recognize the probable nonexistence of Merlin or the fictiveness of fiction. It means only that there is consistency in how he approaches marvels, with an eye to their possibility or impossibility regardless of where he discovers them. In chapter 3, we saw that Oresme did the same when he evaluated the stories of St. Patrick's Purgatory. Merlin's pseudo-historical status is not a problem that William feels the need to resolve, nor is Merlin out of bounds because he appears in Arthurian literature.

Often, the common ground between literature and philosophy is more subtle but still discernible. It is no coincidence, for instance, that a weasel cures another weasel with a herb in Marie de France's *Eliduc*, or that Guildaluec uses the same herb to revive an unconscious Gulliadun; weasels were often associated with resurrection in natural philosophy, and various plants were thought capable of restoring life.[26] The two disciplines have a common store of marvels. This is not to deny that many marvels in romance have no clear philosophical corollary. Light pours from the mouth of Havelock the Dane, indicating his nobility, and both Havelock and Sayf bin Dhī Yazan bear a mole that signifies the same, but such marvels are not of great interest to philosophers. The "ympe-tree" of *Sir Orfeo* is linked at least as strongly to folklore as to philosophy.[27] Still, marvels common in romance, such as unusual gems, metals, and herbs, as well as sorcery and

24. William of Auvergne, *De universo* 2.3.25, 1072aH: "non immerito credi potest."

25. Van der Lugt, *Le ver, le démon et la vierge*, 346.

26. Anna Klosowska surveys some of the key philosophical sources in "Queer/Posthuman in Marie de France's Eliduc," 228–30.

27. See Jirsa, "In the Shadow of the Ympe-tre," 53–55.

prophecy, also captured the interest of natural philosophers, and that fact did not escape the notice of writers from either camp. Some marvels familiar from philosophy are deliberately repurposed in literature, in ways that assume readers' familiarity with them. In the case of the *Thousand and One Nights*, a surprising twist works best if readers know how the marvel typically operates so that they can see how the story departs from convention.

The story focuses on a learned philosopher named Duban who cures a Persian king, Yunan, of leprosy. The feat inspires the king's gratitude and then his suspicion toward Duban because of his awe-inspiring powers. Egged on by an envious vizier, he eventually orders Duban killed. When Duban realizes that he is going to die, he sets up a trap for the king. He asks to be given some of his "scientific and medical texts" before he dies so that he can make gifts of them, identifying one for the king himself.[28] It is, he says, an "especially special" book with one remarkable secret: the recitation of certain lines from it can make a decapitated head answer any question asked of it.[29] Duban offers his own head for this purpose, promising that it will become an oracular head, also called a prophetic head, the same marvel that is associated with Orpheus. The king is enthralled and impatient to see the wonder performed, and when Duban asks the king to spare his life, knowing that he will be denied, the king replies, "You must be killed, especially so that I can see how your head responds to me."[30] The desire to see the marvel forecloses the possibility of mercy, which was not a true possibility in any event. Whetting the king's desire for the marvel, Duban only illustrates the power that he continues to exercise over him. After the executioner kills him, the king prepares his head as he was instructed, but when he goes to open the book, he finds that the pages are stuck together. Duban's decapitated head does actually speak at this moment, but only to tell the king that he needs to wet his fingers in order to separate the pages. The king finds nothing written on them, but we learn that, in the course of wetting his fingers, he has ingested poison that Duban left on the edges of the leaves. The spectacle that the king so desperately wanted to see turns out to be his own death.[31]

28. *Thousand and One Nights*, 16th night, ed. Mahdi, 1:103: "kutuba ʿilmī wa-ṭibbī." Trans. Haddawy, 56.

29. *Thousand and One Nights*, 16th night, ed. Mahdi, 1:103: "khāṣṣu al-khawāṣṣi." Trans. Haddawy, 56. Haddawy among others calls this book the *Secret of Secrets*, but the text says only that it contains a secret (*sirr*), and since the book appears to have nothing written in it, it cannot be identified with any text.

30. *Thousand and One Nights*, 16th night, ed. Mahdi, 1:104: "lā budda min qutilaka wa-khuṣūṣan ḥattā abṣura kayfa takallamanī raʾsuka." Trans. Haddawy, 56.

31. As Barbara Newman reminded me, the poisoned leaves of a book also provide the key to the central mystery of Umberto Eco's *Name of the Rose*.

The story shows that Duban does have prodigious powers, extending even to self-revivification, although he only uses them for ill after the king sentences him to death. That is, he becomes disloyal only after being sentenced to death for being disloyal, one of many ironies in the tale. As for the king, his supposed concern with Duban's faithfulness is undermined by his total faith in the philosopher, following his instructions to the letter and accepting naively that Duban, after having been killed unjustly by him, will perform marvels for him postmortem. Rather than suspicious, the king seems as envious as the vizier, coveting not Duban's status but his knowledge and ability. He too wants to be a producer of spectacular marvels.

Most striking is the role of the promised marvel in the tale. It is expressly rooted in philosophy: Duban selects from a pile of philosophical texts one that is supposed to produce the marvel of the oracular head, a marvel that traveled from Greek myth to Arabic philosophy and, mostly from there, to Latin philosophy. In the Latin West, it was associated with Islamic science, which is why Gerbert of Aurillac, who was reportedly able to create prophetic heads, was supposed (falsely) to have lived among Muslims.[32] The marvel makes the king more eager to do what he was already going to do, and then it does not do what it was supposed to do. The suspense of the tale builds toward its operation, and yet, at the very moment when it is supposed to work, after the king has been convinced that it could actually work, it changes character. The marvel of the oracular head is swapped out, and in its place is left the poisoning of the king. In other words, the plot twist becomes the marvel. The secret of the book is not life after death but simply death, its power based not on any philosopher's great wisdom but on something as mundane as poison. Duban displays his cleverness, but not in the manner we were led to expect.

The story turns, then, from a familiar, albeit spectacular marvel drawn from philosophy to one that is very much about plot. The one fuels the other, as the suspense surrounding the prophetic head is rerouted to the poisoning. As it ends, the story is about surprising reversals of fortune, and it is hard to think of a more characteristically medieval plot arc than that. In the process, the genre of the book that Duban offers the king changes from science to literature. Although supposedly containing advanced learning, it is ultimately a blank canvas that Duban fills with a story of his own devising. He changes the nature of the marvel that sits at the story's center, replacing one that is common within the realm of natural science with one that is unique to literature. As we have seen many times, marvels are typi-

32. See Truitt, *Medieval Robots*, 69–95; and Burnett, "Adelard, Ergaphalau, and the Science of the Stars."

cally other than they seem, and Duban's reversal of expectations satisfies that criterion.

The emphasis on his narrative skill is foreshadowed earlier in the story, when he confronts the king and tells him that he is receiving the crocodile's reward for his good service. The king, predictably, asks to hear the tale about the crocodile and his substandard reward. Such spin-offs are the very life force of the *Thousand and One Nights,* the device that keeps the stories ever multiplying. As an internal story told during negotiations between a fisherman and a jinn, the tale of Duban and Yunan is itself such an offshoot. But Duban replies, "I am not able to fulfill your request in my current circumstances."[33] With his unusual response, Duban resists the rules of the very framed narrative he appears in, putting pressure on the text's fictionality. He insists on the reality of his dire situation, so serious that it leaves no room for storytelling, and commits in another way to misdirection. Duban the unwilling storyteller becomes Duban the master storyteller.

Insofar as it alludes to traditionally philosophical marvels in a way that shows deep familiarity with them and also refocuses attention on narrative, the story of Duban and Yunan invites comparison with the early Castilian *Flores y Blancaflor.* The romance has a strong claim to being the earliest version of the story in Europe, and I give it priority here.[34] In one instance, Flores returns home from his aunt and uncle's house in search of Blancaflor, but his mother the queen tells him that she has died. After watching him prepare to commit suicide, the queen says in desperation that she knows of "a medicine that will revive Blancaflor."[35] As I mentioned with respect to *Eliduc,* many plants were thought capable of restoring health in the Middle Ages (as they provide many medicines now) and, at the furthest extreme, of restoring life. The queen pretends to possess one, placing herself in the tradition of sorceresses like Morgan la Fey and *Partonopeus*'s Melior, both of whom have expert knowledge of plants.[36] What she delivers instead is

33. *Thousand and One Nights,* 16th night, ed. Mahdi, 1:103: "mā yumkinunī battahā fī hādhihi al-waqti alladhī anā fihi." Trans. Haddawy, 55.

34. As Patricia Grieve notes, the publication of the Castilian version was largely overlooked for decades after it appeared (*Floire and Blancheflor,* 23), a situation that she did much to change with her 1997 book. David Arbesú reviews the claims for the priority of the Castilian or French text in *Crónica de Flores y Blancaflor,* 5–24. The Castilian text is by far the most detailed and geographically specific of the known versions, which might also suggest that it precedes the others.

35. *Crónica de Flores y Blancaflor,* ed. Arbesú, 70: "une melezina con que bevira Blancaflor." See, similarly, *Le conte de Floire et Blancheflor* 1043–44, ed. Leclanche.

36. On Morgan as healer, see for instance Geoffrey of Monmouth, *Life of Merlin,* ed. Clarke, 100; and Chrétien de Troyes, *Erec and Enide,* 4219–28, ed. Poirion. On Melior's training in medicinal herbs, see *Partonopeus de Blois,* 4583–88, ed. Crapelet.

the news that Blancaflor is not dead but sold, news that acts as a marvelous elixir insofar as it restores her to life within her son's mind.

Packaging surprising news as a marvel, the queen shows herself to be fluent in their operations. Her comment understands marvels to be what we have often seen them be: surprising possibilities that depend on hidden causes, such as the natural potency of a plant or stone. In this case, the queen exposes not hidden powers but hidden knowledge, a fact that she had previously concealed from her son. Like Duban in the *Thousand and One Nights*, she uses a marvel to frame an unexpected shift in the narrative, one that shares with marvels the power to disorient and surprise their audience. Further, her "medicine" replicates the complicated epistemological status of marvels. Blancaflor is alive but not revived, enslaved but not entombed. The queen's words are true and not, allowing her to disavow responsibility even as she casts herself as a sort of heroine. She seems to recognize that marvels create a conceptual space that accommodates half- or non-truths. At the same time, her reversal in telling the truth where once she had lied becomes equivalent to nature's ability to reverse itself, to bring life out of death. Finally, the characteristic creativity of marvels appears in her ingenuity, not just her scheming but her clever appeal to a marvel that is more appropriate than it might initially seem.

The notion of marvels returns later, when Flores hides in a basket of flowers in order to breach the tower in which Blancaflor is trapped. Blancaflor, who had been despondent, exults when she sees him, and when her friend Gloris observes the change, she says, "I tell you that this flower has great power [*virtud*] in it."[37] The joke alludes to herbal marvels, which is an easy joke to make given Flores's name and the fact that he arrives in a basket of flowers. He is a marvel because of the transformation he effects in Blancaflor, which again likens a surprising change to a medicinal cure. Gloris's joke treats marvels as mysterious but powerful things that operate outside of normal bounds. Flores's improbable pathway into the tower represents the opaque operation of marvels and the hiddenness of their causes. Flores, literally hidden within the flowers, is their special potency abstracted into human form. He is the possibility of a marvel made corporeal and real, its efficacy turned into a visible fact. His entrance into the tower also represents the power of love to work secretly, powerfully, and to some extent unaccountably. That medieval romance often treats love as a marvel is no secret, of course. The author of *Amadas and Ydoine* says so directly: "Love is a wondrous thing: it can perform marvels in an instant. Anyone

37. *Crónica de Flores y Blancaflor*, ed. Arbesú, 92: "digo que esta flor ha grand virtud en si."

who wants to examine Love will discover many marvels in it."[38] However, Flores's status as the specific force of marvelous power, possessed through the purity of his love, shows that the marvelousness of love need not be hackneyed. The author as well as the reader needs to be able to recognize that Gloris draws on it cleverly if they are going to be in on the joke.

THE SUBTRACTION AND ADDITION OF MARVELS IN *SIR ORFEO*

In the examples above, *Flores y Blancaflor* evokes marvels in their absence, while the *Thousand and One Nights* sidelines its marvel and then supplants it. Figuring a space where marvels might be but are not, or are not in their usual forms, the authors shift attention from the marvel to the instability and variability that it represents. In *Sir Orfeo*, the absence of an expected marvel and the addition of an unexpected one continue to focus attention on the audience's familiarity with them, their symbolism, and their reconfigurability. In this case, the poem's marvelous stones reveal a missing marvel. The category of stones includes gems, minerals, rocks, and animals like coral, all appearing without distinction in medieval lapidaries and other works on natural philosophy. Popular outside of romance, where they were worn to provide protection or good luck, they proliferated inside of it. To name only two especially well-known examples, the grail in Chrétien's *Perceval* is studded with precious stones, while the grail in Wolfram von Eschenbach's *Parzival* actually is a stone capable of curing illness and performing myriad other powers, such as making it possible for the phoenix to reconstitute itself. Nonetheless, although *Sir Orfeo* has been, in Jeff Rider's words, "inexhaustibly provocative of interpretation," its stones have not attracted much critical attention.[39]

When Herodis recounts the fairy king's visit to her, she says:

> "Þe king hadde a croun [crown] on hed;
> It nas [was not] of silver, no [nor] of gold red,
> Ac [But] it was of a precious ston
> —As bri3t [bright] as þe sonne it schon;
> &, as son [soon] as he to me cam,
> Wold ich nold ich, he me nam [siezed]."[40]

38. *Amadas and Ydoine*, 298–301, ed. Reinhard: "D'amer est estrange cose, / Mervailes fait en poi de pose. / Ki ben vudra esgarder, / Mainte mervaile i pot noter." Trans. Arthur, 25.

39. Rider, "Receiving Orpheus in the Middle Ages," 365.

40. *Sir Orfeo*, 149–54, ed. Bliss. Future references are to this edition, and are given parenthetically in the text.

This is the only description she provides of the fairy king's appearance. This "myddai fend," a well-known demon in the Latin West, wears a crown made of a single precious stone, and as he approaches her, she loses her ability to refuse him.[41] It is clear that he enchants her, and the only possible means of enchantment that the poet mentions is the crown made of stone. Stones were widely reputed to have such powers, whether to enchant or to release someone from enchantment. Regarding the stone gerachidem, for instance, one lapidary writes that "it always has within it a commanding power that makes a woman unable to deny anything to one who asks."[42] Gems were often presented as tools to bend the will of women. Similarly, in *Amadas and Ydoine*, a demon enchants Ydoine by placing a gem-bearing ring on her finger, and the ring makes her appear to be dead. Arguably, the same happens to Herodis.[43] The fairy king's enchantment turns Herodis from a woman calm, beautiful, and loving into one who is mad, crying and tearing at herself. As the impact of Flores's entrance into the tower is measured through its mood-reversing effect on Blancaflor, so the fairy king's enchantment registers in Herodis's reversed comportment.

It is noteworthy too that, when Herodis is taken, she is placed within a castle itself made "al of precious stones" (366). Presumably its powers are at play in the hall, with its scores of victims frozen in suspended animation. Recall that Orfeo, after he sees Herodis in a group of women hawking, follows her back to the fairy castle immediately. Entering presumably just after she arrives, he nonetheless finds her immobile and lying under an imp-tree, as she was when the fairy king first came to her. The "riche stones" that make fairyland always bright seem also to turn her into a statue the moment she returns (371). The hall of horrors evokes in other ways the special power of stones. The people who are "þouȝt dede [thought to be dead], & nare nouȝt [are not]" are described at uncharacteristic length and provide most of the information we have about the nature of the poem's

41. Hilton, *Scale of Perfection* 2.3416, ed. Bestul. On the demon and the danger of sleeping under trees at midday, see Friedman, *Orpheus in the Middle Ages*, 175–94; and Jirsa, "In the Shadow of the Ympe-tre." The noonday demon (*daemonio meridiano*) is mentioned in Ps 90:6. For Bernard of Clairvaux's well-known interpretation of it, see *Sermones super Cantica Canticorum* 33.11–16, ed. Leclercq et al., 1.2:2883–87.

42. Marbod of Rennes, *Liber lapidum* 30:445–46, ed. Herrera, *Lapidario*, 105: "Huic quoque semper inest impetratoria virtus, / Qua nequeat mulier quicquam prohibere pententi." I preserve the Latin names of the stones because it is not always clear how to translate them.

43. Neil Cartlidge compares the pseudo-death of Ydoine to that of Herodis in "Sir Orfeo in the Otherworld," 216–25.

fairy otherworld (390). They constitute, as Tara Williams writes, the "central marvel" of the poem.[44] Viewed in the context of lapidaries, the victims all suffered preventable tragedies. Succumbing to violence, whether by losing a head or arms or being pierced through with a sword, succumbing to madness, choking, drowning, burning, dying in childbirth, and falling prey to enchantment are all calamities that medieval lapidaries offer means to prevent. Even looking only at the most popular lapidary in medieval England, the eleventh-century *Liber lapidum* of Marbod of Rennes, one can find all of them, some addressed by more than one stone.[45]

When Orfeo enters the fairy king's palace, he finds victims of ten different misfortunes, all in a state of suspended animation. All were stolen from "þis warld" and taken to fairyland "wiþ fairi" (403, 404). They are organized according to mishap: "Sum stode wiþ-outen hade, / & sum non armes nade [ne had]," and so forth (391–92). The repetition in syntax and diction, with "sum" appearing anaphorically in nine of ten consecutive lines, gives the impression of a roll call. Each victim might have benefited from the protection of different stones. Those without arms might have worn corneleus, which "staunches the flow of blood from limbs wherever it occurs."[46] Those suffering the wounds of battle, whether in the form of decapitation or piercing ("þurth þe bodi" they "hadde wounde" [393]), might have carried gagatronica, which makes its wearer victorious in any battle.[47] As we saw earlier, Hercules benefited from it. Presumably those who sit "armed on hors" were similarly unlucky in battle (395). If these victims suffered because of wild animals instead, then orites might have helped them. It repels beasts and also heals the wounds that they cause.[48] Those who choked might have been poisoned, in which case echites is one of many stones that could have saved them.[49] Various stones were reported to calm agitated waters, and if those who drowned did so at sea, then they might have benefited from smaragdus's power to repel tempests.[50] Those burned

44. Williams, *Middle English Marvels*, 18. As Williams notes, there is no scholarly consensus on how to interpret the scene, and she reviews some of the options that have been proposed (15–16).

45. Marbod's lapidary survives in more than two hundred manuscripts and was translated during the Middle Ages into many languages, including French, Spanish, Hebrew, Italian, English, and Icelandic.

46. Marbod of Rennes, *Liber lapidum* 22:340, ed. Herrera, *Lapidario*, 83: "Sanguinis ex membro sistit quocumque fluorem."

47. Marbod of Rennes, *Liber lapidum* 27:400, ed. Herrera, *Lapidario*, 95.

48. Marbod of Rennes, *Liber lapidum* 43:579–83, ed. Herrera, *Lapidario*, 141.

49. Marbod of Rennes, *Liber lapidum* 25:374–79, ed. Herrera, *Lapidario*, 89–91.

50. Marbod of Rennes, *Liber lapidum* 7:157, ed. Herrera, *Lapidario*, 41.

in fire might have turned to zingnite, which puts out fire.[51] In one of the French versions of *Floire et Blancheflor*, the ring that Floire's mother gives him, the one whose gems ward off injury, specifically prevents fire from burning him.[52] Those who went crazy or died in childbirth might have used any number of stones, including peanite, which "helps women in childbirth in the final hour when the decisive moment imperils them."[53] And finally, those like Herodis who were snatched while sleeping under an imp-tree beneath the noonday sun were victims, it seems, of enchantment. Chrisolite, placed in a bracelet and worn on the left arm, "frightens demons and is thought to vex them," while adamant drives away phantasms.[54] Several stones counteract enchantment and phantasies. Bartholomaeus Anglicus, citing Isidore as his source, writes that heliotrope "discerneþ þe folye of enchaunters," whereas jet "helpeþ aȝeins wicchecraft and fordoþ [neutralizes] harde enchauntementz."[55] Gems and stones often direct their powers toward situations whose outcomes might appear random or difficult to control. Where a situation might easily cut one of two ways, then—in a lawsuit, in courtship, in illness—the gem's powers incline in the favorable direction. In this respect, epistite is an emblematic stone because it "keeps the one who carries it safe from twists of fate."[56]

One might object that the author of *Orfeo* did not necessarily have lapidaries in mind when he gathered his victims of misfortune in the fairy king's foyer, because stones alone would not inoculate against such calamities. Charms, relics, herbs, and patron saints offered similar protections, with areas of influence that often overlapped, as stones' powers overlap among themselves. Charms too could protect against conquest in battle; herbs too could offer protection from madness; patron saints too could aid travelers or women in labor. Nonetheless, stones do an especially good job of associating the different victims together. Even a single stone like adamant has powers relevant to many of them. "It works against enemies, insanity, wild beasts, savage men, disputes, quarrels, poisons, and attacks

51. Bartholomaeus Anglicus, *De proprietatibus rerum* 16:103, trans. Trevisa, ed. Seymour, 881.

52. *Le conte de Floire et Blancheflor*, 1216b, ed. Leclanche.

53. Marbod of Rennes, *Liber lapidum* 34:494–95, ed. Herrera, *Lapidario*, 119: "et parientibus auxiliatur, / Ultima quas urget dubii discriminis hora."

54. Marbod of Rennes, *Liber lapidum* 9:190, ed. Herrera, *Lapidario*, 49: "Demones exterret, et eos agitare putatur."

55. Bartholomaeus Anglicus, *De proprietatibus rerum* 16:40 and 16:48, trans. Trevisa, ed. Seymour, 2:847 and 852.

56. Marbod of Rennes, *Liber lapidum* 31:464, ed. Herrera, *Lapidario*, 111: "tutum servat dubia sub sorte gerentem."

of phantasms and of incubi."[57] That list might cover five of the poet's ten misfortunes. Also, whereas herbs and charms are not specifically named in *Orfeo*, stones are.

If viewed through the lens of lapidaries, the people in the hall appear to be differently unlucky, each suffering misfortune of the sort that stones and gems were said to prevent. Not just unlucky, they are unprotected, and therefore easy prey for the fairy king, who instead uses the special power of stones to his advantage. To detect the pattern, a reader would have to be very familiar with marvels, as the author would need to assume that they would be. It is not only in this respect, however, that the poem registers absent marvels. Orfeo's failure to use marvels is the more glaring omission since Orpheus was a famed expert in the powers of stones. In the Middle Ages, he was known not just as a musician who could revive the dead through song or as a creature of myth, but as the supposed author of charms and various works on magic, a sorcerer who was also expert in medicine and astrology. He was an Argonaut, a philosopher, a theologian, and a prophet. Like the Sibyl, Virgil, and others, Orpheus was commonly included among non-Christian prophets and astronomers who were supposed to have foreseen the coming of Christ.[58] He was also well known as an expert on herbs and stones. Although the Greek verse lapidary attributed to him, the *Lithica*, appears not to have been available in Latin for much of the Middle Ages, it influenced those that did circulate, and authors in the Latin West knew about it.[59] Albertus Magnus, for instance, writes that Orpheus believed stones to have divine powers.[60]

Considered in light of his reputation, Orfeo is strikingly without magic. He removes his crown when he leaves for the woods and replaces it only at the poem's end, when his kingdom is restored. No special powers are ascribed to it. Rather, gemless Orfeo invests himself in his harp and, as Seth Lerer argued decades ago, ranks art over sorcery.[61] The harp makes the

57. Albertus Magnus, *De mineralibus* 2.2.1, in *Opera omnia*, ed. Borgnet, 5:31: "valet contra hostes et insaniam et indomitas bestias et feros homines et contra jurgia et rixas et contra venena et incursus phantasmatum et incuborum."

58. Smoller, "'*Teste Albumasare cum Sibylla*,'" 78.

59. As Dorothy Wyckoff notes, the Latin *Damigeron*, often cited as *Evax* in later lapidaries, seems to be derived from the Greek *Lithica* (*Book of Minerals*, 265–66), and it in turn was a key source for Marbod of Rennes, who features prominently in Albertus Magnus's *De mineralibus* (268). As this note suggests, medieval lapidaries were a relatively conservative genre, with authors who tended to compile and comment on preexisting materials.

60. Albertus Magnus, *Mineralium* 2.1.1, in *Opera omnia*, ed Borgnet, 5:24.

61. Lerer, "Artifice and Artistry in *Sir Orfeo*."

fairy king pliable to his will, but there is no hint that Orfeo casts a spell. Rather, the fairy king offers him a boon after he plays, and when he hesitates to release Herodis, Orfeo convinces him by logical argument. Animals may lie at Orfeo's feet, but they choose to do so: "For ioie [joy] abouten him þai teþ [gather]" (274). He exercises power through music and through reason, governing through inspiration and persuasion rather than magic. The poem contrasts the fairy king's sorcery and his seeming dependence on magical stones with Orfeo, who lacks their aid.

Orfeo, then, is without powers the reader might well expect him to have, salient for their absence. That absence does not constitute a rejection of marvels or a recognition of their lack of sophistication. Instead, absent marvels stand out against a backdrop of present ones, of the noonday demon, marvelous cures, and magical rings. They are not disavowed so much as reimagined, like set scripts that invite creative reworking, and they continue to resonate. Indeed, romance itself, as several critics have noted, relies similarly on the reworking of plots.[62] Here, the alterations emphasize the benevolence of Orfeo the nonenchanter, as though he has relinquished an option conventionally available to him. He is also a reminder that magicians were increasingly suspect as time passed.[63] Avicenna's prophet has a pure soul, but magic more often becomes a tool of the wicked and the product of base motivations. Orfeo is contrasted to the fairy king as an emblem of what he might be but is better than. The opposition teaches the reader to look for other missing marvels, which only works at a thematic level if a reader recognizes their absence.

The two absences discussed above—the only implied vulnerability of the victims in the fairy king's hall because they are not protected by stones, and the non-marvel-producing Orfeo—set the interpretive stage for the poem's key addition with respect to marvels. In chapter 4, I described a series of marvelous illusions—men hunting, men fighting, and ladies dancing—that appears in natural philosophy and in literature, namely, in *Sir Orfeo*, Chaucer's *Franklin's Tale*, and *Mandeville's Travels*. Of course, the other examples postdate *Orfeo*, according to its usual dating, but as Claude Lecouteux and Neil Cartlidge have shown, and as we saw in the citations from William of Auvergne, the visions were popular at the time the poet wrote.[64]

It is fitting at this point to pay attention to the poet's transformation of

62. See, for instance, Bruckner, *Shaping Romance*, 37–59.

63. Michael Bailey argues for a general shift from condemning certain magical practices to condemning those who performed them (*Fearful Spirits, Reasoned Follies*, 148–94).

64. Lecouteux, *Chasses fantastiques*; and Cartlidge, "Sir Orfeo in the Otherworld."

the scene. *Sir Orfeo* tells its reader that the eponymous king often sees a series of scenes on hot afternoons, as he sits in the woods. He describes three: first, the fairy king and his men hunt; second, an army of knights appears; and third, knights and ladies dance (283–302). The first two disappear as quickly as they arrive; Orfeo "nist whider þai bi-come" (did not know where they came from) and "nist whider þai wold" (did not know where they went) (288, 296). The third likewise passes him by. It is not clear whether or not they are illusions, but they are familiar marvels. The poet adds a fourth to the familiar trio: a scene of women hawking, and among them Herodis. "Oft" he sees the hunters (282), and "oþer while" he sees the knights and the dancers (289, 297), but "on a day" he sees the group of sixty women hawking (302). The phrasing registers difference: while the other visions appear with some regularity, the vision of the women hawking happens but once, and it jostles Orfeo out of his stupor. He laughs because the hawking reminds him of past joys—"Ich was y-won [accustomed] swiche werk to se" (317)—transporting him to his former life even before he sees Herodis. Familiarity breeds familiarity, and a remembered sport introduces a remembered wife. When he does see her, he stares "ȝern," or eagerly, without uttering a sound, before deciding to pursue her (323). The unusual response that the scene elicits from him, as he laughs and seeks human companionship relinquished many years earlier, registers the oddity of the scene and captures his disorientation. It is unlike the others.

The fourth vision, then, is a one-time variation from what even the poet characterizes as a normal sequence of images. His two alterations—the unfamiliar scene in which she appears departs from familiar ones, and the vision is unique rather than regular—capture Orfeo's surprise at Herodis's appearance. Both build suspense, in retrospect, for the identification of Herodis within a group of otherwise nameless faces. The trilogy of scenes sets the poet's variant in relief, fittingly containing his character, Herodis, and advancing his plot. The final vision thus acts as something of an authorial signature, an imprint that marks the poet's innovation. It can only function in that respect, however, if the reader is so familiar with common marvels that they can detect deviation from the normal path. The poet assumes as much. Chapter 4 cited William of Auvergne's discussion of two of the three illusions here represented and his deliberations about their status. Are they illusions produced by demons, visions of souls in purgatory, or imagination's creations? In *Sir Orfeo*, too, their status is unclear. Are the women as real or unreal as the hunt? Are they fantastic creatures or mortal people? These are not questions that can be answered. Situating fairyland somewhere between illusion and aristocratic play, the marvelous visions both thematize uncertainty and reproduce it.

Fairyland is predictably and similarly indefinable. Orfeo can follow and rescue Herodis, but he reaches her through a "roche" in the ground, exceeding the confines of the normal world (347). Rocks are a common feature in medieval geographies of the fairy or enchanted otherworld. For instance, when the beloved follows her fairy lover in Marie de France's *Yonec*, she passes through an entrance in a hill and arrives in fairyland, in a city where every house is made of silver.[65] As he travels to an alternative world, Orfeo enters an ambiguous space that is in many respects a mirror image of the world above ground. Recall that fairyland stands in for the underworld that Orpheus traditionally visits in order to retrieve Eurydice. It is not entirely natural or entirely supernatural. It is, however, legible. By subtracting expected marvels and adding unexpected ones, the poet treats marvels as a discourse. They can be read sequentially and analyzed coherently, but only by readers who know the language.

MARVELS AND METAMORPHOSIS: THE *THOUSAND AND ONE NIGHTS* AND MARIE DE FRANCE'S *YONEC*

I have argued that authors play with readers' expectations by reinterpreting, removing, and adding marvels. It is a game that suits marvels especially well given their indeterminate status, their maybe realness. Not only changeable, they also represent change, as we see in this final section on marvels that involve transformation. Marie de France's *Yonec*, for instance, takes changeability as one of its central themes. A woman trapped in a tower by a jealous husband wishes that a knight might come to her and alleviate her suffering, as she has heard that knights are wont to do. A tamed hawk, with straps on its feet, appears in response. Wished into being, he enters her room through the window, turns into a man, confesses his great love for her, and tells her not to fear. She hesitates, suspicious of a hawk-turned-knight, and perhaps suspicious of getting what she wanted as well. Presumably worried that dark powers might be in play, she seeks assurance that he is Christian, as Raymondin did from Mélusine and Partonopeu did from Melior. To accommodate her request, the knight, Muldumarec, suggests that she feign illness and call for a chaplain. He then assumes her appearance, and when the chaplain arrives, Muldumarec takes the Eucharist, both wafer and wine. With that testament of faith, the lady joins him in bed.

The fears inspired by Muldumarec's metamorphosis are fittingly resolved by the Eucharist, and not only for doctrinal reasons. Like the knight in hawk or female form, the wafer and wine too differ with respect to

65. Marie de France, *Yonec*, 347, ed. Rychner.

accidents and substance.[66] They are not what they seem to be, and they promise that misleading appearances can be sacred. In other words, the sacrament neutralizes the threat posed by transformation. By taking them, Muldumarec aligns himself with a holy brand of change. By taking them while in altered form, seeming to be the lady, he suggests that his true nature is both benevolent and constant. His alteration is only skin deep.[67] In a characteristic act of inversion, Marie de France flips the beloved's concern. She worried about Muldumarec's transformability, but the lai focuses instead on her own altered appearance. Although "she lost her beauty" during her first seven years of imprisonment, once she falls in love with Muldumarec, her beauty returns: "The great joy she often experienced on seeing her lover caused her appearance to alter."[68] Shifting attention from the knight's changeability to the lady's own, Marie reverses expectations. The shape-shifter inspires less suspicion than the now prettier woman, and the seemingly more mundane transformation poses the greater threat to both of them. The lady's husband "noticed that she was different from her usual self," commenting specifically on her clothing.[69] He sets his sister to spy on her, and when she sees the hawk/knight enter and exit, he places traps on the windowsill that wound Muldumarec fatally. As he dies, he tells his beloved, "I told you what would happen: your appearance would kill us."[70]

On multiple levels, then, *Yonec* plays with change, not only change in its characters but change in the plot, as doubt is redirected from Muldumarec to his beloved. Muldumarec's cross-species metamorphosis is here more innocuous than the wholly typical transformation of the lady in love. The three sorts of change in the tale—the lady's, Muldumarec's, and Christ's in the Eucharist—mark out a range of possibilities. On this continuum, eucharistic transubstantiation is the ideal, and one that Muldumarec approaches. He does not even fall in love in the lai, but reveals that he has long loved the lady; he is ever one in substance, like the consecrated wafer.

66. Sharon Kinoshita and Peggy McCracken also understand the Eucharist here in terms of the tale's interest in different sorts of metamorphosis (*Marie de France: A Critical Companion*, 148–49).

67. In *Metamorphosis and Identity*, Caroline Walker Bynum argues that such transformations are usually superficial.

68. Marie de France, *Yonec*, 47, in *Les lais de Marie de France*, ed. Rychner: "Sa beuté pert"; and 225–27: "Pur la grant joie u ele fu / Que suvent puet veeir sun dru, / Esteit tuz sis semblanz changiez." Trans. Burgess and Busby, *The Lais of Marie de France*, 89.

69. Marie de France, *Yonec*, 229–30, in *Les lais de Marie de France*, ed. Rychner: "s'aparceit / Qu'autrement est k'il ne suleit." Trans. Burgess and Busby, *The Lais of Marie de France*, 89.

70. Marie de France, *Yonec*, 321–22, in *Les lais de Marie de France*, ed. Rychner: "Bien le vus dis qu'en avendreit: / Votre semblanz nus ocireit." Trans. Burgess and Busby, *The Lais of Marie de France*, 90.

Paradoxically, then, the most spectacular sorts of superficial change represent the greatest constancy. Such paradox finds an easy vehicle in marvels, which are supposed to play with appearances. As the Eucharist memorializes Christ's sacrifice, born of love, so Muldumarec's metamorphosis testifies to the purity of his own. The lady is equally enamored, as far as the lai shows, but Muldumarec faults her with his final words. She is placed in an impossible position, unable to control her appearance as he does but, unlike him, watched constantly by an abusive husband who wants to keep her miserable. Her own joy, once she betrays it, destroys her.

In *Yonec*, the transformative power of marvels casts light on the changeability of people, whether their forms alter in major or minor ways. In the final complete story of the Syrian manuscript of the *Thousand and One Nights*, marvels again reflect on lovers and the character of their devotion as their situations alter. In the story, a beautiful young man, a prince and then king named Badr, seeks to marry Jawhara, the daughter of a powerful sea king, after he hears his uncle describe her beauty. Badr is half-human, half-sea creature, with a mother from the sea and a human father. His hybridity is essential to his story, which sees him turn into two sorts of bird before he wins his beloved. His uncle approaches Jawhara's father on Badr's behalf, but, rebuffed, the insulted uncle leads an attack on the sea king and conquers him. Jawhara and Badr each flee the battle, but they happen to arrive at the same destination: a single tree on a secluded island. When Badr looks up and sees a woman in it, he decides that she must be Jawhara, and if not, "then one who is even more beautiful."[71] With the sort of illogic characteristic of such stories, he recognizes her only because she exceeds all units of measurement. He concludes, "My uncle has not done justice to a fortieth part of her charm or a carat of her beauty," and so she does and does not resemble the uncle's description.[72]

The jewel imagery reminds us that her name means "gem," which puts further pressure on the question of her value. She is too beautiful to be assessed properly, and that very indescribability is what makes her recognizable. Although Badr reveals himself as the man on whose account her father was conquered, he expects her to celebrate his arrival, and she, distrustful of him, feigns affection. Easily persuaded that she wants what he

71. *Thousand and One Nights*, 250th night, ed. Mahdi, 508: "fa-hādhī aḥsanu minhā." Trans. Haddawy, *The Arabian Nights*, 492.

72. *Thousand and One Nights*, 251st night, ed. Mahdi, 509: "mā waṣafa khālī rubʿa ʿushra miʿshāra ḥusnihā wa-lā qīrāṭa min jamālihā." Trans. Haddawy, *The Arabian Nights*, 493.

wants, "he did not doubt that she loved him."[73] She descends, embraces him, and then casts a spell on him, turning him into "the prettiest of birds," with white feathers and a red bill and feet.[74] She orders her maid to maroon him on a desert island where he will die, but, moved by Badr's beauty, the maid instead takes him to one that is more lush and provides him with food and water. Now "perched on a tree branch," alone on a secluded island, he is in precisely the position that Jawhara was when he found her.[75] Tree-bound and unable to fly, he is trapped and defenseless. When a birdcatcher arrives, he sees Badr, who, in his avian form, "bewildered the mind and dazzled the eyes."[76] Badr too is an object of adoration, desired for his beauty. Like Jawhara, he is the most beautiful member of his species, so beautiful that others want to possess him. The birdcatcher "marvels" at him and captures him, succeeding where Badr had failed.

Thanks to his marvelous transformation, Badr finds himself in the same plight as Jawhara. In this case, the marvel changes Badr but, more important, it allows Jawhara to switch places with him, to be the one on the ground rather than the one in the tree. His aggressive attempt to possess her inspires her assertion of her own will. Unable to restore her family's lost power, she can at least reduce his stature so that he is as vulnerable as she was, without power and family protection, endangered because of his very desirability. The birdcatcher struggles to part with him, refusing to sell him to the first man who offers and holding out until a king promises solely to admire him, not to eat him. Facing the threat of eternal adoration at the cost of imprisonment, he is rescued by the queen, a powerful sorceress who sees his true nature and restores him to his proper form. Less interested in possessing a valuable object than freeing it, the queen models good behavior, but Badr does not follow her lead. He leaves—only to find himself at the mercy of a third sorceress, named Lab, in the City of Magicians. Passionately attached to her, he reveals his own fickleness and is therefore punished by further transformations.

"When King Badr saw her beauty, he was bewitched," and he loves Queen Lab in spite of his better judgment, but his passion cools as quickly

73. *Thousand and One Nights*, 251st night, ed. Mahdi, 509: "wa-ẓanna anahā 'ashiqatahu." Trans. Haddawy, *The Arabian Nights*, 493.

74. *Thousand and One Nights*, 252nd night, ed. Mahdi, 510: "ahsanu mā yakūnu min al-ṭuyūri." Trans. Haddawy, *The Arabian Nights*, 494.

75. *Thousand and One Nights*, 254th night, ed. Mahdi, 512: "qā'idun fawqa ghuṣnin min aghṣāni al-shajarati." Trans. Haddawy, *The Arabian Nights*, 496.

76. *Thousand and One Nights*, 254th night, ed. Mahdi, 512: "yadhashu al-khāṭira wa-yasbā al-nāẓira." Trans. Haddawy, *The Arabian Nights*, 496.

as it grew.[77] When he watches from the window as she turns herself into a bird in order to mate with a former lover whom she had transformed into a bird as well, he recovers from his bewitchment, and even escapes briefly, but falls back into her snares. She then turns him into "the ugliest of birds."[78] Contrasting with his earlier transformation into "the prettiest of birds," the point is now Badr's culpable changeability, as he readily relinquishes his affection for Jawhara and transfers it to the "more beautiful" and equally fickle Queen Lab.[79] So fixated on beauty, he loses his own. When Badr tries to mollify Queen Lab before she transforms him, he vows, "nothing will change me toward you," tying his own changeability to the tale's many metamorphoses.[80] He is unsteadfast and his failing is reflected in his altered forms.

The magic that transforms Badr on both occasions gives him what he deserves, reflecting the nature of his attachment to the two women. He traps Jawhara and so he is trapped; his affections alter and so he is altered. Badr's debauched relationship with Lab is clearly the more objectionable of the two, and his transformation suggests that it brings out his worst side. The contrast with his earlier transformation also suggests a better fate with Jawhara if he can approach her more graciously, as he eventually does. They live happily ever after, an unchanging fate that suggests Badr has learned to be constant in his virtues. The story's marvels express more clearly than the plot how Badr has erred and how he ought to change. Shape-shifters themselves, marvels here reverse perspectives, identify fickleness, and encourage positive change. In a variety of ways, they symbolize change as effectively as they create it. Whether because of the powers they possess or because they can be reworked endlessly across texts, their own proclivity toward variation makes them powerful symbols of transformation to readers who can understand them in kind.

A book on marvels should not end with the *Thousand and One Nights* without comment, given the text's unique role in shaping Western representations of Islamic cultures. As Travis Zadeh notes, "when writing about the wonders of the Orient, there is no practical way to outrun the penumbra of Orientalism," and so it is a topic to raise rather than one to avoid.[81]

77. *Thousand and One Nights*, 262nd night, ed. Mahdi, 521: "fa-naẓara al-maliku badru ilā ḥusnihā fa-ḥāra aqlahu." Trans. Haddawy, *The Arabian Nights*, 506.

78. *Thousand and One Nights*, 269th night, ed. Mahdi, 530: "aqbaḥi al-ṭuyūri." Trans. Haddawy, *The Arabian Nights*, 515.

79. *Thousand and One Nights*, 262nd night, ed. Mahdi, 521: "aḥsanu."

80. *Thousand and One Nights*, 267th night, ed. Mahdi, 528: "mā yughayyirunī shayun baʿda anki." Trans. Haddawy, *The Arabian Nights*, 513.

81. Zadeh, *Wonders and Rarities*, introduction.

The text was dubbed the *Arabian Nights* when it was first translated into English in the eighteenth century because it was supposed to represent the decadence and otherness of a whole and homogenized culture, and it is important to stress that it does not serve that capacity here. Rather, my aim in including it is to de-exoticize it. It represents no outer limit with respect to marvels, no foil against which the greater rationality of the Latin West might establish itself. Its approach toward marvels is instead based in a shared philosophical tradition that welcomed adaptation and elaboration across disciplines. "Orientalist" literature misrepresented Arabic texts and overstated their dissimilarity from those written in the Latin West, especially with respect to marvels. In this book, I try to break the strong association of marvels with backwardness, foreignness, credulity, and intellectual simplicity.

These final chapters have highlighted qualities of marvels that are familiar from the early ones but with alterations that suit their literary contexts. Still confounding objects and phenomena that invite investigation, they put pressure on the lover who distrusts them and the king who fears them. Given their reliance on hidden and usually inscrutable causes, they are well equipped to conceal secrets, and also to bring hidden desires or motivations to light. Because they resist evidence, they effectively test faith and good judgment. They speak to imagination as much as they emerge from it, and so they reveal not only nature's creativity but that of authors and characters. Defined by motion and change, marvels also represent characters who are not as steadfast as they should be. They lend themselves to ever new interpretations, and that registers in the instability of their textual form. They are infinitely reworkable, as persisting stories about them—about heroic powers; about secret lands like Wakanda and Pandora; about radioactive spiders, the sorcerer's stone, and war-waging trees—all testify. By putting marvels in different disciplines, genres, and cultures in dialogue with one another, I hope to call attention to the complexity of their mechanisms and connotations, and ultimately to the playfulness and creativity of the period that embraced them.

Conclusion

In *Parzival,* Wolfram von Eschenbach introduces a fake source named Kyot, a Provençal writer who supposedly found an account of the grail in Toledo, in a text written in *heidensch* or heathenish script—presumably Hebrew or Arabic—and who then learned the language in order to read it.[1] Composed likewise by a "heathen" named Flegetanis, a distant descendant of Solomon, the text inspires Kyot to research the story further in Latin sources and, finally, to present his findings in French. Insofar as a non-Christian testifies to the truth of a Christian story, the episode is familiar from previous chapters. Laura Smoller points to the common medieval "practice of collecting gentile testimony to Christian truths," whether from pagans like the Sibyl and Orpheus or Muslims like Abū Maʿshar, of course in addition to Jews.[2] The twist in this case is that the astrologer testifies to the validity not of biblical miracles or points of Christian doctrine but of a story from romance. As Jean d'Arras echoes the methods of natural philosophers when he announces that the fairy Mélusine existed, so von Eschenbach appeals to natural philosophy to cast the matter of his thirteenth-century poem as foreseen truth.

At this point, we are well positioned to appreciate the complexity of von Eschenbach's gestures. Rooting his poem in cosmology, he mixes disciplines in order to buoy his central marvel, the grail. Not surprisingly, the topic of marvels leads him to natural philosophy, and natural philosophy in turn establishes the pseudo-seriousness of his fiction. With it, he upsells the marvel and makes it a fated fact. Whereas philosophers often hedge with respect to marvels that only need to be logically possible, the writers of romance like to double down. This is not a firm rule, but as a general pattern, the more fully invented the marvel, the more insistent the claims for

1. Von Eschenbach, *Parzival* 10, ed. Lachmann, 529.20.
2. Smoller, "'*Teste Albumasare cum Sibylla*,'" 78.

its realness. With a less-than-grave tone, then, von Eschenbach casts the quest for the grail as divinely ordained.

Pretending to translate what was already written in the stars, he allows his marvel to cross not just disciplinary but also linguistic barriers with ease, as cosmological signs are translated into Arabic or Hebrew and then into French and finally into German. The circuitous path suggests the transportability of marvels across languages and cultures. At the same time, he reminds us that nature displays nearly poetic creativity when it produces marvels. It is his ultimate source, credited with an inventiveness that fuels his own, but of course playing a part that he wrote for it. In other words, the stars are the fake source behind the fake source, Flegetanis. What would authorize his poem, both its facticity and historicity, is itself concocted, and recognizably so. Perhaps von Eschenbach recognizes that human ingenuity often invents the marvels ascribed to nature, but whatever his motive, the overlapping influences collapse the distinction between poet and nature, inviting readers to appreciate his artfully indirect claim for authorship.

With his multiple sources that are all figments of his imagination, von Eschenbach plays a familiar game with his reader that includes the poem's central marvel. It depends on the philosophical status of marvels as unlikely but not impossible, deserving of serious attention even though they may well be proven false. In romance, authors like to pretend that their purely fictional marvels are still worthy of the same serious attention, and here von Eschenbach likewise exaggerates the credibility of his focal marvel in a manner that signals its constructedness. He evokes the methods of natural philosophers only to point slyly at their fundamental inapplicability. His goal is not to prove the marvel logically possible or to articulate its possible mechanisms, but to echo such efforts in a context that no longer supports them. The author's conviction regarding the marvel registers the inevitable lack of evidence. There is no option to argue that nature might have created these marvels, or to make subtle claims about what might be but probably is not, and so he turns to bald assertion.

The "heathen" source discovered in Toledo also points to the cross-cultural concerns of this book. As we have seen, philosophers in the Latin West regularly attributed theories about marvels and the marvelous imagination to Arabic sources, and it is tempting to credit von Eschenbach with a similar perspective. He certainly sees his philosophical source, whether he wrote in Arabic or Hebrew, as intellectually advanced, if ultimately unable to reap the benefits of his superior insights, and specifically unable to discover the grail. As balm can only be cultivated by Christians, so can the grail only be discovered by them, and even then, only by the best of them. Like any number of wise pagan philosophers who were thought to end up in hell, so Flegetanis has formidable knowledge but not revelation, and he can only draw the map for a treasure that he does not have the purity to find. As in travel literature, so here the world is imprinted with signs that testify to the correct faith and favors those who possess it.

Fake sources have a long and distinguished literary history, but they develop a special bond with medieval romance.[3] Later imitations and evocations of the genre, from Miguel de Cervantes's *Don Quijote* through Umberto Eco's *Name of the Rose* and beyond, strengthen it further. They are appropriate to a genre that likes to tip its hand, to show its reader that its claims are often to be distrusted. As secrets in romance exist only to be exposed, so the same spirit of transparency extends to the frame, where supposed sources are revealed, and also revealed as untrustworthy. In these final pages, I focus on the fake source of *Quijote* and how it too plays with the uncertain truth status of marvels. The text is privileged in literary history because it marks, perhaps, the birth of the novel or a certain type of novel, or a turning point of some sort.[4] One of its seemingly modern or proto-modern features is its skepticism, which is related to the complexity of truth claims in the work.[5] For instance, in the second part of the novel, Quijote meets characters who have read the first part, as well as a pseudepigraphical second part that pretended to have been written by Cervantes and whose author is still unidentified. The characters distinguish the "true, legitimate, faithful" Quijote from the "false, fictitious, apocryphal one," the former presented by Cervantes and the latter not, as though any character might fairly disparage another as "fictitious."[6] Because the Cervantes-authored continuation is valid in a way that the other is not, Cervantes evokes a sense in which literature might be called true in order to pretend that Quijote exists. Rather than emphasize Cervantes's turn away from the romances that the novel pillories and parodies, we might consider a point of continuity with the foregoing analysis: the novel continues to use marvels to complicate judgments about truth and falsehood in ways that support its sophisticated ambiguities.

3. For a brief overview, see Millett, "Chaucer, Lollius, and the Medieval Theory of Authorship," 98–102.

4. See Cascardi, "*Don Quixote* and the Invention of the Novel." Cervantes calls the work a *novela*, a term that was already in use in preceding centuries.

5. See, for instance, Lorca, *Neo-Stoicism and Skepticism*. On skepticism in Cervantes's work more generally, see Fuchs, *Knowing Fictions*.

6. Cervantes, *Don Quijote de la Mancha* 2.61, ed. Rico et al., 1:1131: "el verdadero, el legal y el fiel," "no el falso, no el ficticio, no el apócrifo."

When *Don Quijote* contrasts the "lying books" of romance with the "true history" it presents to its readers, it opposes truth and falsehood only to undermine the opposition.[7] Cervantes's narrator claims to have found the core of the story in Arabic script, in a pile of papers that he bought, again in Toledo, written by a Muslim philosopher (*filósofo mahomético*) named Cide Hamete Benengeli.[8] He then hired a *morisco aljamiado*, a Muslim convert to Christianity, to translate it into Castilian for him.[9] But the story that Cervantes tells about this source is inconsistent: the novel's first part is written in part or entirely by Hamete, but the narrator tells us that the account stops there, excluding the third sally described in the continuation. The narrator writes that he learns a bit about Quijote's death from a separate source, Castilian verses written in Gothic script on parchment and found in the foundations of an old hermitage.[10] But when the second part begins, it names Hamete as its source and proceeds without explanation. Further, as the buried parchment fragments suggest, the sources are old, and yet Quijote is supposed to have lived in the seventeenth century. Otherwise, characters in the novel's second part could not pretend to have read Cervantes's first installment, and Quijote himself could not refer regularly to recent literature and events. The result is that "the time of the knight and the time of the historian are in frank conflict," without possibility of resolution.[11]

Hamete also belongs to the past, to a Toledo that welcomed Arabic philosophers and produced wonders still discoverable years later. The official expulsion of Moriscos from all of Spain in 1609, along with the many local laws against Moorish dress and the owning of Arabic texts and so forth in earlier years, creates a firm contrast between the text's history and its present.[12] The novel, only comprehensible to the narrator thanks to a Morisco

7. Cervantes, *Don Quijote de la Mancha* 1.18 and 1.1, ed. Rico et al., 1:193 and 1:43: "libros mentirosos"; "verdadera historia." There are many other instances where the novel calls itself a "verdadera historia."

8. Cervantes, *Don Quijote de la Mancha* 2.53, ed. Rico et al., 1:1061. Cervantes elsewhere describes him as a historian ("historiador arábigo"), 1.9, ed. Rico et al., 1:108. For a list of fake sources in earlier Spanish literature, including fake Arabic sources, see Mosquera, "Los autores ficticios del 'Quijote,'" 61.

9. Cervantes, *Don Quijote de la Mancha* 1.9, ed. Rico et al., 1:107. "Aljamiado" likely refers to someone who is able to decipher *aljamía*, or romance written in the Arabic alphabet. See, for instance, Muñoz, "'Anduve mirando se parecía por allí algún morisco aljamiado.'" As she notes, *aljamía* survives in about two hundred manuscripts from the fourteenth to seventeenth centuries, hardly a fringe phenomenon (240–41).

10. Cervantes, *Don Quijote de la Mancha* 1.52, ed. Rico et al., 1:591.

11. López-Baralt, "El sabio encantador Cide Hamete Benengeli," 339.

12. On the rising hostility toward Iberian Muslims as well as Jews in the period, see Constable, *To Live Like a Moor*.

that he finds instantly and implausibly before him, is within its time and alienated from it simultaneously. Instead of a mythical Arthurian past, Cervantes turns to a forcibly suppressed Muslim one, and instead of a political utopia centered on a Round Table, he imagines a heterogeneous culture that is both scientifically advanced and filled with marvels.[13] The effect is not to locate the novel's origin in a void, but to define it with concrete historical details that do not line up. As with von Eschenbach, so here constructions are visible as constructions. With his irreconcilable timelines, Cervantes signals that none of them is true and teaches the reader not to trust his claims, even as he insists that his novel is more trustworthy than its romantic predecessors.

At the same time, the narrator maintains an ironic distance from Quijote, who, as the credulous reader of romance, is a figure familiar from literary history. For instance, Chaucer's Nun's Priest swears, "This storie is also [as] trewe, I undertake, / As is the book of Launcelot de Lake, / That wommen holde in ful greet reverence" (3211–13). The Nun's Priest discredits the Lancelot romance, as well as his own story, by ironically comparing himself to the women who believe it with the force of devotion. Their "reverence" forms a contrast with his irreverence and also contributes to the tale's interest in trustworthy and untrustworthy readers. In *Quijote*, however, we get the perspective of the women, as it were. We see how those who empathize with or laugh at Quijote cater to his fantasies, sometimes "so vividly and realistically that there was very little difference between them and the truth."[14] Sancho Panza, long promised an island in return for his service, is actually given a land to govern, and so "deceptions become the truth."[15] Although the novel criticizes uncritical readers of romance—the "ignorant rabble" who "come to believe and hold as true all the absurdities they contain"—their simplicity is complicated by the fact that "truth" is a specious category throughout.[16]

In this context, Cervantes evokes a host of familiar marvels, including the oracular head, the beaver that removes its own testicles, balm, and the lice on a ship that die when it passes the equinoctial line. Whenever Quijote cannot deny that circumstances conflict with his delusions, which happens

13. The scholarship on Cervantes's depiction of Muslims and Moriscos is vast, but a good starting point is Villanueva's *Moros, Moriscos y Turcos de Cervantes*.

14. Cervantes, *Don Quijote de la Mancha* 2.70, ed. Rico et al., 1:1193: "tan al vivo y tan bien hechos, que de la verdad a ellos había bien poca diferencia."

15. Cervantes, *Don Quijote de la Mancha* 2.49, ed. Rico et al., 1:1025: "las burlas se vuelven en veras."

16. Cervantes, *Don Quijote de la Mancha* 1.49, ed. Rico et al., 1:563: "el vulgo ignorante venga a creer y tener por verdaderas tantas necedades como contienen."

often, he blames them on enchanters, experts in confusing the distinction between the way things seem and the way they are. In this way, he supports his fantasy with a genre-appropriate device, playing with marvels in the manner of ʿĀqila or Flores's mother. Some of the marvels, like those concerning the beaver and the louse, are matters of common knowledge, while others are faked (the oracular head) or wished into being (enchantment). They play to the novel's fondness for enigmas. Perhaps the most striking claim is that Quijote saw an array of images in the Cave of Montesinos, a marvel unlike the others because it occurs during sleep, without witnesses. We have good reason to distrust it, but the question of its legitimacy lingers for the rest of the novel. It stands apart because Quijote does not usually make up events from whole cloth; they tend to have some basis in experience, however misconstrued. That the supposed vision occurs while Quijote sleeps in an underground cave calls to mind the disorienting effects of subterranean vapors and deepens the questions around it. Ultimately, there is no way to measure the accuracy of an underground vision experienced by a sleeping fictional character who suffers from a localized form of madness.[17] Further obscuring the matter is the narrator's account of a marginal quotation that expresses Hamete's skepticism toward the episode, along with his commitment to include it "without affirming either its falsity or its truth."[18] It is a familiar caveat in the philosophy of marvels, as we have seen. Together, the perplexing conditions that surround the marvel heighten its unknowability. No matter how many factors conspire to discredit it, it cannot be conclusively disproven, not least because nothing actually happens to a fictional character in the first place. Cervantes plays with such puzzles, and invites the reader to play along.

My point here is not to deny change. For instance, the camaraderie between literature and philosophy that I have described in medieval texts, particularly on the matters of marvels and imagination, is not as easily witnessed in the centuries that follow.[19] Richard Firth Green argues for a distinction between the treatment of fairies in literature, on the one hand, and in philosophy and theology, on the other, and he shows how the two grew

17. On the epistemological questions raised, see Cascardi, "Cervantes and Descartes on the Dream Argument."

18. Cervantes, *Don Quijote de la Mancha* 2.24, ed. Rico et al. 1:829: "sin afirmarla por falso o verdadera."

19. On the marvel-performing imagination in early modern Europe, see Vermeir, "The 'Physical Prophet' and the Powers of the Imagination"; and the collected articles in *Diseases of the Imagination and Imaginary Disease in the Early Modern Period*, ed. Haskell. On the role of Arabic sources in the period's philosophy, see Saliba, *Islamic Science and the Making of the European Renaissance.*

further apart as the Middle Ages proceeded.[20] So with marvels understood more broadly, I think. My purpose, rather, is to sketch in the briefest terms a sort of literary history that does not depend on rupture or on the maturing of readers who become skeptical and sophisticated where they had been credulous and undiscriminating. Because marvels have been used in the service of such triumphant narratives, my hope is that they might instead support an alternative. Well before the writing of *Don Quijote*, marvels trouble truth claims and muddy judgment in ways that invite a reader's scrutiny. They are claims that are supposed to be complicated, and to be recognized as such.

While I have glanced forward in this conclusion, the claims I make in the preceding chapters are specifically about the Middle Ages. There, I have argued, marvels mark out common ground between real and invented things. Unusual by definition, they tend to be unsettling, whether or not they are real. In either case they express creativity, either nature's or a poet's. In these respects, they bear the imprint of imagination, which is closely associated with them and often produces them. Uninterested in distinguishing real from illusory things and phenomena, the faculty instead obscures ontological boundaries, and has a special talent for doing so. In philosophy, we have seen that marvels are nonimpossibilities in the sense that they are logically possible. In literature, authors play with the discourse of nonimpossibility to pretend that the marvels they concoct are possible or more than possible. Their protean nature means that they can be invented and reinvented anew, inviting endless artistic adaptations. Able to inhabit different forms in different disciplines and in different places, they might elicit wonder through their very instability. Because marvels are regularly associated with the Middle Ages or more narrowly with the Islamic world, their conception has colored the understanding of past times and places, often to their detriment. It stands to reason, then, that a more faithful conception might remove an albatross of sorts from around the neck of the societies and genres most directly linked to them.

20. See Green, *Elf Queens*, especially 42–75.

Acknowledgments

Many people have helped to make this book a reality, beginning with the kind souls who invited me to give talks at their universities or at conferences. Those experiences, especially when the project was in its early stages, helped it to find its shape. I thank Paul Bakker at Radboud University, Jen Jahner at the California Institute of Technology; Suzanne Akbari, then at the University of Toronto; Scott Bruce, then at the University of Colorado, Boulder; Anna Kelner, Aparna Chaudhuri, and James Simpson at Harvard University; Eric Ensley, Alex Reider, and Jessica Brantley at Yale University; Markus Rathey, Peggy Olin, and Martin Jean at Yale's Institute of Sacred Music; Kathleen Noll, Katy Breen, and Barbara Newman at Northwestern University; Esther Yu and Michelle Ripplinger at the University of California, Berkeley; Taylor Cowdery and Harry Cushman at the University of North Carolina at Chapel Hill; Joe Stadolnik and Julie Orlemanski at the University of Chicago; Béatrice Delaurenti and Koen Vermeir at L'École des hautes études en sciences sociales; and Jutta Eming at Freie Universität.

This book wouldn't exist at all without two fellowships I received, the first from the Radcliffe Institute for Advanced Study from 2016 to 2017, and the second from Yale's Institute of Sacred Music from 2018 to 2019. I'm still in disbelief that such opportunities exist and only wish that everyone could benefit from them. I had no idea where this book was going when I got to Radcliffe, and the chance to spend a year bumbling around in the library, auditing Arabic classes, and talking with scholars from dozens of different fields was a rewarding and formative experience for me, one whose benefits extend well beyond this book. Yale's Institute of Sacred Music is a second home. Under the kindhearted and expert management of Eben Graves and Martin Jean, my fellowship year introduced me to amazing people across the university, and my office there will forever be my happy place. I am grateful to the Institute for Scholarship in the Liberal Arts at the University of Notre Dame for enabling me to take two fellowships in quick succession.

I also thank the Institute for a publishing subvention, as well as a grant for copyediting that materially supported this publication.

Dozens of people have provided help, whether professional or personal, while I have worked on this book. I especially thank Amy Appleford, Jessica Brantley, Ardis Butterfield, Taylor Cowdery, Harry Cushman, George Edmondson, John Block Friedman, Bruce Holsinger, Shazia Jagot, Maura Nolan, Julie Orlemanski, Sarah Quesada, Jessica Rosenfeld, Christopher Shields, James Simpson, Amanda Skofstad, Vance Smith, Sebastian Sobecki, Yasmin Solomnescu, Laura Spagnoli, Emily Thornbury, Shawkat Toorawa, Ryan Vlasak, Nicholas Watson, and Travis Zadeh. I owe my career to Rita Copeland and David Wallace, who modeled excellence as scholars and advisers, and who continue to be my touchstones in this profession. Steve Justice read the book's early chapters with great care and insight, as Matilda Bruckner did with the later chapters, and as Joe Stadolnik did with the whole thing. Preternaturally talented readers, they all made the book much better. I started to learn the Arabic alphabet the day after I was granted tenure, and without the help of Alexander Key, Luke Leafgren, and Adeel Mohammadi, I don't think I would have gotten far. Without those fellowship years I mentioned, I don't see how I would have been able to persevere, either. I've had the chance to work with astonishingly bright graduate students, including Maj-Britt Frenze, Nathan Phelps, Daniel Hellstrom, and Logan Quigley. All the students in my graduate classes have made me think more deeply about medieval literature, and working with them continues to be one of the best parts of my job. I am deeply grateful to the amazing librarians at Hesburgh Library for fetching me all manner of materials, often obscure, and doing so with professionalism and unerring competence.

I'd also like to give a shout-out to my family, the Karneses (Nancy, Ray, Elaine, John, Nan, Ed, Pam, Mary, Becky, Stephen, Matt, and Jeff), the Lemmerichs (Lucie and Finn), the Otsukas (Lisa, Mike, and Dean), and the Toumajians (David, Anja, Cody, Mark, Leanne, Peter, and Sydney).

My two readers for the University of Chicago Press were spectacularly generous and helpful. Both have identified themselves, and so I warmly thank Barbara Newman and Travis Zadeh for reports that went well beyond the call of duty. Travis even checked my Arabic transliterations, and for such exceptional collegiality in the age of a global pandemic, he deserves some sort of medal. I couldn't imagine two more knowledgeable or insightful readers. It's been a true pleasure to work once again with Randy Petilos and the amazing team at the University of Chicago Press, including Tamara Ghattas, who oversaw editing and production, as well as with

Lys Weiss, copyeditor extraordinaire. Would that I had more books to send their way.

Finally, I thank my husband, Shane Duarte, for his unfailing encouragement, brilliance, and love. This book is dedicated to my twin brother, David Toumajian, and my closest friend, Jessica Rosenfeld. As kids, David and I used to pretend to be the Wonder Twins, even though it's not an especially fun game; once you declare your powers, there's not much else to do, and the guy can only be some form of water. But David has many superpowers: fun-loving, impossibly energetic, charismatic, funny, smart, brave, and thoughtful, he got the better qualities, even though he will always be two minutes younger and therefore two minutes behind me. I met Jessica in graduate school and I wouldn't want to imagine my life or my career without her wisdom, good humor, and kindness. She is the best of friends and the best of people: stalwartly loyal, unflappable, sage, and loving. On a surprising number of occasions, people have confused us with one another, but I appreciate the mistake since I'd like to be as similar to her as possible. Together, the three of them are my people in this life, and I am very lucky to have them in it.

∴

Portions of chapters 1 and 2 appeared in earlier form as "Marvels in the Medieval Imagination," *Speculum* 90, no. 2 (April 2015): 327–65, copyright © 2015 by The Medieval Academy of America, Boston, Massachusetts. Part of chapter 4 appeared in "The Possibilities of Medieval Fiction," *New Literary History* 51, no. 1 (January 2020): 209–28, copyright © 2020 by Johns Hopkins University Press. I thank both journals for permission to print revised versions here.

Bibliography

PRIMARY SOURCES

Abū Ḥāmid al-Gharnāṭī, Muḥammad ibn ʿAbd al-Raḥmān ibn Sulaymān ibn al-Māzinī al-Qaysī. *De Grenade à Bagdad: La relation de voyage d'Abû Hâmid al-Gharnâtî (1080–1168) ou Al-muʿrib ʿan baʿḍ ʿadjâʾib al-Maghrib*. Ed. and trans. Jean-Charles Ducène. Paris: L'Harmattan, 2006.

———. *Al-muʿrib ʿan baʿḍ ʿajāʾib al-Maghrib (Elogio de algunas maravillas del Magrib)*. Ed. and trans. Ingrid Bejarano. Madrid: Consejo Superior de Investigaciones Científicas, 1991.

———. *Abū Ḥāmid el Granadino y su relación de viaje por tierras Eurasiáticas*. Ed. and trans. César E. Dubler. Madrid: Imprenta y Editorial Maestre, 1953.

———. *Tuḥfat al-albāb*. Ed. Gabriel Ferrand. *Journal asiatique* 207, no. 3 (1925): 1–148, and 207, no. 4 (1925): 193–304.

The Adventures of Sayf Ben Dhi Yazan: An Arab Folk Epic. Trans. Lena Jayyusi. Bloomington: Indiana University Press, 1996; reprint, 1999.

Alain of Lille. *Alain de Lille: Textes inédits*. Ed. Marie-Thérèse d'Alverny. Paris: Librairie philosophique J. Vrin, 1965.

Albertus Magnus. *Albertus Magnus, On Animals: A Medieval Summa Zoologica*. Trans. Kenneth F. Kitchell Jr. and Irven M. Resnick. 2 vols. Baltimore: Johns Hopkins University Press, 1999.

———. *Book of Minerals*. Trans. Dorothy Wyckoff. Oxford: Clarendon Press, 1967.

———. *De animalibus liber XXVI, nach der Cölner urschrift*. Ed. Hermann Stadler. 2 vols. Münster: Aschendorff, 1916–20.

———. *Opera omnia*. Ed. Auguste Borgnet. 38 vols. Paris: Vivès, 1890–95.

———. *Opera omnia ad fidem codicum manuscriptorum edenda*. Ed. Bernhard Geyer et al. Monasterii Westfalorum (Münster): In aedibus Aschendorff, 1951–present.

———. "'The Problemata Determinata XLIII' Ascribed to Albertus Magnus (1271)." Ed. James Weisheipl. *Mediaeval Studies* 22 (1960): 303–54.

———. *Questions concerning Aristotle's On Animals*. Trans. Irven M. Resnick and Kenneth F. Kitchell Jr. Washington, DC: Catholic University of America Press, 2008.

Amadas and Ydoine. Trans. Ross G. Arthur. New York: Garland Publishing, 1993.

Amadas et Ydoine: Roman du XIIIe siècle. Ed. John R. Reinhard. Paris: Librairie ancienne Honoré Champion, 1926.

Aquinas, Thomas. *Commentary on Aristotle's Physics*. Trans. Richard J. Blackwell, Richard J. Spath, and W. Edmund Thirlkel. Notre Dame, IN: Dumb Ox Books, 1963; rev. ed. 1999.

———. *In metaphysicam Aristotelis commentaria Sancti Thomae Aquinatis*. Ed. M.-R. Cathala. Turin: Marietti, 1926.

———. *Opera omnia iussu impensaque Leonis XII P.M. edita*. 38 vols. Rome: Ex Typographia Polyglotta, 1882–1976.

———. *Summa contra Gentiles*. Trans. James F. Anderson, Vernon J. Bourke, Charles J. O'Neil, and Anton C. Pegis. 5 vols. Notre Dame: University of Notre Dame Press, 1975.

———. *Summa theologiae: Latin Text and English Translation, Introduction, Notes, Appendices, and Glossaries*. Ed. Thomas Gilby. 61 vols. London: Blackfriars, 1964–81.

———. *Truth*. Trans. James V. McGlynn, Robert W. Mulligan, and Robert W. Schmidt. 3 vols. Indianapolis: Hackett Publishing, 1954; reprint, 1994.

The Arabian Nights. Trans. Husain Haddawy. New York: W. W. Norton, 1990.

Aristotle. *Analytica posteriora: Translationes Iacobi, Anonymi sive 'Ioannis,' Gerardi, et Recensio Guillelmi de Moerbeka*. Ed. Lorenzo Minio-Paluello and Bernard G. Dod. Aristoteles Latinus 4.1–4. Bruges: Desclée de Brouwer, 1968.

———. *The Complete Works of Aristotle: The Revised Oxford Translation*. Ed. Jonathan Barnes. 2 vols. Princeton: Princeton University Press, 1984.

———. *Metaphysica: Lib. I–XIV*. Ed. Gudrun Viullemin-Diem. 2 vols. Aristoteles Latinus 25.3, parts 1–2. Leiden: E. J. Brill, 1995.

———. *Parts of Animals, Movement of Animals, Progression of Animals*. Ed. Jeffrey Henderson; trans. Arthur L. Peck and Edward S. Forster. Loeb Classical Library 323. Cambridge, MA: Harvard University Press, 1937; rev. ed., 1961.

Augustine of Hippo (Sancti Aurelii Augustini). *De civitate Dei*. Ed. Bernhard Dombart and Alfons Kalb. 2 vols. Corpus Christianorum Series Latina 47–48. Turnhout: Brepols, 1955.

———. *Soliloquiorum libri duo; De immortalite animae; De quantitate animae*. Ed. Wolfgang Hörmann. Corpus Scriptorum Ecclesiasticorum Latinorum 89. Vienna: Hoelder-Pichler-Tempsky, 1986.

———. *De Trinitate, libri XV*. Ed. William J. Mountain and François Glorie. 2 vols. Corpus Christianorum Series Latina 50–50A. Turnhout: Brepols, 1968; reprint, 2001.

———. *De utilitate credendi, De duabus animabus, Contra Fortunatum, Contra Adimantum, Contra epistulam fundamenti, Contra Faustum*. Ed. Joseph Zycha. Corpus Scriptorum Ecclesiasticorum Latinorum 25.1. Vienna: F. Tempsky, 1891.

Averroes (Abū al-Walīd Muḥammad ibn Aḥmad ibn Rushd). *De arte poetica: Translatio Guillelmi de Moerbeke*. Ed. Ersa Valgimigli, Ezio Franceschini, and Lorenzo Minio-Paluello. Aristoteles Latinus 33. Bruges: Desclée de Brouwer, 1968.

———. *Talkhīṣ kitāb al-shi'r*. Ed. Charles Butterworth and Aḥmad 'Abd al-Mājid Harīdī. Cairo: al-Hay'ah al-Miṣrīyah al'Āmmah li-l-Kitāb, 1986.

Avicenna (Abū 'Alī al-Ḥusayn ibn 'Abdallāh Ibn Sīnā). *Avicenna's De anima (Arabic Text): Being the Psychological Part of Kitāb al-shifā'*. Ed. Fazlur Rahman. London: Oxford University Press, 1960.

———. *Avicennae De congelatione et conglutinatione lapidum, Being sections of the Kitāb al-shifā'*. Ed. and trans. Eric J. Holmyard and Desmond C. Mandeville. Paris: Paul Geuthner, 1927.

———. "'L'épître sur la disparition des formes intelligibles vaines après la mort' d'Avicenne: Édition critique, traduction et index." Ed. and trans. Jean R. Michot. *Bulletin de philosophie médiévale* 29 (1987): 152–70.

———. *Liber de anima seu Sextus de naturalibus: Édition critique de la traduction latine médiévale*. Ed. Simone van Riet. 2 vols. Louvain: E. Peeters, 1968–72.

———. *Livre des directives et remarques (Kitāb al-ʾišārāt wa l-tanbīhāt)*. Trans. and ed. Amélie-Marie Goichon. Paris: J. Vrin, 1951.

———. *Le livre des théorèmes et des avertissements (Kitāb al-ishārāt wa-l-tanbīhāt)*. Ed. Jacobus Forget. Leiden: Brill, 1892.

———. "Risāla fī al-fiʿl wa-l-infiʿāl." In *Majmūʿ Rasāʾil al-Shaykh al-Raʾīs Abī ʿAlī al-Ḥusayn ibn ʿAbdallāh ibn Sīnā al-Bukhārī*. Hyderabad: Maṭbaʿat Jamʿīyat Dāʾirat al-Maʿārif al-ʿUthmānīyah, 1934.

Bacon, Roger. *Fr. Rogeri Bacon Opera quaedam hactenus inedita*. Ed. John S. Brewer. 3 vols. London: Green, Longman, and Roberts, 1859.

———. *Opera hactenus inedita Rogeri Baconi*. Ed. Robert Steele. 16 vols. Oxford: Clarendon Press, 1909–41.

———. *The Opus majus of Roger Bacon*. Ed. John Henry Bridges. 3 vols. Oxford: Clarendon Press, 1897–1900.

———. *The Opus majus of Roger Bacon*. Trans. Robert Belle Burke. 2 vols. Philadelphia: University of Pennsylvania Press, 1928.

Bartholomaeus Anglicus. *De proprietatibus rerum*. Ed. Baudouin van den Abeele. Vol. 1. Turnhout: Brepols, 2007.

———. *On the Properties of Things: John Trevisa's Translation of Bartholomaeus Anglicus, De proprietatibus rerum: A Critical Text*. Ed. Michael C. Seymour. 3 vols. Oxford: Clarendon Press, 1975–88.

Bernard of Clairvaux. *Sancti Bernardi Opera*. Ed. Jean Leclercq, Charles H. Talbot, and Henri M. Rochais. 9 vols. Rome: Editiones Cistercienses, 1957–77.

Biblia Sacra iuxta Vulgatam Clementinam. Ed. Alberto Colunga and Lorenzo Turrado. 11th ed. Madrid: Biblioteca de Autores Cristianos, 2002.

Bibliorum Sacrorum cum Glossa Ordinaria. Ed. François Feuardent, Jean Dadré, and Jacques de Cuilly. 7 vols. Venice: Apud Magnam Societatem, 1545–1603.

al-Bīrūnī, Abū al-Rayḥān Muḥammad ibn Aḥmad. *Chronologie orientalischer Völker (Al-athār al-bāqiya ʿan al-qurūn al-khālīya)*. Ed. Eduard Sachau. Leipzig: Brockhaus, 1878.

———. *The Chronology of Ancient Nations: An English Version of the Arabic Text of the Athâr-ul-Bâkiya of Albîrûnî, or Vestiges of the Past*. Trans. Eduard Sachau. London: W. H. Allen & Co., 1879.

Bonaventure. *Opera omnia*. 10 vols. Quaracchi Editions. Rome: Ex Typographia Collegii S. Bonaventurae, 1882–1902.

Bradwardine, Thomas. *De causa Dei contra Pelagium, et De virtute causarum, ad suos Mertonenses, libri tres*. Ed. Sir Henry Savile. Facsimile reprint of 1618 edition. Frankfurt am Main: Minerva, 1964.

Burchard of Mount Sion. *Descriptio terrae sanctae*. In *Peregrinatores medii aevi quatuor*, 1–100. Ed. Johann C. M. Laurent. Leipzig: J. C. Hinrichs, 1864.

———. *Description of the Holy Land*. Trans. Denys Pringle. In *Pilgrimage to Jerusalem and the Holy Land, 1187–1291*, 241–320. Burlington, VT: Ashgate, 2011.

Casaubon, Meric. *A Treatise Proving Spirits, Witches, and Supernatural Operations, by Pregnant Instances and Evidences: Together with Other Things Worthy of Note*. London: Brabazon Aylmer, 1672.

Cervantes Saavedra, Miguel de. *Don Quijote de la Mancha: Edición del Instituto*

Cervantes (1605, 1615, 2015). Ed. Francisco Rico, Joaquín Forradellas, and Gonzalo Pontón. 2 vols. Madrid: Real Academia Española, 2015.

Chartularium Universitatis Parisiensis. Ed. Heinrich Denifle, Emile Châtelain, Charles Samaran, and Émile van Moé. 4 vols. Paris: Ex typis fratrum Delalain, 1889–97.

Chaucer, Geoffrey. *The Riverside Chaucer*. Ed. Larry Benson. 3rd ed. Boston: Houghton Mifflin, 1986.

Chrétien de Troyes. *Arthurian Romances*. Trans. William W. Kibler and Carleton W. Carroll. London: Penguin Books, 1991; reprint, 2004.

———. *Oeuvres complètes*. Ed. Daniel Poirion, with the collaboration of Anne Berthelot, Peter Dembowski, Sylvie Lefèvre, Karl Uitti, and Philippe Walter. Paris: Gallimard, 1994.

———. *Romans*. Ed. Michel Zink et al. Paris: Librairie générale française, Le Livre de poche, 1994.

Christine de Pizan. *Le chemin de longue étude*. Ed. and trans. Andrea Tarnowski. Paris: Librairie générale française, 2000.

Comestor, Petrus. *Historia scholastica*. Ed. Jacques-Paul Migne, Patrologia Latina 198, cols. 1053–1844. Paris: Imprimerie catholique, 1855.

Le conte de Floire et Blancheflor. Ed. Jean-Luc Leclanche. Paris: Librairie Honoré Champion, 1980.

Crónica de Flores y Blancaflor. Ed. David Arbesú. Tempe: Arizona Center for Medieval and Renaissance Studies, 2011.

Dante Alighieri. *Purgatorio*. Ed. and trans. Robert M. Durling and Ronald L. Martinez. Oxford: Oxford University Press, 1996.

Il De mirabilibus mundi *tra tradizione magica e filosofia naturale*. Ed. Antonella Sannino. Florence: SISMEL, Edizioni del Galluzzo, 2011.

De mundo: Translationes Bartholomaei et Nicholai. Ed. William L. Lorimer and Lorenzo Minio-Panuello. Bruges: Desclée de Brouwer, 1965.

al-Dimashqī, Shams al-dīn. *Manuel de la cosmographie du moyen âge*. Ed. and trans. August F. Mehren. Copenhagen: C. A. Reitzel, 1874; reprint, Frankfurt am Main: Institute for the History of Arabic-Islamic Science, 1994.

———. *Nukhbat al-dahr fī ʿajāʾib al-barr wa-l-baḥr*. Ed. August F. Merhen. Saint Petersburg: Académie impériale des sciences, 1866.

Dominicus Gundissalinus. *De divisione philosphiae*. Ed. Ludwig Baur. Münster: Aschendorff, 1903.

Duns Scotus, John. *Doctoris subtilis et Mariani Ioannis Duns Scoti Ordinis Fratrum Minorum Opera omnia*. 21 vols. Ed. Pacifico M. Perantoni, Carolus Balić, Barnaba Hechich, and Josip Percan. Vatican City: Typis Polyglottis Vaticanis, 1950–2015.

An Eleventh-Century Egyptian Guide to the Universe: The "Book of Curiosities." Ed. and trans. Yossef Rapoport and Emilie Savage-Smith. Leiden: Brill, 2014.

English Mediaeval Lapidaries. Ed. Joan Evans and Mary S. Sarjeantson. Early English Text Society o.s. 190. London: Oxford University Press, 1933.

Flores y Blancaflora. In "Leyendas medievales españolas del ciclo carolingio." Ed. José Gómez Pérez. *Anuario de filiogía* 2–3 (1963–64): 7–136.

Four Romances of England: King Horn, Havelok the Dane, Bevis of Hampton, Athelston. Ed. Ronald B. Herzman, Graham Duke, and Eve Salisbury. Kalamazoo, MI: Medieval Institute Publications, 1999.

Geoffrey of Monmouth. *Life of Merlin. Vita Merlini*. Ed. and trans. Basil F. L. Clarke. Cardiff: University of Wales Press, 1973.

Gerald of Wales. *Giraldi Cambrensis Opera*. Ed. John S. Brewer, James F. Dimock, and Sir George F. Warner. 8 vols. London: Longman, 1861–91.

Gervase of Tilbury. *Otia imperialia: Recreation for an Emperor*. Ed. and trans. Shelagh E. Banks and James W. Binns. Oxford: Clarendon Press, 2002.

Al-Gharnāṭī. See Abū Ḥāmid al-Gharnāṭī.

Al-Ghazālī, Abū Ḥāmid Muḥammad ibn Muḥammad al-Ṭūsī. *Algazel's Metaphysics: A Mediaeval Translation*. Ed. Joseph T. Muckle. Toronto: St. Michael's College, 1933.

———. *Maqāṣid al-falāsifa: fī al-manṭiq wa-al-ḥikma al-ilāhīya wa-al-ḥikma al-ṭabīʿīya*. Ed. Muḥyī al-Dīn Ṣabrī al-Kurdī. Cairo: al-Maṭbaʿah al-Maḥmūdiyah al-Tijārīyah bi-al-Azhar, 1936.

Giles of Rome. *Errores Philosophorum: Critical Text with Notes and Introduction*. Ed. Josef Koch; trans. John O. Riedl. Milwaukee: Marquette University Press, 1944.

Glaive-des-couronnes (Sayf al-Tījān): Roman traduit de l'arabe. Trans. Nicolas Perron. Paris: Benjamin Duprat, 1862.

Gower, John. *Confessio amantis*. Ed. Russell Peck; trans. Andrew Galloway. 3 vols. Kalamazoo, MI: Medieval Institute Publications, 2000–2004.

Gratian. *Decretum Gratiani, Emendatum et variis lectionibus simul et notationibus illustratum*. Ed. J.-P. Migne. Patrologia Latina 187. Paris: Apud Garnier Fratres, 1891.

Hayton of Corycus. *Flos historiarum*. Ed. Édouard Dulaurier, Jean Dardel, Charles Kohler, Charles Schefer, Louis de Mas Latrie, and M. Gaston Paris. *Recueil des historiens des croisades*: Documents Arméniens. 2 vols. Paris: Imprimerie nationale, 1869–1906.

———. (Hetoum) *A Lytell Cronycle: Richard Pynson's Translation (c. 1520) of* La fleur des histoires de la terre d'Orient *(c. 1307)*. Ed. Glenn Burger. Toronto: University of Toronto Press, 1988.

Hilton, Walter. *The Scale of Perfection*. Ed. Thomas H. Bestul. Kalamazoo: Medieval Institute Publications, 2000.

Ibn Baṭṭūṭa, Shams al-Dīn Abū ʿAbdallāh Muḥammad ibn ʿAbdallāh al-Lawātī al-Ṭanjī. *The Travels of Ibn Battuta, A.D. 1325–54*. Ed. and trans. Charles Defrémery, Beniamino R. Sanguinetti, Hamilton A. Gibb, Charles F. Beckingham, and A. David Bivar. 5 vols. London: Hakluyt Society, 1958–2000.

———. *Voyages d'Ibn Battūta: Texte arabe accompagné d'une traduction*. Ed. and trans. Charles Defrémery and Beniamino R. Sanguinetti, with Vincent Monteil. 4 vols. Paris: Éditions Anthropos, 1968–69.

Ibn Ḥawqal, Abū al-Qāsim ibn ʿAlī al-Naṣībī. *Configuration de la terre (Kitab surat al-ard)*. Trans. Johannes H. Kramers and Gaston Wiet. 2 vols. Paris: Éditions G.-P. Maisonneuve & Larose, 1964.

———. *Kitāb ṣūrat al-arḍ*. Beirut: Dār Maktabat al-Ḥayāh, 1964.

Ibn Khurdādbih (Khurradādbih), Abū al-Qāsim ʿUbaydallāh ibn ʿAbdallāh. *Kitāb al-masālik wa'l-mamālik*. Ed. Michael Jan de Goeje and Fuat Sezgin. Leiden: Brill, 1889; reprint, Frankfurt am Main: Institute for the History of Arabic-Islamic Science at Johann Wolfgang Goethe University, 1992.

Ibn Rushd. See Averroes.

Ibn Sīnā. See Avicenna.

Isidore of Seville. *Isidori Hispalensis Episcopi Etymologiarum sive originum libri xx*. Ed. Wallace M. Lindsay. 2 vols. Oxford: Clarendon Press, 1911.

———. *Traité de la nature*. Ed. Jacques Fontaine. Bordeaux: Féret & Fils, 1960.

Itinera et relationes Fratrum Minorum saeculi XIII et XIV. Ed. Anastasius van den Wyngaert. Sinica Franciscana 1. Florence: Apud Collegium S. Bonaventurae, 1929.

Jacques de Vitry. *Historia orientale. Historia orientalis*. Ed. and trans. Jean Donnadieu. Turnhout: Brepols, 2008.

al-Jāḥiẓ, Abū ʿUthmān ʿAmr ibn Baḥr. *Le cadi et la mouche: Anthologie du Livre des animaux*. Ed. and trans. Lakhdar Souami. Paris: Éditions Sindbad, 1988.

———. *Kitāb al-ḥayawān*. Ed. ʿAbd al-Salām Muḥammad Hārūn. 7 vols. Cairo: Maktabat Muṣṭafā al-Bābī al-Halabī, 1958.

Jean d'Arras. *Mélusine; Or The Noble History of Lusignan*. Ed. and trans. Donald Maddox and Sara Sturm-Maddox. University Park: Pennsylvania State University Press, 2012.

———. *Mélusine ou La noble histoire de Lusignan: Roman du XIVe siècle*. Ed. and trans. Jean-Jacques Vincensini. Paris: Librairie générale française, 2003.

John of Plano Carpini. *Mission to Asia*. Ed. Christopher Dawson. Toronto: University of Toronto Press, 1980; reprint, 2003.

———. *Storia dei Mongoli*. Ed. Enrico Menestò. Spoleto: Centro Italiano di studi sull'alto medioevo, 1989.

al-Kindī, Abū Yūsuf Yaʿkhūb ibn Isḥākh. "Al-Kindī: *De Radiis*." Ed. Marie-Thérèse d'Alverny and Françoise Hudry. *Archives d'histoire doctrinale et littéraire du moyen âge* 61 (1974): 139–260.

———. *De radiis: Théorie des arts magiques*. Trans. Didier Ottaviani. Paris: Éditions Allia, 2003.

———. *Liber de somno et visione*. In *Die philosophischen Abhandlungen des Jaʿqūb ben Isḥāq al-Kindī*, 12–27. Ed. Albino Nagy. Beiträge zur Geschichte der Philosophie und Theologie des Mittelalters, vol. 2, part 5: Münster: Aschendorff, 1897.

———. *The Philosophical Works of al-Kindī*. Ed. and trans. Peter E. Pormann and Peter Adamson. Oxford: Oxford University Press, 2012.

———. "Risālat fī māhīyat al-nawm wa-l-ruʾyā." In *Rasāʾil al-Kindī al-falsāfīya*, 1:293–311. Ed. Muḥammad ʿAbd al-Hādī Abū Rīdah. 2 vols. Cairo: Dār al-Fikr al-ʿArabī, 1950–53.

Langland, William. *Piers Plowman: The Three Versions*. Ed. George Kane, E. Talbot Donaldson, and George H. Russell. 3 vols. Berkeley: University of California Press, 1988–97.

Llull, Ramón. *Nova edició de les obres de Ramón Llull* (NEORL). Ed. Fernando Domínguez Reboiras. Palma de Mallorca: Patronat Ramón Llull, 1990–.

———. *Obra escogida*. Trans. and ed. Pere Gimferrer. Barcelona: Penguin, 2016.

Mandeville, John. *The Book of John Mandeville*. Ed. Tamarah Kohanski and C. David Benson. Kalamazoo, MI: Medieval Institute Publications, 2007.

———. *The Book of John Mandeville, with Related Texts*. Ed. and trans. Iain Macleod Higgins. Indianapolis: Hackett Publishing, 2011.

———. (Jean de Mandeville) *Le livre des merveilles du monde*. Ed. Christiane Deluz. Paris: CNRS Éditions, 2000.

Map, Walter. *De nugis curialium, Courtiers' Trifles*. Ed. Montague R. James, Christopher Brooke, and Roger A. B. Mynors. Oxford: Clarendon Press, 1983.

Marbod of Rennes (Marbodo de Rennes). *Lapidario, Liber lapidum*. Ed. and trans. María Esthera Herrera. Paris: Les belles lettres, 2005.

Marco Polo. *The Description of the World*. Trans. Arthur C. Moule and Paul Pelliot. 2 vols. London: Routledge, 1938.

———. *Milione; Le Divisament dou monde: Il Milione nelle redazioni toscana e franco-italiana.* Ed. Gabriella Ronchi. Milan: Arnaldo Mondadori, 1982.

Marie de France. *Les lais de Marie de France.* Ed. Jean Rychner. Paris: Librairie Honoré Champion, 1966.

———. *The Lais of Marie de France.* Trans. Glyn S. Burgess and Keith Busby. 2nd ed. London: Penguin Books, 1999; reprint, 2003.

———. *Saint Patrick's Purgatory: A Poem by Marie de France.* Trans. Michael J. Curley. Binghamton, NY: Medieval and Renaissance Texts and Studies, 1997.

al-Masʿūdī, Abū al-Ḥasan ʿAlī ibn al-Ḥusayn. *Les prairies d'or (Kitāb murūdj adh-dhahab wa-maʿādin al-djawhar).* Ed. and trans. C. Barbier de Meynard and Abel Pavet de Courteille. 9 vols. Paris: Imprimerie impériale, 1861–77.

———. *Les prairies d'or (Kitāb murūdj adh-dhahab wa-maʿādin al-djawhar).* Ed. and trans. C. Barbier de Meynard, Abel Pavet de Courteille, and Charles Pellat. 5 vols. Paris: Société asiatique, 1962–89.

Middle English Verse Romances. Ed. Donald B. Sands. New York: Holt, Rinehart & Winston, 1966.

The Middle English Versions of Partonope of Blois: Edited from the manuscripts. Ed. Adam F. T. Bødtker. Early English Text Society e.s. 109. London: Kegan Paul, 1912.

More, Henry. *The Immortality of the Soul, so farre forth as it is demonstrable from the knowledge of nature and the light of reason.* London: J. Flesher, 1659.

Neckham, Alexander. *Alexandri Neckam, De naturis rerum libri duo. With the poem of the same author, De laudibus divinae sapientiae.* Ed. Thomas Wright. London: Longman, Roberts & Green, 1863.

Odoric of Pordenone (Odoric de Portu Naonis). *Relatio.* In *Itinera et relationes Fratrum Minorum saeculi XIII et XIV*, 381–495. Ed. Anastasius van den Wyngaert.

———. *The Travels of Friar Odoric.* Trans. Sir Henry Yule. Grand Rapids, MI: William B. Eerdmans Publishing, 2002.

Oresme, Nicole. *Nicole Oresme and the Astrologers: A Study of His* Livre de divinacions. Ed. and trans. George W. Coopland. Cambridge, MA: Harvard University Press, 1952.

———. *Nicole Oresme and the Marvels of Nature: A Study of His* De causis mirabilium *with Critical Edition, Translation, and Commentary.* Ed. and trans. Bert Hansen. Toronto: Pontifical Institute of Mediaeval Studies, 1985.

———. *Nicole Oresme and the Medieval Geometry of Qualities and Motions: A Treatise on the Uniformity and Difformity of Intensities known as* Tractatus de configurationibus qualitatum et motuum. Ed. and trans. Marshall Clagett. Madison: University of Wisconsin Press, 1968.

Ovid. *Heroides, Amores.* Ed. Jeffrey Henderson; trans. Grant Showerman and G. P. Goold. 2nd ed. Loeb Classical Library 41. Cambridge, MA: Harvard University Press, 1977.

———. *Metamorphoses, Volume 1: Books 1–8.* Ed. Jeffrey Henderson; trans. Frank J. Miller and G. P. Goold. 3rd ed. Loeb Classical Library 42. Cambridge, MA: Harvard University Press, 1977.

Partonopeus de Blois. Ed. Georges A. Crapelet. 2 vols. Paris: De l'imprimerie de Crapelet, 1834.

Patrologia latina (*Patrologiae cursus completus,* Series Latina). Ed. Jacques-Paul Migne. 221 vols. Paris: J.-P. Migne, 1844–1905.

Pliny. *Natural History.* Ed. and trans. William H. S. Jones, Harris Rackham, and

D. E. Eichholz. 10 vols. Loeb Classical Library 330, 352–53, 370–71, 392–94, 418–19. Cambridge, MA: Harvard University Press, 1938–63.

Al-Qazwīnī, Zakarīyā ibn Muḥammad. *'Ajā'ib al-makhlūqāt wa-gharā'ib al-mawjūdāt.* Ed. Fārūq Sa'd. Beirut: Dār al-Āfāq al-Jadīdah, 1973.

La Queste del Saint Graal: Roman du XIIIe siècle. Ed. Albert Pauphilet. Paris: Librairie Honoré Champion, 1965.

The Quest of the Holy Grail, from the Old French Lancelot-Grail Cycle. Trans. and ed. Judith Shoaf. Peterborough, ON: Broadview Press, 2018.

Rhetorica ad Herennium. Ed. and trans. Harry Caplan. Loeb Classical Library 403. Cambridge, MA: Harvard University Press, 1954.

Robert de Boron. *Merlin and the Grail: Joseph of Arimathea, Merlin, Perceval: The Trilogy of Prose Romances Attributed to Robert de Boron*. Trans. Nigel Bryant. Woodbridge: D. S. Brewer, 2001.

———. *Le roman du graal: Manuscrit de Modène*. Ed. Bernard Cerquiglini. Paris: Union générale d'édition, 1981.

Rolle, Richard. *The* Incendium amoris *of Richard Rolle of Hampole*. Ed. Margaret Deanesly. London: Longmans, Green & Co., 1915.

Le roman de Partonopeu de Blois. Ed. and trans. Olivier Collet and Pierre-Marie Joris. Paris: Librarie générale française, 2005.

Ṣā'id al-Andalusī (Abū al-Qāsim Ṣā'id ibn Aḥmad ibn 'Abd al-Raḥmān al-Taghlibī). *Kitâb Tabaqât al-Umam ou Les catégories des nations*. Ed. F. Louis Cheikho. Beirut: Imprimerie catholique, 1912.

———. *Science in the Medieval World: "Book of the Categories of Nations."* Ed. and trans. Sema'an I. Salem and Alok Kumar. Austin: University of Texas Press, 1991.

Sayf ibn Dhī Yazan. See *Sīrat Fāris al-Yaman al-Malik Sayf ibn Dhī Yazan*.

al-Shiblī, Badr al-Dīn Muḥammad bin 'Abdallāh. *Ākām al-marjān fī aḥkām al-jānn*. Ed. Edward Badeen. Beirut: Klaus Schwarz Verlag, 2017.

Simon de Saint-Quentin. *Histoire des Tartares*. Ed. Jean Richard. Paris: Paul Geuthner, 1965.

Sīrat Fāris al-Yaman al-Malik Sayf ibn Dhī Yazan. 4 vols. Cairo: al-Maktabah wa-al-Maṭba'ah al-'Uthmānīyah, 1930.

Sir Gawain and the Green Knight. Ed. J. R. R. Tolkien, Eric V. Gordon, and Norman Davis. 2nd ed. Oxford: Clarendon Press, 1967.

Sir Orfeo. Ed. Alan J. Bliss. 2nd ed. Oxford: Clarendon Press, 1966.

Solinus. *C. Iulii Solini, Collectanea rerum memorabilium*. Ed. Theodor Mommsen. Berlin: Weidmann, 1958.

Thomas of Cantimpré (Thomas Cantimpratensis). *Liber de natura rerum: Editio princeps secundum codices manuscriptos*. Ed. Helmut Boese. Berlin: Walter De Gruyter, 1973.

The Thousand and One Nights (Alf Layla wa-Layla), From the Earliest Known Sources: Arabic Text Edited with Introduction and Notes. Ed. Muhsin Mahdi. 3 vols. Leiden: Brill, 1994.

Vincent of Beauvais. *Speculum quadruplex, sive Speculum maius*. 4 vols. Graz: Akademische Druck & Verlagsanstalt, 1964–65.

Virgil. *Eclogues, Georgics, and Aeneid 1–6*. Trans. H. Rushton Fairclough and G. P. Goold. Loeb Classical Library 63. Cambridge, MA: Harvard University Press, 1999.

William of Auvergne. *Guilielmi Alverni Opera omnia*. 2 vols. Paris: Andrew Prellard, 1674; reprint, Frankfurt am Main: Minerva, 1963.

William of Boldensele. *Guillaume de Boldensele sur la Terre sainte et l'Égypte (1336), Liber de quibusdam ultramarinis partibus de Guillaume de Boldenselen, 1336. Suivi de la traduction de Jean de long, 1351.* Ed. Christiane Deluz. Paris: CNRS éditions, 2018.

William of Rubruck (Guillelmus de Rubruc). *Itinerarium Guillelmi de Rubruc.* In *Itinera et relationes Fratrum Minorum saeculi XIII et XIV*, 147–332. Ed. Anastasius van den Wyngaert.

———. *The Mission of Friar William of Rubruck: His Journey to the Court of the Great Khan Möngke, 1253–1255.* Trans. Peter Jackson. London: Hakluyt Society, 1990.

Wolfram von Eschenbach. *Parzival.* Ed. Karl Lachmann; trans. Peter Knecht. Berlin: Walter De Gruyter, 2003.

———. *Parzival.* Trans. Arthur T. Hatto. London: Penguin, 2004.

SECONDARY SOURCES

Abu-Deeb, Kamal. *The Imagination Unbound: Al-Adab al-ʿAjāʾibi and the Literature of the Fantastic in the Arabic Tradition: Arabic Text with English Introduction.* London: Saqi, 2007.

Adamson, Peter. *Al-Kindī.* Oxford: Oxford University Press, 2007.

Adamson, Peter, and Peter Pormann, eds. and trans. *The Philosophical Works of al-Kindī.* Oxford: Oxford University Press, 2012.

Adamson, Peter, and Richard C. Taylor, eds. *The Cambridge Companion to Arabic Philosophy.* Cambridge: Cambridge University Press, 2005.

Ahmed, Shahab, *What Is Islam? The Importance of Being Islamic.* Princeton: Princeton University Press, 2016.

Akbari, Suzanne Conklin. *Idols in the East: European Representations of Islam and the Orient, 1100–1450.* Ithaca: Cornell University Press, 2009.

Akbari, Suzanne Conklin, and Amilcare Iannucci, eds. *Marco Polo and the Encounter of East and West.* Toronto: University of Toronto Press, 2008.

Alonso, Manuel. "Influencia de Algazel en el mundo latino." *Al-Andalus* 23, no. 2 (1958): 371–80.

Álvarez, Marco Antonio Santamaría. "La muerte de Orfeo y la cabeza profética." In Bernabé and Casadesús, eds., *Orfeo y la tradición órfica*, 1:105–35.

Ashe, Laura, ed. *Early Fiction in England: From Geoffrey of Monmouth to Chaucer.* London: Penguin, 2015.

———. "1155 and the Beginnings of Fiction." *History Today* 65, no. 1 (15 January 2015): 41–46.

———. *Fiction and History in England, 1066–1200.* Cambridge: Cambridge University Press, 2007.

Bailey, Michael. *Fearful Spirits, Reasoned Follies: The Boundaries of Superstition in Late-Medieval Europe.* Ithaca: Cornell University Press, 2013.

———. "The Feminization of Magic and the Emerging Idea of the Female Witch in the Late Middle Ages." *Essays in Medieval Studies* 19 (2002): 120–34.

Bakker, Paul J. J., ed. *Averroes' Natural Philosophy and Its Reception in the Latin West.* Leuven: Leuven University Press, 2015.

Baldwin, John. *Aristocratic Life in Medieval France: The Romances of Jean Renart and Gerbert de Montreuil, 1190–1230.* Baltimore: Johns Hopkins University Press, 2000.

Bale, Anthony. "Places, Real and Imagined." In Bale and Sebastian Sobecki, eds.,

Medieval English Travel: A Critical Anthology, 17–25. Oxford: Oxford University Press, 2019.

———. "'Ut legi': Sir John Mandeville's Audience and Three Late Medieval English Travelers to Italy and Jerusalem." *Studies in the Age of Chaucer* 38 (2016): 201–37.

Barbezat, Michael. "In a Corporeal Flame: The Materiality of Hellfire before the Resurrection in Six Latin Authors." *Viator* 44, no. 3 (2013): 1–20.

Bartlett, Robert. *The Natural and Supernatural in the Middle Ages: The Wiles Lectures given at the Queen's University of Belfast, 2006*. Cambridge: Cambridge University Press, 2008.

Beckett, Katharine Scarfe. *Anglo-Saxon Perceptions of the Islamic World*. Cambridge: Cambridge University Press, 2003.

Berlekamp, Persis. *Wonder, Image, and Cosmos in Medieval Islam*. New Haven: Yale University Press, 2011.

Bernabé Pajares, Alberto, and Francesc Casadesús, eds. *Orfeo y la tradición órfica: Un reencuentro*. 2 vols. Madrid: Akal, 2008.

Bernstein, Alan. "Esoteric Theology: William of Auvergne on the Fires of Hell and Purgatory." *Speculum* 57, no. 3 (1982): 509–31.

Bevilacqua, Alexander. *The Republic of Arabic Letters: Islam and the European Enlightenment*. Cambridge, MA: Belknap Press of Harvard University Press, 2018.

Bezzola, Reto R. *Les origines et la formation de la littérature courtoise en Occident (500–1200)*. 3 vols. Paris: Librairie Honoré Champion, 1958–67.

Black, Deborah L. "Avicenna on the Ontological and Epistemic Status of Fictional Beings." *Documenti e studi sulla tradizione filosofica medievale* 8 (1997): 425–53.

———. "Estimation (*Wahm*) in Avicenna: The Logical and Psychological Dimensions." *Dialogue* 32, no. 2 (1993): 219–58.

———. "Imagination and Estimation: Arabic Paradigms and Western Transformations." *Topoi* 19 (2000): 59–75.

———. "Rational Imagination: Avicenna on the Cogitative Power." In Luis Xavier López-Farjeat and Jörg Alejandro Tellkamp, eds., *Philosophical Psychology in Arabic Thought and the Latin Aristotelianism of the 13th Century*, 59–81. Paris: J. Vrin, 2013.

Blatherwick, Helen. *Prophets, Gods and Kings in Sīrat Sayf ibn Dhī Yazan: An Intertextual Reading of an Egyptian Popular Epic*. Leiden: Brill, 2016.

Bloom, Jonathan. *Paper before Print: The History and Impact of Paper in the Islamic World*. New Haven: Yale University Press, 2001.

Blumenthal, Henry J. "Neoplatonic Interpretations of Aristotle on 'Phantasia.'" *Review of Metaphysics* 31, no. 2 (1977): 242–57.

Boglioni, Pierre. "Saints, miracles et hagiographie chez Guillaume d'Auvergne." In Franco Morenzoni and Jean-Yves Tilliette, eds., *Autour de Guillaume d'Auvergne (+1249)*, 323–39. Turnhout: Brepols, 2005.

Bonino, Serge-Thomas. "Le rôle de l'image dans la connaissance prophétique d'après saint Thomas d'Aquin." *Revue Thomiste* 89 (1989): 533–68.

Bramon, Dolors. *El mundo en el siglo XII: Estudio de la versión castellana y del "original" Árabe de una geografía universal: "El tratado de al-Zuhrī."* Barcelona: Editorial AUSA, 1991.

Brentjes, Sonja. *Teaching and Learning the Sciences in Islamicate Societies (800–1700)*. Turnhout: Brepols, 2018.

Brooks, David. "The Great Escape." *New York Times*, 22 April 2008.

Bruckner, Matilda Tomaryn. "Natural and Unnatural Woman: Melusine Inside and Out." In Laine E. Doggett and Daniel E. O'Sullivan, eds., *Founding Feminisms in Medieval Studies: Essays in Honor of E. Jane Burns*, 21–32. Cambridge: D. S. Brewer, 2016.

———. *Shaping Romance: Interpretation, Truth, and Closure in Twelfth-Century French Fictions*. Philadelphia: University of Pennsylvania Press, 1993.

Bundy, Murray Wright. *The Theory of Imagination in Classical and Mediaeval Thought*. Urbana: University of Illinois, 1927.

Burnett, Charles. "Adelard, Ergaphalau, and the Science of the Stars." In Burnett, ed., *Adelard of Bath: An English Scientist and Arabist of the Early Twelfth Century*, 133–45. London: Warburg Institute, 1987.

———, "Antioch as Link between Arabic and Latin Culture in the Twelfth and Thirteenth Centuries." In Isabelle Draelants, Anne Tihon, and Baudouin van den Abeele, eds., *Occident et Proche-Orient: Contacts scientifiques au temps des Croisades*, 1–78. Turnhout: Brepols, 2000.

———. "Arabic into Latin: The Reception of Arabic Philosophy into Western Europe." In Adamson and Taylor, eds., *The Cambridge Companion to Arabic Philosophy*, 370–404.

———. *Magic and Divination in the Middle Ages: Texts and Techniques in the Islamic and Christian Worlds*. Aldershot, UK: Variorum, 1996.

———. "Master Theodore, Frederick II's Philosopher." in Burnett, *Arabic into Latin in the Middle Ages: The Translators and Their Intellectual and Social Context*, 225–85. Farnham, UK: Variorum, 2009.

———. "The Translating Activity in Medieval Spain." In Salma Khadra Jayyusi, ed., *The Legacy of Muslim Spain*, 1036–58. Leiden: Brill, 1992.

Burns, E. Jane. "A Snake-Tailed Woman: Hybridity and Dynasty in the *Roman de Mélusine*." In Burns and Peggy McCracken, eds., *From Beast to Souls: Gender and Embodiment in Medieval Europe*, 185–220. Notre Dame, IN: University of Notre Dame Press, 2013.

Bynum, Caroline Walker. *Dissimilar Similitudes: Devotional Objects in Late Medieval Europe*. New York: Zone Books, 2020.

———. *Metamorphosis and Identity*. New York: Zone Books, 2001.

———. "Metamorphosis, or Gerald and the Werewolf." *Speculum* 73, no. 4 (1998): 987–1013.

———. "Miracles and Marvels: The Limits of Alterity." In Franz J. Felten and Nikolas Jaspert, eds., *Vita religiosa im Mittelalter: Festschrift für Kaspar Elm zum 70*, 799–817. Berlin: Duncker & Humblot, 1999.

———. "Wonder." *American Historical Review* 102, no. 1 (1997): 1–26.

Byrne, Aisling. *Otherworlds: Fantasy and History in Medieval Literature*. Oxford: Oxford University Press, 2016.

Calasso, Giovanna. "Constructing and Deconstructing the *dār al-islām/dār al-ḥarb* Opposition." In Calasso and Lancioni, eds., *Dār al-Islām/dār al-ḥarb*, 21–47.

Calasso, Giovanna, and Giuliano Lancioni, eds. *Dār al-Islām/ dār al-ḥarb: Territories, People, Identities*. Leiden: Brill, 2017.

Camille, Michael. *The Gothic Idol: Ideology and Image-Making in Medieval Art*. Cambridge: Cambridge University Press, 1989.

Campany, Robert Ford. *Strange Writing: Anomaly Accounts in Early Medieval China*. Albany, NY: SUNY Press, 1996.

Campbell, Mary. "'The Object of One's Gaze': Landscape, Writing, and Early Medieval Pilgrimage." In Scott D. Westrem, ed., *Discovering New Worlds: Essays on Medieval Exploration and Imagination*, 3–15. New York: Garland Publishing, 1991.

———. *The Witness and the Other World: Exotic European Travel Writing, 400–1600*. Ithaca: Cornell University Press, 1988.

Caroti, Stefan. "Éléments pour une reconstruction de la philosophie de la nature dans les *Quodlibeta* de Nicole Oresme." In Jeannine Quillet, ed., *Autour de Nicole Oresme: Actes du Colloque Oresme organisé à l'Université de Paris XII*, 85–118. Paris: Vrin, 1990.

Carruthers, Mary. *The Book of Memory: A Study of Memory in Medieval Culture*. Cambridge: Cambridge University Press, 1990.

Cartlidge, Neil. "Sir Orfeo in the Otherworld: Courting Chaos?" *Studies in the Age of Chaucer* 26 (2004): 195–226.

Cascardi, Anthony J. "Cervantes and Descartes on the Dream Argument." *Cervantes: Bulletin of the Cervantes Society of America* 4, no. 2 (1984): 109–22.

———. "*Don Quixote* and the Invention of the Novel." in Cascardi, ed., *The Cambridge Companion to Cervantes*, 58–79. Cambridge: Cambridge University Press, 2002.

Chism, Christine. "Facing the Land of Darkness: Alexander, Islam, and the Quest for the Secrets of God." In Markus Stock, ed., *Alexander the Great in the Middle Ages: Transcultural Perspectives*, 51–75. Toronto: University of Toronto Press, 2016.

———. "Memory, Wonder, and Desire in the *Travels* of Ibn Battuta and Ibn Jubayr." In Nicholas Paul and Suzanne Yeager, eds., *Remembering the Crusades: Myth, Image, and Identity*, 29–49. Baltimore: Johns Hopkins University Press, 2012.

Clagett, Marshall. *The Science of Mechanics in the Middle Ages*. Madison: University of Wisconsin Press, 1959.

Cohen, Jeffrey Jerome, ed. *The Postcolonial Middle Ages*. New York: St. Martin's Press, 2000.

———. *Stone: An Ecology of the Inhuman*. Minneapolis: University of Minnesota Press, 2015.

Compagni, Vittoria Perrone. "Artificiose operari: L'immaginazione di Avicenna nel dibattito medievale sulla magia." In Maria Bettetini and Francesco D. Paparella, with Roberto Furlan, eds., *Immaginario e immaginazione nel medioevo: Atti del convegno della Società Italiana per lo Studio del Pensiero Medievale (SISPM), Milano, 25–27 Settembre 2008*, 271–96. Turnhout: Brepols, 2009.

Constable, Olivia Remie. *To Live Like a Moor: Christian Perceptions of Muslim Identity in Medieval and Early Modern Spain*. Philadelphia: University of Pennsylvania Press, 2018.

Cook, Robert. "Chaucer's Franklin's Tale and *Sir Orfeo*." *Neuphilologische Mitteilungen* 95, no. 3 (1994): 333–36.

Cooper, Helen. *The English Romance in Time: Transforming Motifs from Geoffrey of Monmouth to the Death of Shakespeare*. Oxford: Oxford University Press, 2004.

Copeland, Rita. *Rhetoric, Hermeneutics, and Translation in the Middle Ages: Academic Traditions and Vernacular Texts*. Cambridge: Cambridge University Press, 1991.

Corbin, Henry. "Mundus imaginalis ou l'imaginaire et l'imaginal." *Cahiers internationaux du symbolisme* 6 (1964): 3–26.

Courtenay, William. *Capacity and Volition: A History of the Distinction of Absolute and Ordained Power*. Bergamo: P. Lubrina, 1990.

Crane, Susan. "Chivalry and the Pre/Postmodern." *postmedieval* 2, no. 1 (2011): 69–87.
Crick, Julia. "Geoffrey of Monmouth, Prophecy and History." *Journal of Medieval History* 18, no. 4 (1992): 357–71.
Dalché, Patrick Gautier. "Géographie arabe et géographie latine au XIIe siècle." *Medieval Encounters* 19, no. 4 (2013): 408–33.
d'Alverny, Marie-Thérèse. "Algazel dans l'Occident Latin." In d'Alverny, *La transmission des textes philosophiques et scientifiques au Moyen Age*, 3–24. Ed. Charles Burnett. Aldershot, UK: Variorum, 1994.
———. "L'Introduction d'Avicenne en Occident." In *Avicenne en Occident: Recueil d'articles de Marie-Thérèse d'Alverny réunis en hommage à l'auteur*, 12–16. Paris: Vrin, 1993.
Daston, Lorraine, and Katharine Park. *Wonders and the Order of Nature, 1150–1750*. New York: Zone Books, 1998.
Davidson, Herbert A. *Alfarabi, Avicenna, and Averroes on Intellect: Their Cosmologies, Theories of the Active Intellect, and Theories of the Human Intellect*. New York: Oxford University Press, 1992.
Delaurenti, Béatrice. "La fascination et l'action à distance: Questions médiévales." *Médiévales* 50 (2006): 137–54.
———. "Les franciscains et le pouvoir du regard (1277–1295): Une question quodlibétique attribuée à Raymond Rigauld." *Études franciscaines* n.s. 9 (2016): 147–86.
———. "Pratiques médiévales de réécriture: Le cas de la doctrine avicennienne du pouvoir de l'âme en dehors du corps." *Aevum* 90 (2016): 351–76.
Deluz, Christiane. *Le livre de Jehan de Mandeville: Une 'Géographie' au XIVe siècle*. Louvain-la-Neuve: Institut d'études médiévales de l'Université Catholique de Louvain, 1988.
Denoix, Sylvie. "Des culs-de-sacs heuristiques aux garde-fous épistémologiques ou comment aborder l'aire culturelle du 'monde musulman.'" *Revue des mondes musulmans et de la Méditerranée* 103–4 (2004): 7–26.
DeVun, Leah. *Prophecy, Alchemy, and the End of Time: John of Rupescissa in the Late Middle Ages*. New York: Columbia University Press, 2009.
Dewender, Thomas. "Imaginary Experiments (*procedere secundum imaginationem*) in Later Medieval Natural Philosophy." In Pacheco and Meirinhos, ed., *Intellect et imagination dans la philosophie médiévale* 3:1823–33.
Dolnikowski, Edith Wilks. *Thomas Bradwardine: A View of Time and a Vision of Eternity in Fourteenth-Century Thought*. Leiden: Brill, 1995.
Dronke, Peter. *Fabula: Explorations into the Uses of Myth in Medieval Platonism*. Leiden: Brill, 1974.
———. *Medieval Latin and the Rise of European Love-Lyric*. 2 vols. Oxford: Clarendon Press, 1965–66.
Dubost, Francis. "Merveilleux et fantastique au moyen âge: Positions et propositions." *Revue des langues romanes* 100, no. 2 (1996): 1–35.
Duhem, Pierre. *Le système du monde: Histoire des doctrines cosmologiques de Platon à Copernic*. 10 vols. Paris: A. Hermann, 1913–59.
Eamon, William. *Science and the Secrets of Nature: Books of Secrets in Medieval and Early Modern Culture*. Princeton: Princeton University Press, 1994.
Eco, Umberto. *From the Tree to the Labyrinth: Historical Studies on the Sign and Interpretation*. Trans. Anthony Oldcorn. Cambridge, MA: Harvard University Press, 2014.

Elders, Leo. "Les rapports entre la doctrine de la prophétie de Saint Thomas et le *Guide des égarés* de Maïmonide." *Divus Thomas* 78, no. 4 (1975): 449–56.

Elliott, Dyan. *Fallen Bodies: Pollution, Sexuality, and Demonology in the Middle Ages.* Philadelphia: University of Pennsylvania Press, 1999.

El-Zein, Amira. *Islam, Arabs, and the Intelligent World of the Jinn.* Syracuse: Syracuse University Press, 2009.

Encyclopaedia of Islam (online resource). Ed. Martijn T. Houtsma, Peri J. Bearman, Kate Fleet, et al. Leiden: Brill, 1913–present.

Even-Ezra, Ayelet. *Ecstasy in the Classroom: Trance, Self, and the Academic Profession in Medieval Paris.* New York: Fordham University Press, 2019.

Fahd, Toufic. *La divination arabe: Études religieuses, sociologiques et folkloriques sur le milieu natif de l'Islam.* Leiden: Brill, 1966.

———. "Génies, anges et démons en Islam." *Sources orientales* 8 (1971): 155–214.

Fanger, Claire. "Things Done Wisely by a Wise Enchanter: Negotiating the Power of Words in the Thirteenth Century." *Esoterica* 1 (1999): 97–132.

Fattori, Marta, and Massimo Bianchi, eds. *Phantasia—imaginatio: V° colloquio internazionale, Roma 9–11 gennaio 1986.* Rome: Edizioni dell'Ateneo, 1988.

Fletcher, Alan J. "*Sir Orfeo* and the Flight from the Enchanters." *Studies in the Age of Chaucer* 22 (2000): 141–77.

Fradenburg, L. O. Aranye. "Simply Marvelous." *Studies in the Age of Chaucer* 26 (2004): 1–27.

———. "The Wife of Bath's Passing Fancy." *Studies in the Age of Chaucer* 8 (1996): 31–58.

Fraser, Kyle. "Roman Antiquity: The Imperial Period." In David J. Collins, ed., *The Cambridge History of Magic and Witchcraft in the West: From Antiquity to the Present,* 115–47. Cambridge: Cambridge University Press, 2015.

Freedgood, Elaine, *Worlds Enough: The Invention of Realism in the Victorian Novel.* Princeton: Princeton University Press, 2019.

Freedman, Paul, and Gabrielle Spiegel. "Medievalisms Old and New: The Rediscovery of Alterity in North American Medieval Studies." *American Historical Review* 103, no. 3 (1998): 677–704.

French, Roger K., and Andrew Cunningham. *Before Science: The Invention of the Friar's Natural Philosophy.* Brookfield, VT: Scolar Press, 1996.

Friedman, John Block. *The Monstrous Races in Medieval Art and Thought.* Cambridge, MA: Harvard University Press, 1981.

———. *Orpheus in the Middle Ages.* Cambridge, MA: Harvard University Press, 1970.

Friedman, John Block, and Kristen Mossler Figg, eds. *Trade, Travel, and Exploration in the Middle Ages: An Encyclopedia.* New York: Garland, 2000.

Friedman, John Block, Kathryn Giogoli, and Kristen Figg. *Book of Wonders of the World: Secrets of Natural History, ms. fr. 22971: Original held in the Bibliothèque Nationale de France, París.* Burgos, Spain: Siloé, 2018.

Frisch, Andrea. *The Invention of the Eyewitness: Witnessing and Testimony in Early Modern France.* Chapel Hill: University of North Carolina Press, 2004.

Frye, Northrop. *The Secular Scripture: A Study of the Structure of Romance.* Cambridge, MA: Harvard University Press, 1976.

Fuchs, Barbara. *Knowing Fictions: Picaresque Reading in the Early Modern Hispanic World.* Philadelphia: University of Pennsylvania Press, 2021.

Gallagher, Catherine. "The Rise of Fictionality." In Franco Moretti, ed., *The Novel*, 1:336–63. 2 vols. Princeton: Princeton University Press, 2006.
Ganim, John. "The Myth of Medieval Romance." In R. Howard Bloch and Stephen G. Nichols, eds., *Medievalism and the Modernist Temper*, 148–66. Baltimore: Johns Hopkins University Press, 1996.
Ganim, John M., and Shayne Legassie, eds. *Cosmopolitanism and the Middle Ages*. New York: Palgrave Macmillan, 2013.
Gaunt, Simon. "Can the Middle Ages Be Postcolonial?" *Comparative Literature* 61, no. 2 (2009): 160–76.
———. *Love and Death in Medieval French and Occitan Courtly Literature*. Oxford: Oxford University Press, 2006.
Giffen, Lois Anita. *Theory of Profane Love among the Arabs: The Development of the Genre*. New York: New York University Press, 1971.
Goldie, Matthew Boyd. *Scribes of Space: Place in Middle English Literature and Late Medieval Science*. Ithaca: Cornell University Press, 2019.
Grant, Edward. *The Foundations of Modern Science in the Middle Ages: Their Religious, Institutional, and Intellectual Contexts*. Cambridge: Cambridge University Press, 1996.
———. *The Nature of Natural Philosophy in the Late Middle Ages*. Washington, DC: Catholic University of America Press, 2010.
———. "Scientific Thought in Fourteenth-Century Paris: Jean Buridan and Nicole Oresme." In Madeleine Pelner Cosman and Bruce Chandler, eds., *Machaut's World: Science and Art in the Fourteenth Century*, 105–24. New York: New York Academy of Sciences, 1978.
Green, Richard Firth. *Elf Queens and Holy Friars: Fairy Beliefs and the Medieval Church*. Philadelphia: University of Pennsylvania Press, 2016.
Greene, Virginie. *Logical Fictions in Medieval Literature and Philosophy*. Cambridge: Cambridge University Press, 2014.
Grieve, Patricia E. *Floire and Blancheflor and the European Romance*. Cambridge: Cambridge University Press, 1997.
Griffel, Frank. "Al-Ghazali." In Edward N. Zalta, ed., *The Stanford Encyclopedia of Philosophy (Fall 2008 Edition)* (online resource). http://plato.stanford.edu/archives/fall2008/entries/al-ghazali/.
———. *Al-Ghazālī's Philosophical Theology*. New York: Oxford University Press, 2009.
Gutas, Dimitri. *Avicenna and the Aristotelian Tradition: Introduction to Reading Avicenna's Philosophical Works*. 2nd ed. Brill: Leiden, 2014.
———. *Greek Thought, Arabic Culture: The Graeco-Arabic Translation Movement in Baghdad and Early 'Abbāsid Society (2nd–4th/8th–10th Centuries)*. New York: Routledge, 1998.
———. "Imagination and Transcendental Knowledge in Avicenna." In James Montgomery, ed., *Arabic Theology, Arabic Philosophy: From the Many to the One. Essays in Celebration of Richard M. Frank*, 337–54. Leuven: Peeters, 2006.
———. "Intellect without Limits: The Absence of Mysticism in Avicenna." In Pacheco and Meirinhos, eds., *Intellect et imagination dans la philosophie médiévale*, 1:351–72.
Hamesse, Jacqueline. "*Imaginatio* et *phantasia* chez les philosophes du XIIe et du XIIIe siècle." In Fattori and Bianchi, eds., *Phantasia—imaginatio*, 153–81.
Hanna, Ralph. "Mandeville." In A. S. G. Edwards, ed., *Middle English Prose: A Critical*

Guide to Major Authors and Genres, 121–31. New Brunswick, NJ: Rutgers University Press, 1984.

Haq, Syed Nomanul. *Names, Natures and Things: The Alchemist Jābir ibn Ḥayyān and His Kitāb al-Aḥjār (Book of Stones)*. Boston: Kluwer, 1994.

Harb, Lara, *Arabic Poetics: Aesthetic Experience in Classical Arabic Literature*. Cambridge: Cambridge University Press, 2020.

Harf-Lancner, Laurence. *Les fées au Moyen Âge: Morgane et Mélusine, La naissance des fées*. Paris: Librairie Honoré Champion, 1984.

———. "Littérature et politique: Jean de Berry, Léon de Lusignan et le *Roman de Mélusine*." In Danielle Buschinger, ed., *Histoire et littérature au Moyen Age: Actes du colloque du Centre d'études médiévales de l'Université de Picardie, Amiens, 20–24 mars 1985*, 161–71. Göppingen: Kümmerle Verlag, 1991.

Haskell, Yasmin Annabel, ed. *Diseases of the Imagination and Imaginary Disease in the Early Modern Period*. Turnhout: Brepols, 2011.

Hasse, Dag Nikolaus. *Avicenna's* De anima *in the Latin West: The Formation of a Peripatetic Philosophy of the Soul, 1160–1300*. London: Warburg Institute, 2000.

———. "Influence of Arabic and Islamic Philosophy on the Latin West." In Edward N. Zalta, ed., *Stanford Encyclopedia of Philosophy (Fall 2008 Edition)*. http://plato.stanford.edu/archives/fall2008/entries/arabic-islamic-influence/.

———. "King Avicenna: The Iconographic Consequences of a Mistranslation." *Journal of the Warburg and Courtauld Institutes* 60 (1997): 230–43.

———. "The Soul's Faculties." in Pasnau, ed., *The Cambridge History of Medieval Philosophy*, 1:305–19.

Hasse, Dag Nikolaus, and Amos Bertolacci, eds. *The Arabic, Hebrew, and Latin Reception of Avicenna's Metaphysics*. Berlin: Walter de Gruyter & Co., 2011.

Heath, Peter. "Romance as Genre in *The Thousand and One Nights*." *Journal of Arabic Literature* 18 (1987): 1–21 and 19 (1988): 1–26.

———. *The Thirsty Sword: Sīrat ʿAntar and the Arabic Popular Epic*. Salt Lake City: University of Utah Press, 1996.

Heng, Geraldine. *The Invention of Race in the European Middle Ages*. Cambridge: Cambridge University Press, 2018.

Hernández, Raquel Martín. "Literatura mágica y pseudocientífica atribuida a Orfeo." In Bernabé and Casadesús, eds., *Orfeo y la tradición órfica*, 1:365–77.

Higgins, Iain Macleod. *Writing East: The "Travels" of Sir John Mandeville*. Philadelphia: University of Pennsylvania Press, 1997.

Hunt, Tony. "Aristotle, Dialectic, and Courtly Literature." *Viator* 10 (1979): 95–130.

Ingham, Patricia Clare. *The Medieval New: Ambivalence in an Age of Innovation*. Philadelphia: University of Pennsylvania Press, 2015.

Jacobs, Martin. *Reorienting the East: Jewish Travelers to the Medieval Muslim World*. Philadelphia: University of Pennsylvania Press, 2014.

Jagot, Shazia. "Fin' Amors, Arabic Learning, and the Islamic World in the Work of Geoffrey Chaucer." PhD diss., University of Leicester, 2014.

Janssens, Jules. "Al-Ghazālī and His Use of Avicennian Texts." In Miklós Maróth, ed., *Problems in Arabic Philosophy*, 37–49. Piliscsaba, Hungary: Avicenna Institute of Middle Eastern Studies, 2003.

Jirsa, Curtis R. H. "In the Shadow of the Ympe-tre: Arboreal Folklore in *Sir Orfeo*." *English Studies* 89, no. 2 (2008): 141–51.

Jolivet, Jean. *L'intellect selon Kindī*. Leiden: Brill, 1971.

Justice, Steven. "Did the Middle Ages Believe in Their Miracles?" *Representations* 103, no. 1 (2008): 1–29.
Karnes, Michelle. *Imagination, Meditation and Cognition in the Middle Ages*. Chicago: University of Chicago Press, 2011.
———. "Marvels in the Medieval Imagination." *Speculum* 90, no. 2 (2015): 327–65.
———. "Medieval Latin Rhetoric and the Internal Senses." In Jill Ross and Frédérique Woerther, eds., *The Cambridge History of Rhetoric*, vol. 2. Cambridge: Cambridge University Press, forthcoming.
———. "The Possibilities of Medieval Fiction." *New Literary History* 51, no. 1 (2020): 209–28.
———. "Wonder, Marvels, and Metaphor in the *Squire's Tale*." *English Literary History* 82, no. 2 (2015): 461–90.
Kay, Sarah. *The Place of Thought: The Complexity of One in Late Medieval French Didactic Poetry*. Philadelphia: University of Pennsylvania Press, 2007.
Kaye, Joel. *Economy and Nature in the Fourteenth Century: Money, Market Exchange, and the Emergence of Scientific Thought*. Cambridge: Cambridge University Press, 1998.
———. "Law, Magic, and Science: Constructing a Border between Licit and Illicit Knowledge in the Writings of Nicole Oresme." In Ruth Mazo Karras, Joel Kaye, and E. Ann Matter, eds., *Law and the Illicit in Medieval Europe*, 225–37 and 298–303. Philadelphia: University of Pennsylvania Press, 2008.
Kelly, Douglas. "The Domestication of the Marvelous in the Melusine Romances." In Donald Maddox and Sara Sturm-Maddox, eds., *Melusine of Lusignan: Founding Fiction in Late Medieval France*, 32–47. Athens: University of Georgia Press, 1996.
———. "*Matiere* and *genera dicendi* in Medieval Romance." *Yale French Studies* 51 (1974): 147–59.
Kemal, Salim. *The Philosophical Poetics of Alfarabi, Avicenna and Averroës: The Aristotelian Reception*. New York: Routledge, 2003.
Kennedy, Kathleen. "Moors and Moorishness in Late Medieval England." *Studies in the Age of Chaucer* 42 (2020): 213–51.
Kennedy, Philip F., ed. *On Fiction and* Adab *in Medieval Arabic Literature*. Wiesbaden: Harrassowitz, 2005.
Key, Alexander. *Language between God and the Poets: Maʿnā in the Eleventh Century*. Berkeley: University of California Press, 2018.
Khanmohamadi, Shirin. *In Light of Another's Word: European Ethnography in the Middle Ages*. Philadelphia: University of Pennsylvania Press, 2014.
Kieckhefer, Richard. *European Witch Trials: Their Foundations in Popular and Learned Culture, 1300–1500*. Berkeley: University of California Press, 1976.
———. *Forbidden Rites: A Necromancer's Manual of the Fifteenth Century*. University Park: Pennsylvania State University Press, 1998.
———. *Magic in the Middle Ages*. New York: Cambridge University Press, 1989.
———. "The Specific Rationality of Medieval Magic." *American Historical Review* 99, no. 3 (1994): 813–36.
Kiessling, Nicolas K. *The Incubus in English Literature: Provenance and Progeny*. Pullman: Washington State University Press, 1977.
King, Charles W. *The Natural History, Ancient and Modern, of Precious Stones and Gems and of the Precious Metals*. London: Bell & Daldy, 1865.
King, Peter. "Rethinking Representation in the Middle Ages: A Vade-Mecum to Medi-

eval Theories of Mental Representation." In Henrik Lagerlund, ed., *Representation and Objects of Thought in Medieval Philosophy*, 81–100. Aldershot, UK: Ashgate Publishing Group, 2007.

Kinoshita, Sharon. "Reorientations: The Worlding of Marco Polo." In John Ganim and Shayne Legassie, eds., *Cosmopolitanism and the Middle Ages*, 39–57.

Kinoshita, Sharon, and Peggy McCracken, *Marie de France: A Critical Companion*. Cambridge: D. S. Brewer, 2012.

Klosowska, Anna. "Queer/Posthuman in Marie de France's *Eliduc*: Sanctuaires à répit, Female Couples, and Human/Animal/Bare Life." *FKW/Zeitschrift für Geschlechterforschung und Visuelle Kultur* 54 (2013): 76–87.

Knapp, James F., and Peggy A. Knapp. *Medieval Romance: The Aesthetics of Possibility*. Toronto: University of Toronto Press, 2017.

Knight, Stephen. *Merlin: Knowledge and Power through the Ages*. Ithaca: Cornell University Press, 2009.

König, Daniel G. *Arabic-Islamic Views of the Latin West: Tracing the Emergence of Modern Europe*. Oxford: Oxford University Press, 2015.

Kruger, Steven F. *Dreaming in the Middle Ages*. Cambridge: Cambridge University Press, 1992.

Kukkonen, Taneli. "Faculties in Arabic Philosophy." In Dominik Perler, ed., *The Faculties: A History*, 66–96. Oxford: Oxford University Press, 2015.

———. "Ibn Sīnā and the Early History of Thought Experiments." *Journal of the History of Philosophy* 52, no. 3 (2014): 433–59.

———. "Plenitude, Possibility, and the Limits of Reason: A Medieval Arabic Debate on the Metaphysics of Nature." *Journal of the History of Ideas* 61, no. 4 (2000): 539–60.

Lampert-Weissig, Lisa, ed. *Medieval Literature and Postcolonial Studies*. Edinburgh: Edinburgh University Press, 2010.

Landy, Joshua, and Michael T. Saler, eds. *The Re-enchantment of the World: Secular Magic in a Rational Age*. Stanford: Stanford University Press, 2009.

Lassner, Jacob. *Demonizing the Queen of Sheba: Boundaries of Gender and Culture in Postbiblical Judaism and Medieval Islam*. Chicago: University of Chicago Press, 1993.

Lavezzo, Kathy. *Angels on the Edge of the World: Geography, Literature, and English Community, 1000–1534*. Ithaca: Cornell University Press, 2006.

Lecouteux, Claude. *Chasses fantastiques et cohortes de la nuit au Moyen Âge*. Paris: Imago, 1999.

———. "Introduction à l'étude du merveilleux médiéval." *Études germaniques* 36, no. 3 (1981): 273–90.

Leemhuis, Fred. "Can you Marry a Djinni? An Aspect of the *djinn* as Persons." In Hans G. Kippenberger, Y. B. Kuiper, and Andy F. Sanders, eds., *Concepts of Person in Religion and Thought*, 217–28. Berlin: Walter de Gruyter & Co., 1990.

Leff, Gordon. *Bradwardine and the Pelagians: A Study of His 'De causa Dei' and Its Opponents*. Cambridge: Cambridge University Press, 1957.

Legassie, Shayne. *The Medieval Invention of Travel*. Chicago: University of Chicago Press, 2017.

Le Goff, Jacques. *L'imaginaire médiéval: Essais*. Paris: Gallimard, 1985.

———. *The Medieval Imagination*. Trans. Arthur Goldhammer. Chicago: University of Chicago Press, 1988.

———. "L'Occident médiéval et l'océan indien: un horizon onirique." In *Pour un autre*

Moyen Âge: Temps, travail et culture en Occident, 18 essais, 280–98. Paris: Gallimard, 1977.

Lemay, Richard J. *Abu Ma'shar and Latin Aristotelianism in the Twelfth Century: The Recovery of Aristotle's Natural Philosophy through Arabic Astrology.* Beirut: American University of Beirut, 1962.

Lerer, Seth. "Artifice and Artistry in *Sir Orfeo*." *Speculum* 60, no. 1 (1985): 92–109.

Lester, Anne. "The Coffret of John of Montmirail: The Sacred Politics of Reuse in Thirteenth-Century Northern France." *Peregrinations* 4, no. 4 (2014): 50–86.

Lindberg, David. *The Beginnings of Western Science: The European Scientific Tradition in Philosophical, Religious, and Institutional Context, Prehistory to A.D. 1450.* 2nd ed. Chicago: University of Chicago Press, 2007.

———. *Roger Bacon's Philosophy of Nature: A Critical Edition, with English Translation, Introduction, and Notes, of* De multiplicatione specierum *and* De speculis comburentibus. Oxford: Clarendon Press, 1983.

———. *Theories of Vision from al-Kindi to Kepler.* Chicago: University of Chicago Press, 1976.

Lobsien, Verena Olejniczak. "Faculties and Imagination." in Dominik Perler, ed., *The Faculties: A History*, 140–49. Oxford: Oxford University Press, 2015.

Lochrie, Karma. "Provincializing Medieval Europe: Mandeville's Cosmopolitan Utopia." *PMLA* 124, no. 2 (2009): 592–99.

López-Baralt, Luce. "El sabio encantador Cide Hamete Benengeli: ¿fue un musulmán del Al- Andalus o un morisco del siglo XVII?" In Ruth Fine and Santiago López Navia, eds., *Cervantes y las religiones*, 339–60. Frankfurt am Main: Vervuert Verlagsgesellschaft, 2008.

Lorca, Daniel. *Neo-Stoicism and Skepticism in Part One of* Don Quijote*: Removing the Authority of a Genre.* Lanham, MD: Lexington Books, 2016.

Louth, Andrew. *Greek East and Latin West: The Church AD 681–1071.* Crestwood, NY: St. Vladimir's Seminary Press, 2007.

Lynch, Kathryn. "East Meets West in Chaucer's Squire's and Franklin's Tales." *Speculum* 70, no. 3 (1995): 530–51.

Lyons, Malcolm C. *The Arabic Epic: Heroic and Oral Story-Telling.* 3 vols. Cambridge: Cambridge University Press, 1995.

———. *The Man of Wiles in Popular Arabic Literature: A Study of a Medieval Arab Hero.* Edinburgh: Edinburgh University Press, 2012.

Maier, Anneliese. *On the Threshold of Exact Science: Selected Writings of Anneliese Maier on Late Medieval Natural Philosophy.* Trans. Steven D. Sargent. Philadelphia: University of Pennsylvania Press, 1982.

Mallette, Karla. *European Modernity and the Arab Mediterranean: Toward a New Philology and a Counter-Orientalism.* Philadelphia: University of Pennsylvania Press, 2010.

Marrone, Steven. "William of Auvergne on Magic in Natural Philosophy and Theology." In Jan A. Aertsen and Andreas Speer, eds., *Was ist Philosophie im Mittelalter? Qu'est-ce que la philosophie au Moyen Âge? What Is Philosophy in the Middle Ages?* 741–48. Berlin: W. de Gruyter, 1998.

Martínez Martín, Leonor. "Teorías sobre las mareas según un manuscrito arabe del siglo XII." *Memorias de la Real Academia de Buenas Letras de Barcelona* 13 (1971): 135–212.

McCracken, Peggy. *The Curse of Eve, the Wound of the Hero: Blood, Gender, and Medieval Literature.* Philadelphia: University of Pennsylvania Press, 2003.

McGinn, Bernard. "'*Teste David cum Sibylla*': The Significance of the Sibylline Tradition in the Middle Ages." In Julius Kirshner and Suzanne F. Wemple, eds., *Women of the Medieval World: Essays in Honor of John H. Mundy*, 7–35. New York: Basil Blackwell, 1985.

Mehtonen, Päivi. "Poetics, Narration, and Imitation: Rhetoric as Ars aplicabilis." In Virginia Cox and John Ward, eds., *The Rhetoric of Cicero in Its Medieval and Early Renaissance Commentary Tradition*, 289–312. Leiden: Brill, 2006.

Menocal, María Rosa. *The Arabic Role in Medieval Literary History: A Forgotten Heritage*. Philadelphia: University of Pennsylvania Press, 1987.

———. *Shards of Love: Exile and the Origins of the Lyric*. Durham, NC: Duke University Press, 1994.

Menocal, María Rosa, Raymond P. Scheindlin, and Michael A. Sells, eds. *The Literature of Al-Andalus*. Cambridge: Cambridge University Press, 2000.

Metlitzki, Dorothee. *The Matter of Araby in Medieval England*. New Haven: Yale University Press, 1977.

Michaud-Quantin, Pierre. *Études sur le vocabulaire philosophique du Moyen Age*. Rome: Edizioni dell'Ateneo, 1970.

Michot, Jean R. *La destinée de l'homme selon Avicenne: Le retour à Dieu (maʿād) et l'imagination*. Leuven: Aedibus Peeters, 1986.

Mikkelson, Jane. "Flights of Imagination: Avicenna's Phoenix (ʿAnqā) and Bedil's Figuration for the Lyric Self." *Journal of South Asian Intellectual History* 2 (2019): 28–72.

Millett, Bella. "Chaucer, Lollius, and the Medieval Theory of Authorship." *Studies in the Age of Chaucer, Proceedings* 1 (1984): 93–103.

Minio-Paluello, Lorenzo. "Michael Scot." In Charles C. Gillespie, ed., *The Dictionary of Scientific Biography*, 11:361–65. 18 vols. New York: Charles Scribner's Sons, 1970–90.

Minnema, Anthony. "A Hadith Condemned at Paris: Reactions to the Power of Impression in the Latin Translation of al-Ghazālī's *Maqāṣid al-falāsifa*." *Mediterranea* 2 (2017 for 2016): 145–62.

Minnis, Alastair J. "Medieval Imagination and Memory." In Minnis and Ian R. Johnson, eds., *The Cambridge History of Literary Criticism, Vol. 2: The Middle Ages*, 239–74. Cambridge: Cambridge University Press, 2005.

Miquel, André. *La géographie humaine du monde musulman jusqu'au milieu du 11e siècle*. 4 vols. Paris: Mouton (vols. 1–3); Paris: F. Paillart (vol. 4), 1967–88.

Mittman, Asa S. *Maps and Monsters in Medieval England*. New York: Routledge, 2006.

Molland, A. G. "Roger Bacon as Magician." *Traditio* 30 (1974): 445–60.

Mosquera, Santiago Fernández. "Los autores ficticios del 'Quijote.'" *Anales Cervantinos* 24 (1986): 47–65.

Mottahedeh, Roy. "*ʿAjāʾib* in *The Thousand and One Nights*." In Richard G. Hovannisian and Georges Sabagh, eds., *The Thousand and One Nights in Arabic Literature and Society*, 29–39. Cambridge: Cambridge University Press, 1997.

Moureau, Sébastien. "Les sources alchimiques de Vincent de Beauvais." *Spicae: Cahiers de l'Atelier Vincent de Beauvais* n.s. 2 (2012): 5–118.

Muñoz, Nuria Martínez de Castilla. "'Anduve mirando se parecía por allí algún morisco aljamiado.'" In Muñoz and Rodolfo Gil Grimau, eds., *De Cervantes y el Islam*, 235–46. Madrid: Sociedad estatal de conmemoraciones culturales, 2006.

Murdoch, John E. "From Social into Intellectual Factors: An Aspect of the Unitary Character of Late Medieval Learning." In Murdoch and Edith Dudley Sylla, eds., *The Cultural Context of Medieval Learning: Proceedings of the First International*

Colloquium on Philosophy, Science, and Theology in the Middle Ages, September 1973, 271–339. Dordrecht: D. Reidel, 1975.

Al-Musawi, Muhsin J. *The Medieval Islamic Republic of Letters: Arabic Knowledge Construction*. Notre Dame, IN: University of Notre Dame Press, 2015.

———. *Scheherazade in England: A Study of Nineteenth-Century English Criticism of the Arabian Nights*. Washington, DC: Three Continents, 1981.

Newman, Barbara. *God and the Goddesses: Vision, Poetry, and Belief in the Middle Ages*. Philadelphia: University of Pennsylvania Press, 2003.

———. "What Did It Mean to Say 'I saw'? The Clash between Theory and Practice in Medieval Visionary Culture." *Speculum* 80, no. 1 (2005): 1–43.

Ngai, Sianne. *Our Aesthetic Categories: Zany, Cute, Interesting*. Cambridge, MA: Harvard University Press, 2012.

Nirenberg, David. *Neighboring Faiths: Christianity, Islam, and Judaism in the Middle Ages and Today*. Chicago: University of Chicago Press, 2014.

Norris, Harry T. "Sayf b. Ḏī Yazan and the Book of the History of the Nile." *Quaderni di studi arabi* 7 (1989): 125–51.

North, John D. *Chaucer's Universe*. Oxford: Clarendon Press, 1988.

———. "Medieval Concepts of Celestial Influence: A Survey." In Patrick Curry, ed., *Astrology, Science and Society: Historical Essays*, 5–17. Suffolk, UK: Boydell Press, 1987.

Oberman, Heiko A. *Archbishop Thomas Bradwardine, A Fourteenth Century Augustinian: A Study of His Theology in Its Historical Context*. Utrecht: Kemink & Zoon, 1957.

Orlemanski, Julie. "Who Has Fiction? Modernity, Fictionality, and the Middle Ages." *New Literary History* 50, no. 2 (2019): 145–70.

Ormsby, Eric L. *Ghazali: The Revival of Islam*. Oxford: Oneworld, 2008.

Ottaviani, Didier. "Le prophétie comme achèvement intellectuel à la fin du moyen âge." *Nouvelle revue du XVIe siècle* 21, no. 1 (2003): 11–24.

Ouyang, Wen-Chin. "Solomon's Ring in the Arab Literary Imaginary." In Nuha Alshaar, ed., *The Qur'an and* Adab*: The Shaping of Literary Traditions in Classical Islam*, 433–71. Oxford: Oxford University Press, 2017.

Pacheco, Maria Cândida de Costa Reis Monteiro, and José F. Meirinhos, eds. *Intellect et imagination dans la philosophie médiévale: Actes du XIe congrès international de philosophie médiévale de la Société internationale pour l'étude de la philosophie médiévale*. 3 vols. Turnhout: Brepols, 2006.

Pagden, Anthony. *European Encounters with the New World: From Renaissance to Romanticism*. New Haven: Yale University Press, 1993.

Park, Katharine. "Meanings of Natural Diversity." In Edith Sylla and Michael McVaugh, eds., *Texts and Contexts in Ancient and Medieval Science: Studies on the Occasion of John E. Murdoch's Seventieth Birthday*, 134–47. Leiden: Brill, 1997.

Pasnau, Robert, ed. *Cambridge History of Medieval Philosophy*. 2 vols. Cambridge: Cambridge University Press, 2010.

Perler, Dominik. "Faculties in Medieval Philosophy." in Perler, ed., *The Faculties: A History*, 97–139. Oxford: Oxford University Press, 2015.

Peters, Edward. *The Magician, The Witch, and the Law*. Philadelphia: University of Pennsylvania Press, 1978.

Phillips, Kim M. *Before Orientalism: Asian Peoples and Cultures in European Travel Writing, 1245–1510*. Philadelphia: University of Pennsylvania Press, 2014.

Pinault, David. *Story-Telling Techniques in the Arabian Nights*. Leiden: Brill, 1992.

Pines, Shlomo. "The Arabic Recension of the *Parva naturalia* and the Philosophical Doctrine concerning Veridical Dreams according to *al-Risala al-Manamiyya* and Other Sources." *Israel Oriental Studies* 4 (1974): 104–53.

Pingree, David. "The Diffusion of Arabic Magical Texts in Western Europe." In Biancamaria Scarcia Amoretti, ed., *La diffusione delle scienze islamiche nel Medio Evo europeo (Roma, 2–4 ottobre 1984)*, 58–102. Rome: Accademia nazionale dei Lincei, 1987.

Pinto, Ana. *"Mandeville's Travels": A "Rihla" in Disguise*. Madrid: Editorial Complutense, 2005.

Pinto, Karen. *Medieval Islamic Maps: An Exploration*. Chicago: University of Chicago Press, 2016.

Poirion, Daniel. *Le merveilleux dans la littérature française du Moyen Âge*. Paris: Presses universitaires de France, 1982.

Power, Amanda. *Roger Bacon and the Defence of Christendom*. Cambridge: Cambridge University Press, 2013.

Prendergast, Thomas, and Stephanie Trigg. *Affective Medievalism: Love, Abjection, and Discontent*. Manchester, UK: Manchester University Press, 2019.

Quillet, Jeannine. "Enchantements et désenchantements de la Nature selon Nicole Oresme." In Albert Zimmermann and Andreas Speer, eds., *Mensch und Natur im Mittelalter*, 1:321–29. 2 vols. New York: De Gruyter, 1991–92.

Rahman, Fazlur. *Prophecy in Islam: Philosophy and Orthodoxy*. London: George Allen & Unwin, 1958; reprint, Chicago: University of Chicago Press, 2011.

Rajabzadeh, Shokoofeh. "The Depoliticized Saracen and Muslim Erasure." *Literature Compass* 16, nos. 9–10 (2019), no pagination.

Rampling, Jennifer. *The Experimental Fire: Inventing English Alchemy, 1300–1700*. Chicago: University of Chicago Press, 2020.

Rapoport, Yossef, and Emilie Savage-Smith. *Lost Maps of the Caliphs: Drawing the World in Eleventh-Century Cairo*. Chicago: University of Chicago Press, 2018.

Rashed, Marwan. "Natural Philosophy." In Adamson and Taylor, eds., *The Cambridge Companion to Arabic Philosophy*, 287–307.

Ribémont, Bernard. *De natura rerum: Études sur les encyclopédies médiévales*. Orléans: Paradigme, 1995.

Rider, Jeff. "Receiving Orpheus in the Middle Ages: Allegorization, Remythification, and *Sir Orfeo*." *Papers on Language and Literature* 24, no. 4 (1988): 343–66.

Rikharðsdottir, Sif. *Medieval Translations and Cultural Discourse: The Movement of Texts in England, France and Scandinavia*. Rochester, NY: D. S. Brewer, 2012.

Robertson, Kellie. *Nature Speaks: Medieval Literature and Aristotelian Philosophy*. Philadelphia: University of Pennsylvania Press, 2017.

Robinson, Cynthia. *In Praise of Song: The Making of Courtly Culture in al-Andalus and Provence, 1005–1134 A.D.* Leiden: Brill, 2002.

Rodinson, Maxime. "La place du merveilleux et de l'étrange dans la conscience du monde musulman médiéval." In Mohammed Arkoun, ed., *L'étrange et le merveilleux dans l'islam médiéval: Actes du colloque tenu au Collège de France à Paris, en mars 1974*, 167–87. Paris: Éditions J. A., 1978.

Roest, Bert. "Divinations, Visions, and Prophecy according to Albertus Magnus." In Renée Nip, H. Van Dijk et al., eds., *Media Latinitas: A Collection of Essays to Mark the Occasion of the Retirement of L. J. Engels*, 323–28. Turnhout: Brepols, 1996.

Sahner, Christian C. "From Augustine to Islam: Translation and History in the Arabic Orosius." *Speculum* 88, no. 4 (2013): 905–31.

Said, Edward W. *Orientalism*. New York: Penguin, 2003.

Saif, Liana. *The Arabic Influences on Early Modern Occult Philosophy*. New York: Palgrave Macmillan, 2015.

Saif, Liana, Francesca Leoni, Matthew S. Melvin-Koushki, and Farouk Yahya, eds. *Islamicate Occult Sciences in Theory and Practice*. Leiden: Brill, 2020.

Saler, Michael T. "Modernity and Enchantment: A Historiographic Review." *American Historical Review* 111, no. 3 (2006): 692–716.

Saliba, George. *Islamic Science and the Making of the European Renaissance*. Cambridge, MA: MIT Press, 2007.

Saunders, Corinne J. *Magic and the Supernatural in Medieval English Romance*. Woodbridge, UK: D. S. Brewer, 2010.

Savage-Smith, Emilie, and Marion B. Smith. "Islamic Geomancy and a Thirteenth-Century Divinatory Device: Another Look." In Savage-Smith, ed., *Magic and Divination in Early Islam*, 211–76. Aldershot, UK: Ashgate, 2004.

Shank, Michael H. "Naturalist Tendencies in Medieval Science." In Peter Harrison and Jon H. Roberts, eds., *Science without God? Rethinking the History of Scientific Naturalism*, 37–57. Oxford: Oxford University Press, 2019.

Shulman, David D. *More Than Real: A History of the Imagination in South India*. Cambridge, MA: Harvard University Press, 2012.

Shyovitz, David I. *A Remembrance of His Wonders: Nature and the Supernatural in Medieval Ashkenaz*. Philadelphia: University of Pennsylvania Press, 2017.

Sirat, Colette. "Les traducteurs juifs à la cour des rois de Sicile et de Naples." In Geneviève Contamine, ed., *Traduction et traducteurs au moyen âge*, 168–91. Paris: Editions du Centre national de la recherche scientifique, 1989.

Smith, A. Mark. "Perception." In Pasnau, ed., *Cambridge History of Medieval Philosophy*, 1:334–45.

Smoller, Laura Ackerman. "'*Teste Albumasare cum Sibylla*': Astrology and the Sibyls in Medieval Europe." *Studies in History and Philosophy of Biological and Biomedical Sciences* 41 (2010): 76–89.

Sobecki, Sebastian. "New World Discovery." In *Oxford Handbooks Online*. Oxford: Oxford University Press, 2015, no pagination.

Søndergaard, Leif, and Rasmus Thorning Hansen, eds. *Monsters, Marvels, and Miracles: Imaginary Journeys and Landscapes in the Middle Ages*. Odense: University Press of Southern Denmark, 2005.

Spiegel, Gabrielle M. "Forging the Past: The Language of Historical Truth in Middle Ages." *History Teacher* 17, no. 2 (1984): 267–83.

———. "Maternity and Monstrosity: Reproductive Biology in the *Roman de Mélusine*." In Laine E. Doggett and Daniel E. O'Sullivan, eds., *Founding Feminisms in Medieval Studies: Essays in Honor of E. Jane Burns*, 100–124. Cambridge: D. S. Brewer, 2016.

Sullivan, Karen. *The Danger of Romance: Truth, Fantasy, and Arthurian Fictions*. Chicago: University of Chicago Press, 2018.

Tachau, Katherine. *Vision and Certitude in the Age of Ockham: Optics, Epistemology, and the Foundations of Semantics, 1250–1345*. Leiden: Brill, 1988.

Taylor, Jamie. *Fictions of Evidence: Witnessing, Literature, and Community in the Late Middle Ages*. Columbus: Ohio State University Press, 2013.

Teske, Roland. *Studies in the Philosophy of William of Auvergne, Bishop of Paris (1228–1249)*. Milwaukee: Marquette University Press, 2006.

Thijssen, Johannes M. M. H. "Late-Medieval Natural Philosophy: Some Recent Trends in Scholarship." *Recherches de théologie et philosophie médiévales* 67, no. 1 (2000): 158–90.

Thorndike, Lynn. *A History of Magic and Experimental Science*. 8 vols. New York: Columbia University Press, 1923–58.

———. "Imagination and Magic: The Force of Imagination on the Human Body and of Magic on the Human Mind." In Eugène Tisserant, ed., *Mélanges Eugène Tisserant*, 7:353–58. 7 vols. Vatican City: Biblioteca apostolica vaticana, 1964.

Tomasch, Sylvia, and Sealy Gilles, eds. *Text and Territory: Geographical Imagination in the European Middle Ages*. Philadelphia: University of Pennsylvania Press, 1998.

Toorawa, Shawkat. "Wâq al-wâq: Fabulous, Fabular, Indian Ocean (?) Island(s)." *Emergences* 10, no. 2 (2000): 387–402.

Tornesello, Natalia. "From Reality to Legend: Historical Sources of Hellenistic and Islamic Teratology." *Studia Iranica* 31, no. 2 (2002): 163–92.

Torrell, Jean-Pierre. *Recherches sur la théorie de la prophétie au Moyen Âge, XIIe–XIVe siècles: Études et textes*. Fribourg: Éditions universitaires Fribourg Suisse, 1992.

Touati, Houari. *Islam and Travel in the Middle Ages*. Trans. Lydia G. Cochrane. Chicago: University of Chicago Press, 2010.

———. *Islam et voyage au Moyen Âge: Histoire et anthropologie d'une pratique lettrée*. Paris: Éditions du Seuil, 2000.

Travaglia, Pinella. *Magic, Causality, and Intentionality: The Doctrine of Rays in al-Kindī*. Florence: SISMEL Edizioni del Galluzzo, 1999.

Truitt, Elly. *Medieval Robots: Mechanism, Magic, Nature, and Art*. Philadelphia: University of Pennsylvania Press, 2015.

———. "The Virtues of Balm in Late Medieval Literature." *Early Science and Medicine* 14, no. 6 (2009): 711–36.

Vance, Eugene. *From Topic to Tale: Logic and Narrativity in the Middle Ages*. Minneapolis: University of Minnesota Press, 1987.

Van der Lugt, Maaike. *Le ver, le démon et la Vierge: Les théories médiévales de la génération extraordinaire*. Paris: Les belles lettres, 2004.

Van Gelder, Geert J. H, and Marlé Hammond, eds. Takhyīl: *The Imaginary in Classical Arabic Poetics*. Cambridge: Gibb Memorial Trust, 2008.

Veenstra, Jan R. *Magic and Divination at the Courts of Burgundy and France: Text and Context of Laurens Pignon's* Contre les devineurs *(1411)*. Leiden: Brill, 1998.

Vermeir, Koen. "Castelli in aria: Immaginazione e spirito della natura in Henry More." *Lo Sguardo* 10 (2012): 99–124.

———. "Imagination between Physick and Philosophy: On the Central Role of Imagination in the Work of Henry More." *Intellectual History Review* 18, no. 1 (2008): 119–37.

———. "The 'Physical Prophet' and the Powers of the Imagination. Part I: A Case-Study on Prophecy, Vapours and the Imagination (1685–1710)." *Studies in History and Philosophy of Biological and Biomedical Sciences* 35, no. 4 (2004): 561–91.

Villanueva, Francisco Márquez. *Moros, moriscos y turcos de Cervantes: Ensayos críticos*. Barcelona: Bellaterra, 2010.

Vinaver, Eugène. *Form and Meaning in Medieval Romance.* Cambridge: Modern Humanities Research Association, 1966.

Vines, Amy N. *Women's Power in Late Medieval Romance.* Cambridge: D. S. Brewer, 2011.

Von Hees, Syrinx. "The Astonishing: A Critique and Re-reading of ʿAǧāʾib Literature." *Middle Eastern Literatures* 8, no. 2 (2005): 101–20.

Wacks, David A. *Framing Iberia:* Maqāmāt *and Frametale Narratives in Medieval Spain.* Leiden: Brill, 2007.

Wade, James. *Fairies in Medieval Romance.* New York: Palgrave Macmillan, 2011.

Walzer, Richard. "Al-Fārābī's Theory of Prophecy and Divination." *Journal of Hellenic Studies* 77, no. 1 (1957): 142–48.

Warner, Marina. *Stranger Magic: Charmed States and the Arabian Nights.* London: Chatto & Windus, 2011.

Watson, Gerard. *Phantasia in Classical Thought.* Galway: University of Galway Press, 1988.

Watson, Nicholas. "Desire for the Past." *Studies in the Age of Chaucer* 21 (1999): 59–97.

Weisheipl, James A. "Aristotle's Concept of Nature: Avicenna and Aquinas." In Lawrence D. Roberts, ed., *Approaches to Nature in the Middle Ages,* 137–60. Binghamton, NY: Center for Medieval and Early Renaissance Studies, 1982.

———. *Nature and Motion in the Middle Ages.* Washington, DC: Catholic University of America Press, 1985.

Weiskott, Eric. "English Political Prophecy and the Problem of Modernity." *postmedieval* 10, no. 1 (2019): 8–21.

Westrem, Scott D. *Broader Horizons: A Study of Johannes Witte de Hese's Itinerarius and Medieval Travel Narratives.* Cambridge, MA: Medieval Academy of America, 2001.

Williams, Tara. *Middle English Marvels: Magic, Spectacle, and Morality in the Fourteenth Century.* University Park: Pennsylvania State University Press, 2018.

Wohlman, Avital. *Thomas d'Aquin et Maïmonide: Un dialogue exemplaire.* Paris: Éditions du Cerf, 1988.

Wolfson, Harry A. "The Internal Senses in Latin, Arabic, and Hebrew Philosophic Texts." *Harvard Theological Review* 28, no. 2 (1935): 69–133.

Yeager, Suzanne M. "The World Translated: Marco Polo's *Le Devisement dou monde, The Book of Sir John Mandeville,* and Their Medieval Audiences." In Akbari, Iannucci, and Tulk, eds., *Marco Polo and the Encounter of East and West,* 156–81.

Zadeh, Travis E. "Commanding Demons and Jinn: The Sorcerer in Early Islamic Thought." In Alireza Korangy and Daniel J. Sheffield, eds., *No Tapping around Philology: A Festschrift in Honor of Wheeler McIntosh Thackston Jr.'s 70th Birthday,* 131–60. Wiesbaden: Harrassowitz, 2014.

———. *Mapping Frontiers across Medieval Islam: Geography, Translation, and the ʿAbbasid Empire.* London: I. B. Tauris, 2011.

———. "Postscript: Cutting Ariadne's Thread, or How to Think Otherwise in the Maze." In Saif et al., eds., *Islamicate Occult Sciences in Theory and Practice,* 607–50.

———. "The Wiles of Creation: Philosophy, Fiction, and the ʿAjāʾib Tradition." *Middle Eastern Literatures* 13, no. 1 (2010): 21–48.

———. *Wonders and Rarities: The Marvelous Book That Traveled the World and Mapped the Cosmos.* Cambridge, MA: Harvard University Press, forthcoming.

Zambelli, Paola. "L'immaginazione e il suo potero: Desiderio e fantasia psicosomatica o transitiva." In Zambelli, ed., *L'ambigua natura della magia: Filosofi, streghe, riti nel Rinascimento*, 53–75. Milan: Il Saggiatore, 1991.

Zumthor, Paul. "Dire le voyage au Moyen Âge." *Liberté* 35, nos. 4–5 (1993): 79–94.

———. "The Medieval Travel Narrative." *New Literary History* 25, no. 4 (1994): 809–24.

———. "Merlin: Prophet and Magician." in Peter Goodrich and Raymond H. Thompson, eds., *Merlin: A Casebook*, 129–59. New York: Routledge, 2003.

Index

Abraham ibn Daud, 43
Abu-Deeb, Kamal, 10n41, 28n5
Abū Maʿshar, 16, 100, 121–22, 204
action at a distance, 58, 60–71, 73
Adamson, Peter, 6n19, 40n54, 40n55
Aeneid. *See* Virgil.
Ahmed, Shahab, 6, 7n24
Akbari, Suzanne Conklin, 7n28, 112n1, 115n17, 116n21
Alain of Lille, 85–86
Albertus Magnus, 4n13, 11, 23, 29, 37, 60n6, 69–70, 71, 86, 90n28, 104, 105; on demons, 53–54; on fossils, 24, 108–11; on the Minotaur, 97, 102; on the powers of stones and gems, 19–20, 83–84, 88–89, 107, 195; on prophecy, 48, 49n100, 51n111; on witchcraft, 32n15, 54
alchemy, 25, 72, 139
Alexander the Great, 99, 100, 101, 102, 119, 142, 148
aljamiado, 207
Alonso, Manuel, 42, 43n68
Álvarez, Marco, 145n17
Amadas and Ydoine, 150, 171–72, 190–91, 192
Amazons, 25, 127n74
Anaxagoras, 104–5
Aquinas, Thomas, 9, 14, 17–18, 23, 37, 39, 57n132, 60n7, 71; on demons, 53n120, 54n123; on natural philosophy, 37, 81; on prophecy, 35, 48–52
Arbesú, David, 189n34
Aristotle, 3, 10, 17, 18, 27, 49n99, 60, 66, 98, 151, 152, 154, 184; on imagination, 30, 68; on nature and natural philosophy, 37, 86; translations of, 33, 36
Ashe, Laura, 20n97, 146n18
Aucassin et Nicolette, 147
Augustine, 13, 49n103, 64, 91n31, 102, 105, 120, 143; on marvels, 77n83, 92, 143; on nature, 14, 38n47, 85–86
automata, 13, 18n84, 25, 30
Averroes (Ibn Rushd), 3, 68n44
Avicenna (Ibn Sīnā), 18, 23, 24, 51, 52n117, 65n31, 66, 77n83, 84n2, 100; on fictive beings, 90–92; on fossils, 24, 108–9, 110; on imagination, 28, 29n6, 31, 32, 40n55, 44, 45–46, 47n90, 50, 51, 58, 60, 71n57, 76, 91–92; on imaginative prophecy, 42–47, 48, 49, 51, 196; on motive prophecy, 60, 67–70, 79, 80

Bacon, Roger, 38, 80, 90, 132–33, 138n121, 176; multiplication of species doctrine of, 61, 64–66, 67n38
Bailey, Michael, 32n15, 179n143, 196n63
Bale, Anthony, 134–35
balm, 116, 127, 205, 208
Bamford, Heather, 147n22
Barbezat, Michael, 56n130
Bartholomaeus Anglicus, 38n47, 194
Bartlett, Robert, 13n53, 14n61, 66n32
basilisk, 13, 37, 65, 66, 72, 132, 181
beaver, 22–23, 208, 209
Beckett, Katharine Scarfe, 5n15
Bennett, Jane, 181n7, 182
Benson, David, 113n3, 137n116
Berlekamp, Persis, 2, 4
Bernard of Clairvaux, 192n41

Made in the USA
Columbia, SC
06 November 2023

25580154R00141